Feminism
<u>is</u> Sexism

JP Tate

ISBN-13: 978-1500906269 / ISBN-10: 1500906263

Author's Note: Wherever possible I have used online references rather than bibliographical notes so that the reader has immediate access to those references and doesn't have to buy another book to confirm a point or see an example.

Other Books by JP Tate

<u>Fiction</u>
The Most Hated Man
The Identity Wars: Utopia is Dystopia
The Curious Tales of Mr Mayhew and Mr Broker
Dutiful: a love story of consensual sadomasochism
An Exile's Tread on Forbidden Soil (Iron Blade # 1)
No Brotherhood but that of Our Fathers (Iron Blade # 2)
A War for Generations Yet Unborn (Iron Blade # 3)

<u>Non-Fiction</u>
Sex-Objects: a little book of liberation
All God Worshippers Are Mad: a little book of sanity

Contents

Preface

If you are laughing derisively or sneering contemptuously at the title of this book, then *you* have endorsed, consciously or unconsciously, the dominant sexism of the society in which you live. If you choose to read this book, then by the end of it you may understand *why* it was sexist of you to react in the way that you did. You may acquire a clearer insight into what genuine impartial sex equality really means, and you might even become a better person. Now who could object to that?

We all know who would object to that, so let's forestall a few of the usual mindless objections.

Circumventing Those Entrenched in Denial

Feminists parrot ideology. Consequently, there are a number of predictable knee-jerk reflex responses that they will make to a polemical book of this sort, probably without bothering to read it. The title alone will be sufficient for them to spew bile all over the pages. So let's just clear away some of their predictable detritus before we begin.

Knee-Jerk Reflex 1: *Any attack upon feminism is backlash! It's backlash!! It's BACKLASH!!!!!!!*

This dismissal of all criticism was very popular with feminists in the 1970s and 1980s. But just shouting the word 'backlash' is not an argument and it proves nothing. Feminists have always treated the word 'backlash' as a magic word that makes all criticism disappear in a puff of pixie dust.

The position they take is this: (a) Any non-feminist who criticises feminism can only be motivated by the prejudice of misogynist sexism. No other motivation is conceivable or possible. (b) Any argument motivated by prejudice is invalidated by that prejudice. (c) Therefore, all criticism of feminism by a non-feminist is invalid and can legitimately be dismissed out of hand.

For decades feminism has dismissed without discussion any criticism of itself from outside of its own echo chamber, refusing to engage with the criticism on the spurious grounds that it was merely 'backlash' against feminism and therefore illegitimate. Only the supremely dishonest could allow themselves to get away with this puerile strategy. It is like some 1930s Stalinist accusing every critic of being a counter-revolutionary.

The premise that misogyny is the only possible motivation for opposing feminism is utterly false. This book argues in favour of gender equality, that is why it is anti-feminist. Anyone who supports a genuinely impartial gender equality must be against feminism because (as we shall see) it is feminism itself which is opposed to gender equality.

Knee-Jerk Reflex 2: *Any talk about defending men from the injustices of misandrist sexism is really just an attack upon women and women's rights! It's just more misogyny!*

This is like saying that a defence of adult's civil rights must necessarily be an attack upon children's civil rights, or that defending white people from racist abuse must necessarily be a racist attack upon black people. But any rational person knows that moral principles must be applied impartially. If you endorse a principle of racial equality, then you must apply it to everyone in defence of everyone, not just to people of a certain colour. If you endorse a principle of sex equality, then you must apply it to both sexes in defence of both sexes, not just to people of one sex. Impartiality is fundamental to moral principles as such. A principled defence of men is not an attack upon women.

By endorsing the principle of sex equality, a person is committing themselves to opposing both misandry and misogyny. To pretend that opposing misandry makes you guilty of misogyny is not a moral position, it is a blind refusal to apply the moral principle impartially. Anyone who treats a defence of men as necessarily being an attack upon women has no intellectual or moral integrity. They are lying both to themselves and to everyone else.

Besides, if feminists insist upon believing that any defence of men is necessarily an attack upon women, then why has feminism been claiming for more than four decades that feminism is a defence of women but is not an attack upon men? What blatant hypocrisy.

So why is this reflex response employed? Why does feminism treat any defence of men as an attack upon women? Two reasons. The first is that feminism has enjoyed total domination over the politics of gender debate for nearly half a century and it has no intention of sharing power with anyone else. Secondly, feminism is a zero-sum view of the world. A zero-sum game is a situation in which one participant's gains are exactly balanced by the losses of the other participant, and where their own losses are exactly balanced by the gains of the other participant. (Imagine two people playing poker; whatever one player wins, the other loses.) For one side to gain, the other side must lose. Feminism applies this to their sex-war of men against women and women against men. To them, any attempt to defend men from misandrist sexism as an attempt to gain something for men, and on their zero-sum model this equates to a loss for women. So feminism doesn't want any gains in equality for men, only for women. But for anyone who is not fighting the feminist sex-war, a genuine impartial sex equality is not a zero-sum game at all, it is the liberation of both sexes.

Knee-Jerk Reflex 3: *Feminism speaks on behalf of all women, therefore any attack upon feminism is an attack upon women!*

Feminism does not speak on behalf of all women, it merely claims to. If a Marxist claims to speak on behalf of all the workers of the world, does that mean that an attack upon

Marxism is an attack upon working class people? Of course not. It may *seem* that way to Marxists because they take it upon themselves to be the voice of the working class, just as it *seems* that way to feminists because they take it upon themselves to be the voice of all women, but the reality is that an attack upon a particular ideology need not in any way be an attack upon the people that they claim to represent. The Prime Minister in 10 Downing Street might believe that he represents the British people but that doesn't mean that any attack upon the Prime Minister is therefore an attack upon the British people.

Just as the terms 'Marxists' and 'working class people' are not synonymous, so too, the terms 'feminists' and 'women' are not synonymous. A person can be a woman without being a feminist and a person can be a feminist without being a woman, so *any criticism of feminism is precisely that*, it is a criticism of the misandrist ideology called feminism. This means that it is a criticism of men who are feminists but it is not a criticism of women who are not feminists. Women don't have to be feminists any more than voters have to be conservatives. It's a choice. Feminism is a political ideology, whereas being female is simply a biological/anatomical classification. The two are not remotely the same. An attack upon one does not imply an attack upon the other.

Feminism's conflation of itself with women is like some cold war American militarist equating Stalinism with the Russian people or equating Maoism with the Chinese people. Russians are no longer Stalinists but they're still Russians. The Chinese are no longer Maoists but they're still Chinese. Ideologies and people are not the same thing.

This book is a polemic against the most sexist ideology in the world: feminism. Hopefully, honest sex-equalitarian women will recognise the truth in what is said in these pages, to whatever extent they think that it is true, and will engage with the ideas fairly.

<u>Knee-Jerk Reflex 4</u>: *Any man who speaks against feminism does so because he feels threatened by strong women and therefore all his criticisms are nothing but the expression of his own character deficiencies and male inadequacy!*

Notice how this unsubstantiated assertion is shielded from rational refutation by its not being based on anything rational. It simply traduces all male critics of feminism. It is a crude smear. It is an emotional vilification derived from the feminist negative gender-stereotype of male inadequacy.

This, quite deliberately, produces a situation in which men are never allowed to protest against feminist oppression because it is taken for granted that no such oppression could possibly exist and therefore any such protest results solely from the man's personal shortcomings and can legitimately be dismissed out of hand.

Also, have you noticed how whenever someone is speaking of a man feeling threatened by a strong woman, it is always said as a *criticism of the man*, as if the threat could never possibly be a genuine one; that it could only ever be due to his personal weakness (and therefore constitutes a failure to be traditionally 'manly', an assumption which covertly imposes a requirement for men to live up to the 'real man' rules of traditional masculinity).

But whenever someone is speaking of a woman feeling threatened by a strong man, it is again always said as a *criticism of the man*. Feminist hypocrisy takes it for granted that the woman's feelings of being threatened are legitimate and serious, and that the man must actually be guilty of posing some threat to the woman merely because she feels threatened, whereas any man's feelings of being threatened by a woman are simply laughed to scorn as absurd and he is ridiculed as an 'unmanly' wimp. This feminist double-standard is based on the traditionally sexist view of the two sexes.

<u>Knee-Jerk Reflex 5</u>: *You can't criticise feminism because feminism is not one thing. Feminists disagree with one another and don't all hold the same position. There are many feminisms, so which are you criticising?*

This is an outrageously disingenuous way of sidestepping criticism, but how often have you heard it? You criticise something said by a feminist and another feminist says 'I'm a feminist and I don't think that, so that's not what feminism is'. In other words, you can criticise the feminist beliefs of Ms Smith but that isn't a criticism of feminism itself, or you can criticise the feminist beliefs of Ms Jones but that doesn't count as a criticism of feminism, only of Ms Jones' version of it.

If one type of feminist wants to disagree with another type of feminist about what feminism is, or ought to be, then that's a disagreement *within feminism*. It's of no account to anyone from outside the ideology who is criticizing *feminism as such*. If radical feminists, liberal feminists, eco-feminists, equity feminists, and so on, disagree with each other about policy and practice, that doesn't mean that there isn't an ideology and a political movement called 'feminism' which can quite rightly and properly be criticised.

So, in this book, when I use a phrase like 'feminism says' or 'feminism holds to the position that', the reader should understand that I am speaking of things commonly said by feminists and positions routinely held by feminists. I am not, of course, claiming that *every single person* who ever identified themselves as a feminist must therefore have said this, or that every single person who self-identifies as a feminist must therefore have held this position. I am simply mentioning something said by, or a position held by, orthodox feminist opinion or mainstream feminist society or some influential feminist. I am referring to feminism as an ideology and a political movement.

If the reader can find one particular feminist who said something different in one particular feminist book, or if the reader is aware of one school of feminism which holds to a slightly different position on a particular topic, this does not mean that *all those feminists* who *do* say what I'm attributing to 'feminism' are in some way unrepresentative of feminism, or that feminism is not guilty of what those feminists have said and done. Feminism may be a broad church but it is still a major pillar of the state religion of contemporary society (i.e. political correctness), and can be criticised in general terms.

Anyone who believes in patriarchy theory is a feminist, anyone who believes that women have been oppressed by men and that action must be taken to redress this oppression is a feminist, and anything that is said, done, advocated, or legislated *with a presumption of the basic tenets of feminism* is being said, done, advocated, or legislated by feminists. Feminism is a political movement of such immense power that it entirely dominates all discussion of the politics of gender. To suggest that there is no such thing as 'feminism' because there are only 'different types' of feminism is shamefully dishonest.

Not all Marxists agree on every point of Marxism (far from it), so does that mean that no one can criticise Marxism? Not all liberals agree on every point of liberalism, so does that mean that no one can criticise liberalism? Not all conservatives agree on every point of conservatism, so does that mean that no one can criticise conservatism? *Every* ideology can and should be criticised rigorously. No one is above criticism. Marxism, liberalism, conservatism, Christianity, Islam, fascism, socialism, anarchism, and you name it; they all can and should be criticised. All of them. And so can bloody feminism.

Failing to Circumvent Entrenched Denial

Will this book be accused of misogyny? Will it be accused of attacking women? Will the word 'backlash' be thrown at it? Of course it will. These false accusations will be made, as they are always made, in order to dismiss the book without any discussion of the issues it attempts to address about a genuine, principled and impartial sex equality. But none of these infantile feminist-reflex accusations are true. If the reader has a mind of their own, they will not be fooled by the usual presumptive dismissals. Of course, if the reader does *not* have a mind of their own . . . . then that would explain why they are incapable of changing their mind. Their mind doesn't belong to them, it belongs to feminism.

The feminist reactionaries of the present political establishment who review this book will not address any of the points of argument it raises because they never take seriously any criticism of themselves. Instead, they will trash the book in its entirety in haughty tones of contemptuous dismissal. They will not engage in any dialogue with an anti-establishment critic, they will denounce that critic as a misogynist, a woman-hater, a rape apologist, a wicked monster of male oppression, and all the other unjust and unsubstantiated abuse that they always employ whenever anyone dares to disagree with them. It is who they are.

But what about everyone else? This book argues that feminism *is* sexism. Most people have been taught to believe the opposite, that feminism opposes sexism. It is a very difficult thing for a person to admit that they were wrong about something in which they have made an emotional investment over a long period of time. If they have invested themselves deeply in a set of ideas only to discover that those ideas are false, the realisation makes them feel like a fool. All this time they've been believing something that wasn't true. It makes them feel as if the life they've been living was a sham; that by changing their minds about their former beliefs they have thereby invalidated their lives. All this time they'd been believing one thing and living their lives by it, and now they realise that the truth is something else entirely.

Changing your mind about your faith in feminism is like changing your mind about a religious faith. If you've spent forty years living in accordance with the doctrines of, say, Catholicism and then come to realise that atheism is true, it's painful. Forty years of your life wasted on a falsehood. That's a hard thing to face. It's exactly like that when trying to get people to change their minds about feminism.

Changing your mind can sometimes take a great deal of courage and intellectual integrity. If you, reader, have been fooled by the lying propaganda of hypocritical sexist feminism, you will need to draw upon your courage and your intellectual integrity now.

Chapter One

Traditional Sexism

Traditional sexism in the society previous to the society we live in now (i.e. the society before second wave feminism) was always a two-edged sword. It always cut both ways. Boys were raised from the cradle to be 'brave little soldiers' just as girls were raised from the cradle to be 'good little homemakers'. Boys were culturally indoctrinated to believe that when they went off to war it would be heroic and glorious. Girls were culturally indoctrinated to believe that their wedding day would be the happiest day of their life. But when the young man was in a military uniform up to his knees in dirty water in a trench, and the young woman was in an apron up to her elbows in dirty water at a kitchen sink, they both discovered that they had been lied to.

It is crucial to understand that traditional sexism always victimized *both* sexes because all of the gratuitous privileging of women that feminism has perpetrated is so often mistakenly believed to be justified on the grounds that it is a necessary rectification of a traditional societal imbalance that favoured men. We are constantly told that the obsessive and systemic policy of advantaging women over men in all areas of life through feminist legislation and a multiplicity of affirmative action programmes is nothing more than a means to cast aside the disadvantage that women previously suffered. The reason that so many otherwise intelligent people have been so catastrophically conned by feminism is their belief that traditional sexism was all one-way traffic and so in the present day women and men must be treated *unequally* in order to make them equal.

But the historical truth is that misandrist sexism is as old as misogynist sexism. This is a very difficult thing for those who have been subjected to the ideological oppression of feminism

10

to grasp. After more than four decades of second wave feminism *their minds are closed to the possibility of error* in what they have been taught to believe. Those under 40 years of age have never known any interpretation of history contrary to the feminist interpretation of history. They have been raised from the cradle to accept it as true, just as the boys and girls of earlier generations were raised to be brave little soldiers and good little homemakers, trapped within the orthodoxy of the culture into which they have been born.

Some readers may already have baulked at the use of a phrase like "the ideological oppression of feminism" and thrown this book aside in contemptuous disgust. Their cultural indoctrination to one point of view and *one point of view only* does not permit them the freedom of an open mind. Their minds are closed and shuttered and padlocked. They cannot bring themselves to admit even the possibility that what they have obediently believed all their life may not be true.

For those readers who are willing to read further, what follows may seem strange if you haven't come across it before. Although there are more and more people speaking out against feminist oppression, if what you read in these pages strikes you as a bizarrely abnormal perspective on society, this simply means that the political establishment, in which feminism is such a key player, has thus far successfully stopped you from hearing anti-establishment opinions. After all, you live in a society in which feminist beliefs and values frame the laws passed by government and where feminist beliefs dominate the media, where education has been feminised, where employment practices have been feminised, where social services have been feminised, where even police procedures have been feminised, where *every arm of the state* has been systemically feminised.

[Author's note: when I use the word 'feminised' I mean 'made consistent with feminist beliefs'. I do not use the word 'feminised' to mean 'now involves female participation' or 'now better reflects a feminine sensibility', I use it to mean 'operates in accordance with feminist ideology'.]

11

If you don't believe this, then try instituting a government policy, or an educational programme, or an employment practice, or a police procedure that is contrary to feminism. You'll have no chance. Feminism is in power. Face it, if *an ideology exercises power in every arm of the state*, then that ideology is a part of the political establishment. It is *not* a part of a 'progressive counter-culture', it *is* the culture. You live in it. This is why the argument I make in this polemical book may strike you as odd. The feminist reactionaries of the establishment have exercised the power of veto over what you are allowed to hear in the hope of exercising a similar power of veto over what you are allowed to think.

So, as you read, remind yourself that the conventional assumptions and presuppositions about the politics of gender do not apply in the argument that follows. For example, it will not be blithely taken for granted that sexism is a male crime, or that only women suffer sexism, or that men are the problem and women are the solution, or that men are violent and women are not, or that women are intrinsically better human beings than men. This book endorses *impartial sex equality* and so it does not pander to any culturally orthodox presuppositions about gender. Instead we shall begin by taking a swift overview of traditional sexism without indulging in any conventional feminist prejudice.

What Is Sexism?

When we look back over history we see a proliferation of many different societies with a diverse range of beliefs and values. But one constant feature amongst all this diversity has been the way that societies have assigned gendered identities and gendered social roles to women and men. It is this aspect of society that gives rise to sexism. So if we want to examine traditional sexism soberly and sensibly we had better be clear on what we mean when we identify something as being an instance of 'sexism'. When I speak of sexism in this book I am referring to the *societal imposition* of these gendered identities and social roles, where *cultural norms* psychologically condition women and men to see themselves in a certain way and constrain the social roles which women and men can occupy. I am not referring to gendered roles necessitated by evolutionary survival, nor to the presence of evolutionary psychology in people's thinking, both of which occur naturally, but rather to the *social enforcement* of gendered identities and roles.

To clarify this by examples, it is not sexism that humans prefer physically beautiful sexual partners because a preference for physical beauty (symmetrical features, broad-shouldered men, long-legged women) is something that evolution has built-in to humans as an indicator of physical health, an asset to survival, and good breeding potential. This is not sexist because it is a naturally occurring aspect of human psychology, not a political injustice. However, when this evolutionary preference is *socialised* in ways that empower beautiful people unfairly (e.g. pretty women getting jobs as television weather forecasters because viewers would rather hear about the weather from someone who is physically attractive even though weather forecasting has nothing to do with beauty or sex appeal) then this is sexism because people are being unjustly excluded from those jobs for cultural/commercial reasons (i.e. more viewers).

Similarly, it would not be sexism for men to wish to impress women with a display of what in evolutionary terms would be 'masculine' traits (e.g. a physically capable protector) but it is sexism when *society makes those traits compulsory* (e.g. men being culturally expected and legally required to fight in wars because it is their 'manly duty') or when men are taught to fear displaying any 'effeminate' traits because their culture insists they must conform to the tough guy role models of John Wayne or Clint Eastwood in a cowboy movie.

If this basic contention is accepted, that gender dispositions derived from evolutionary inheritance are not sexist but the societal imposition of gender is sexist, then determining whether something is sexist or not is actually quite tricky. Feminism's long-standing habit of sweepingly and thoughtlessly attributing misogynist sexism to everything with

13

which they are dissatisfied has misled people into thinking that sexism is easily identified. In fact, it is often quite problematic.

For example, stiletto high heel shoes make a woman's legs appear longer and exaggerate the femaleness of her movements, which emphasises *evolutionary traits* which make her more sexually desirable. At the same time she might be living in a society which *pressures* women into wearing high heels to exaggerate their 'femininity'. So if an individual woman chooses to wear stiletto heels it might be sexism or it might not be, depending upon why she is wearing them. She might be freely choosing to enhance her natural sex-appeal, or she might be submitting to a cultural expectation.

Or, to take another example, the traditional male sex-object for women was the high-status high-income man; the success-object. But in the present society women are far more financially independent than in the past and it is noticeable that the current male sex-object in popular culture is moving much more toward the good looking hunk with his six-pack muscularity. (Compare the physicality of Brad Pitt and Tom Cruise to that of Humphrey Bogart and James Stewart.) So when women sexually objectify a good-looking hunk, this might simply be the appeal of male physical beauty that is a part of women's evolutionary psychological inheritance.

On the other hand, the greater emphasis on male physical beauty in recent years due to women's greater financial independence is creating increased *social pressure* on men to conform to an additional gendered norm. This is encapsulated in the popular 1989 "Gillette, the best a man can get" television commercial   https://www.youtube.com/watch?v=ThDBf14qPsc   where the male ideal is presented as being *not only* the traditional success-object *and* the traditional sporting hero *and* the traditional family man *but now* he has to be physically gorgeous too. This multiple imposition of gender is an egregious case of misandrist sexism. Yet which of the two cognitive influences is in operation when a woman sexually objectifies a good-looking hunk, evolutionary psychology or culturally conditioned sexism, is tricky to establish. It's the old question of the interplay of nature and nurture.

It is evident that classifying something as sexism is a much more subtle and nuanced task than the crude gender generalisations of feminism have led people to believe. We have to take great care with the disambiguation of identity/behaviour that is derived from our evolutionary inheritance and identity/behaviour that is induced by a societal imposition. Feminism, in contrast, continually indulges itself in attributing sexism as the motivation behind anything and everything that it *wants* to label as sexism.

Just as in the proliferation of diverse societies throughout history where the one constant feature has been the way that societies have assigned gendered identities and social roles to women and men, contemporary feminist society also commits this offence. Feminism's approach to the politics of gender as a sex-war has actually made it *the chief perpetrator of a societal imposition* of gender identities in present-day society, with its emphatic gender-stereotypes of male guilt and female innocence.

In any discussion of domestic violence feminism will cast men in the role of perpetrator and women in the role of victim, even though this is not a true picture of domestic violence. In any discussion of rape feminism will cast men in the role of the sexually predatory male and women in the role of the imperilled female living in a 'rape culture', although the reality of women forcing men into sex and men forcing women into sex would require a gender-neutral definition of what constitutes rape. Feminism relies very heavily on its ideological attribution of gender identities that portray a world of oppressed women and male oppressors. It does everything it can to psychologically condition women into seeing themselves as oppressed, just as its propaganda constantly promotes a degraded and debauched picture of men. Mainstream feminism is constantly telling us what 'men' are like and how they behave, and what 'women' are like and how they behave. As I hope to make clear, feminism is guilty of a gross societal imposition of gender and is therefore *guilty of sexism*, not opposed to it. For the last half-century feminism has been a part of the problem, not the solution.

The Bifurcation of Society

The traditional bifurcation of human society, the division of labour on the basis of gender, was not pursued as an end in itself. Its purpose was, firstly, to secure society's basic survival by ensuring a sufficient number of children survived to adulthood and, secondly, to advantage the political/economic ruling class who were in power at the time. If material circumstances permitted the ruling elite to modify gender roles to better serve their political/economic interests, they would do so. For example, when societies were structured to include a slave class the female slaves might be found working at the same labour as the male slaves, working for their owners in whatever way advantaged those owners. The economic ruling class in a slave society did not say that female slaves were too delicate and ladylike to work at agricultural labour in the cotton fields. Society's gender beliefs have always been tailored to pursue the interest of those in power.

It was similar in feudal societies where female serfs and female peasants didn't get to live like a pampered middle-class domestic goddess complaining about her lack of career opportunities and the glass ceiling, the feudal ruling class exploited its workers of both sexes ruthlessly. It was again similar for the working class under capitalism. People were made to serve the economic interest of those who had power over them, with some women (and children) being used as factory-fodder alongside the men.

Yet, despite these sporadic modifications, historically society has had a fairly consistent gendered bifurcation of social roles for the overwhelming majority of human beings all the way back into prehistory. Why? For two main reasons: (1) certain work needed a man's greater physical strength, whilst women were often limited to work that could be performed whilst they were pregnant or breast feeding, and (2) human children are hugely dependent during the early years of their lives and require a great deal of looking after if they are to survive to adulthood.

This is why feminism has arisen at precisely the time in history that it has. The *contraceptive revolution* of the 1960s and 1970s was a change in the material circumstances of society that permitted women to have sex without getting pregnant. This was a socially transformative invention of enormous magnitude, on the same kind of scale of importance as the invention of the wheel, the printing press, or the internal combustion engine. Birth-rates in cultures where the contraceptive revolution has occurred have dropped dramatically and, as the crucial enabling factor in women's liberation, it was 'the pill' that sparked the modification of gender roles that began in the sixties and has continued since.

In addition, the *technological revolution* of the 1980s and 1990s is a change in the material circumstances of society that permits women to engage in the public workplace equally with men. When the Soviet Union made its flag they put a hammer and sickle on it. The hammer was a symbol of the urban proletariat and the sickle was a symbol of the agricultural proletariat. The hammer and sickle are 'muscle' tools, it needs strength to wield them. But if someone made a workers' flag today, what tool would best symbolize the workplace? A computer keyboard. A pregnant woman can operate a keyboard just as effectively as the strongest of men. His physical strength is no longer relevant in most workplaces. Nor need a woman be pregnant if she doesn't wish to be, she has reliable contraception and society's survival doesn't have a problem with under-population, it has a problem with global over-population.

It is these two changes in the material circumstances of society that has enabled the ideology of second-wave feminism to be created. *It could not have been created before*. The political ascendancy of feminism has occurred at precisely the same time as the contraceptive revolution and the technological revolution. *This is not a coincidence.* It is now in the interest of the economic ruling class to exploit women in the public workplace as much as it has always exploited men because the material circumstances now allow for that exploitation.

But prior to the 1960s this was not an option. Societal survival and the interest of the ruling class meant that ordinary people were made to conform to the gender roles society required of them. What were the child mortality rates for the 12th century or the 14th century, let alone the 7th century BC or whenever? Both societal survival and ruling class privilege depended upon a sufficient number of workers being raised to adulthood for the next generation. This material circumstance of human biology forced women into a child-rearing role and forced men into a family-provider role from prehistory onwards. Every type of society needed its child-bearers to be its child-raisers, and needed its non-child-bearers to support the family through the products (or wages) of his work.

With pregnancy and maternity being a slow process of procreation, one child per birth over several births, evolutionary nature itself left men with the primary role of working on behalf of women and children to earn the daily bread and bring it home to their families. How could the children (or indeed the women) have survived if he had not done so? The family was society's *survival unit.* It was the means by which the next generation could be born and raised. Nature cast men into the role of breadwinner and head of the household *to take personal responsibility for keeping the women and children alive.* It did not serve a 'male interest' for the man to be required to serve women and children in this way, so this was not some patriarchal plot by a conspiratorial brotherhood of men who wanted to oppress women. For nearly all of the history of the human species gender bifurcation was simply a necessary response to the material circumstances of the struggle for survival.

As societies developed and progressed the evolutionary division of labour was systemically formalised by the cultural norms which served the interest of the ruling elites because without ordinary men and women occupying these gendered roles the political rulers would not have had the next generation of workers to exploit to maintain their position of wealth and power. Thus men were socialised to be farmers, artisans, soldiers, industrial workers, etc., (factory-fodder in peace time and cannon-fodder in war time) while women were primarily baby-incubators, childcare workers, and domestic servants.

This was the fundamental basis of the gender-bifurcation of society but it is not the whole story. To properly understand traditional sexism we need to examine in greater detail the ways in which society systemically formalised this bifurcation through an imposition of gender-identities as the psychological underpinning of these social roles; the ways in which human personality traits were culturally gendered to facilitate the allocation of social roles to women and men as two distinct classes of person. This examination is quite easily done because there is a wealth of evidence.

Sometimes traditional sexism produced insulting stereotypes that victimised women and men in the same way. For example, male bodybuilders were stereotyped as being stupid because they were very physically developed. The assumption being, apparently, that if a man is physically developed it is therefore impossible for him to be intellectually developed as well, and vice versa. This generated the caricatures of the weedy intellectual and the stupid he-man, where the latter equated stupidity with excessive maleness. So much so, that a piece of traditional weight-training equipment became synonymous with stupidity: the 'dumb-bell'. And in exactly the same way that the man who was perceived as being extremely masculine (the he-man) was insulted this way, his counterpart, the woman who was perceived as being extremely feminine (the tits and ass glamour girl) was also assumed to be stupid. Just how close the parallel is in this particular example is evident when we remember that the classic icon of the female air-head bimbo is the 'dumb blonde'. It's right there in the language: the very male dumb-bell and the very female dumb blonde.

19

However, this similarity of insult was not the usual practice in traditional sexism. On the contrary, standardly traditional sexism victimized both sexes by imposing gendered social roles in which, speaking broadly in terms of cultural norms, what was *forbidden* to one sex was *compulsory* for the other sex, thereby enforcing preconceived notions of gender 'difference'. We hear this expressed in the traditional phrase 'the opposite sex'. Women and men were not usually described as 'the other sex', they were socially polarised as the *opposites* of one another. This phrase 'the opposite sex' is a denial of (or at least, does not adequately acknowledge) the common humanity shared by women and men, and is therefore sexist against both sexes; it is misandrist and misogynist.

Why is it sexist against both sexes? Because under the traditional imposition of gendered social roles and gendered identities the position of the human individual was one of being deprived of the freedom to be a whole person. Human individuals of both sexes were forced to live only half of their humanity; to be half a human. Cultural norms of gender meant that some attributes common to both women and men were compulsory for men and forbidden to women, and some attributes common to both women and men were compulsory for women and forbidden to men. (This is not to say that people actually managed to successfully achieve whatever was held to be compulsory for them, merely that they were constantly pressured to try to achieve it and to not admit any failure to achieve it.)

Examples of this polarisation of the sexes are both obvious and innumerable. It would take a very long time to compile an exhaustive list but the flavour of this bifurcation of the human species is readily apparent if we consider a few examples:

Things that were *compulsory for men* included:

- Being strong in all circumstances
- Being capable; being successful at whatever endeavour he is engaged in

- Being dominant in social interactions, especially over other men
- Being physically brave
- Expressing 'masculine' physicality (e.g. sport)
- Earning or having money; being a financial provider
- Having social status
- Being protective toward women
- Being a 'gentleman' who defers to a lady
- Taking the sexual initiative
- Being good at fucking
- Being heterosexual

Things that were *compulsory for women* included:

- Being submissive to men, at least in public
- Being nurturant
- Being interested in domestic concerns
- Expressing 'feminine' physicality (e.g. being pretty; sex appeal)
- Being a virgin prior to marriage
- Being 'ladylike' in conduct and deportment
- Having babies (unless 'barren')
- Being a good mother
- Being heterosexual

Things that were *forbidden to men* included:

- Failure
- Showing any form of weakness
- Being dependent (e.g. a 'kept man', a 'mommy's boy')
- Needing help
- Displaying any form of behaviour held to be 'effeminate'
- Admitting to being a virgin
- Being interested in domestic concerns (unless a professional, e.g. chefs)
- Losing in competition with a female
- Intruding upon an area of life considered to be a female purview

Things that were *forbidden to women* included:

- Expressing anger
- Being physically violent in public
- Being independent (unless wealthy or a 'career-woman')
- Displaying any form of behaviour held to be 'manly'
- Taking the sexual initiative
- Admitting to her own sexual appetites
- Sexual promiscuity
- Intruding upon an area of life considered to be a male purview

And so on and so on. Let us not make the crass mistake of trying to *compete in victimology* but acknowledge what really matters, that both sexes were tightly constrained by rules of what was compulsory, permissible, and forbidden. Men may have felt that women had the easier ride; women may have felt that men had the easier ride. Both may have resented their lot in life. The male factory worker may have bemoaned how his whole life was spent earning money for the wife and kids. The housewife may have bemoaned how her whole life was spent servicing her family as a domestic servant. Comparative victimology is not the issue that impartial sex equality addresses. The point that matters is that both sexes had their humanity constrained by the imposition of socially enforced gender identities. The widespread belief that traditional sexism was all one-way traffic, that it advantaged men and disadvantaged women, is the foundation stone of feminism and it is a lie.

Unfortunately, whilst the reader will certainly be very familiar indeed with the sexism that women have suffered, they may be largely unfamiliar with (and often profoundly ignorant of) the sexism that men have suffered. For this reason there is no need whatsoever to recount for the umpteenth time the issues of misogynist sexism; we have all heard those recounted daily for forty years. What we need to address are those issues of misandrist sexism which have been consistently and conspicuously ignored by an entire culture. This is a very necessary, if heretical, undertaking and it is in large measure what this book is about because once traditional misandry is properly understood it becomes glaringly obvious how feminism is guilty of *perpetuating* traditional misandry; that feminism *is* sexism.

Misandry is Not Trivial

Anyone reluctant to abandon the dogma that women are the martyrs of herstory may feel a desire at this point either to dismiss any consideration of misandrist sexism on the grounds that it never existed or to belittle the oppression suffered by men under traditional sexism on the grounds that it was trivial compared to that endured by women. This would be an example of what I mean by comparative victimology and, as it is an entrenched habit-of-mind amongst the 'politically correct', perhaps we should deal with it straight away by asking the question: of all the innumerable sexist cultural norms that existed in traditional society, which was the single most extreme sexism of all?

The value of asking this question is that the answer, contrary to the expectation of any feminist reader, is one type of traditional misandry. The answer is war and the misandrist *double-standard about the value of human life* that war exemplifies. Every time one government has declared war upon another government men have been called upon *as men* to fight and die in it. The traditional gender construct of the 'real man' required a man to display patriotic fervour in rushing to volunteer. It was held to be his 'manly duty' and if he failed in this, he failed in his manhood.

It was not held to be a womanly duty. Families did not send their daughters to be maimed and murdered in warfare, they sent their sons. It was young men (and so many of them were little more than boys they were so young) who were *socially expected and legally required* to fulfill a gendered social role of being ripped apart by shrapnel, riddled with machine gun

23

bullets, poisoned with mustard gas, disemboweled by bayonet (or knife or sword or spear), decapitated by axe or torn in two by a roadside bomb.

Any refusal to fight was punished by severe social condemnation. The psychological pressure society used to coerce men into uniform is readily apparent in recruitment posters such as "Here's Your Chance. It's Men We Want" http://www.archives.gov.on.ca/en/explore/online/posters/pics/16180_your_chance_770 .jpg (where the underlining of the word "men" means 'real men' as well as identifying which sex is expected to join up) and the ubiquitous "Daddy, What Did You Do in the Great War?" http://cockelshells.files.wordpress.com/2011/01/daddy.jpg which exploits a father's love for his children in applying emotional blackmail.

Women were encouraged to send men to their deaths. Here is the text of a poster from 1915 that makes it very clear how the government understood the power that women had over men which could be deployed to coerce men into fulfilling the masculine gendered social role:

"TO THE YOUNG WOMEN OF LONDON. Is your 'best boy' wearing khaki? If not, don't YOU THINK he should be? If he does not think that you and your country are worth fighting for – do you think he is WORTHY of you? Don't pity the girl who is alone – her young man is probably a soldier fighting for her and her country – and for YOU. If your young man neglects his duty to his king and country, the time may come when he will NEGLECT YOU. Think it over – then ask him to JOIN THE ARMY TODAY."

http://www.telegraph.co.uk/women/womens-life/11003194/WW1-in-pictures-Poster-women-of-World-War-One.html?frame=2992601

Boys were raised to fear being thought a coward, and alleged 'cowardice' in uniform could mean execution by firing squad. Society has always imposed upon men an idea of masculinity that identified maleness with the capacity to fight. *Nobody ever gave a woman a white feather.*

The nationwide 'white feather campaign' in Britain during the world war of 1914 -1918 is as clear-cut an instance of the *social imposition* of a gendered role to the extreme detriment (e.g. death, maiming, shell-shock, etc.) of the victim as could be found anywhere in history. http://en.wikipedia.org/wiki/White_feather It also highlights the fact that when we speak of 'society' imposing gendered social roles, we must remember that this imposition was perpetrated by the women in society as well as the men.

The white feather campaign is a graphic demonstration of how one of men's main motivations for submitting to military service was to earn the respect of women, and of how easily men can be manipulated into doing their 'manly duty' when pressured into it by women. Handing out the white feather was a form of street activism conducted by women whose goal was to *shame men* into enlisting in the British Army by presenting a white feather symbolising cowardice to any young man they met who was not wearing a military uniform.

This appallingly misandrist campaign was endorsed and practiced by many of the suffragettes, including two of the leading militant feminists of the day, Emmeline and Christabel Pankhurst. That suffragettes, the feminist 'first-wave', were prominent in handing out white feathers to send men to a death by sexism, is grounds enough for us to understand that the extreme hypocrisy of feminists is not merely a feature of the second wave. These suffragettes were acting completely in accord with traditional misandry, as Emmeline Pankhurst made perfectly clear in her public statements. She said that the reason men must risk their lives in this war was *the protection and defence of women*.

"The least that men can do is that every man of fighting age should prepare himself to redeem his word to women, and to make ready to do his best, to save the mothers, the wives and daughters of Great Britain from outrage too horrible even to think of. We have the right to say to the men 'Fight for your country, defend the shores of this land of ours, fight for your homes, for the women, and for the children'."

The "outrage too horrible even to think of" is, of course, ravishment by the beastly Hun. So when a man must "redeem his word to women", this is the obligation of his gendered social role to lay down his life so that a woman may be spared suffering. Then, as now, female pain was considered more serious than the loss of male life. Men, ever the expendable sex, must be willing to die so that women like Pankhurst can remain safe at home to cast their votes in elections. (I'll address the issue of the suffragettes and 'votes for women' at the end of this chapter.)

Women are killed in warfare, certainly, but (with some notable exceptions) they are killed as a result of being in the wrong place at the wrong time. They are living in the town that the enemy troops invade; they are living inside a house that gets hit by an aerial bomb, and so on. Men are killed in war because it is their gendered social role to get killed in wars. It is this fact that makes the wholesale slaughter of male human beings in warfare an instance of *sexism*. If a man or a women is unlucky enough to be run over by a bus when crossing the road, their death is a tragic misfortune but it is not the result of sexism. If society coerces men from the cradle to be willing to volunteer for war, if it imposes a social construct of gender that requires them to fight in battle, or even more conspicuously, if it legally imposes conscription upon men for a national service that includes combat, then this is death by sexism. Misandrist sexism is lethal. Men die of sexism. They always have.

This is so obviously the case that it wouldn't need to be argued, but for the fact that feminism has been entrenched in denial about it for as long as feminism has existed. Yet history (what feminism calls 'patriarchy') is crammed full of evidence. Go back in time as far as you like, the imposition of a social construct of gender to motivate men to fight in wars is conspicuously evident. Around 61AD Queen Bouddica of the Iceni tribe in Britain is reported by the Roman historian Tacitus as giving an inspirational speech to her army on the eve of her final battle (in which the men of her army were slaughtered). Tacitus writes of her saying:

"'But now,' she said, 'it is not as a woman descended from noble ancestry, but as one of the people that I am avenging lost freedom, my scourged body, the outraged chastity of my daughters . . . . If you weigh well the strength of the armies, and the causes of the war, you will see that in this battle you must conquer or die. This is a *woman's* resolve; as for *men*, they may live and be slaves." [my italics]

The phrase "my scourged body, the outraged chastity of my daughters" is a reference to Boudicca having been publicly whipped by the Romans and her two underage daughters having been raped by the Romans. The men of their tribe must avenge them. The contemptuous sneer in speaking of men living as slaves while a *woman* is prepared to fight and die clearly expresses the idea that if she, a woman who does *not* have a duty to fight nonetheless intends to do so, then how *shameful* it would be for any man to *fail* to fight.

It doesn't actually matter to the point I'm making here whether Boudicca actually said this as stated or whether Tacitus is inventing to dramatise his account of the battle because *either way* it shows that the attitude of telling men they have a duty to protect women and a gendered social role to fight in wars was present in the society of the time. It was used to make men risk their lives in war, then as now. Then as always.

The closest female equivalent to this is death during pregnancy and childbirth. Society imposed upon women *the expectation* of motherhood and no one knows how many women have died during childbirth throughout history, just as no one knows how many men have died in warfare. Insofar as social pressure coerced women into motherhood, it can be argued that sexism played a role in deaths during pregnancy and childbirth. But it wasn't society that gave women a womb. If men had been born with wombs, social pressure to give birth would not have been gendered. Death during pregnancy and childbirth is a sex-specific fatality but it is one caused fundamentally by biology

27

and anatomy. To that extent, therefore, it is not a straightforward example of sexism. It is a mixture of the natural dangers of childbirth (an evolutionary circumstance) and the social pressure that encouraged women to risk them. We should also remember that society was not intending to sacrifice women's lives in childbirth. Midwives and doctors did everything they could to deliver mother and child safely and healthily. It is hardly equivalent to lining men up in uniformed rows and marching them directly into cannon fire or machine-gun bullets. Men were sent to war in the certainty that large numbers of them would not return.

Society has always treated men as the expendable sex. The ruling class are pursuing imperialist expansion? Send the men to die. Your homeland is being invaded? Send the men to die. Capitalism must be defended? Send the men to die. Bolshevism must defeat capitalism? Send the men to die. The diplomats cannot come to an agreement? Send the men to die. War is androcide. Simply put, 'manly duty' = 'gendered social role'. Not only has this been true throughout history, it is still the case.

Example 1 (1970s): In Washington DC there is a memorial to the American veterans of the Vietnam war called "The Wall". It is dedicated: "In honor of the men and women of the armed forces of the United States who served in the Vietnam war. The names of those who gave their lives and of those who remain missing are inscribed in the order they were taken from us." Listed on the monument are 58,272 names of the American dead and missing in action from that war. *8 of them are women.* http://thewall-usa.com/women.asp

Example 2 (1980s): During the Falklands/Malvinas war, 649 Argentine military personnel, 255 British military personnel and 3 Falkland Islanders died. We know that three of the people killed were women because if we look up the Falklands dead online the gender of the three women is always mentioned. Can you guess which three? Yes, that's right, the three civilians. The people who were in the wrong place at the wrong time, killed in this instance by 'friendly fire'. But what about all

28

the people who died in the line of duty? Usually online resources don't tell us the gender of the military dead. Why not? Is it because it is taken for granted that they will all be men? Numerous websites tell us that 255 British servicemen and 3 female civilians were killed, and we're told that the dead included paratroopers, commandos, marines, sailors, airmen, officers, NCOs, privates, and even laundrymen. But in the absence of an actual gender breakdown we can note that when a website lists the names of the British military dead http://www.roll-of-honour.com/cgi-bin/falklands.cgi the names of the military casualties are male.

Example 3 (2000s): At the time of writing, the gender inequality of the British military fatalities in the war in Afghanistan is 444 men and 3 women. The government and the media never seem to mention this. They prefer to speak of the 'men and women' serving their country and sacrificing their lives. If the gender imbalance were 444 female soldiers dead and 3 male soldiers, do you think that someone would have mentioned the fact? Do you think that the media would have been full of it? Do you think that there would have been feminist campaigns and rallies and marches about it? But the reality is that it is 444 men and 3 women. And the rest is silence. Did *you*, reader, notice the gender imbalance when you were reading or listening to the news reports? http://www.bbc.co.uk/news/uk-10634173

The reason for this gender imbalance is that the Ministry of Defence has a policy of not putting women into close combat. They serve at or near the front line, and this is why some brave women have given their lives in the service of their country, but the MoD does not use women as combat troops. The excuses given for this never include the *political consequences* of employing women as combat troops. Instead, apologists say that the reason for keeping women out of combat is that these fit, strong, active, athletic young women are too weak and girly to be able to carry their equipment; a combat soldier's kit is too heavy for women. Or they say that male soldiers will be so concerned to protect female soldiers in combat that it will undermine military effectiveness. Or they say that when women and men are physically tested on a level playing field (i.e.

without the women being given an artificial advantage) all the men beat all the women, so women in combat would make the fighting troops sub-standard. Even those who do advocate women being given combat roles talk about it in terms of giving women the 'opportunity' to fulfill these roles.

The elephant in the room that no one ever mentions is: what would be the political consequences? The sexist double-standard about the value of human life means that if large numbers of male dead are sent home in coffins or body bags, society says 'how tragic' and the war continues. But what would the public reaction be if there were large numbers of *female dead* being sent home in coffins or body bags? Society would see an eruption of campaigns, marches, rallies and protests demanding that the war must end and end now! Sending women to their deaths in large numbers would not be so socially acceptable. The military know this. They know that if women and men had impartial sex equality in the armed forces, then *political opposition to wars would be massively increased* because female lives are held to be so much more valuable, so much less expendable, than male lives.

This isn't going to happen any time soon, even if the Ministry of Defence were to change its policy, because at present women make up about 9% of the British armed forces, so even if women have the 'opportunity' to serve in combat the numbers are likely to be low. Nonetheless, the armed forces of Canada and New Zealand are said to have no restrictions on women serving in combat roles and the Australian army is currently opening up all military roles to women, including those that were previously considered too dangerous. The United States military is currently deliberating over whether it will use female personnel in combat roles in future, so maybe the British armed forces will eventually get around to doing so.

But, of course, even if women are given the opportunity of taking a combat role in the future and some women *choose* to take it, that is a very different thing from the *compulsory* conscription of men into military service that we have seen in the past. And, you might be surprised to discover, that we can still see in the present. Societies the world over find it easy to view their male population as combatants, even without a war. This includes European countries. Austria, Cyprus, Estonia, Finland and Greece still have male military conscription. Incredibly, Switzerland, who haven't had a war since god knows when, still has male conscription. France suspended military conscription in 1996 and ended it in 2001. Poland imposed military conscription upon its young men until 2008. Germany ended conscription in 2011.

Israel is the only country in the world which requires women to perform compulsory military service and Israel is a special case, being a small population under a constant state of siege from the countries that surround it. It is difficult to even imagine western nations ever making military service including combat roles compulsory for women. Having said that, Norway has a form of conscription currently in operation and in 2013 the Norwegian Parliament voted to extend conscription *to women*, so who knows?

One conclusion that we might draw from the history of war as androcide, with its presumption of the male combatant and the female non-combatant, is that if you wanted a gender theory of history, it would have to conform to the seemingly universal belief in male expendability. Rather than beginning a gender theory of history with the idea of male privilege and empowerment, which would be completely contrary to the centuries of evidence for this attitude of the expendability of male lives, a much more sensible and realistic place to start would be the way that societies all over the world all through history have shown that they will do anything to keep women alive to produce the next generation of babies; that *keeping women and children alive* has been the central preoccupation of every society since primordial times.

I am not suggesting that anyone should adopt a gender theory of history based upon this because I wouldn't want anyone to adopt any kind of gender theory of history. I'm just saying that if you feel driven to have a gender theory about history, then this would be the reasonable place to start: with every society's need to *preserve and protect the people with the wombs* to ensure the next generation. That has been the actual gender privilege practiced by pretty much every society under the sun. It still is, even though the world is now so overpopulated.

But feminism takes a different view, of course. So what is the feminist position on this lethal misandrist sexism that has killed untold millions of men over the centuries? The typical feminist response that we can expect, is to be told that war cannot be sexism against men because it is men who start all the wars. In fact, it is not *men* who start wars, that is a feminist lie, it is *governments* and ruling classes who start wars. Again the response will doubtless be the same; that governments were made up of men, so it was still men who started all the wars. Do you see how this relies upon treating all men as one indivisible group of people? That's the mind-set of feminists engaged in a sex-war with men as the enemy.

But, as we shall see in chapter two when we look at patriarchy theory, just because the office-holders in government are male, that doesn't mean that 'men' (as a class of persons) are making the political decisions. German men didn't decide to invade Poland in 1939, the German government did. British Men didn't decide to declare war on Germany as a result, the British government did. Blaming men for war is blaming the victims.

This, however, will count for nothing to anyone who holds to the feminist gender-stereotype of the insatiably violent male. The much-lauded feminist heroine Andrea Dworkin famously wrote:

"Men love death. In everything they make, they hollow out a central place for death, let its rancid smell contaminate every dimension of whatever still survives. Men especially love murder. In art they celebrate it, and in life they commit it. They embrace murder as if life without it would be devoid of passion, meaning, and action, as if murder were solace . . ." [Dworkin (1988) "Letters from a War Zone", p214]

32

So there we are then, now we know. Men just can't help killing themselves by the millions because they are so much in love with death. What a very plausible explanation. How astonishingly ignorant would a person have to be, ignorant about men and ignorant about men's experiences, to believe this radical feminist view?

Recognising the misandry of war reveals the enormous difference between the attitude of someone who believes in genuine sex equality and the attitude of someone who endorses the feminist agenda. If you wanted to take action to *decrease the amount of war in the world*, one important way you might go about this would be by liberating men from traditional misandry; by opposing the cultural norm that treats all men as if they were combatants by nature and conscripts them into military service, either formally or informally, on the basis of their sex alone. The more that this cultural expectation upon men to fight is removed from the society they are living in, the less war there is likely to be. The urgently necessary emancipation of men through a vocal opposition to misandrist gendered social roles is the attitude that a sex-equalitarian would take in their opposition to war.

But feminism is an obstacle to progress in this regard because it has always been more concerned to *blame men for war* and deny any need for men's liberation and deny that misandry even exists. Feminists seem to find blaming men much more self-satisfying.

The Sexist Double Standard About the Value of Human Life

I said above that the single most extreme example of sexism there has ever been is war and the misandrist double standard about the value of human life that war exemplifies. This double-standard extends far beyond the male gendered social role in warfare. Female lives are held to be of more value than male lives *as a general rule* in both traditional society and contemporary society.

33

If you, reader, are forty or fifty years of age, ask yourself how many times in your life you have heard news reports on television or in the press about death and destruction in various guises around the world in which the news announcer or headline writer said that 'women and children' were among the dead? The phrase 'including women and children' is an established form of words in news reporting because it has been used so many times. By adding the words 'including women and children' to the report on the death toll the reporters clearly indicate that they think this makes the disaster even worse; even more serious and tragic. But why would the disaster have been less tragic, less serious, if only men had died? Are adult male lives so much less valuable than the lives of adult females? That's the clear, unequivocal implication. It's the reason why you've never read or heard a headline about the dead 'including men and children'.

Valuing *children's* lives over *adult* lives is a separate issue and a whole other argument, but the perennial 'including women and children' specifically values women's lives more highly than those of men and the phrase has been around for generations. It goes way back into the past. So this demonstrates just how misandrist traditional society (the so-called 'patriarchy') was against men. A sexist double-standard about the value of human life itself is the ultimate in sexism. Could anything be more sexist than that?

This practice is beginning to be abandoned in news reports now and it is not so routine as it once was. Yet it is still a fairly common occurrence. For example, "Women and children dead after migrant boat capsizes" http://www.mirror.co.uk/news/world-news/lampedusa-migrant-boat-capsizes-leaving-2362868#.UuZlm_unxkg Why are the deaths of the women who drowned more significant than the deaths of the men who also perished? Or "More than 800 Syrian detainees in Egypt, including women and children" https://www.middleeastmonitor.com/news/africa/7890-more-than-800-syrian-detainees-in-egypt-including-women-and-children If the 800 detainees had all been men, would the injustice have been any less?

34

In the first Gulf War in 1990 Saddam Hussein took hundreds of foreigners hostage to use them as human shields. In an attempt to appease criticism from around the world, and amid a propaganda fanfare, he released all the women and children being held hostage. The men being held hostage were not released. http://articles.latimes.com/1990-09-02/news/mn-2041_1_western-women

I remember thinking at the time that it wasn't surprising that a person like Saddam Hussein would have such a *traditional* attitude to gender roles, but what was so revealing about the incident was the way that everyone in the West *also took it for granted* that if anyone was going to be released, then naturally it should be the women and children. We might all agree that the children are the most innocent people in any such situation but that doesn't detract from the innocence of the adult hostages. Are the female civilians in some way more innocent than the male civilians? No, it's just that if anyone is going to be left at risk of death, everyone *takes it for granted* that it should be the men, the most expendable ones, because that's their traditional gendered social role.

The examples are legion. Recently the news media reported an agreement to release the women and children from the devastated city of Homs in the Syrian civil war, but the men are not to be released. http://www.aljazeera.com/news/middleeast/2014/01/women-children-can-leave-syria-homs-2014126171622446761.html The Assad government will release the women, who are assumed to be non-combatants, but not the men because cultural norms treat all men as if they were *combatants by nature*.

Many of the reports using the phrase 'including women and children' are from war zones and perhaps feminism would attempt to excuse the devaluing of innocent men's lives by saying that as the soldiers committing the killings are male, then men should also be the ones killed instead of innocent women and children. But this commits the feminist fallacy of treating all men as one homogenous group who are collectively guilty. Even if you think the soldiers are guilty, the civilian men are as innocent as the civilian women. However, this is a distinction that feminists rarely make. In feminism's sex-war,

35

men are just men and they're all the same. Indeed, as we shall see in chapter 2, patriarchy theory creates a problem for the very concept of *an innocent man*.

But what about an innocent *boy?* The children are innocent, right? Or does the sexist double-standard about the value of human life extend to boys and girls? In February 2014 NBC News ran a story from Reuters which said:

"Gunmen from Islamist group Boko Haram stormed a boarding school in Nigeria overnight and killed 29 pupils . . . Many of the victims died as the school was burned to the ground. 'Some of the students' bodies were burned to ashes,' Police Commissioner Sanusi Rufai said."

If you were not aware of this news item at the time, then the lapse might be explained by a later line in the news report: "All those killed were boys. No girls were touched, Rufai said." http://www.nbcnews.com/news/world/29-boys-killed-boko-haram-attacks-boarding-school-nigeria-n37991

In September of the previous year over 40 students, all boys, had been shot dead in their college in the town of Gujba. These were two incidents of mass murder among many acts of deadly violence. For years Boko Haram has been committing atrocities in pursuit of their jihad. In April 2014 The Guardian newspaper reported:

"So far, 2014 has been the bloodiest year of their insurgency: at least 1,500 have been killed in dozens of attacks, and it's only April. This compares to 2,100 deaths between 2009 and 2013." http://www.theguardian.com/world/2014/apr/17/boko-haram-will-keep-killing-and-nigerias-leaders-are-powerless

But something else happened in April. Boko Haram abducted 260 schoolgirls from a school in Chibok. The girls were still alive, they hadn't been shot or been burned alive like the boys, but there was talk of sex-slavery and forced marriages. Suddenly the whole world was erupting into social media campaigns to #BringBackOurGirls. Nowhere more so that in the feminist West. Twitter went wild. Hollywood movie stars got involved. The president's wife Michelle Obama got involved. It was a celebrity frenzy.

The story got such a rush of media momentum that the ultra politically correct comedian John Stewart did a piece on the abduction in which he mocked the grinning black leader of Boko Haram, Abubakar Shekau, (as well as joking about the name of President Goodluck Jonathan) in a way that his regular audience would have considered borderline racist under any other circumstances. During his piece to camera, Stewart described the abduction of the girls as "one of the most horrifying atrocities any people or country could suffer". Really, John? So are we supposed to believe that abducting girls is a more horrifying atrocity than burning boys alive?

The glaring gender double-standard was so extreme that even some people *outside* of Men's Rights activism noticed it. Kill boys and the world barely rouses itself to comment; abduct girls and incite a global response of strident outrage demanding that something must be done. Yet in the end #BringBackOurGirls came to nothing because, of course, what does Boko Haram care about Infidel twitter campaigns? All the campaign really proved was the age-old sexism of the double-standard about the value of female lives compared to the value of male lives, and the traditional imperative to protect females. If you want anyone to give a damn about you, then you better be born a girl.

Another example of the double-standard about the value of human life is the issue of workplace fatalities. The United States Bureau of Labor http://www.bls.gov/iif/oshcfoi1.htm#2011 says that in 2012 there were 4,383 workers who died from employment injuries. Over 90% of them were men. This is not a freak statistic. In 2011 there were 4,693 workers who died from employment injuries and, you guessed it, over 90% of them were men. In 2010? Over 90% of workers who died from employment injuries were men. Are you seeing a pattern here? In 2009? Over 90% were men. And so on. Men suffer the overwhelming majority of workplace deaths and injuries because it's overwhelmingly men who do the dangerous jobs.

Here's a question: have you heard these statistics before? *Year after year after year people of one sex suffer over 90% of deaths from workplace injuries?* I mean, we've had more than forty years of high-profile feminist agitation, and feminism is supposed to be all about sex equality and opposing gender inequality, especially gender inequality in the workplace, isn't it? But have you heard any feminists campaigning on this issue of deaths in the workplace? No, neither have I. Sadly, year after year, over 90% of these dead workers committed the unpardonable sin of having been born the wrong sex, so who cares if they're dead.

What about in the UK? According to the Guardian newspaper http://www.theguardian.com/news/datablog/2013/may/07/men-gender-divide-feminism men are 20 times more likely to have a fatal injury at work than women. Yet the UK Health & Safety Executive (HSE) statistics on fatalities in the workplace 2012/13 is a typical expression of society's casual devaluation of male human life. http://www.hse.gov.uk/statistics/fatals.htm Although men suffer the vast majority of deaths in the workplace, nowhere in this document is there a breakdown of the statistics by gender. Download the pdf file and search for the words 'gender' or 'male' or 'men' (as I did). The search comes up empty.

Do you think that this would be the case if the vast majority of deaths in the workplace were female? The HSE's workplace injuries web pages do mention gender in connection with violent assault (where it says that in interviews conducted by the Crime Survey for England and Wales 1.2% of women and 1.6% of men reported being victims of violence at work). http://www.hse.gov.uk/statistics/causinj/violence/index.htm After all, violence against women is a feminist issue, so gender needs to be mentioned in that connection. But when men are suffering gender-inequality at the cost of their lives the powers-that-be are blind and mute. They see nothing and they say nothing. No wonder most people aren't aware of these issues.

The Sexist Double Standard About Human Pain

Imagine it's 1940. A ten year old girl scrapes her knee and is crying, so an adult rushes to her side to comfort her, cooing words of reassurance. A ten year old boy scrapes his knee and is crying so an adult tells him to stop crying like a girl and be brave like a man. The girl learns that displaying her vulnerability brings sympathy and support. The boy learns that displaying his vulnerability brings censure. (It is important to remember this when listening to feminists demanding special treatment and protection for women, because feminism constantly plays upon this old expectation that 'female vulnerability' entitles them to sympathy and support. Feminism presents an image of all the women in the world being like crying ten year old girls with scraped knees.)

I mention this 1940s scenario simply to make the obvious point that each child was being groomed by society to accept a gendered attitude regarding human pain. Women had society's permission to cry like a child, men absolutely did not. From childhood onwards, traditional ideas of gender promoted a deliberate *social insensitivity* toward male pain. There was a misandrist double-standard about human pain which viewed female pain as pitiable whilst treating male pain callously. The double-standard persists to the present day. If you don't believe me, ask yourself the following question: do you find testicular pain funny? Traditional society did and so does contemporary society.

Question: How many times have you personally seen a comedy entertainment in which a man is hit in the testicles as a joke to be laughed at?

Answer: Too many hundreds of times to count. Thousands of times probably.

Question: How many times have you personally seen a comedy entertainment in which a woman is hit in the vagina as a joke to be laughed at?

Answer: Zero? Have you ever seen this in comedy entertainment?

If you enjoy this brand of comedy, ask yourself why you think that male genital pain is something to laugh at; to take humorous pleasure in? Then ask yourself why you think female genital pain isn't funny. The answer is: your misandrist sexism. You have a culturally induced double-standard about human pain. For anyone who believes in impartial sex equality the issue is clear. It has to be both or neither. Either *both* male and female genital pain is funny or *neither* is.

If you are so intellectually dishonest that you are in denial about this, then check out the example of 'funny' violence against men in the first television commercial on this video in Vinny Mac's excellent "Misandry in the Media" series http://www.youtube.com/watch?v=cg0uWls9qnw&feature=c4-overview&list=UUIEO_w-8_voXDymte5KYw_A in which a two minute commercial spends half of its air time, a full minute, showing a woman beating the shit out of a man for the amusement of the audience at home.

Those readers who are not in denial will know from your own direct experience that you live in a culture which treats male pain as humorous and amusing. But only if the pain is male.

If you take the position that 'funny' violence against men is not an important issue of sex equality because it is too trivial or because it's just a laugh, then you will doubtless have no objection to increased levels of comedy violence against women in future. Indeed, you might see an increased occurrence of slapstick violence against women in comedies as a good sign. Laughing at female pain will be movement toward greater sex equality and when the audience laughs as readily at a woman being punched in the tits as they do at a man being kicked in the balls, you will surely feel that we have made some genuine progress toward greater equality in public attitudes about violence.

You will, won't you? Or will you feel that female pain is in some unspecified way 'different'?

Male pain has always been more socially acceptable than female pain in the history of entertainment because male pain has always been more socially acceptable in every aspect of society. After all, boys have to be groomed into men who will march off to war. So in addition to being amused by men in pain, society is also excited by men in pain. Violence has been a staple ingredient of film entertainment from its earliest beginnings. Overwhelmingly the violence in cinema has been, and continues to be, directed at male characters. For generations movies have delighted in depicting men being bombed, shot, stabbed, punched, kicked, thrown off buildings, set on fire, and otherwise physically violated. Action movies are largely 'violence against men' movies. Slapstick silent comedies were largely 'violence against men' comedies. War movies are, undeniably, 'violence against men' movies. Even romantic-comedies can involve violence against men. (See chapter 6.)

Despite this, in the 1980s there was a feminist campaign against 'violence against women in cinema'. This was particularly targeted at things like rape scenes in movies because the idea was to draw attention to male violence against females. The actual amount of violence against women in cinema was a tiny, tiny fraction of the total amount of violence in cinema but this glaringly obvious fact was entirely ignored because the violence against men was perceived as being male-on-male violence and was viewed with the same attitude as that felt toward gangster-on-gangster violence: if the mafia are killing each other, who cares, so long as innocent citizens are not being hurt. To feminism, men suffering beatings from other men is not a cause for concern. Remember, in the feminist universe all men are one homogenous lump, so there is no important distinction to be made between male victimizers and male victims. The man being punched in the face is indivisible from the man that is punching him because all men are 'men'.

But what about female violence against men? Sorry, that doesn't count. Apparently, that isn't violence. How many times on the cinema screen have you seen a woman slap a man across the face *without him slapping her back*? Very occasionally he does, but mostly he doesn't. He just stands there and takes it. He has to 'suck it up' like a man, as they say. It is a long-standing cinematic tradition that women are allowed to hit men across the face with impunity. As Bogart said to Peter Lorre after he was slapped by Mary Astor in The Maltese Falcon:

"When you get slapped, you'll take it and like it."

This grotesquely conspicuous and yet *politically invisible* sexist double-standard was brought to its ludicrous apogee with the introduction into movies in the 1990s of the character of the female tough guy who doesn't have to take a beating herself. It has long been an axiom of tough guy movies that the tough guy has to take a severe beating at some point during the film to show how tough he is. How many times have you seen Bruce Willis or Sylvester Stallone or Arnold Schwarzenegger or Jeanne Claude Van Damme suffer a bloody bruising beating during the course of an action film? I personally cannot watch the Rocky movies because the level of prolonged and appalling violence that Rocky is always required to suffer in the ring is too extreme for me.

But when the female tough guy appeared she was shown 'kicking ass' against her male opponents without ever taking a serious beating herself. After all, if you punch one of Charlie's Angels in the face it would smudge her glamorous cosmetics. Society was still conditioned to have a double-standard about male pain and female pain. A cinema audience would cheerfully watch a man getting repeatedly punched in the face, kicked in the teeth, smashed with an iron bar, etc., and enjoy the movie. But if the same things had been done to a female tough guy the audience would have started to feel uncomfortable. They were quite prepared to watch a woman kicking ass against a man but they would've become a little queasy if a man were kicking ass against a woman in the same way. The violence inflicted upon her mustn't be too severe because she was a girlie tough guy.

42

This is why, when the female tough guy was fighting male villains, *she* would repeatedly hit *him* with bone-crunching impact but he wouldn't hit her back *too much* because that's "violence against women". In movie fights the male villain tended to *grab* the female tough guy, *wrestle* her, *throw* her against a wall, and things like that, rather than just punching her solidly in the face over and over as he would have done to a male tough guy.

The farcical nonsense of having a female tough guy who mustn't be hit back because "she's a girl" has begun to be modified a bit in recent years but the double-standard is still very much in place. So much so, that if we were to suggest that there should be as just as many female tough guys in movies as male tough guys, and that *the women should take the same brutal beatings that the men take*, this equality might provoke some horror. We might be accused of being misogynist monsters for even suggesting such an equality. And if such films were actually made, what would the feminist response be? Would there be a feminist campaign group protesting outside the cinema trying to get the film banned because of its unacceptable level of "violence against women"?

There are signs that the situation is beginning to change slowly. In recent years the female tough guy has had to take a few hard knocks here and there. For a graphic example of this changing attitude (from a different medium) compare the image of the Lara Croft of the past who doesn't have a scratch or bruise on her body http://kgvreflections.files.wordpress.com/2013/12/lara-croft-tomb-raider-6374056-1600-1280.jpg with the Lara Croft of the present http://wasduk.files.wordpress.com/2013/12/lara-croft-2013.jpg who is bleeding and bandaged and covered in dirt. Perhaps before too long the female tough guys will get the stuffing knocked out of them in exactly the same way that the male tough guys do.

In this connection I should offer a word of recognition for the film "GI Jane". Contrast two films both made by Ridley Scott: "Thelma and Louise" (1991) and "GI Jane" (1997). The former was hailed by the critics as some kind of splendid breakthrough in anti-sexist movie-making. The latter was dismissed mainly, it seems, because the critics never have a good word to say about the actor who starred in it, Demi Moore. (She received the 1997 Golden Raspberry Award for Worst Actress for this film.) The film critics could not have been more wrong about these two movies. The truth is that "Thelma and Louise" is a massively and crudely sexist film with wall-to-wall sexist stereotypes, whilst it was "GI Jane" that was actually the significant breakthrough in anti-sexist movie-making.

What makes "Thelma and Louise" so appallingly sexist? The characters in the script. Just look at all the feminist negative male stereotypes it contains.

- The bullying abusive husband who, naturally, is no good at sex.

- The young stud who is good at sex and so, naturally, is totally untrustworthy and a thief.

- The rapist who attacks in the shadows of a lonely parking lot.

- The nice guy cop who conforms to the newly-minted 1980s imposed male gender role of the concerned and empathic 'new man' and who is therefore utterly ineffectual.

- The menacing-looking Nazi-type uniformed cop who turns into a squealing crybaby when the roles are reversed.

- It even includes the leering, lecherous truck driver! Is anything more of a sexist stereotype than the lecherous truck driver? But he's in "Thelma and Louise" along with all the others.

(If you're interested, contrast this movie with the French film "Baise Moi" to see what a *non-sexist* version of "Thelma and Louise" would be like.)

What makes "GI Jane" an important breakthrough in anti-sexist movie-making? The female action hero gets the shit kicked out of her. She takes exactly the same kind of severe beating that a male action hero would routinely take. The film even uses this beating to raise the issue of how male marines might be weakened in an interrogation situation if a female marine was being tortured. The male marines might endure torture themselves without giving away information to the enemy but they would spill their guts if a female marine were being tortured because *the male imperative to protect women* would be too strong for them to resist. "GI Jane" was a film that deserved a lot of credit for being brave enough to tackle the issue of the sexist double-standard about human pain.

Misandrist Chivalry

I've just mentioned 'the male imperative to protect women'. This may sound odd to any readers under forty years of age who have never known any other society than feminism. Aren't we all told every day, year in and year out, decade after decade, that men are domestically and sexually violent toward women, and an ever-present *threat* to women? Hasn't feminism taught us over and over that men have always oppressed women and kept them downtrodden? How could someone raised under feminism possibly take seriously the idea that throughout history men have *protected* women?

But remember some of the points we have already considered above. Throughout human evolution social survival has depended upon ensuring that the next generation are born and raised, so the need to protect *the people with the wombs and the breast milk* is an inherited instinct in men, a part of their evolutionary psychology. This has been used to socially gender male conduct. As we have seen, if you want to exert psychological pressure on men to coerce them into volunteering for a war, what do you do? You tell them that they'll be *defending their wives and sweethearts*, and they buy into this because there is an age-old societal belief that men have a duty to protect women. This has been so central to how people have been conditioned to think for centuries that it is hardly surprising that when we look at the cultures of the past

45

we repeatedly see cultural norms in which men are protective toward women.

These cultural norms have included all forms of protection. The most explicit is protection from physical danger, whether it is by escorting a woman home after dark or defending her in a violent altercation or whatever. The social reinforcement of this masculine role to place himself between a woman and harm can be found in every popular entertainment in which a male hero rescues a damsel in distress, going all the way back to the gallant knight who rescues the princess in the tower. But the burden of financial responsibility that men have taken on behalf of women and children is also a form of protection, as is the code of etiquette called chivalry.

Traditional society included cultural norms of chivalrous behaviour that were so misandrist that they seem difficult to credit as real, now that these aspects of chivalry have largely been consigned to the past. The rules of 'gentlemanly conduct' imposed a whole catalogue of required conduct to which men had to conform (although this applied slightly less to men of the working class, who were no doubt too shagged out from hard work to bother with this malarkey).

A man was expected to stand up whenever a woman in his company was standing, which is why he was also expected to offer a lady his seat if he had one and she didn't. A man was expected to handle heavy objects for a woman, which is why he had to pull out her chair for her when she sat down. He was expected to open doors for her, and to stand between her and the road when walking in the street to protect her from the hustle and bustle of the traffic. He had to make sure that he arrived first on a date/appointment and not complain when she arrived late because if she had arrived first and he had been late, then she would have been left waiting alone and unprotected in a public place. He had to offer her his arm so that he could 'escort' her from one place to another. He was required to put himself in harm's way to defend her honour and protect the little lady from anyone who might disrespect her. In any number of ways he was forever dancing attendance upon her courteously as her knight in shining armour.

All of these courtesies express the same idea: that a gentleman always puts *consideration for the ladies* ahead of any consideration for himself or other men. The essence of gentlemanly conduct is *deference to the ladies* and it entailed a great deal of bowing-and-scraping to women. It was a code of etiquette designed to turn every man into the servant of every woman (or at least, every women of their own social class). As such, its female-supremacist character might be expected to appeal to feminists and, indeed, there are a few feminists who are such monumental hypocrites that they believe that men should still, in this day and age, adopt a chivalrous 'gentlemanly' attitude toward women even though women have long since ceased to be ladies. But for most feminists the code of etiquette that I've just described would either be ignored as trivial or would be classified as misogyny for treating women as if they were all needy and incapable. And in both cases, whether pro-chivalry or anti-chivalry, feminists will be blind to its misandry.

So, for any reader who still doesn't get it, let's consider just one of these examples of required conduct and spell it out. *Men being expected to stand up in the presence of women* is not so very different from black people in 1960s America being required to sit at the back of the bus; an indignity which gave rise to the civil rights 'freedom riders'. Some people will sneer at this analogy or even find it objectionable. They will say that the two things are not analogous because sitting at the back of the bus was an expression of a wider systemic racism. But that is very much the point that I'm making, men having to stand in the presence of women was an expression of a wider systemic misandry. Having to sit at the back of the bus or having to stand in the presence of women might both appear trivial on the surface but neither is trivial when placed in context. Let's use the tool of role reversal.

Imagine that there was a cultural rule which said that women were not allowed to sit in the presence of men who were

47

standing; that a woman was not permitted to sit down until *after* the men in her company were seated. A woman must stand up whenever a man enters the room and she must remain standing until *he* has sat down. If another man enters the room she must again stand up until such time as he has sat down. If the first man gets to his feet to leave, then she too must stand and remain standing until he has left the room because she is *not allowed* to be seated in the presence of a man who is standing. Travelling home that evening, footsore and weary, she must surrender her seat on the bus to a man because there are no other seats available for him to sit down in, so she must give him her seat because she is not permitted to sit if he is standing.

Does it still sound trivial? If such a cultural rule existed for women, feminists would scream from the rooftops that it was abominably sexist male-supremacism and proof positive that men were the most despicable monsters on the face of the earth. But as it was men who were told that they must abide by a rule which said that no gentleman was permitted to sit if a lady was standing, apparently that was nothing to get upset about. Is this really so very different from being required to sit at the back of the bus? Isn't it worse? If you had to choose between these two indignities, which would you choose? Either you had to sit at the back of the bus or you were obliged to stand if any member of the other sex was standing. Which would you choose?

And as for the context of a wider systemic misandry, this rule of social conduct was not an arbitrary and isolated case. It was a part of a whole system of cultural norms and behavioural etiquette that expected men to protect and provide for women. Chivalrous conduct wasn't an atypical add-on feature of traditional society, it was an expression of *the prevailing attitudes about gender*. Perhaps the most important point of which to take note when considering the social custom of chivalry is that it had *no advantage to men*. On the contrary, it might cost a man dearly to protect a woman. Gentlemanly conduct only advantaged women. Yet it is almost archetypal as a 'traditional' mode of behaviour. Under traditional sexism, women and men were both advantaged and disadvantaged in their different ways under the gendered bifurcation of society.

Why did men submit to the indignity and insult of chivalry? At its deepest psychological level chivalry is the socialised expression of an evolutionary inheritance. As we've already considered, over millennia in which people lived in a dangerously hostile state of nature humans evolved with gender roles because the child-bearers were less able to defend themselves than the other sex, so adaptation for survival developed in that other sex (males) genetic selection for the abilities needed to protect the child-bearers. If the offspring did not live long enough to reach adulthood and themselves produce offspring, then the species would have become extinct. The species survived because males evolved to protect females and progeny.

But this instinct to protect women that men may have within their evolutionary psychology relates to chivalry only at the deepest psychological level. As a code of etiquette, as a set of behavioural norms, men submitted to the rules of chivalry because they were socialised to accept it and conform to it. It was a part of the imposed gendered social roles that both men and women were culturally conditioned to obey.

Remembering the definition of sexism given at the beginning of this chapter, that gender dispositions derived simply from evolutionary inheritance are not sexist but the *societal imposition* of gender is sexist, chivalry is clearly misandrist (and in a back-handed way, misogynist too, in that it infantilizes women) precisely because it is a socially enforced code of rules and norms. I'm not just pointing out the obvious, that opening doors for women as if they weren't able to use door handles without assistance has nothing to do with the survival of the species. It goes much further.

Society has, as we have seen, a belief in the superior value of female lives. Chivalry is a part of this elevation of women to a status of superior value. By treating women *as if* they were children, women's lives were given the superior value *that the lives of children have* for most people. Since women's lives are not, in fact, more valuable than men's lives, a code of etiquette was adopted for *the pretence that women are as valuable as children*. Treating women as 'ladies' was like treating women as children, the poor helpless darlings. This is why we find the loss of female lives being spoken of as if women were people of superior value with the old phrase 'including women and children'. If some women and men are killed in a plane crash, the deaths of these women are of no account for the overall survival of the species. When society treats their deaths as being more tragic than the deaths of men this is an expression of the systemic misandry of which chivalry was a part.

Chivalry, like any code of etiquette, is cultural not natural. That is why it had to be socially reinforced. This reinforcement took the form of conformity to chivalry being *a source of respect for men*. This is one of the classic techniques by which society imposed gendered social roles on both sexes. If you want women to perform domestic duties in the home, make it a source of respect for women so that they become house-proud. Then they'll cook and scrub for all they're worth in order to earn the respect they derive from their domestic abilities. If you want men to take financial responsibility for women and children, make it a source of respect for men to be good financial providers. Then they'll devote their lives to working six days a week with overtime until they drop dead at the age of sixty-five. Chivalry was also imposed using this technique. Traditionally, men protected women and were rewarded with respect. They were respected by the women.

You can see this social reinforcement in operation in the phrase 'no man should ever hit a woman'. This is an appeal to the traditional idea of male honour. Culturally it was *dishonourable* for a man to hit a woman. However much she provoked him he was supposed to restrain himself from lashing out because the masculine code of honour meant that he must never hit a woman. The phrase 'no woman should ever hit a man' wasn't used in the same way because traditionally women were required to conform to a different code of honour to that required of a man (which required, for example, a greater sexual chastity than men). These codes of honour were, again, a source of pride and self-respect. This answers our question for us: men submitted to the indignity and insult of chivalry because in traditional society *it wasn't perceived as* an undignified insult, it was perceived as a source of honour and respect (just as chastity was a source of honour and respect for women).

In traditional society the respect of women was one of the things that men valued most highly (as well as the respect of other men). Indeed, we might say that 'respect' was to men what 'love' was to women. If you look at the classic scenarios of romance and adventure, popular literature directed at a female readership is all about a woman winning a man's love, and popular literature directed at a male readership is all about a man winning the admiration and respect of a woman. In popular romantic fiction, the heroine overcomes some obstacle to their love and when they embrace at the end of the story she knows that she has won his heart forever. In popular adventure stories, the hero saves the damsel in distress from the villain and when they embrace at the end she looks up at him with adoring eyes because he's the personification of the male protector.

Traditionally, if a deceitful man wanted to manipulate a woman, his most effective way of doing so might be to convince her that he had fallen in love with her and she with him. A woman might do anything for the man she loved. If a deceitful woman wanted to manipulate a man, her most effective way of doing so might be to convince him that he was her hero. A man might do anything for the woman who respected him enough to place her trust in him and rely upon him for help.

These classic scenarios are a reflection of a social reality. If society wanted to manipulate men into serving the interests of women it would do what, in fact, it did do: make chivalry a source of respect, honour and pride for men. Then they'll be chivalrous. Then they'll defer to the ladies like a proper little gentleman. This was very much a part of traditional society.

But can you, reader, living in a contemporary feminist society that systemically *disrespects* men, even imagine such a thing as women expressing their respect for men? Can you imagine the women in the culture of the present day actually *showing men respect for their manhood?*

In a feminist society in which women habitually pour scorn upon men, condescendingly and contemptuously, for being immature boys obsessed with games, for being selfish and inconsiderate domestic incompetents, for being irresponsible commitment-phobes, and for being absurdly macho, etc., etc., the old respect for manhood has been torn to shreds and thrown into the rubbish bin with the rest of the garbage. In a feminist society in which men are labelled as the oppressor, as rapists, as domestically violent abusers, and as potential paedophiles, etc., etc., is the idea of showing respect for men *as men* even imaginable?

If not, then what place does chivalry have in contemporary society? For how long are men going to show greater consideration to women than they do to other men, and put themselves at risk even to the point of sacrificing their own lives and limbs, for the sake of feminist women who continually *disrespect* them and gender-stereotype them as the predatory, abusive, oppressive male even whilst accepting their protection? Chivalry insists that a gentleman always defers to a lady, but the 'lady' was a cultural feature of traditional society. She no longer exists. In feminist society *there are no ladies, there are only women.* Chivalry puts women on a pedestal, but that pedestal is contrary to sex equality.

Chivalry is dead. Bury it.

There is no greater embodiment of chivalry than the conduct of the men on the passenger liner Titanic which sank in the North Atlantic ocean in 1912. This incident is held up as the foremost example of men sacrificing their lives in accordance with the unwritten code of 'women and children first'. Now compare and contrast. In 1994 the ferry Estonia sank in the Baltic Sea. The 989 passengers and crew were multinational and multiethnic but the majority came from Sweden, Estonia, Latvia, and Finland. The final death toll was 852 by drowning and hypothermia due to exposure in the water. The 137 who survived were mostly *young adult males of strong physical constitution*. Women, the elderly, and children fared less well. Only seven people over the age of 55 survived, and no one under the age of 12 survived.

On the Titanic, where male self-sacrifice was observed, *70% of the women* survived but only *20% of the men*. On the Estonia, where male self-sacrifice was apparently not observed, 5.4% of the women survived and 22% of the men.

Are All Men Sluts?

One of the most painful burdens carried by men under traditional sexism was the requirement that men must take the sexual initiative with women. Untold generations of boys and young men have suffered the agonies of having to muster the courage to take the sexual initiative, only to find that they are too shy, or they get shot down in flames by the woman's rejection. Every time a man expressed a romantic or sexual interest in a woman he was, in emotional terms, placing his head on the chopping block, and time after time, down came the axe to cut his fucking head off.

In traditional society the person who took the sexual initiative was much more likely to be turned down than they would be these days because, of course, we are talking about sexual relations *before* the contraceptive revolution. Not only did women have to be more careful about sex because of the fear of pregnancy, they were also living in a culture that smeared girls who were even thought to be promiscuous as 'sluts'. This was a time when young men who were virgins had to pretend that they were not, and young women who were not virgins had to pretend that they were. The customs of the time required women to put up a show of resistance to seduction (the very concept of seduction presupposes some resistance). The angst-ridden young man who was expected to take the sexual initiative was very likely to suffer rejection.

Women, in contrast, had the advantage of being in the empowered position of *decision*. She got to say yes or no. This traditional power accorded to women is still reflected in every feminist discussion of rape in the present day where the sole issue under discussion is *the consent of the woman*, the decision-maker, never the consent of the man, as if the decision whether or not to have sex was always *hers alone*.

(Traditional attitudes to sex are very much a part of feminism in this regard, as is the way that feminists discuss heterosexual sex as if the male were the *active* participant and the female were the *passive* participant, as if hetero sex was something that *he* did *to* her and was therefore all his fault. These days some feminists even claim that if a woman was drunk when she consented, then it doesn't count as consent. The man, drunk or sober, is always held accountable for his actions but he's also held accountable for *her* actions as well. If she gets drunk, he's held responsible for what she does whilst intoxicated. How *passive* can you get! Covertly, feminism borrows heavily from the code of chivalry in the way that it treats women as if they were children who are not responsible for their own actions and have to be protected by men. In this way, the extreme misandry of feminism indirectly produces a considerable amount of feminist misogyny.)

Given their traditional gendered requirement to take the sexual initiative, it is scarcely surprising that men have been painted as being sexually aggressive. It also helps explain why young men can sometimes be clumsy and boorish in their approach to potential sexual encounters. Adopting a swaggering demeanour of pushy over-confidence may be a mask for fear of rejection, but it would usually be taken as evidence of male sexual aggressiveness and therefore condemned. As so often, men were given this onerous gendered social role and were then condemned for carrying it out. Few things can have caused young males more angst, remorse, and self-contempt over the generations. One of the few benefits that men might consider themselves to have received from the gender revolution of the last forty years is that these days there are an increasingly large number of young women who don't wait virginally to be asked and then play hard to get (because that was *their* traditional gendered role) but instead will vocalise their own sexual appetites and take the sexual initiative with the boys.

It has not only been a complaint made by feminists, it has also been a complaint made by women, that it is terribly unfair and sexist that society has had such double-standards about sexual promiscuity; that if a woman was sexually promiscuous people would call her a slut whereas if a man was sexually promiscuous people would not call him a slut. Actually, it is no longer the case in mainstream western society that women are demeaned as sluts if they have a lot of sexual partners. That *used to be* the case but it is not any longer, as you will know if you've been paying attention to the world around you. This particular complaint is a useful issue to address, however, because it highlights the way in which the average contemporary misandrist pig is blind to the insults paid to men.

One reason (it is not the only reason but it is one reason) why men traditionally have not been called sluts is that society has taken it for granted that *all men are sluts*. It was, and still is, popularly believed that all men will stick their cocks into anything that holds still long enough; that no man can truly be trusted to stay sexually faithful to his wife or partner because given the chance he will be skirt-chasing and looking to get his end away. So one reason why *the word* 'slut' has not been used against men is that it would be superfluous. If you believe that all adult males are by nature sluts, then to call someone a man is *already* to call him a slut. His being a slut is taken as a given when you call him a man.

If a wife does not trust her husband around other women because 'we all know what *men* are', then that wife believes that she is married to a slut. The implication is right there is the phrase 'we all know what *men* are'. Moreover, she is in the position of believing that any man she had married, however

55

different his character might have been from her actual husband, would also have been a slut because (join in the chorus) 'we all know what *men* are'. This misandrist sexism is so commonplace, so completely ordinary and conventional, that many people don't even see it. But it's right in front of their face.

These days people like to give explanations for universal male sluttishness based on evolutionary psychology; that the genetic imperative makes men want to disperse their seed as widely as possible whereas evolution has made women sexually monogamous. But no one thinks that women must therefore be incapable of being promiscuous. There is any amount of unreliable pop-research which claims women commit more infidelity or less infidelity or the same amount of infidelity as men. Yet although people do not think that women are inescapably monogamous, they do seem to think that men are inescapably sluts. It's what they're accustomed to thinking.

The idea that most men are *not* sluts; that most men are *not* sexually aroused by every women they meet; that most men would refuse sex with the majority of women they meet because the men are not attracted to those women; these ideas are completely alien to the average misandrist pig. There are still women in the world who think that if a man *doesn't* want to sleep with her, then *he must be gay*. The idea, for example, that he finds her sexism against him repulsive and he doesn't want to sleep with her because he's not attracted to a woman with such a bigoted personality, is something that wouldn't occur to her.

A straightforward recognition that some men and women *are* sluts, and that some men and women *are not* sluts, is apparently simply too radical an idea for people to accept. They prefer to go on believing that *all men are sluts*. Why would they prefer that? They must know lots of men who do not chase after women. They must have met lots of men who are intimidated by sex and would prefer a nice cup of tea, thank you. They may even themselves *be* a man who meets any number of women that he does not want to have sex with

56

because he doesn't find them sexually arousing. Yet still they prefer to go on believing that all men, as men, are sluts.

People often believe whatever they are told to believe, even if it is contrary to their own direct experience. Years ago people were told that 'research' had shown that men think about sex every seven seconds. People took this ludicrous claim seriously, as if they thought it plausible. What morons. How could anyone, man or woman, possibly think about sex every seven seconds? Men wouldn't be able to read this book if they stopped every seven seconds to think about sex; they'd never reach the end of a page. I wouldn't have been able to write it if I glazed over every seven seconds to think about sex. Feminist society's negative gender-stereotype of men as creatures who are only interested in football, lager and Kylie Minogue's bum would itself collapse if there were no time to pay attention to a ninety minute football match because the men watching it were thinking about sex every seven seconds. Yet this 'research' claim was *taken seriously*.

Many years later in 2011 some researchers from Ohio State University did their own study and came up with an average figure of 19 times per day. http://www.eurekalert.org/pub_releases/2011-11/osu-sds112811.php (I'm not endorsing this figure, just quoting it.) Whereas if men were thinking about sex every 7 seconds, that would add up to around 12,240 sexual thoughts per day. That people were prepared to believe this nonsense demonstrates just what extreme levels of total bullshit they are prepared to believe about sexuality in men.

The incredibly crass sexist caricature of men as creatures who are *by nature* sluts is more than just an offensive travesty. It is the kind of thing which causes people to take seriously the bizarrely absurd feminist fantasies about how all men are rapists or potential rapists, and about how women have to live in a male 'rape culture'. An idea as stupid as 'rape culture' could never gain any traction if people weren't already predisposed to the widespread misandrist belief that all men walk around with permanent erections looking for someone to stick it into.

One reason (again, it is not the only reason but it is one reason) why the word 'slut' was used pejoratively against women was the belief that women are *not* all sluts. The woman who behaved sluttishly was seen as disgracing her sex because it was assumed that women were not inclined to promiscuity like men, it was taken for granted that women in general were the sexually fastidious and sexually faithful gender.

I would certainly agree that *the word* 'slut' may not be used very often about men but it is not the use of the word that matters, it is the *belief* that all men are sluts which matters. Getting rid of this sexist caricature of the 'horny male' is imperative in today's society in which every discussion of sexual consent and rape omits to mention the issue of male consent to sex because male consent is taken for granted. The issue of sexual consent is *enormously important* and it cannot be discussed in an impartial sex-equalitarian way until society discards its present belief that the issue of male consent can simply be ignored because men are all a bunch of sluts.

Misandrist Homophobia

Given the traditional gender-stereotype which views men as voraciously promiscuous heterosexuals with one-track minds in constant pursuit of women, it is not surprising that homophobia has itself been an example of misandrist sexism. Nor is it surprising that in a modern society ruled by political correctness, this is seldom if ever mentioned in discussions about homophobia.

The current ruling elite classify male homosexuals (as one group within LGBTI) as a victimized vulnerable group and classify white male heterosexuals as the guilty victimizers who oppressed everyone else. So it tends to pass by unnoticed that the centuries-long prejudice against male homosexuals is entirely consistent with the rest of traditional misandrist sexism; that the dominant homophobia in traditional society was directed against men and was one very prominent example of the way that men were persecuted for failing to conform to the social imposition of gender. It is therefore worthwhile to spend a moment reminding ourselves that this was an important example of misandry.

Until the 1980s when gay men introduced an ultra-butch fashion of leather biker outfits and lumberjack chic and Arab dictator moustaches, mainstream society's standard misrepresentation of the male homosexual was the classic limp-wristed, mincing caricature of fussy effeminacy. Gay men were thought of as a kind of pretend woman. In other words the popular idea of a gay male was the absolute personification of a man's failure in manhood under the traditional social construct of masculinity. (It may be that the ultra-butch image of the 1980s was, in part, an ironic response to this, coinciding as it did with gay liberation.) Gay men lived in fear of public assault and criminal prosecution if their secret became known and they would try to avoid this by avoiding effeminacy; they could 'pass for straight'. Safety lay in appearing 'manly' in the required manner, an outward show of conformity with the constraints of gender imposed upon all men, straight or gay.

All of this is well-known, yet such is the resistance to even talking about misandry in feminist society that discussions of this sexist persecution of men never seem to speak of it *as a sexist persecution of men*. Instead, it's spoken of as the persecution of homosexuals *by men* under 'patriarchy', although this misreading of history is itself homophobic since it implicitly treats gay men as if they were not as much *men* as any other men.

Homophobia is, of course, a larger issue than the persecution of male homosexuals. But in the past (in the West) lesbianism was not the target of the majority of homophobia because of the old-fashioned notion that men were sexual creatures whereas women were non-sexual creatures. The belief that women did not have any sexuality (the 'lie back and think of England' attitude in which women submitted to the bestial appetites of men for the sake of patriotic procreation) meant that although prejudice against lesbians was very real, it was less publicly overt than prejudice against gay men.

This is not to say that there was no social persecution of lesbians, merely that the persecution of male homosexuals was much more conspicuous. Misogyny could bring disapprobation upon women for showing any signs of active sexuality, and a culture that was busy disapproving of overt signs of *heterosexual* lust in women had less time for singling out homosexual lust in women for special disapprobation. There is a famous, although probably apocryphal, story that lesbianism was not mentioned when the criminal law relating to male homosexuality was being discussed with Queen Victoria because Her Majesty refused to believe that there were any female homosexuals. Whether the story is true or not doesn't matter because the point here is the attitude of society at the time which the story reflects. Laws constraining sexual behaviour were laws which targeted men. Then *as now*, in fact.

The 'social purity' movement of the late 19th century was the Victorian version of the kind of political alliance of feminists and illiberal conservatives that we're familiar with today. They wanted to place greater legal restraints on expressions of male lust such as prostitution and pornography. (It is worth noticing that feminists, with their abiding fear of sexuality in men, have always been the natural allies of illiberal conservatives in matters of sex, as with feminism's campaigns against pornography in recent decades. Both groups view sexuality in men as something inherently dangerous that has to be caged like a beast.) In 1885 the social purity movement was behind a major revision of UK law to protect women and girls from the beastly excesses of male sexuality, but the Labouchere Amendment to the act created an offence of 'gross indecency' that made all sexual acts between men illegal. Not for the last time, the desire to legislate for the protection of females resulted in the criminalization of males, on this occasion the criminalization of homosexual men.

Traditional sexism made male homosexuality a criminal offence. Female homosexuality was not. This is an important difference. There was a powerful cultural taboo against lesbianism but you didn't go to prison for it. (In the present day there are a lot of countries where lesbians are victimized by anti-homosexuality laws alongside gay men, but this wasn't the case in traditional western cultures.) The criminalization of male homosexuality could be very extreme. In the state of Virginia in 1779 Thomas Jefferson attempted to pass a law under which men who engaged in sodomy were to be punished with castration, as a *liberalisation* of the law which had previously punished the 'crime' with the death penalty. He failed and the penalty for sodomy remained death. Consensual sexual acts between men only began being decriminalized in the US and the UK in the 1960s (1962 and 1967).

Another reason for the greater persecution of homosexuality in males than in females, in addition to the old belief that men were 'active' sexually and women were 'passive' sexually, was the emphasis on the sexual act of 'sodomy'. The law in this regard in the centuries preceding the late 19th century tended to criminalize buggery/sodomy rather than homosexuality. The term sodomy could include any sexual act deemed to be 'unnatural' or 'immoral' but it was rarely applied to heterosexual couples so it's fairly clear that what the law targeted was anal and oral sex between men. In this way, in practice, the law was really about the criminalization of homosexual men and this also placed the focus of traditional homophobia on gay males rather than lesbians.

But the point I particularly wish to call attention to is that the disparity in homophobia as it related to women and men was not merely a matter of criminal law, nor was its impact limited to homosexuals. Although gay men were clearly the chief victims of homophobia, it is important to note that cultural norms applied *the fear of being perceived* as homosexual more severely upon men than upon women.

By this I mean that *heterosexual* men suffered a greater impact from the prejudice against homosexuals than did heterosexual women. The legal and cultural focus on male homosexuality gave men in society a widespread pervasive fear of being perceived as effeminate *because effeminacy was equated with homosexuality.*

For example, in traditional society two women could walk down the street hand-in-hand without attracting any undue attention, especially young women. Women had the freedom to be tactile with one another. But if two men were to walk down the street hand-in-hand, they would be sneered at as a couple of queers. For two men to be touching one another as they walked down the street they would have to be singing football songs whilst having an arm around each other's shoulders, preferably when drunk, to make it acceptably 'manly'.

Girls could pet and cuddle one another in public without any assumption of homosexuality; it was just girls being girls. But the only sociably acceptable way for boys to be affectionate in public was to playfully punch one another because then it was 'roughhousing' and suitably manly. Men did not have the same freedom to be tactile with one another that women had because men's behaviour was much more likely to be assumed to be sexual in nature than women's behaviour.

Indeed, women could even *ballroom dance* with one another (e.g. if no man had plucked up the courage to take the initiative and ask them to dance). If two men had waltzed together on the dance floor of the local ballroom, they would probably have gone home with broken noses and black eyes. Two men dancing together was featured in comedy movies as a thing to be laughed at. You, reader, will have seen films in which a man and a woman are dancing together when another man taps them upon the shoulder, says "Excuse me", and then instead of dancing off with the woman he dances off with the man. The cinema audience's laughter is a measure of how culturally taboo this would have been in real life. That's why you've never seen a film in which a women and a man are dancing together when another woman taps them on the shoulder, says "Excuse me", and then instead of dancing off with the man she dances off with the woman. Why would the audience have found that funny? Women were *allowed* to dance together in real life.

Ironically, it was the very invisibility of lesbianism in mainstream culture that gave heterosexual women this greater freedom from the fear of being thought homosexual. The overly 'manly' woman was socially disapproved of, for she was failing to conform to the imposition of 'feminine' gender and her 'masculine' behaviour was frowned upon as inappropriate for a lady, parallel to the taboo on women smoking in public. Such things were unladylike. But there was not the immediate assumption that any such woman must therefore be a lesbian.

It was even possible for Marlene Dietrich, in the 1930 movie "Morocco", to appear on screen dressed 'as a man' (i.e. in trousers, top hat, tailed coat, and tie) and kiss another women without this spelling the end of her career. On the contrary, she was nominated for an Academy Award for best actress. The movie, and most of all *that scene*, made her name famous in America and turned her into a movie icon. Can you imagine Gary Cooper, her co-star in "Morocco", appearing on screen in an elegant evening gown and kissing a man? What would the audience reaction have been? I doubt he'd have been nominated for an Oscar. Men only wore 'drag' in comedies when they could be laughed at.

Just think of the plethora of abusive slang there has been for homosexuality that was applied to men but not to women. Queer, fairy, pansy, faggot, poof, left-footer, brown-hatter, nancy boy, bender, queen, sod, bugger, bum-boy, fruit, sissy, etc. There is abusive slang for lesbians in the present day but not much in the past. The insult with which lesbians were punished in traditional society was that of being utterly disregarded as if they didn't exist. But the commonplace and prolific verbal abuse relating to male homosexuality under traditional sexism was so ubiquitous that its effects spilled over on to heterosexual men. This did not happen by accident.

The fear of an accusation of homosexuality was a powerful tool for society's *enforcement* of the social constructs of masculinity on heterosexual men. He had to be constantly on guard against showing any tender feelings or emotional sensitivity that he might have because it was dangerous to display those things in public. For men, to be at all effeminate was to be assumed to be gay, the taboo was so strong. Imagine trying to sell a toiletries product like moisturiser to men in the 1940s. Imagine an Englishwoman saying goodbye to another woman by kissing her on the cheek; could two *Englishmen* have done that? This is what I mean when I say that homophobia had a much greater negative impact upon the lives of *heterosexual* men than it did upon the lives of *heterosexual* women. It imposed much more severe constraints. It inflicted a higher level of fear.

This is a point that is steadfastly ignored by feminist political correctness because feminism wants to *blame* heterosexual men for homophobia, so it cannot admit that heterosexual men were amongst the victims of homophobia. But the truth is that the oppression of male homosexuals was a part of the *misandrist oppression of all men*.

At a time when homosexuality could not be openly referred to on the cinema screen, the ridiculing of male 'sissy' characters could be found in innumerable films up to and including the 1970s. The sissy was written into the movie for cheap laughs because he was understood by the audience to be gay. Alternatively, the sissy was sometimes seen as sexless, a creature from another universe, set apart by his androgyny. (Kenneth Williams and Charles Hawtrey, both gay in real life, had screen images of this kind.) But the sissy generally has an implied homosexuality that is punished by the audience with malicious laughter.

It is interesting to compare the sissy with the similarly vilified 'mummy's boy' because there appears to have been no assumption of homosexuality in regard of the mummy's boy. His behaviour is not viewed as effeminate, he is ridiculed simply because he has failed to meet the requirements of 'real' manhood. He is too dependent and helpless in still needing his mummy, too lacking in go-it-alone self-assertiveness, to be properly 'masculine'. His sin is the sin of *weakness*; a human trait that was forbidden to men. That a sexist cliché like the mummy's boy sits so readily alongside other objects of derision like the effeminate sissy and the man in drag, is revealing of how traditional homophobia went far beyond prejudice against homosexuals. It was a part of the systemic societal imposition of gender upon men, in being the *polar opposite* of the required list of attributes assigned to male physicality: brave in the face of danger, stoical in the face of pain, never showing weakness, dominant over other men, successful at work in the financial provision for his family, capable with tools, a winner at sport and a winner at sex (scoring goals and scoring with women) and so on. The stronger the ridicule and contempt thrown at male effeminacy, the stronger was the need for all men to abide by the cultural gendered norms of manliness.

Feminism has always had an ideological difficulty with gay men because they don't fit the feminist gender stereotype of men any more than they fitted the gender stereotype of men found in traditional sexism. On the one hand, gay men are *men*, and we all know what feminism says about men. But on the other hand, gay men can hardly be accused of being sexually predatory upon women and the perpetrators of 'rape culture'. Also, they are a designated oppressed social group.

For feminists, gay men *are* men but they are *not* 'men' in inverted commas. When a feminist is making a sweeping generalization about how appalling 'men' are, she doesn't mean gay men. Only heterosexual men are 'men' and therefore guilt-objects who are to blame for everything. But, aside from the reversal in direction of who is the object of blame, notice how similar this distinction is to traditional sexism. It's like the old prejudice that gay men are not 'real men'. For feminism gay men aren't 'real' men either, their political status is more like being honorary women. And how similar is that to traditional sexism's caricatured view of the effeminate gay man as a kind of pretend woman?

Universal Suffrage

Before we end this brief survey of traditional sexism and move on to feminism's re-writing of history as the oppression of women by men we should, perhaps, mention the issue that for many people symbolises traditional sexism and makes them view it solely in terms of misogyny and never in terms of misandry. This is the slack-brained belief that in history *men had the vote and women didn't*, therefore men were politically enfranchised and women weren't.

First, let's disabuse ourselves of the false idea that in the past men had the vote. Throughout most of history societies all across the planet were politically structured as monarchies, feudal systems, slave societies and the like, so the issue of voting rights doesn't arise for most of history. Let's move right along to western 'democratic' societies in the 19th century and use England as the example.

In England in the early 19th century less than 3% of the total population had the vote, which means that approximately 6% of men had the vote and 94% of men did not. After the Reform Act of 1832 one in seven men had the vote (because suffrage was limited to men who occupied property with an annual value of £10 or more) so a little over 14% of men had the vote and a little under 86% did not. By the 2nd Reform Act in 1870 two out of five men had the vote, so 40% of men had the vote and 60% did not. The 3rd Reform Act of 1884 gave the vote to 60% of men, and 40% of men were still disenfranchised because of a property qualification on voting. Votes for women were introduced in 1918, thirty four years later.

http://www.nationalarchives.gov.uk/pathways/citizenship/struggle_democracy/getting_v ote.htm

This 1918 law, the Representation of the People Act, is very interesting because one of the issues it addressed was that *men who did not have the right to vote were nonetheless expected to fight and die for their country* in World War 1. These men were legally required to fight in the war but they were not in a position to vote for or against the government that sent them to their deaths. So when Emmeline Pankhurst and the suffragettes paused in their advocacy of 'Votes For Women' momentarily to hand out white feathers of cowardice to young men who were not in uniform in order to shame these boys into risking their lives to protect the women of Britain, they might have asked themselves how many of the men they were coercing into combat actually did not have the vote either.

From 1918 men over 21 years of age had the right to vote (without any property restrictions). Only 40% of women had the right to vote because of property restrictions and their having to be over 30 years of age. Women had equal voting rights with men (all men and women over 21 without any property restrictions) from 1928. http://en.wikipedia.org/wiki/Suffrage

But notice the age qualification. Men were conscripted to fight in the war from the age of 18. Their right to vote began at 21. So even after the 1918 and 1928 acts, men between 18 and 20 years of age were expected to lay down their lives for a country that did not give them the right to vote. When was the voting age lowered to 18? *In 1969, that's when.* So men between 18 and 20 years of age had to serve in World War 2 without having the right to vote for or against the government that sent them to their deaths.

During World War 2 women were also conscripted into national service but not into combat. From 1942 all men between 18 and 51 years of age and all women between 20 and 30 years of age were subject to conscription but the women had a choice between military service and working in industry, so women were not required even to serve in the armed forces, let alone in combat. This meant that women over 21 could vote equally with men but without an equal requirement to fight for their country and women over 30 could vote equally with men without even being subject to conscription. But men between 18 and 20 years of age had to fight and die without the right to vote.

Is this the history of women's suffrage that you are accustomed to hearing?

Second, let's consider whether having the right to vote actually bestows political enfranchisement. We can all agree that (some) men getting the vote sooner than women was a clear case of sexism of which we can all disapprove. But let's not pretend that votes for women was the most important issue in the history of sexism. Men suffering a misandrist double-standard about human pain and women having a gendered social role for motherhood, or husbands having financial responsibility for their wives and wives being under their husbands authority, were all much more important. After all, there are now more *female* voters in the UK electorate than there are *male* voters, yet feminists are still pretending that we live in a patriarchal society in which women are oppressed by men. So even feminists must agree that the right to vote is far less important in the politics of gender than the suffragettes appeared to believe.

Or, to take an American example, from 1870 voting rights in the USA were expanded to include citizens regardless of race, colour, or "previous condition of servitude" (i.e. slavery). It wasn't until 1920 that the US electorate included citizens of both sexes. If this means that for fifty years black men could vote in American elections but white women couldn't, are we to assume that *black men were more politically empowered than white women*? The idea is surely laughable, given all the other factors present in the culture of the time. This example is one way to appreciate how the right to vote is not sufficient in itself to constitute political enfranchisement and, consequently, how universal suffrage is not as significant an element of political empowerment as it is usually presented as being.

In the nearly seventy years since the second world war the number of people in the UK electorate who voted in general elections has never been higher than 84%. In the last three general elections it hasn't been higher than 65%. In 2001 it dropped to 59%. http://www.ukpolitical.info/Turnout45.htm In 2011 nearly 18% of the eligible electorate were not even registered to vote. Is anybody surprised? As the anarchists used to sloganize: 'if voting changed anything, they'd abolish it'.

These days, for anyone who disagrees with political correctness, there seems little reason or opportunity to vote. All three major parties in the UK are staunchly politically correct and have been for years, so we can only vote for parties with whom we disagree. And that's the crux of the matter. If there is no party to *vote for*, of what value is a vote? To be politically enfranchised in party politics it's not enough to have a vote, you have to have someone to vote for. If all three parties are the same, you can't even vote negatively, voting for someone you don't actually agree with but who at least isn't as bad as the other lot. In my lifetime I've never come across a politician who represented me, who expressed my beliefs and values. Not one, not ever. The vote? It doesn't mean you're politically enfranchised.

So let's not kid ourselves that shouts of 'Votes for Women!' in 1913 should exercise any undue influence over our thinking in a serious discussion of sexism in society, past or present.

Chapter Two

Patriarchy Theory

Now we need to contrast the historical account of traditional misandry argued above with feminism's Patriarchy Theory to see which account of the past is the more plausible, the more rationally convincing and supported by evidence. These two versions of history are mutually exclusive so one of them *must* be wrong. In chapter 1 we addressed how there was a bifurcation of traditional society by gender. Patriarchy theory also presents a bifurcation of society into two classes of persons by gender: the oppressors and the oppressed, the victimizers and the victims, the guilty and the innocent, each of which is co-extensive with the males and the females respectively.

In presenting us with a view of history which holds that one half of the population of the world has oppressed the other half of the population of the world, the feminist theory of 'patriarchy' does what traditional gender-theories have always done, it divides humanity into 'the people who are like this' and 'the people who are like that'. It *has to* do this in order to achieve its primary purpose, which is the ascription of systemic blame; holding 'men' as a class of persons responsible for all the iniquities of society.

I shall argue that the fundamental beliefs of patriarchy theory are false. Moreover, they are so childishly false that it is easy to demonstrate their falsehood. Although whole libraries of feminist books have been written which are entirely dependent upon a belief in patriarchy theory, it only takes a few pages to show it to be false. Once mature common sense recognizes that patriarchy theory is a puerile fabrication, whole libraries of feminist books that are irrevocably based upon that theory can be put into the shredder for paper recycling.

Let's consider five beliefs that provide the foundation of any orthodox version of patriarchy theory and which could therefore be said to be basic to the theory. Some feminists may not believe all of these but any feminist must believe at least one of them. Most feminists would probably believe all five. The point here is that these are the kind of beliefs which must be true in order for patriarchy theory to be true. If these beliefs are false, then patriarchy theory is false. The theory cannot stand unless you can prove one or more of these fundamental ideas about 'patriarchy'.

The Basics of Patriarchy Theory

(1) Men ruled society?

No, they didn't. This fallacy is perpetuated by the deliberate conflation of two propositions which are actually quite different; so different, in fact, that the first is true and the second is false.

(a) The people who have ruled society have (mostly) been men. True.

(b) Men have ruled society. False.

The first statement is true because, when we look at the people who have been in positions of power where they could be said to be amongst the rulers of society (politicians, the aristocracy, the senior clergy, corporate executives, etc.) we find that nearly all of them have been men.

The second statement is false because it either treats *all men*, men as a class of persons, as having been in those positions of power (which is ludicrously untrue) or it treats their maleness as the reason *why* those individuals occupied those positions of power and implies that the way they behaved whilst in power was *governed* by their maleness. Both of which assumptions are false. The logical error in the conflation of the two propositions will be even more obvious if you try it this way:

71

(a) The people who have ruled society have habitually worn clothes. True.

(b) People who habitually wore clothes have ruled society. False.

The first proposition in each case identifies an attribute common to those who ruled society. They have mostly been men and they have habitually worn clothes. The second proposition in each case *identifies that attribute as the significant reason why* they ruled society. It says that they ruled *because* they were men and *because* they wore clothes. Neither of these contentions is true.

The reason that the proposition 'men have ruled society' is false is that it speaks of 'men' as if *being male* were a sufficient condition to bestow upon a person the power to rule society and/or that when in power *these men made their decisions on the basis of their maleness*. This would mean that Catholic rulers did not rule on the basis of their Catholicism; that Protestant rulers did not rule on the basis of their Protestantism; that Liberal rulers did not rule on the basis of their Liberalism; that Marxist rulers did not rule on the basis of their Marxism, and so on.

It would mean that Fidel Castro (a man) made his political decisions for the same reasons as Richard Nixon (a man) and for the same reasons as Mahatma Gandhi (a man) and the Emperor Hirohito of Japan (a man) and Sitting Bull of the Lakota (a man). More than that, it would also imply that Golda Meir made her political decisions in a very different way from David Ben-Gurion, and that Margaret Thatcher's political views had nothing in common with Winston Churchill's. Were the political priorities of George Bush Jr (a man) really closer to those of Vladimir Lenin (another man) than they were to the political priorities of Condoleezza Rice?

Patriarchy theory is a political interpretation of history that ignores *all the actual politics* in history.

72

It should hardly be necessary to argue against the proposition that maleness was a sufficient condition to bestow political power upon someone, or that throughout history men as a class of persons have ruled society, as this is patently nonsense. Untold generations of men who were feudal serfs and peasant labourers and slaves and coal miners and bus drivers and chimney sweeps and railway engineers have lived in a world that they did not make and could not change. The overwhelming majority of male human beings who ever lived could tell you that they never had any say in ruling society.

Nearly all men throughout history have actually lived politically powerless lives in which society has treated them as expendable workers and even more expendable soldiers. It is demonstrably not true that men as a class of persons have ruled society and it is easy to see that they haven't. Women may have been largely *excluded* from the political governance of society because they were women but men were not *included* in government because they were men. Those who occupied positions in political government did so because of characteristics other than their maleness; it was because they were from wealthy families, they were socially connected, they were Old Etonians and Oxbridge graduates, they were members of the dominant religion, etc. Their maleness was not relevant at all, except insofar as it meant they weren't excluded for being female. But most men *were* excluded for reasons other than their gender.

It would make far more sense to say that, for example, people from the top 20% of financial income have ruled society if they were not excluded for being female or excluded for being an atheist or for being something else which would exclude them. The ruling class is an economic class because that's where the power lies, in control over the generation of wealth. So if a member of that economic class is a man, he is not a member of that class *because* he is a man. If he were, then all men would be in that class. It is not the *maleness* of the people who have ruled society which placed them in that enviable position. It would be preposterous to believe that a titled woman like Lady Muck of Toffee-Nosed Towers had no say in the ruling of society, poor oppressed creature, but that her under-footman and her chauffeur *did* rule society. It would be silly to believe that the middle-class suffragette had no say in ruling society but that the garbage man who emptied her dustbins *did* rule society. Yet feminists speak of 'men' ruling society as if half the population of society were members of the ruling class exercising power over the other half.

The truth, as any sensible grown-up knows, is that apart from a handful of rich and powerful people the rest of the population of the world was born into a society which they did not create and which they did not have the power to change. Men and women both. Once born, they were culturally conditioned to fulfill whatever role the society required of them. If men were born into a society that needed peasant labourers, then men were peasant labourers. If women were born into a society that needed cottage industry weavers and spinners, then women spun wool in their cottages. If society needed urban factory workers, then men and women were urban factory workers. Yet patriarchy theory attributes power to the powerless, if the powerless happen to be male.

The unprincipled nature of feminism is evident when we notice that the people who habitually treat all men as having exercised 'male power', simply because a tiny minority of men were in positions of power, are the very same people who would screech in protest if anyone were to treat all Muslims as terrorists simply because a tiny minority of Muslims are terrorists.

But we all know how feminists would shift their ground if confronted with this argument. When this reading of 'men have ruled society' is shown to be false, feminism adopts an alternative reading of the proposition to make it mean that the men who ruled society were in some way the *representatives* of all men as a class of persons. They admit grudgingly that it is not true that *all* men were in positions of power but claim that the tiny number of men who were in positions of power were deliberately exercising that power to promote the gendered interests of their own sex; in some kind of collective 'male interest'. The revised contention is that those in power were male and because of this they ruled *on behalf of all men*; that this was 'male power'.

(2) Men ruled in the gendered interests of men?

This belief is perhaps the single most important falsehood to address in patriarchy theory because if it fails then patriarchy theory fails so badly that anyone should be able to see that the theory is utterly wrong. If traditional society was not ruled in the gendered interests of men, then nothing is left of the idea of men's political oppression of women.

But before addressing this, it might be worthwhile to ask ourselves why the claim is made in the first place. Why does feminism believe that if the people in positions of power are men, then they must be pursuing a collective male interest? I would suggest that it is because *feminists are themselves fighting a sex-war against men and they assume that men must have been fighting one too.*

Feminists continually tell us that they are speaking and acting in the interest of all women, and that they are fighting to defend all women. As a result of this attitude they take it for granted that their enemy, men, must have a similar attitude; that just as feminists are partisan in favour of women, male rulers must have been similarly partisan in favour of men. Because feminism wants to advantage women and degrade men, it assumes that its enemy must have wanted to advantage men and degrade women. Feminism attributes its own motivations to its adversary. This is *projection*.

This view of the feminist psyche is supported by what feminists have done since gaining power themselves. Having seized command of the cultural establishment and the legislative system, all feminist legislation is devoted to the sole cause of what they see as a collective female interest. Like all deeply prejudiced and hypocritical people, it would be natural for feminists *to assume that their enemies must hate them as*

75

much as they hate their enemies. And, as feminism identifies itself with women, their assumption is that their enemies hate women. This is why so many feminists describe 'patriarchy' in terms of men's 'hatred of women'. They know that all the political power to which they themselves have access is deployed in favour of women, so they take it for granted that in the past when the people in office happened to be male, those men must have pursued a male interest.

Feminism is putting the cart before the horse. It is not because men have traditionally been fighting a war against women that feminism is now fighting its war against men. Rather it is because feminism is fighting a war against men, and wishes to present that struggle as a *defensive* war, that it posits the existence of a traditional male war against women, a war called 'patriarchy'.

Let's consider a few arguments which refute the claim that traditionally men ruled in a gendered male interest. The first we have already mentioned, that we cannot ignore *all the actual politics* in history. Political rulers have, beyond reasonable dispute, self-consciously ruled in the declared interest of causes that were not gendered.

When the Bolsheviks seized power from the Tsarist regime, they were very clear on the collective interest they wished to serve, that of the proletariat. Not the collective interest of men as a gender. When the White Army fought a civil war to win back Russia for the Tsar, they were not acting in a 'male interest' any more than Queen Mary Tudor ("Bloody Mary") was acting in a 'female interest' when she sought to undo the Protestant reformation and restore England to Catholicism. When the Algerians fought a brutal eight year war of independence against French colonialism, Algerian men weren't uniting in a gendered interest with Frenchmen to oppress Algerian and French women, the life-and-death issue was one of national identity.

History is full of competing political ideologies, causes, utopian visions, nationalisms, and ethnic community interests. These myriad political agendas cannot possibly be reduced to the painfully crude analysis that all these agendas covertly served a 'male interest'.

And on those occasions when political leaders do adopt a specifically gendered interest, it always seems to be the interest of *women* that they are concerned about. For example, these days we are very familiar with politicians in western countries expressing concern over the way that Islamic countries treat women (from a perspective that is horrified by female genital mutilation and women not being allowed out of the house on their own). At the same time, politicians in Islamic countries also express their concern over the way that western countries treat women (from a perspective that sees casual sex outside of marriage and the wearing of sexy clothes as being degrading to women). But neither side ever spares a thought about how both types of cultures treat their men (except when those men are homosexual). When have political leaders, or anyone else, ever cared a damn about men? Men are expected to cope without help from anyone else.

The second argument is equally straightforward. The men who occupied positions of political power in the past were always very concerned to protect women as the so-called 'weaker sex'. Why was this? Well, consider. These political leaders lived in the innumerable generations *before* the contractive pill. They lived in the countless generations *before* the workplace was a hive of keyboard-based technology. They lived in the generations when for the vast majority of workers paid employment meant using a hammer, a sickle, a saw, a shovel, or the strength or your own back and arms. The paid employment that women could do just as well as men were mostly things like weaving on the looms of the dark satanic mills or domestic service in the homes of the wealthy.

In a situation where women could only avoid pregnancy by not having sex and where most work was based upon having a certain level of muscle-power, *if women and men had been treated equally and competed against each other on a level playing field*, then the women would have been at a serious disadvantage and would probably have starved or had to resort to prostitution. Indeed, prostitution was a commonplace fate for women who had lost their male partner.

So the male politicians, whether they were the Caesars of Rome or the Victorian gentlemen of Westminster, *acted to protect women by making them the responsibility of men.* Gender roles meant that men were expected to provide for women. Men were expected to defend women if they were in physical danger. Men were expected to take on the responsibilities of being the head of the household and ensuring that the women and children did not starve.

Now let's be very clear on this. I am *not* saying that this system actually did protect women in every case. Of course not, it failed repeatedly, as all systems fail. *Nor* am I saying that this 'protection' wasn't oppressive to women in many ways. Certainly it was, just as it was also oppressive to the men who had these heavy burdens of responsibility placed upon them, not by choice but as a result of societal expectation; an imposed gendered social role.

What I *am* saying is that when in the past the people in political power were almost all men, they plainly did *not* rule in the interests of men. A 'male interest' would have been best served by *not* having gender roles. In a straight competition for individual survival, under the material circumstances of the time (with no reliable contraception and most jobs requiring physical strength), women would have been enormously disadvantaged compared to men. If so-called 'patriarchal' society *had not* imposed gender roles, men would have been much better off and women would have been much worse off. Gender roles were never about achieving male power, they were about ensuring female survival.

Again, let's be clear. I am *not* saying that traditional sexism was good for women. It was oppressive to both women and men. *Nor* am I saying that all women benefited from traditional gender roles. Many women were left homeless and hungry (as were many men).

78

What I *am* saying is that in the absence of the belief that men had a gendered duty to protect and provide for women, in the absence of gender roles that raised children within family units, in the absence of politically imposed heterosexual cultural norms that men and women should live together as husband and wife, in the absence of these societal conventions women as a class of persons would have been in a much worse position. Women would have suffered a worse fate *without* gender roles in place than they did *with* gender roles in place. And *that is why* society had gender roles.

Those past centuries were not times of politically correct cultural taboos. They were not times of universal human rights. They were not times which had a welfare state. In the absence of the kind of security and affluent material conditions of life that people in today's society take for granted, would pregnant and breast-feeding women have thrived *on their own?* Did they thrive, in the societies of the past, when their man was killed down the coal pit or killed in the factory or killed in a war? In the absence of a welfare state women went 'on the parish', dependent upon Christian charity (if 'charity' is the word).

Even today, in the women-first world of 21st century girl-power, if there was a major crash of capitalism and the welfare state ceased to exist, who would be the greater loser by it, women or men? In the brutal aftermath of such a crash of capitalism, how long would it take for girl-power women to start imposing a traditional gendered social role on men, telling them that they had a manly responsibility to protect women and children? In the past, without the modern state welfare system, those in political power were very concerned that men should be given this responsibility for women. This was *not* done in the interest of men.

I am *not* saying that the politicians of the past were right to do this. *Nor* am I suggesting that there should be any kind of return to the ways of the past. (Absolutely not. Quite the contrary. I am a lifelong advocate of sex equality and I am totally opposed to the idea that men should protect women just because they're women. Women are not entitled to any

79

protection that men aren't equally entitled to. Men should refuse *in principle and in practice* to submit to the traditional sexism which says that men ought to sacrifice their own interests in order to protect women.) I am merely considering whether political power in the past was exercised in a 'male interest' through the imposition of gender roles. The answer is no, it wasn't.

Feminists have often described traditional marriage as a form of 'slavery' for women but in the absence of the gendered social roles of which marriage was such an important part, women could have been reduced to the position of *actual real slavery*. After all, apart from (a) societal gender roles, and (b) men's desire to father children, what would there have been to stop men from enslaving women? The answer is: morality. But when life is harsh and times are tough, morality is a slender reed upon which to place all your hopes.

No doubt the slave-owners of ancient Rome considered themselves to be moral people. It didn't stop them from practicing slavery. No doubt the slave-owners of 18th century Mississippi considered themselves to be good Christian folk. It didn't stop them from practicing slavery either. And let's remember what those same feminists who think that marriage was a form of 'slavery' for women have been telling us about men for the last several decades; that men are predatory rapists and paedophiles, inherently violent warmongers and women-haters who are in love with death. If these feminists really believe that men hate women, then what would have stopped these testosterone-fuelled predators from *literally enslaving* womankind, with manacles on her wrists instead of a ring on her finger?

If the rulers of traditional society had operated a *level playing field* for individual women and men pursuing their own interests, under the material conditions that prevailed for millennia, it would have been a sorry lookout for most women. But with the rulers of society imposing and enforcing traditional gender roles, women could share in their men's income and status, they could be comfortable middle-class housewives, they could find paid employment in jobs that society held to be 'appropriate' (schoolteachers, secretaries, shopkeepers, etc) and rare women could become successful businesswomen, women could find a husband to take care of them financially and they could inherit his wealth when he died, they could give birth and raise children within a secure family environment, they could live under a much greater level of personal security than they might have been forced to accept otherwise. I'm not trying to paint a rosy picture of how marvellous a life this was, merely to *contrast it* with the appalling horror of what life might have been like for women in the absence of gendered social roles.

This may be the single most important thing to understand in any discussion about patriarchy theory, and if the reader takes nothing else away with them from reading this book, then let it be this: in total contradiction of everything that most people believe they know about traditional sexism, the social imposition of gender roles was *more in the interest of women than of men* because without gender roles women would probably have starved or been enslaved in the material circumstances of those times. For people in the feminist-dominated, technologically advanced, entitlement culture of the present day to understand history, they must stop thinking ideologically and start thinking realistically. Patriarchy theory is a lie.

We also have to take into account the effects of the presence of evolutionary inheritance in social relations. Evolution made men competitors for sex with women. In evolutionary terms, women wanted the most high-status super-capable man under whose protection she could raise her children. Men competed with each other to be that man. This continued right through traditional society. Men were rivals for status and money in order to win/earn the women they wanted. (This was famously encapsulated in the quote from "Scarface" where Al Pacino says: "You got to make the money first. Then when you get the money, you get the power. When you get the power, then you get the woman.") This underlying evolutionary psychology sets men against one another, always exerting pressure against a unified male interest, and it means that women and men have evolved psychological dispositions which expect men to exercise such power as they personally have to protect women.

Even so, this evolutionary inheritance is not sufficient by itself to ensure such protective behaviour. That is why there was a societal imposition of the masculine social role, because evolutionary psychology isn't strong enough on it's own to guarantee the widespread practice of male protection of females. We see this in all the individual instances where women do suffer at the hands of men (e.g. where domestic violence and rape is perpetrated by males) where not even the *combination* of evolutionary psychology, societal gender constraints, and the political law has been sufficient to hold back an individual man from abusing rather than protecting an individual woman.

So the presence of evolutionary inheritance does not change the picture of what society might have been like for women if gender roles and political laws for the protection of women had not been in place. What a consideration of evolutionary psychology *does* do is to give us another argument against the claim that society was ruled by men in a 'male interest' because it shows us that, in evolutionary terms as well as societal terms, there has never been a biological brotherhood of men with a shared 'male interest' where men took care of each other. The idea of a 'band of brothers' is only found amongst soldiers who fight alongside one another in the same troop in combat or men who play for the same sports team or some small scale grouping of that sort, it is not found in society as a whole. Men have, by and large, not cared about other men because men have been born and raised to be rivals. On a biological level as well as a cultural level, men have competed *against* one another, not stood together in pursuit of a collective 'male interest'.

So we now have three arguments to say that, although the people in political office and commercial power were men, they did not rule in a 'male interest'. But there is a fourth argument that should not be overlooked: *it is not in men's interest to die.* If you believe that in the past those in power ruled in the interests of men, then you have to explain how it is that the sexist double-standard about the value of human life *favours women*, and how it is that men and only men had the gendered social role to be murdered and maimed in every war. You would have to argue that the mass slaughter of men was somehow in their own interest. Which is patently ridiculous. What kind of doublethink would be necessary for a person to believe that traditional society repeatedly imposed horrific obligations of annihilating self-sacrifice upon men but that the victims of this mass androcide were the privileged ones because society was ruled in their collective interest? Yet feminism must perform this doublethink because it *cannot* acknowledge the systemic misandry of traditional society as that would contradict the 'male interest' theory of 'patriarchy'.

The efforts of feminists to perform this kind of doublethink have caused them to *endorse* gender beliefs far more than to *oppose* them. Feminism treats each man as one instance of maleness who is representative of all men, and each woman as one instance of femaleness who is representative of all women. In this way it can hold all men guilty of 'male power' and thereby cling on to a theory of 'patriarchy'.

For example, when Peter sexually objectifies a woman by looking at her breasts he is deemed guilty of 'the male gaze' (supposedly an expression of male hatred for women which reduces them to body parts). It is not *Peter's* gaze, you'll notice, it is the *male* gaze. But when Susan sexually objectifies a man by looking at his muscular buttocks she is not deemed guilty of sexual objectification because, not being a male, she isn't guilty of the male gaze. By treating each person as one representative instance of their sex (i.e. by imposing gender), guilt becomes universal for males and innocence becomes universal for females. Also, every man is thereby cast in the role of a soldier in the alleged war against women.

But this ideological position requires a massive belief in gender. To believe that men 'gaze' in one way but women

83

'gaze' in another, so that the gaze which objectifies is *gendered*, requires that feminism keep itself ignorant of the fact that women sexually objectify men. Similarly, to treat each instance of male violence against women as being stereotypical of maleness, whilst treating each instance of female violence against men as being atypical and subject to rationalization, requires that feminism keep itself ignorant of the fact that women can have personalities that are just as violent, abusive, combative and confrontational as their male counterparts. Like most bigotry, feminism's misandry is based upon ignorance; ignorance about men and ignorance about women.

Feminism has to view women and men as if they were not unique individuals with a common humanity but rather two separate species where each person is merely one cell in a gendered collective. In this way, when an individual man transgresses this can be taken to indicate how all mankind is guilty because that individual man is one instance of maleness as a whole, and when a woman suffers this can be taken to indicate how all womankind is victimized. By adopting this position *feminism has perpetrated an imposition of gender* that exceeds even the traditional beliefs in gender that feminism purports to condemn. In treating each man as nothing more than one cell in a collective maleness it has assumed both a gendered uniformity in male humanity that does not exist and a *uniformity of interest* amongst all men which also does not exist. But feminism is willing to do this so that it can continue to believe that it is fighting against 'male power' in accordance with patriarchy theory.

(3) Capitalism is male power?

One tired old excuse feminism offers for the claim that men had, and still have, all the power in society is that the modern world is ruled by big business and corporate financial empires and the like, and the senior executives of these commercial institutions are predominantly male. It will be pointed out, for example, that 83% of FTSE 100 board members are men https://www.gov.uk/government/publications/women-on-boards-2013-second-annual-review and, on the basis of the raw numbers alone, this be assumed to be evidence of male power (remembering that feminism treats each male as *representative* of maleness as such, or as *one instance* of maleness). This gives rise to the notion that the system itself is 'masculine' and that the iniquities of the system are the result of its 'masculine' character. The proposed solution is 'feminization'; getting more women into these positions of commercial power so that they can make the system reflect female gendered values and norms of behaviour.

[Author's Note: I am using 'feminized' here in the feminist sense of the word, not my own sense of the word that I have used previously. For me, feminised means 'made consistent with feminist beliefs' or 'operates in accordance with feminist ideology' but when feminists use the word they generally mean something like 'now involves much greater female participation and therefore now better reflects feminine norms of behaviour'. For clarity, I'll spell the word as 'feminized' for *their* use of the word and 'feminised' for *my* use of the word.]

But the belief that the maleness of these capitalists is their most significant characteristic is entirely dependent upon the presupposition that these capitalists got to their position of commercial power *because* they are men. The fact that the people at the top of the business hierarchy do not include nearly all of the male population but do include some women, makes a nonsense of the presupposition.

In contrast, the common sense view is that only people who devote their entire lives to the pursuit of their career, who value commercial super-achievement more highly than anything else, working sixty hour weeks, never seeing their children, and focusing their personal goals solely on their financial success, are likely to get a seat at the table amongst the FTSE 100 board members. That's why such a tiny percentage of the population, male or female, are included amongst their number. (e.g. The Occupy Movement's "1%".) In other words, only people who devote their entire lives to the *traditional male gendered social role* and have great success in that social role are likely to become FTSE board members. It is hardly surprising if more men are willing to do this than women in a society which still judges the merit of a man by that traditional gendered social role. The male 'success-object' is still desired by very many women.

In addition, given women's greater freedom of movement between the workplace and the domestic sphere, the greater status that mothers acquire from parenthood than do fathers, and so on, it is also not surprising that women may be less inclined to make the sacrifices in other areas of their lives that are required if someone is to climb the greasy pole all the way to the very top. But feminism has no truck with common sense and prefers to believe that it's all about the machinations of patriarchal oppression keeping female bums off boardroom seats.

In any case, regardless of whether you take the common sense point of view or not, the real question here in regard of the idea that 'capitalism is male power' is: what difference does it make whether the FTSE board members are female or male since they occupy their positions of corporate power and influence not *as men* or *as women* but *as capitalists*? If the FTSE board members were 100% female or 100% male, nothing would change because in both cases the board members would still be 100% capitalists.

The point here is analogous to the presidency of Barack Obama. When Obama was elected for his first term of office there was a lot of hallelujah rejoicing in celebration that a 'black President' had been elected. He was President Messiah, come to save us all. As a result, he received very little criticism from the so-called liberal media during his first term. All the critics who'd been pissing abuse over 'stupid' George 'W' for the previous eight years bit their tongues and bit their lips to avoid saying anything negative about a 'black President'. Any of his political opponents who criticised Obama were, inevitably, immediately accused of being motivated by racism.

But in Obama's second term, a trickle of criticism started from the so-called liberal media about Obama's use of drone strikes, Guantanamo Bay remaining open, the Internal Revenue Service (IRS) illegally targeting his Tea Party political opponents who applied for tax exempt status, and so on.

The critics began to understand what they should have known from the outset, that *in the phrase 'black President' the operative word is 'President'*. Presidents do what Presidents do, it doesn't matter what colour they are. It will be the same when America elects its first female President. People who believe that gender is biologically determined will be singing and dancing in the streets in the expectation that a female in the White House will change the whole nature of politics. But it won't. It didn't when Margaret Thatcher was elected Prime Minister in Britain (things just got even worse). It didn't when Indira Gandhi was elected Prime Minister of India, or when Julia Gillard was elected Prime Minister of Australia. So when America gets its first female President, how long will it take Americans to realise that *in the phrase 'female President' the operative word is 'President'*.

Only a female-supremacist would claim that if the FTSE 100 board members were 100% *female capitalists*, then this would produce a more benign and less venal capitalism than if they were 100% male capitalists. You would have to believe that women were intrinsically more moral human beings than men to think that 'more women on the board' = 'more benevolence and less venality'.

Ever since feminism was invented it has been making the same crass mistake: it judges each human being either solely or primarily on their biological sex, rather than judging them on all their other attributes. Your expectations of the business practices of a female capitalist should be based primarily on her being a capitalist, not upon her being female, because her being a capitalist is much more relevant to her business practices. A person who makes it to the FTSE 100 board will probably have to be ambitious, combative, avaricious and ruthless. What possible difference could it make to the exercising of power if the capitalists are ambitious, combative, avaricious and ruthless *men* or if they are ambitious, combative, avaricious and ruthless *women*? But a feminist gender-supremacist believes in female virtue and male vice, hence the naïve notion that women in positions of power can make the world a better place by changing the system to reflect female gendered values and norms of behaviour.

Anyone who *isn't* a gender-supremacist will understand that capitalists behave like capitalists *because that's what they are*, regardless of sex. So a predominance of males on the FTSE 100 board members doesn't mean that power resides with men. It's not a 'masculine' system. Capitalism doesn't care about women and men, it cares about *profit*. This is why even the UK government's pro-feminist 2011 policy paper on this issue, the "Women on Boards: Review", is at pains to point out that:

"The issues debated here are as much about improving business performance as about promoting equal opportunities for women. There is a strong business case for balanced boards . . . . This business case is backed by a growing body of evidence. Research has shown that strong stock market growth among European companies is most likely to occur where there is a higher proportion of women in senior management teams. Companies with more women on their boards were found to outperform their rivals with a 42% higher return in sales, 66% higher return on invested capital and 53% higher return on equity." https://www.gov.uk/government/publications/women-on-boards-review

It's called capitalism, dummy. It's all about the money. It has nothing to do with 'male power'.

(4) Men had all the personal power?

If the theory of 'male power' doesn't work when it's understood to mean that 'men ruled society', and if it also doesn't work when it's understood to mean that 'those in power ruled in a male interest', then a fallback position which feminism sometimes employs is to change the meaning of 'male power' once again. This time it's revised to mean that 'men in society had more personal freedom and independence'. In other words, men had more power over their lives because they had more access to the workplace to earn a living; that men were financially independent but women were not.

Notice how watered down 'male power' has become by this stage in the defence of the theory of 'patriarchy'. Instead of men oppressing women from on high in the seats of government, we are now asked to view men as individual oppressors of individual women in a situation where 'the personal is political'. Yet, although this is an extremely diluted version of patriarchy theory, feminism has milked this cow for all it's worth. So much so, that many people seem to view traditional society as being male-supremacist simply on the basis of men having more access to the workplace.

But this doesn't stand to reason. The people of an oppressor class do not spend their whole lives working to support and provide for the well-being of the oppressed class. Oppressors make the oppressed work for them, they don't themselves work for the benefit of the oppressed. Her work in the home may have benefited him (as well as herself) but his work outside of the home benefited her (as well as himself). Nor does an oppressor class sacrifice their own lives to ceaseless toil in the hope of being rewarded with the love and respect of the oppressed class. How could women have been an oppressed class when the alleged oppressor was working his guts out to support them?

It's a very peculiar idea to see the mule who is pulling the cart as an image of *mule-supremacism* or to see the role of a beast of burden as being an image of personal empowerment. It might make sense to see the cart-driver with the whip in their hand as the person who has the power. It might make sense to see the people who own the merchandise being transported in the cart as being the people who have the power. But it makes no sense at all to see the poor bloody mule who's doing the arduous work of pulling that cartful of merchandise to market as being *the one who has the power* in this situation. The workplace has, throughout history, been a place of exploitation. Whether it's feudal serfs or capitalist wage-slaves, the workforce has been brutally exploited by those who are really in power. The fact that men had a gendered social role which gave them greater access to the workplace is not evidence of the empowerment of men, it is a measure of the exploitation that they have suffered.

Let's not make the mistake that middle-class feminists living comfortable conservative lives generally make, the mistake of assuming that the workplace is all about personal self-fulfilment through a rewarding career. For untold generations of men the workplace was all about toil and sweat, it was all about aching muscles and sore backs, it was all about indignity and debasement on the bottom rung of the ladder. There is no dignity in labour when you're the mule who is pulling the cart.

If you, reader, are resistant to this idea that men were the sweated labour of traditional society, it may be that you're thinking something like: 'but what about all those working class women who had to work outside of the home? Haven't you read Orwell's "The Road to Wigan Pier" where he talks about women and children having to work down coal mines?' The problem with this objection is that it actually reinforces my argument. Think about it. This objection draws attention to the dreadful working conditions that women suffered *when they did the same jobs that the men were doing*. The objection actually acknowledges how appalling were the lives of the men who did those jobs. To anyone who believes in sex equality, by saying it is shocking that women had to suffer in this way we are also saying it is shocking that men had to suffer in this way. The objection acknowledges that these men had a terrible working life in the gendered role assigned to them by society. It was a role that people would be appalled to find women having to fulfill working alongside men.

So when someone raises this objection, they have already tacitly admitted that society condemned very many men to a

90

terrible life, in complete contradiction of the fantasy tale of male privilege known as patriarchy theory. Why don't feminists recognise this? Because feminists don't believe in sex equality. To a feminist, condemning a *man* to a life of ceaseless drudgery down a coal mine and an early death coughing his guts out with black lung disease is entirely different to condemning a *woman* to the same fate. A feminist will only be interested in complaining about how that despotic tyrant of a male coal miner expected his poor oppressed wife, who didn't have to slave in the bowels of the earth hewing coal, to have his dinner on the table when he arrived home exhausted after his shift. The privileged patriarchal bastard.

How many times over the last half-century have we been told that 'men kept women in the kitchen'? It is one of the most commonplace caricatures of male oppression that women were *forced* into the home, imprisoned within the domestic sphere whilst men frolicked gaily in the public sphere. What were these men actually doing in the public sphere? Some of them were digging up the roads, some were delivering the mail, some were wading through sewage down in the sewers, some were selling meat in a butchers shop, some were walking the streets selling insurance door-to-door, some were swinging a pickaxe to lay cables, some were loading up lorries and some were endlessly driving those lorries up and down the highways, some started their working lives as children and some were still employed as night-watchmen in their old age. The privileged bastards.

Feminism asserts that traditional marriage oppressed women *and only women*. It is spoken of as a ceaseless drudgery suffered by women under a male head of the household. It ignores the fact that the head of the household was largely excluded from his own home and hearth, denied the chance to raise his own children, because he were always *out at work* all day. One of the main sources of paid employment for women in the past was domestic service. How many female servants scrubbing the floors of their employer's house dreamt of the day when they might get married and have a house of their own so that they could cook and clean *their own* home instead of someone else's? Given the choice, would you rather spend your life out at work doing a job you hate, a tiresome chore that you *waste your life* doing in order to earn money, or would you rather spend your life maintaining the home comforts and raising your children? If you answer the question honestly, you may find yourself questioning the old chestnut that women were *forced* into the domestic sphere by men. In the past men didn't have the choice, they *had* to go out to work, at whatever job they could get.

Some men in the past were bachelors so what money they were able to earn by the sweat of their brow they could largely spend on themselves, the lucky fellows, but the cultural norm was marriage and a family. Husbands and fathers didn't get to spend their wages on themselves. They had the obligations of gendered manhood. The traditional idea that the man goes out to work to earn the money whilst the woman stays at home to do the domestic work carries no implication that the person earning the money is therefore the one with the power. Who *earns* the money is of far less importance than *upon whom the money is spent.* (Who has the power – the prostitute giving £40 blow-jobs or the pimp that she gives the money to?) Most men worked, not just for themselves, but for their families. If the husband is paying all the bills, then *his* money is also *his wife's* money and *his children's* money.

The dissolute man who drank away his wages in the pub, leaving his wife and kids without the money for food, was a despised creature. He was a failure as a man. In his drunkenness, he had not met his gendered obligations. The man who couldn't earn enough money to keep a roof over the heads of his family, even if it was no fault of his own, was a failed man. Working class men were frequently out of work and unemployed men had a hard time holding on to their dignity and sense of themselves as men. Unemployment was a kind of symbolic castration for men during times of economic recession and depression. How could they be 'proper' men if they didn't fulfill their obligations as the family breadwinner? And when working class women had to go out to work because the family needed more money than the husband was able to earn on his own, this was again considered shaming for him. How many men uttered the phrase 'no wife of mine is going to have to go out to work'? The societal expectation that men had to get out into the world and earn money was so extreme that (in peacetime) society measured manhood in terms of financial income and status. A man without money in his wallet was a *failed* man. Any such man was obliged to feel ashamed of himself. The financial independence that was largely forbidden to women was compulsory for men. This is why no 'real man' could live off a woman. It was his gendered social role to provide the cash and if he failed in this and lived off of her money, then he was a 'ponce' or a 'kept man' and socially despised accordingly. He could not even let a woman pay for a round of drinks in the pub or pay for a meal on a date. It was considered shameful for him to let her pay.

It wasn't so much that men had *more access* to the workplace, it was that men had a gendered social role which *required them* to have a job and earn money. It follows, of course, that if society imposes a gendered social role upon men to spend their lives in the workplace, then society must also give them access to the workplace. Men had more access *because* they had the obligations of their gender. This is not 'male power', it is male duty.

That's why when those men who hadn't been killed in world war two returned from the killing fields where their friends had been slaughtered, they claimed their old jobs back from the women ("Rosie the Riveter") who had been doing those jobs while the men had been dying in their gendered social role abroad. Those returning men were now expected, in accordance with the societal role that they were required to fulfill, to earn a living for themselves and for their wives and for their children. How could men pay for everything, as they were expected to pay for everything, if women had their jobs?

How can factory-fodder discharge the responsibilities of a financial provider unless he has a job in the factory? How can a work-unit hand over his wage packet to his wife at the end of every week's labour unless he has work?

We can certainly admit that some men could find self-fulfilment in a career and we can further admit that bachelors did have an advantage over spinsters in the matter of financial independence. But the point that counts is that *this was not the cultural norm*. Patriarchy theory has to prove *systemic* male power and the *systemic* oppression of women. Nothing of that sort can be proved by the greater financial independence of bachelors or a few middle-class men who found their careers rewarding. After all, many women may have found their domestic lives and the raising of their children to be profoundly self-fulfilling and rewarding, so does that prove women enjoyed systemic 'female power' and perpetrated a systemic oppression of men? No, it does not in either case.

This prompts a very different view of the relationship between feminism and 'patriarchy'. Taking a realistic perspective on how going out to work in paid employment was for very many men a waste of their lives in futile drudgery performed for no other reason than to earn money, we might think that on the whole it was a more rewarding and self-fulfilling life to be a housewife and mother than it was to be a coalman or an advertising file clerk or a factory foreman or a warehouse labourer. But traditional society did not describe it that way. Instead it would speak of a woman being 'just a housewife' as if that was an inferior position to paid employment. Now, notice how *feminism has implicitly endorsed* this idea that to be 'just' a housewife was the weaker, less important role by speaking of a housewife and mother as occupying a role that was little more than a form of domestic slavery. This description uses *the same values* as so-called patriarchal society in treating the role of paid employment as bestowing the position of power and advantage in a marriage. Feminism is using 'patriarchal' values here.

A real rejection of 'patriarchal' values might have been to say that women in traditional society were the lucky ones who had access to a more rewarding and self-fulfilling life raising their children than the poor men who had to slave away at jobs they hated. But feminism's years of agitation for female access to the workplace implicitly endorses the idea that paid employment was the route to a better life. The idea that the advantaged position might be to stay home and raise your children rather than to work as a taxi driver, stressed out and frustrated, sitting in a traffic jam all day every day, is an idea that mainstream feminism could not have entertained. It would mean that perhaps women had not been *forced* into the domestic sphere. It would mean that paid employment never was the position of privilege and power that feminism presented it as being. Why not ask a modern working-class woman interminably scanning an endless line of customer's groceries through the checkout at a supermarket if her job makes her feel powerful and self-fulfilled?

(4b) Personal power comes in many guises.

If we set aside ideology and take a realistic view, we can observe that personal power comes in many different forms and is exercised in many different ways. In the past these different forms of power have often been gendered. At it's most basic biological level men have had muscle power and women have had reproductive power. Feminism's fear of men is often expressed in terms of how men are on average physically stronger than women. This gender inequality, however, is not sexism since it is not a societal imposition of gender but a product of evolution. Another consequence of evolution is that women have wombs and men do not, so nature denies a man the opportunity to bear his own children himself. Every man is totally dependent upon a woman to have his children for him. (I always laugh when I hear a woman say: 'It's so unfair; women can't have children after middle-age but Charlie Chaplin had a child when he was in his eighties'. Chaplin did *not* have a child, his very much younger wife of child-bearing age had the child. And how many men in their eighties have wives that young?)

Men's dependence upon women for their children is very disempowering for men, certainly for those men who have a compelling paternal instinct, and even more so if they are gay. With feminism's usual hypocrisy it sometimes describes this male disempowerment as 'womb envy' in order to show men in a negative light, but feminism never describes women's attitude to men's on average greater physical strength as 'muscle envy'.

A common example of women's exercise of power is encapsulated in the phrase 'beauty is power' (although this is not limited to women). This is usually understood as referring to erotic power. That is clearly one aspect of the power of beauty. Would anyone seriously deny that sex-appeal is a potent form of empowerment? The beautiful can use their beauty to get their own way and twist other people around their little finger. Gold diggers even use beauty as a form of exchange for material wealth.

Emotional appeal is also very powerful. Foreign aid charities do not make television commercials in which a knowledgeable person speaking directly to camera gives the hard statistics about financial deprivation in Africa. They don't make that sort of commercial because it wouldn't be very effective in securing donations. The television commercials that foreign aid charities actually do make show heart-rending images of helplessly starving African children with a compassionately sombre voiceover saying 'you could save this child's life for only £20 a month'. The emotional appeal of that starving child is going to be a thousand times more powerful than any facts and figures.

Emotional appeal has also served women well as a source of personal power. A performance or an admission of 'little girly' female helplessness has always been an effective way to get a man to do what she wants. It is the woman's traditional tool to manipulate men. 'I'm a poor weak women so some big strong man must take care of me'. 'I'm a defenceless woman so my interests must be put first'. 'I'm a powerless and vulnerable woman so men must make my protection their priority'. This is the refrain of the traditional misandry called chivalry. The more child-like a woman is, the more she can exercise power over the 'protective male'. Women are not children, but an affectation of childishness has functioned as a source of power for women that has never been available to men. It is a part of the explanation of traditional ideals of feminine beauty, with things like lack of body hair, big eyes and small facial features, daintiness and delicacy. All these things add to the child-like appeal of the classically beautiful woman. This is sometimes called neoteny. https://www.youtube.com/watch?v=C46rSlfTum4

(This is also a part of the explanation of why people view violence done to a woman as being a much worse crime than violence done to a man. Violence to a woman is perceived as being closer to violence done to a helpless child. It is noticeable that when the media describe an assault upon a woman, the adjective used is very often 'defenceless'. The attack is said to have been perpetrated upon a 'defenceless woman'.)

Society as a whole, and men in particular, have always found it very difficult to resist the desire to help a crying woman. Traditionally, pathos has empowered women. A pathetic man has been an object of derision and contempt; a pathetic woman has been an object of sympathy and concern. Whatever strength and personal power men may have is instantly put at the service of a woman when she exposes her weakness and helplessness. In this way, men's strength is often *women's* strength since it is placed at their disposal. This is nicely expressed in the famous comment made by Warren Farrell: "The weakness of men is the facade of strength; the strength of women is the facade of weakness". [Farrell (1993), "The Myth of Male Power"] Any readers who are not yet familiar with the books of Warren Farrell are strongly recommended to acquaint themselves with his work.

But there is a disadvantage to the protective power of an affectation of female defencelessness, which is that traditionally women were not seen as authority figures because child-like attributes do not support an image of authority. A person who frequently employs their own alleged powerlessness as a means to acquire power from others in the form of compassion and assistance is unlikely to inspire confidence as an authoritative leader. What bestows power with one hand, disempowers with the other hand.

And this leads us to a crucial understanding of the character of feminism. As the reader will already have worked out for themselves, female 'vulnerability' is the tool that feminism constantly uses in its own exercise of power. Feminism's incessant claims of victimhood on behalf of all women is precisely an appeal/demand for women to receive forms of protection and advantage that are *not available to men*.

Feminism deploys this political weapon over and over. It says that women have special needs because of their 'vulnerability', so all political and cultural decisions must take this into account by favouring women with the privilege of special protection in the workplace, in the home, in the law courts, in their personal relationships, and everywhere else. Feminism makes its demands on the basis that the 'vulnerability' of women *entitles them to have their needs prioritised*. Why must all political action be focused upon women and none of it focused upon men? Because women suffered the martyrdom of male oppression in history. Because they were excluded from many areas of paid employment. Because they are forced to live in a 'rape culture'. Because they live with domestically violent women-haters. Because they are made to carry the burden of child-rearing. Because because because because.

Feminism exploits this form or power relentlessly, spewing out an endless stream of women's alleged victimization and therefore their entitlement to priority treatment. *The most prominent misogyny of which feminism is guilty is the political infantilism of women*; the perpetration of a gender stereotype of woman as victim, of woman as vulnerable, of woman as child.

Feminism even exploits the traditional prejudice of women's gendered entitlement to special protection when it seeks to invalidate all criticism of itself by claiming that any criticism of feminism is actually 'an attack upon women'. Traditionally, any attack upon 'defenceless' women was always viewed as being morally indefensible, therefore by insisting that any criticism of feminism is an attack upon women feminists can pretend that any criticism of feminism is always morally indefensible.

It is not true that in traditional society men had all the personal power. Patriarchy theory's simple deception is to *define* personal power in terms of the ways that men had more power than women and to ignore the ways that women had more power than men. Having defined personal power in terms of the types of power that men had, the theory then claims that men had all the power. We have to remember that feminism originated in the writings and political activism of privileged middle-class women who were complaining about the type of power that *they didn't have*. They type of power which *they did have* was never mentioned because they weren't complaining about that.

(4c) A male contraceptive pill.

It is worthwhile to look more closely at the issue that I referred to in the previous section as 'reproductive power'. A reliable oral contraceptive for women was invented way back in the 1950s but science still hasn't made a reliable oral contraceptive for men. Have you ever wondered why? Feminists would claim that it is just another example of the patriarchy trying to control women's bodies and control their fertility because that interpretation conforms to their 'male power' theory. But think about it. A reliable oral contraceptive pill was an incredibly empowering thing for women and it was developed under what feminism calls the patriarchy. In fact, the contraceptive pill gave women (and only women) reliable control over their own fertility for the first time in history. If there were a male contractive pill, then men could equally control their own fertility. They would be in a position to only father children if they chose to.

In 1951 a young man called Carl Djerassi synthesised norethindrone and, in collaboration with his colleagues biologist Gregory Pincus and physician John Rock, invented the first oral contraceptive. In doing so he empowered women far more than Betty Friedan, Simone de Beauvoir and Germaine Greer combined. Yet, if you were to ask the average girl-power feminist who Carl Djerassi is, do you think that they would recognise his name?

Ironically, from his own encounters with her Djerassi says that "Germaine Greer was always a vociferous opponent of the pill" http://www.theguardian.com/lifeandstyle/2007/apr/15/healthandwellbeing.features1?gu ni=Article:in%20body%20link   This, of course, is because feminist theory requires that the pill be seen as 'men' exercising control over women's bodies, rather than what it actually is, the most liberating and empowering thing that was ever done for women in the history of the world.

Why haven't men been similarly empowered? The conspicuous absence of a male oral contraceptive is not due to any scientific difficulties. Commercial corporations could produce one if they chose to, so why don't they? They could make billions from such a product, and since when have corporations been known to turn down money? Governments could produce one if they chose to, so why don't they?

One of the excuses given for not creating a male contraceptive pill is that men can't be trusted with anything as important as contraception. Men, we are told, might claim to be on the pill when they weren't or might not remember to take their pill but lie to women about this, and so women couldn't trust men to tell the truth. This excuse is as revealing as it is breathtaking. Firstly, it describes the position that men are already in, that of having to trust women if they are relying on the pill as their method of contraception. Secondly, it takes the gender-supremacist position that women are more responsible and more honest than men, as well as treating the reproductive security of women as being important whilst the reproductive security of men is unimportant. And thirdly, it completely ignores the obvious fact that just because the man is on the pill *that doesn't stop the woman from being on the pill also*. Both the woman and the man can take their own pills and each can thereby exercise an equal control over their own fertility.

Another excuse is that men don't need an oral contraceptive because they already have the condom. This is like saying that women don't need an oral contraceptive because they already have the diaphragm; that there is a physical 'barrier' contraceptive available, therefore an oral contraceptive is unnecessary. Does the diaphragm negate the need for a female oral contraceptive? Of course not. Does the condom negate the need for a male oral contraceptive? Of course not. We are talking about equal empowerment, equal control over one's own fertility. So what is the real reason that a male oral contraceptive is still denied to men?

Now follow this closely. At the moment, women have a reliable means to exercise control over their own fertility and men don't. If men were given the same empowerment over their own fertility that women already have, then women would no longer be in an advantaged position. So from a feminist point of view this looks like it would *disadvantage* women in that, in comparison with men, women would have less power than they currently have. If women lose their position of advantage compared to men, feminism views this as women being disadvantaged.

But, in fact, a male contraceptive pill would not mean that women were disadvantaged compared to men, it would actually put women into a position of *equality with men* in this respect. Men would be raised up to the level of power that women already have. Instead of women having more power over fertility than men have, a male oral contraceptive would mean that women would have *the same level of power* over fertility as men. This is a clear example of how, from a feminist perspective, women being in an advantaged position over men is presented as if that were sex equality, whereas a genuine impartial sex equality is presented as if it were female disadvantage. Do you see that?

And that's why we still don't have an equivalent male contraceptive pill: because not only does the political system we live under *not* want men to have control over women's fertility, it doesn't even want men to have control over their own fertility. Neither did the so-called patriarchal system of the 1950s. The establishment, then and now, doesn't want men to have the power to choose whether or not they become fathers. If a man has sex with a woman but doesn't want the sex to result in pregnancy, male oral contraception would give him that freedom of choice *even without the woman's permission*. In other words, it would give him equality of choice with the woman. It's already true that *he* can't have a child without *her* consent. A male pill would mean that *she* couldn't have a child without *his* consent. He could no longer be trapped into marriage or into child support by an 'accidental' pregnancy. In respect of their own fertility, men would no longer be disadvantaged compared to women and women would no longer be more empowered than men (except, of course, in regard of their possession of a womb, but that's nature not sexism). That's why, in the second decade of the twenty-first century, there still isn't a male contraceptive pill; it's because the political establishment doesn't want men to have an equal choice with women and equal control over their own fertility. They prefer men to remain disadvantaged. They prefer to maintain a situation in which women exercise control over male fertility. The truth is the exact opposite of the feminist lie.

Society's decision-makers see it as being *in women's interest* that there should not be a male oral contraceptive, therefore there isn't a male oral contraceptive. If a male pill were seen as being in women's interest, you can bet your boots that there would be one, along with a government-funded campaign to encourage men to take it. Society is governed much more in the perceived female interest than in a male interest. The age-old traditional sexist belief that men's interest can quite properly be sacrificed in the interest of protecting women is alive and thriving in feminist society. This is an example, and a particularly important one, of how men in positions of political power *do not* act in a male interest.

Feminism's fixation on what sex a person happens to be gives their ideology a bizarre view of political representation. It acts and speaks as if what sex a politician happens to be makes a difference to their politics. But what actually matters about a politician is not what sex they are, what matters is *how they legislate based upon what they believe*. Who would be so foolish as to vote for a politician whose political views they disagreed with simply because they were of the same sex as that politician? This is so screamingly obvious that even people

as brainwashed as feminists ought to be able to see it. After all, a feminist would vote for Barack Obama but she wouldn't vote for Sarah Palin. Obama's maleness means nothing because he is an overt and committed feminist. Palin's femaleness means nothing, even if she calls herself a 'conservative feminist', because her political views are contrary to feminist orthodoxy.
http://www.theguardian.com/commentisfree/2008/sep/12/sarahpalin.feminism

Yet when feminism is demanding more women in parliament there is always the underlying suggestion that this will mean that women in society will be better represented as a result of having more female MPs. There is in this an assumption that female politicians will be, to some degree, pro-women. But no parliamentary politician in my lifetime has ever been pro-man. Feminist orthodoxy assumes that if a politician is male and I am male, then that politician must in some way represent *me*. All my life the houses of parliament have had lots of men sitting as MPs but not a single one of them have ever represented *me*. What matters about politicians is what they believe and how they legislate, nothing else. It means absolutely nothing that lots of men have had seats in parliament. None of them have ever had my beliefs and values, and none of them have ever legislated in my interest. The fact that they happen to be the same sex as me does not make them my representatives. *Being male is not a political position.*

Perhaps the feminist belief, derived from patriarchy theory, that being male *is* a political position explains why it is generally assumed that a female politician will be pro-women in her political views. This is conventionally seen as being *a good thing*, although to a sex-equalitarian it simply means that the politician is sexist. To be pro-women is sexist, just as to be pro-men would be sexist. (Not that any politicians ever are pro-men.) To adopt a political position in which you deliberately favour one sex over the other is unequivocally sexist. Why do people think that it's not sexist for a politician to be pro-women? Because they have swallowed the lie of patriarchy theory and think that being pro-women is necessary to achieve equality; that people have to be treated *unequally* in the name of equality.

(5) Males ruled females by violence and the threat of violence?

We have been working our way through various versions of what 'patriarchy' or 'male power' is supposed to mean, beginning with the most unsophisticated and then examining increasingly more devious versions. These have been: (a) men have ruled society, (b) those who ruled society ruled in a male interest, (c) capitalism is another name for male power, and (d) men have had more personal power than women. All of these have been found to be false, and quite obviously false. We have now reached our last variation on a theme, a really watered-down and weaker version of 'patriarchy', namely that (e) men ruled over women through physical violence and threats of violence.

This final version clings to patriarchy theory by claiming that even if men were not the ruling class of society, women were still oppressed by men because in every economic class the men within that class ruled over the women in that class. How? By using brutality and intimidation. Is this true? Have men as a class of persons used their physical strength and alleged predilection for violence to threaten, bully and coerce women into a position of submission? Is this still the case? Lurid media headlines are certainly eager to paint that picture of men. Mainstream contemporary feminism, with its twin obsessions of rape and domestic violence, talks about little else these days. Is this the reality?

Consider your own experience of the world. Men let women get away with offences that they would never tolerate from other men. Picture a scene at a university event where someone is due to speak whom the organised feminist students on campus will not tolerate to speak. Perhaps the speaker intends to say something unforgivably provocative like 'in addition to women having rights, men ought to have rights too', or 'in addition to women being equal with men, men ought to be equal with women' or something similarly reprehensible in its ideological incorrectness. The organised feminist students turn up at the event to set off the fire alarm and scream aggressively at anyone who dares to try to enter the event, to bully them and drive them away by means of hate-filled chanting and outrageously deceitful claims about how it's the inoffensive and patiently reasonable speaker who is guilty of hate-speech, not themselves, and that anyone who wants to listen to the speaker is therefore a rape apologist and a woman-hater. From your own experience, how would you expect the men being insulted and abused to react?

For example, listen to the smiling in-your-face feminist (at 3.56 on this video) at the University of Toronto protest against Warren Farrell http://www.youtube.com/watch?v=iARHCxAMAO0 who says to a remarkably self-restrained man that: "You should be fucking ashamed of yourself, you're fucking scum, you are fucking scum, a fucking rape apologist, incest-supporting, woman-hating fucking scum. Fucking scum, just another . . . you know what though, why would you pay money to fucking support a fucking rape apologist if you weren't fucking one. Fucking scum." (It need hardly be said, of course, that Farrell is *not in any way* a rape apologist and has never said anything that could remotely be thought to justify the label of rape apologist.)

If those aggressively abusive feminists insulting men to their face *actually genuinely believed* that the men they are calling such vile names were in fact inherently violent women-haters, do you think the feminists would be hurling insults so freely? After all, if men really were so innately violent and so motivated by a hatred of women, how would the men react to such incendiary insults? They'd go crazy with rage and physically attack the women who are insulting them, right? Yet the feminists spewing misandrist filth at these men are supremely confident that there is no possibility of this happening. These immature, cloistered, ideologically indoctrinated university feminists would never dare to risk shouting such inflammatory remarks if they honestly thought that there was an imminent probability of their being beaten to a bloody pulp.

This is a classic modern example of feminist doublethink. It says: men are violently abusive misogynists compelled by their intrinsic nature to commit violence against the women they hate but it is perfectly safe for me, a 130lb woman to insult this man to his face in the most obscene manner because *he would never hit a woman*. This doublethink is a combination of the female students believing slavishly in academic feminist ideology whilst having learned, from the reality of their own lives, that society has always taught men that it is irredeemably dishonourable for a man to hit a woman. The female students know that this traditional cultural norm is securely in place for their protection and they are relying upon it for their safety when they abuse men in public.

Traditional sexism was very explicit in its view that it was far worse for a man to punch a woman in the face than it was for him to punch another man in the face. This misandry is still very much in force in today's society, which still holds violence against women to be worse than violence against men. It is very much a part of the sexist double-standard about human pain. Not only have men as a class of persons *not* used systemic violence to force women into submission, in comparison with the way that men have been treated, women have always had a *privileged* position where violence is concerned and feminists exploit this.

Feminists love to talk about how men are so much more physically powerful than women, creating an alternative history in which women were an entire class of fragile defenceless waifs living in constant abject terror under the bruising fists of despotic patriarchs. But in real history the great majority of men (not all of them, of course, there is a genuine issue of domestic violence committed and suffered by both sexes) have always taken their gendered responsibility to protect women far too seriously to make use of any physical superiority they may have had to even a tiny fraction of the extent that *they could have if they had chosen to*.

If men as a class of persons were really the uncivilized beasts described by feminists, then *feminism would never have come into existence in the first place* because the suffragettes would have had the shit kicked out of them by their husbands and fathers, not to mention the general male public. It wouldn't have been a matter of force-feeding suffragettes on hunger strike in prison, it would have been a case of suffragettes being punched senseless in the streets and dead suffragettes floating in the River Thames. And when second wave feminism arrived telling everyone what rapists and wife-beaters and misogynists men are, there would have been a series of violent assaults committed against all the leading feminists.

If men are what feminists *say* men are, then this is what would have happened. This did not happen, therefore men are *not* what feminists say men are. It didn't happen then and it doesn't happen now. Feminist women can and do routinely insult men, describing men in terms of the most obscenely negative gender-stereotype, without coming to any physical harm. But if this gender-stereotype of what-men-are-like were at all accurate, then feminists would never get away with it. So the stereotype is demonstrably wrong. Ask yourself, how is it that a group of women can walk the public street on a 'Take Back the Night' march without any outraged misogynist men committing any violence against them? Clearly, men are not what the 'Take Back the Night' march *says* they are. If they were, then the march would rapidly be turned into a riot by the angry 'male oppressor' counter-demonstration.

Come to think of it, *have you ever seen or heard of a male counter-demonstration to any public feminist action*? I don't remember any. When feminists in the 1970s attended public rallies with banners declaring 'Sisterhood is Powerful', were there ever any counter-demonstrations from men with placards saying 'Down with Sisterhood'? Forty years later, did the 'Slutwalk' marches in 2011 produce any organised response from men with banners declaring 'Yes, You're a Bunch of Sluts'? These things never happen.

This is the crucial evidence: the so-called male oppressor is silent and passive. Can you think of *any* organized anti-feminist demonstrations by men in the last four decades? You'll find anti-abortion protests outside of abortion clinics but that's the (largely religious) pro-life movement protesting a single issue,

107

it's not men protesting against feminism. You'll find excluded fathers protesting against misandrist custody courts but, again, that's a single issue (and a fairly recent development). What violent or even vociferous male response has there been to decades of feminists publicly insulting men? When has the 'male oppressor' *ever* taken to the streets in the western world to demand a return to traditional society? When have you *ever* heard a news broadcast that said 'a feminist rally took place in London today and fifteen women were taken to hospital after they were attacked by raging misogynists'? How many feminist campaigners at the end of a rally or march have received medical treatment because anti-feminist men have broken the women's noses or punched their teeth out? How often do you hear about a group of men charging into a feminist bookshop and smashing the place up? And yet feminism continually says that men are testosterone-fuelled misogynists who oppress women by violence and the threat of violence. If so, shouldn't we expect every public feminist action to result in bloodshed? But it seems they never do.

Most men go to extraordinary lengths of lip-biting to avoid doing any violence to women, even in the face of extreme feminist provocation. It's important to understand what this means. The feminist claim that men habitually and systemically use violence to exert 'male power' over women *is refuted by feminism itself*. If what feminism says about men and male violence were true, then feminism would never have existed because men like that would never have allowed it to exist, they would have crushed it. But feminism *does* exist, therefore feminism *must* be wrong about men. *Feminism disproves itself.* The ideology of feminism is so ridiculously stupid that it is effectively self-refuting.

Patriarchy Theory is Refuted by Historical Fact

The basic tenets of patriarchy theory seem to bear no relation to the world that the theory purports to describe. Yet feminism continues to thrive. So what do feminists out there in the big wide world think patriarchy (or sometimes 'heteropatriarchy') is? Here is an example from a feminist blog:

"Men's power lies in every single relation between men and women, not primarily in the state or by owning the means of production. It's important to have a perspective that sees both the structure at large and at the same time see the individuals and actors creating it - there is no male power without the men exercising it; men's violence against women is also not an isolated phenomenon but a part of the structural violence that men as a group use against women as a group. - Very often when speaking of the realities of this oppression, "exceptions" and the "good men" are mentioned, making a theoretical difference between individual / group / system. Creating a difference between men as individuals and the acts and institutions of men, does not make a lot of sense. - *Men as a group hate women, and express this hatred through rape, murder, sexual harassment, and other sexualized behaviors . . . . All men have power over all women: over all women as a* group and specifically over a few that they are in close relation to." [original emphasis]
http://sosiaalikeskus.wordpress.com/2010/09/27/gendered-heteropatriarchy-on-separatism-and-sexism/

The imbecilic crudity of this would cause people to laugh out loud if the theory were a part of an ideology outside of political correctness. For a theorist to claim that "all men have power over all women" or that "men as a group hate women" is so idiotically contrary to the evidence of people's actual lives that it would beggar belief that anyone could be fool enough to assert such things, if it were not for the fact that we've been hearing assertions just like this for more than forty years. The sensible response to this sort of theory would be to classify it with the theories about how the lizard aliens of the illuminati are secretly running the world or how the leader of some small religious cult was really the second incarnation of Christ.

You'll notice that the theory is designed so that there is no way out of guilt-object status for men. Men as a group are guilty. Men as individuals are guilty. The exercise of male power "lies in every single relation" between the sexes. There are no exceptions. Guilt is presented as being intrinsic to maleness in everything men do. No matter how much power an individual woman has, she is still perceived as being a victim simply because she is a woman. No matter how powerless an individual man is, he is still classified as being one of the victimisers simply because he is a man.

So there is no point in mature adults trying to have a dialogue with the advocates of this childishness. What is there to discuss? Instead, we should address a few more arguments that will further justify casting patriarchy theory into the rubbish bin so that society can get on with moving toward a genuine impartial sex equality. To begin, we could look at a couple of facts about social history *that could not be true if patriarchy theory were true*. Since they are true, this necessarily means that patriarchy theory is not true. Consider these two brief points and then ask yourself if you can still lend any credence to the theory of 'patriarchy'.

(1) If patriarchy theory were true, then it would not have been the case that female lives were held to be more valuable than male lives and men would not have had a gendered social role to put themselves in harm's way, and sometimes even sacrifice their own lives, in order to protect women.

Let's be clear, I'm not saying that men always did this, I'm merely saying that there was a *cultural norm* which stated that men ought to do this; that it was a part of the male role in society to place more value on the safety of a woman than on his own safety. Patriarchy theorists say that traditional society was ruled by men in their own interest, and that men as a group hate women, and that women as a class of persons were oppressed by men as a class of persons. So this cultural norm of valuing the safety of women more highly than the safety of men *could not have existed* in a society ruled by men who hated women and systemically oppressed them. Otherwise you would have to argue that an *oppressor* class valued the lives of the *oppressed* class more highly than they valued their own lives. This would be utterly incredible. Can you imagine white racists in 1850s America valuing the lives of black Americans more highly than they valued their own white lives and having a cultural norm in which white people believed that they should always sacrifice themselves in order to protect black people? *Oppressor classes do not behave that way toward oppressed classes.* What slave-owner would put the safety of his slaves ahead of his own safety? The single fact of the existence of this cultural norm that men should put themselves in harm's way to protect women is, by itself, sufficient to refute patriarchy theory. But that fact does not stand alone.

(2) Traditional society imposed a political structure in which the overwhelming majority of men found themselves living in a society in which they were treated inhumanly as work-units from adolescence to old age (if they didn't get killed by a workplace injury before reaching old age). This was a political and economic system which operated on the basis of the ruthless and relentless exploitation of male bodies. It rendered nearly all men powerless in the society in which they lived, reducing them to factory-fodder and canon-fodder. They shared their lives of ceaseless toil with women of their own class under the oppression of *the minority of men and women* who constituted the economic and political ruling class. Under socio-economic systems such as feudalism and capitalism men were *not* one social group. A baron was a baron and a peasant was a peasant. The political interests of men in one economic class were in conflict with the political interests of men in another economic class, they did not share a 'male power'.

This means that any political theory dependent upon the idea that men were one class of persons, men as a common group with shared interests, beliefs, values and attitudes, is false. Otherwise you would have to argue that men of the economically oppressed class *identified with the men who oppressed them but did not identify with the women who shared their oppression.* You would have to argue that a rich mill-owner felt that he had more interests in common with his impoverished male mill-hands than he had with his own wife and daughters; that he shared 'power' with the men who slaved in his mill but he did not share 'power' with his pampered wife and daughters. The absurdity of this should be sufficient to show that patriarchy theory is not an accurate interpretation of history. It could only be found the slightest bit credible by someone who believes in a *natural biologically determined gendering of the sexes* where there is some unspoken covert brotherhood of men and sisterhood of women derived simply from their biology. Anyone who holds that gender identities are social constructs must reject the idea that there is a biological brotherhood of something called 'male power' which all men held in common. Patriarchy theory is dependent upon this idea, therefore patriarchy theory is false.

The way that a brotherhood of 'male power' is inconsistent with a social construct theory of gender means that any feminist who believes gender to be a social construct should therefore cease to be a feminist because *feminism is dependent upon patriarchy theory and patriarchy theory is dependent upon biological determinism*. Also, if gendered identities and social roles were not social constructs, at least in part, then on my account of what sexism means (the *societal imposition* of those identities and roles) there wouldn't be any such thing as sexism! Instead, there would simply be a biological sex-war; the very same sex-war that feminism believes in and is fighting. (I will return to the issue of the way that feminism coverts endorses the idea that gender is biologically determined in chapter 4.)

But arguments like the two above that are based upon the actual position that men occupied in traditional society will have no effect upon feminists because historical facts mean absolutely nothing to feminism. Its revisionist history can believe anything that suits its political agenda and dismiss anything that is contrary to it. The extreme nature of this re-writing of history can be jaw-dropping in its absurdity. For example, the male feminist organisation NOMAS included on their website a short article by Dr Robert Brannon, a gender studies professor, about how *radical feminists ended black slavery in America*. He says:

"It is widely believed that human slavery was ended in the United States by Abraham Lincoln's 'Emancipation

112

Proclamation'. This is not true. Human slavery was ended in America primarily by a grass-roots petition campaign led by radical feminists." http://nomas.org/lincoln-did-not-free-the-slaves-the-little-known-story-of-how-feminists-ended-slavery/

Now, someone not deluded by feminist ideology might think that what really ended slavery in America was the self-sacrifice of the white and black men in the Union Army who fought against the Confederate Army. It was losing the civil war that forced the southern states to accept the end of slavery. If there had been no war, or if the south had won the war, then slavery would not have ended in the 1860s no matter how many proclamations Lincoln made or how many petition campaigns were organised. Men in blue uniforms ended slavery at the cost of their own lives and at the cost of the terrible physical and psychological wounds they suffered as soldiers. This is so obviously true that Brannon effectively admits it himself at one point, even though it completely refutes the main contention of his article. He says:

"There had been a string of Confederate victories on the battlefield, and it seemed to most of the public that the slave-holding South was about to win its battle to secede. In that event, no slaves at all would be freed." http://nomas.org/lincoln-did-not-free-the-slaves-the-little-known-story-of-how-feminists-ended-slavery/

Yet, despite this admission, no credit is given in the article to the tens of thousands of ordinary men who actually ended slavery in America at the cost of their lives and limbs. Instead, credit is given to the "National Woman's Loyal League" who *collected signatures* in support of ending slavery. I do not think it is going too far to describe Brannon's article as being deluded by feminist ideology. It could only have been written by a professional academic.

A high-profile example of the feminist establishment's disregard of historical truth in favour of their political agenda is Mary Seacole in the Crimean war. She appears to have been more businesswoman than nurse, selling food and alcohol and other comforts to the troops, yet in recent years her name has almost eclipsed that of Florence Nightingale (whose own Crimean medical reputation may have been inflated) as the heroine of the Crimean campaign. Nightingale's primary contribution was probably the way that she drew attention to the deplorable conditions under which the men of the army had to live and fight. As so often, more men died of disease than died in battle, and the officer class were neglectful of the proper care and attention for their soldiers. Nightingale played a significant role in that she was a well-connected, upper-class Victorian lady who could get letters published in the Times newspaper to publicly shame the government into sending out a Sanitary Commission. This is what brought about an improvement in the pestilential conditions the soldiers had been suffering.

But what view of these events are children in today's society given by feminist revisionist history? The historical narrative given to schoolchildren across the western world is all about how women and black people were 'written out' of history. https://www.youtube.com/watch?v=eADLWvWqK5Q What matters to the politically correct establishment of the present day (whose concern for the soldiers' agonies seems as minimal as that of the ruling class of the time) is that Seacole is a positive black/female role-model. Feminists and multiculturalists don't care a damn whether their claims about Seacole are true or not, they just want to exploit her memory for their own political purposes.

Leaving aside those, such as professional academics, whose high-income livelihood is dependent upon pretending that patriarchy theory is true, why do ordinary everyday feminists believe the embarrassingly immature claims of patriarchy theory? There are probably two main reasons, neither of them creditable:

(a) Cultural conformity; they live in a culture that believes in the theory uncritically and in which anyone who even suggests that it might be wrong is punished with social disapprobation for their heresy. (b) Privilege; feminist power is based upon a victimology which *needs* men as a class of persons to be held guilty. Without believing in the male oppressor and the female oppressed, without believing in the special status of women as victims, feminism would have no excuse for demanding privileged treatment for women.

Male Suicide

Any evidence that refutes patriarchy theory is simply ignored or denied by feminists. They live entrenched in denial because anything they don't want to believe is therefore 'backlash'. They treat any criticism *of feminist ideology* as if it were a criticism *of women* and therefore 'misogyny'. They prefer to believe the ubiquitous and persistent old assertion that 'it's a man's world'. This sentiment is the traditional version of what has since become patriarchy theory. It is the crass assumption, which goes largely unchallenged in mainstream culture, that men are the privileged sex and that 'women have to be twice as good to get half as far' (usually with the gender-supremacist addition 'fortunately this is not difficult'). The general idea is that men are irresponsibly living a life of selfish ease and get a free ride whilst women have to make up for what men fail to do in order to make the world go round.

If anyone is stupid enough to believe these misandrist clichés, they might want to ask themselves why men in this society kill themselves far more often than do women. After all, if everything is so much easier for privileged males, shouldn't they have less reason to reach the level of desperation in which a person would rather die than live another day?

Perhaps a female-supremacist will simply take this higher male suicide rate as evidence of how inadequate and feeble men are compared to women. But, *in the absence of a gender-supremacist attitude*, a sensible person would conclude that if one sex is committing suicide far more often than the other sex, then it is the sex that is killing themselves more often who are having a tougher time in life; that if there is a privileged sex, then it is probable that it is the sex who are committing suicide far less often.

115

The UK Office for National Statistics says that "suicide and injury/poisoning of undetermined intent" is the leading cause of death for men between 20 and 34 years of age. It accounted for a quarter (26%) of *all deaths* of men of that age in 2012. It's also the leading cause of death for men between 35 and 49 years of age. It's the second leading cause of death for boys between 5 and 19 years of age.

http://www.ons.gov.uk/ons/rel/vsob1/mortality-statistics--deaths-registered-in-england-and-wales--series-dr-/2012/info-causes-of-death.html

The 2013 Samaritans report, 'Suicide: facts and figures' states that "Across the UK, male suicide rates are consistently higher than female rates. [In] England and Scotland the male suicide rate is approximately 3 times higher than the female rate. In Wales the male suicide rate is approximately 4 times higher than the female rate. In Northern Ireland the male suicide rate is approximately 5 times higher than the female rate."

http://www.samaritans.org/support-us/why-support-samaritans/facts-and-figures-about-suicide

It's worth remembering these statistics the next time you hear a feminist tell a man to "check your privilege". Just imagine the constant barrage of sympathy and concern that would fill the media based upon innumerable academic papers written by feminist researchers if these figures were reversed; if there were three to five times as many women committing suicide as men. But not when it is three to five times as many men committing suicide as women. There are no high-profile campaigns to defend and protect men. Remind me, which is the privileged sex? This is the same old double-standard about the value of human life.

The National Institute of Mental Health in the USA states that in 2007 almost four times as many males as females died by suicide, that nearly five times as many males as females aged 15 to 19 died by suicide, and that just under six times as many males as females aged 20 to 24 died by suicide.

http://www.nimh.nih.gov/health/publications/suicide-in-the-us-statistics-and-prevention/index.shtml#factors

Pause for a moment to drink that in: on the 2007 figures, young

American men aged 20 to 24 are committing suicide almost *six times as often* as American women of the same age. Shouldn't that be one of the most high-profile issues of gender inequality in America? Isn't it much more important that how many women get to be the CEOs of major business corporations? Aren't the lives of these desperate young men more valuable than the career opportunities of rich powerful women? Apparently not. Society has never valued the lives of the expendable sex. We should remember that men, especially young men, are also the group in society most likely to be murdered. "From 2002 to 2011, the average homicide rate for males was 3.6 times higher than the rate for females." [Alexia Cooper & Erica Smith, "Homicide in the U.S. Known to Law Enforcement", 2011] http://www.bjs.gov/index.cfm?ty=pbdetail&iid=4863 Between the much higher male suicide rate and the much higher rate of male victims of homicide, there is an epidemic of male death. But it is not the type that feminism talks about, it is an epidemic of male death where *men are the victims*.

The Canadian government's 'Statistics Canada' states that "During [2009] a total of 2,989 males committed suicide (17.9 deaths per 100,000) compared to 901 females (5.3 deaths per 100,000). As these data show, males were three times more likely to commit suicide than females. The much higher rate of male suicide is a long-term pattern in Canada. At all points in time over the past 60 years, males have had higher rates of suicide than females." http://www.statcan.gc.ca/pub/82-624-x/2012001/article/11696-eng.htm Did you notice the phrase "over the past 60 years"? This is nothing new. Men were being driven to suicide much more often than women in traditional society, even *before* second-wave feminism.

In Australia, the government-funded national media initiative Mindframe states that "In 2011, 1727 males (15.3 per 100,000) and 546 females (4.8 per 100,000) died by suicide . . . . Suicide accounted for 1.5% of death from all causes in 2011. In males 2.3% of all deaths were attributed to suicide, while the rate for females was 0.8%." http://www.mindframe-media.info/for-media/reporting-suicide/facts-and-stats

Interestingly, Mindframe also states that "For those of Aboriginal and Torres Strait Islander descent, the relative age standardised suicide rate is 2.5 times higher for males and 3.4 times higher for females than for the corresponding non-Indigenous population."

Ask yourself this: if someone suggested that the higher suicide rates for the indigenous Aboriginal population of Australia were evidence of how they are discriminated against and suffer a more difficult life than the non-indigenous population, do you think that this suggestion would be accepted as true by the politically correct establishment? Of course it would, they'd find the suggestion entirely consistent with their political sympathies. But what if you made *exactly the same argument* for the higher suicide rates for men, that men are discriminated against and suffer a more difficult life than women? The establishment elite would deny that suggestion until they were blue in the face.

Those in authority over us try to avoid the issue of the much higher male suicide rate by disguising it with theories as to why the suicide rate is much higher for men. They say, for example, that women might attempt suicide as often as men but fail to actually kill themselves as often. This is the 'men are more successful at suicide' theory. But we could equally well theorize that women live, and have always lived, in a society which allows them to make a plaintive 'cry for help', whereas men live, and have always lived, in a society that rigorously forbids them from making a 'cry for help, because traditional gender roles do not permit men to show weakness. In which case, the female 'cry for help' attempted suicides might look like they weren't genuine attempts.

But all of this theorising about why people commit suicide is ultimately beside the point. What really matters is *the contradiction* between the suicide rates and patriarchy theory. If men were/are the oppressor and women were/are the oppressed, then how can it be that the oppressors are killing themselves three or four times more often than the oppressed? How can the oppressors have *more reason to want to die* than the oppressed do? This goes against all sense and reason. If patriarchy theory were true, then women would have higher suicide rates than men because an oppressed class are always going to have more reason to end their lives than an oppressor class. In fact, men have much higher suicide rates than women, therefore patriarchy theory is not true.

Unfalsifiable Ideology

The reader may have been wondering how feminism accounts for all the oppression and misandry that men have suffered throughout history. Surely they cannot have entirely ignored such a colossal amount of historical evidence? Surely someone must have drawn their attention to the way that the overwhelming majority of men have been ruthlessly economically exploited, and the way that men have been butchered in their millions in warfare fulfilling their gendered social role, and the way that men have themselves been *denied* the protection that they have been expected to *provide* for women? Feminism must have commented upon this and tried to explain this away, mustn't it? There is, in fact, a standard feminist response to all the pain and exploitation that men have endured under traditional sexism. It is this: 'Patriarchy hurts men, too'.

Breathtaking, isn't it. 'Patriarchy hurts men, too'. Instead of seeing all this evidence as a refutation of patriarchy theory, they blithely *take it for granted* that patriarchy theory *must be true* and conclude that 'patriarchy hurts men, too'. This is then used as an excuse for claiming that men should also be feminists and oppose 'patriarchy' because men will be better off, will live healthier and more satisfying lives, if they put an end to their own masculine systems and masculine behaviour.

But notice how glaringly 'patriarchy hurts men, too' is inconsistent with the most basic fundamentals of the theory of 'patriarchy'. If society was ruled by men, if it was ruled in a male interest, if men had all the power, how could it possibly be the case that men would be better off without patriarchy? If men were the privileged, advantaged oppressor class, how could it possibly be the case that the overwhelming majority of men were hurt by patriarchy? Anyone with any intellectual integrity would see immediately that if men would be better off without traditional sexism, and if men were hurt (indeed, mass murdered and maimed) by traditional sexism, then traditional sexism *could not possibly have been* what patriarchy theory *says* it was. Men would certainly be far better off if traditional sexism did not exist, that's why we can be equally certain that patriarchy theory is false.

But feminists cannot admit that traditional misandrist oppression refutes patriarchy theory because their whole ideology is based upon that theory. They cannot admit that these facts about history disprove the feminist interpretation of history because if they did, they would have to cease to be feminists. Their ideology requires them to believe in patriarchy theory no matter how much contrary evidence there is to refute it. So instead they treat 'patriarchy' *as a given*, they treat 'patriarchy' *as if it were irrefutable*, and then they magnanimously acknowledge that sometimes men can also suffer as a result of 'patriarchal oppression'.

This, I would argue, is an example of the difference between a *theory* and an *ideology*. If a person holds to a theory and is presented with evidence to the contrary which shows that their theory cannot be true as stated, then they must either revise their theory to take account of the contrary evidence or, if this is not possible, they must abandon their theory. If they refuse to do either, if they hold to their theory no matter how much evidence there is to disprove it, then it is no longer a theory, it has become an ideology. An ideologue never admits that they are wrong, they simply ignore or reinterpret contrary evidence to somehow make it fit their ideology. Any lame excuse will do, so long as they can go on pretending that their ideology is a true picture of the world. Hence, 'patriarchy hurts men, too'.

To take a contemporaneous example. The ideology of multiculturalism holds that as society becomes ever more multiethnic people from different cultures will recognise that their common humanity with people from other cultures is more significant to them than their ethnic differences and so a multicultural society will enjoy a much greater level of ethnic harmony that a largely monocultural society.

Yet in the UK, fifty years of ever-increasing multiculturalism has brought with it fifty years of ever-increasing ethic conflict and division. There have been race riots. There is ethnic apartheid in divided cities. The young people of the different ethnic communities are frequently described as being disaffected and alienated. There are even Jihadis who want to murder the kufr. Some might think that this *disproves* multiculturalism's theory about how a multiethnic society promotes ethnic harmony. But not the multiculti ideologue. They cannot admit that their ideology has been refuted by the actual consequences of their political programme. So instead, they hold that the increasing levels of ethnic disharmony are all caused by white racism; that 'racism is endemic to white people'. They believe this because it makes the ethnic disharmony *consistent with their ideology*.

Again, some might object that if white people were as endemically racist as multiculturalists say they are, then multiculturalism would never have been allowed to happen in the first place. A population of endemically racist people would never have permitted it. Since multiculturalism has taken place and continues to take place, we must conclude that white people were not endemically racist. It's a reasonable conclusion. But not to a multiculti. Whatever 'explanation' fits their ideology must be the correct one. Blaming all ethnic conflict on white people is the only way that they can explain away the fact that multiculturalism has not increased ethnic harmony in society in the way that, back in the 1960s, 70s, and 80s, their theory said it would. It therefore must be the correct explanation.

A theory is refutable by evidence and argument to the contrary. It is falsifiable. An ideology is not. It is believed by the ideologue regardless of whether it has been shown to be false. To an ideologue, *their faith* is irrefutable, even when it's been refuted. Just as evidence and argument has no effect upon a devout religious believer, neither does it have any effect upon a secular ideologue. Just as a multiculti must believe that multiculturalism is unfalsifiable, feminists must believe that feminism is unfalsifiable. Feminists, by definition, *must* believe in patriarchy theory. It is the foundation of their ideology. It can never be admitted that this theory is false. So feminists will continue to believe in it. No matter what.

The Matriarchy

When feminists say that men are to blame for all the wrongdoing in the world, that *everything is men's fault*, they usually sound like a kid from the 1960s saying that everything wrong with the world is the fault of 'people over thirty'. Although 'people over thirty' do not all share a political stance, and 'people over thirty' do not have a common interest as a group, just as 'men' do not all share a political stance and do not have a common interest as a group, it is exhilarating for an immature adolescent to feel that those old people, the 'people over thirty', are the one's who have made a mess of the world and that it's up to the *untarnished* young to set things right. Revolution now, the kids are alright! This sort of scapegoating makes its appeal on a purely emotional level, as the kind of thing that you feel is true 'in your gut', even though as a political theory it's strictly for the kids (or anyone else who feels themselves to be *unsullied* by any of the guilt for the wrongdoings of the world, like feminist women).

But although that may be the usual impression created by sweeping statements about 'patriarchal' society, in contrast, sometimes when feminists are speaking of 'The Patriarchy' they make it sound as if there was (and still is) some kind of international conspiracy by a brotherhood of men endlessly scheming together to oppress women. Governments, capitalists, religions, monarchies, and political activists, were all combined in the grand conspiracy to degrade women to an inferior social position. This international conspiracy of men has the same status and credentials as a slightly earlier theory by another bunch of fanatics about the 'international conspiracy of

Jews' (who presumably held their secret meetings in the smoke-filled room next door to the international conspiracy of men), with *the same spurious reason given in support of each theory*, that it was men/Jews who occupied the significant positions of power in society.

If 'The Patriarchy' is described in terms of an international conspiracy of men, most feminists will baulk and say that, no, no, that's not what they mean by 'The Patriarchy' (because the idea is so inexpressibly silly) and that what they mean by patriarchal society is much more subtle and nuanced than that. But perhaps the question we should be asking is: what about 'The Matriarchy'? There is plenty of evidence for a matriarchal conspiracy. There *is* an international sisterhood who scheme together to oppress men. It's called feminism. Feminist literature fills libraries with anti-male propaganda which is then employed in creating legal systems, government legislation, workplace practices, and family relations which systemically disadvantage and degrade men to the status of inferiors. The colossal quantity of feminist literature published over the last half-century constitutes a very public international ideological programme of political action, and perhaps the only thing that stops it from being a 'conspiracy' in the fullest sense of the word is that there was nothing covert about it. They conspired right out in the open.

Chapter Three

Feminism Stopped Us From Achieving Equality

One of the most common causes of quarrels and discord is proximity. For those in sustained relationships, the person most likely to be on the end of our ratty, griping, irritable behaviour is the person we live with, and the person most likely to get on our nerves is, again, the person we live with. Why? Because they're *always there*. We wake up with them, we eat with them, we go to bed with them, we go on holidays with them, and sometimes it seems like there's just no way of getting away from them. We can't nag our boss because they might fire us. We can't have a screaming fit at someone on the commuter train because we don't even know them. We can't vent our rage at the commissioner of taxes because they are just some anonymous bureaucrat that we'll never get to meet face to face. We can't revenge ourselves upon the spammer who litters our email inbox with spam messages because they live in Africa or Eastern Europe or somewhere miles away. But our darling partner in life, they're always on hand and in the firing line.

In traditional society there was a strong cultural norm for people to live as heterosexual couples. As a result, when proximity got to work, the person you were most likely to be quarrelling with was your partner of the so-called opposite sex. So men got to thinking that they could have an interesting, enjoyable little life if it wasn't for the woman they lived with putting the skids on things all the time. And women got to thinking that they could have a contented, rewarding little life if it wasn't for the man they lived with putting a block on things all the time. Men got to feeling that everything was *her* fault and women got to feeling that everything was *his* fault. And although this was quite normal in its way, it was also very childish.

Then along came second wave feminism which proclaimed from every media outlet that *men* were the oppressor, that *men* were the guilty ones, that *men* were the inconsiderate, selfish ones, that *men* were the domestically incompetent, irresponsible ones, that *men* were the problem. And all over the western world exultant women spun round on their heel, pointed an accusatory finger at their man and declared 'You see, I *told* you everything was *your* fault!'

And this was the spirit in which second wave feminism exploded onto the political scene in the 1970s.

Feminism's Perversion of the Freedom Movement of the 1960s

The 1960s was, by a long way, the most moral decade of the twentieth century. I say this because I am a liberal and my political views therefore focus largely on individual freedom and societal equality. The sixties was the decade that decriminalised male homosexuality, spoke out against men being drafted into the military (in America at least), championed individual life-choices, promoted greater tolerance, and produced a youth culture that advocated peace and love. Compare that to the fascistic thirties promoting hatred or the Thatcherite eighties promoting avarice. The sixties stand out as a moral beacon in the last century.

Men grew their hair shoulder length then added a beard and accompanied that with a casting off of the restrictive old suit, collar and suffocating tie to replace them with the freedom of long flowing garments like smock shirts, kaftans, and bell-bottom flares. Whereas men had once been forbidden any form of jewellery, now they sported love beads and astrological star-sign medallions. The old proscription, fear and avoidance of anything that might be accused of being effeminate had begun to be abandoned and the liberation of men burst forth in a multi-coloured blossoming of flower-power in which the cultural requirement placed upon men that they be drab and dull was overthrown.

125

Society's age-old expectation and requirement that men be the financial provider, the wage-earner, was an oppression from which young men were taking the early steps toward freeing themselves with a hippy culture that placed free self-expression and self-exploration above the grinding concern with earning money. This meant that, at a time when women wanted more access to the workplace so that they might provide financially for themselves, men were in a position to welcome more women in the workplace as the complementary other side of the coin to men being freed from the burden of having to be the breadwinner.

Most powerfully of all, it became much more possible for men to reject the call to war. The youth culture of peace and love enabled young men to have the confidence to defy their gendered social role of being cannon fodder. *Draft-dodging could and should have been the embryo of a men's liberation movement.* And they could have had women's support in men's liberation. There is a great example of this.

Back in 1915 during the Kaiser's war there was a ubiquitous recruitment poster which exploited the traditional imposition of gender upon men with the slogan "Women of Britain Say Go!" http://upload.wikimedia.org/wikipedia/en/a/ac/1915_Women_of_Britain,_say_Go!.jpg The poster implies that it is every man's duty to protect the womenfolk and that no women would respect a man who failed in his duty. But in 1968 the singer Joan Baez and her two sisters appeared on a poster which was a superb counter to the 1915 poster, with the slogan "Girls Say Yes to Boys who Say No" (Proceeds of the sale of this poster go to the draft resistance) http://oaj.oxfordjournals.org/content/32/1/121/F7.large.jpg. Not only does the 1968 poster recognise that a significant reason for young men to accept the traditional gendered social role that murders and maims them is that they want to impress women and be admired by women (traditionally, how many young women wanted to fuck a coward?) but more than that *it unites women and men* behind an issue that belongs not in a women's liberation campaign but rather in a men's liberation campaign.

126

This is a perfect example of what the action for sex equality that came out of the 1960s freedom movement *should have been*; women and men united in opposing the traditional sexist imposition of gender upon either women or men. There was even a women's protest group in Australia called Save Our Sons (SOS) from 1965 to 1972 demanding the repeal of the National Service Act of 1964, which conscripted men who were not yet eligible to vote. http://nvdatabase.swarthmore.edu/content/australian-women-protest-conscription-during-vietnam-war-save-our-sons-sos-1965-1972

In 1972 the singer songwriter Dory Previn released the tremendous "Don't Put Him Down", an insightfully sympathetic song about the stress men experience over the pressure to perform sexually. Dory Previn, in case you haven't heard of her, is *female*. (Previn also wrote the equally brilliant "Angels and Devils the Following Day", a song about how a woman with two male lovers was wounded more painfully by the sensitive and gentle lover than she was by the rough, even physically bruising, lover. Who would write a song of such maturity these days?) In 1974 Harry Chapin had a hit single with "The Cat's in the Cradle", a song of agonising pathos about how each generation of fathers suffer the fate of missing out on spending precious time with their sons because the fathers are so busy taking care of business. The lyrics of the song were based upon a poem written *by his wife*, Sandy. Can you imagine a modern girl-power pop singer performing a song with lyrics that displayed such an empathy for men?

I mention these songs to emphasize how it was entirely possible for the 1960s freedom movement to have developed along lines where women and men could be sympathetic and understanding toward each other's oppression by traditional sexism. There need never have been a feminist sex-war. Instead of more than four decades of women being encouraged to view men as their adversaries, four decades of sleeping with the enemy, four decades of men being degraded as immature, selfish Homer Simpsons and sexually predatory rapists, *we could have had* four decades in which women and men learned about the difficulties and injustices that each sex suffered under the old society. As a result, a genuinely impartial sex equality could have blossomed and, by the end of the twentieth century, we might all have been living in a truly sex-equalitarian society.

The freedom movement of the 1960s should have set us on the path to the liberation of both women and men. But in those years of the early seventies another political force was growing in power. One that viewed men as the repository of all that is wrong with the world. One that believed men were the source of all vice and women were the source of all virtue. One that understood nothing about men because the role that men played in this ideology was to be the scapegoat for every grievance, and you can't afford to have any sympathy or understanding for a scapegoat, not if it is to serve its function. This ideology was called feminism. Its very name declares its partiality. It states up front that it takes sides, and whose side it is on. Its partisanship declares a sex-war. And the opportunity for impartial sex equality was snuffed out at its birth in favour of the hypocritical blame-culture of an ideology that appropriated the discourse of equality for itself.

"We take the woman's side in everything. We ask not if something is 'reformist', 'radical', or 'moral'. We ask: is it good for women or bad for women?" ["Principles". New York Radical Women, in "Sisterhood is Powerful", Morgan (ed) 1970.]

This catastrophic attitude of taking sides can be seen as arising out of the politics of the late 1960s. It was a time of direct and personal political action. When the students fought the police in the streets, when the barricades went up in Paris, when black and liberal Americans marched for civil rights, when the young opposed the Vietnam war, when workers went on strike against the bosses, when the Left challenged the Right, when the long-haired confronted the short-haired, when youth counter-culture demanded a different world from that of the old, the late 1960s exemplified a politics that asked the question: on which side of the barricade will you take your stand? The perception was that there was a good side and a bad side, and one's own morality depended upon being *on the correct side*. There was an idea that to be moral meant taking sides. This made sense at the time because back then the Left were still engaged in class politics.

But during the twenty years between 1970 and 1990 the Left transformed itself from a politics whose fundamental interpretation of the world was a *class-analysis* into the Pseudo-Left whose fundamental interpretations of the world were a *gender-analysis* and a *race/ethnicity-analysis*. The Pseudo-Left abandoned class politics (especially after the end of the cold war) and replaced it with the 'politics of identity'. Simultaneously, as young left-wingers turned into middle-aged pseudo-left-wingers taking up professional positions in the state machine as university lecturers and local government officials and welfare counselors and so on, what had been the progressive counter-culture transformed into the new *reactionary establishment:* political correctness. But although their politics had changed fundamentally from a class-orientation to a gender/ethnicity-orientation, their attitude of taking sides remained.

This is why the current establishment elite of the politically correct are so unshakably convinced that they occupy the high moral ground. They believe that they are *on the correct side*. It has turned them into a bunch of dictatorial, zero-tolerance, micro-managing, po-faced authoritarians who constantly impose speech-codes and cultural taboos and bureaucratic regulations, curtailing everyone's freedom on the grounds of gender sensitivity and ethnic sensitivity and even ecological sensitivity. Instead of being a freedom movement it has become an anti-freedom movement which is incessantly declaring more and more things to be ideologically 'unacceptable'. The establishment culture of political correctness is massively condescending to ordinary citizens, treating us like children who must be schooled in 'correct' thinking, because the Pseudo-Left elite believe that they are *the people who know best*.

In fact, the politically correct entirely lack self-knowledge. They are blind to the sexism in feminism, blind to the racism in multiculturalism, and they persist in the absurd belief that they

129

are the 'progressive counter-culture' as if we were still living in the 1960s. If they were to admit to themselves that they are the establishment culture which exercises control over the entire political state machine and mainstream media, and that they are imposing their own beliefs and values upon society from the top down, then their romanticised self-image of the feminist multiculti freedom-fighter would be exposed for the sham that it is. Their vanity could never permit this. So they delude themselves into believing that they are still 'progressive' even while they impose their cultural orthodoxy with reactionary intolerance. Feminism, like multiculturalism, is an ideology that knows no mercy. Its perpetrators are convinced that the authoritarian imposition of their closed-minded 'correctness' is good for society and that everyone will come to agree with them in the end.

In this cause they have turned the whole of mainstream politics into an exercise in social engineering. But to engineer a new society you must socially engineer the people who are to be the population of that society. Hence, the speech-codes, the cultural taboos, the bureaucratic regulations, and the politically correct thought-police. Hence, the *tyranny of niceness*. Feminism began with the daughters of middle-class domestic matriarchs whose term of universal approbation was 'nice'. Their mothers wanted a *nice* house with a *nice* garden in which to raise their *nice* children who would attend a *nice* school and grow up to find *nice* jobs and meet a *nice* girl or a *nice* boy to marry so that they could live in *nice* houses and have *nice* children in their turn. *Feminist matriarchs simply applied their mothers' values to political society as a whole.* They have imposed their cultural tyranny of niceness with the same air of po-faced propriety and genteel authoritarianism with which middle-class mothers formerly imposed their domestic tyranny. Political government is now a case of 'mother knows best'.

So now all the citizen-children of society must play nicely together. There mustn't be any boisterous independence of mind. There mustn't be any male naughtiness. That is 'challenging' behaviour and mother's authority must never be challenged. Incredibly, the tyranny of niceness has even been applied to warfare. Western governments still insist that wars must be fought, but under the influence of feminism they now further insist that wars must be fought *nicely*. A soldier standing at a checkpoint watching a truck approaching him and wondering if the vehicle is full of explosives mustn't refer to the enemy as 'towelheads' because that would be racist. Just because the soldier is under continual and imminent threat of being killed by the enemy, that's no reason for him to be *impolite*. After all, western armies no longer fight wars to defeat the enemy, they fight wars to win the hearts and minds of the foreign population so that they can see what nice people we are and will like us. So that in future we can all play nicely together.

There is no realism or adulthood in the naïve world-view of the current establishment. But that doesn't matter because they have the power to legislate their will. In the end, all that matters is who has the power. Not that they would admit this. The new authoritarianism does not recognise itself as such because their arrogant and illiberal enforcement of their own narrow set of beliefs and values is, for them, the *correct* side to be on. They believe that's what gives them the moral high ground. It derives from the mistaken idea that in order to be moral one must take sides.

But the opposite is true, to be moral one must *apply moral principles impartially*, one must be unbiased, one must be non-partisan, one must *not* take sides. The concept of equality itself presupposes impartiality, of *not* favouring one group over another. How can equality ever be possible if one group is held to be above criticism and the other group is demonised as always being in the wrong? Yet in every feature of the political landscape the current cultural and political elite are committed to taking sides. They are on the side of the Palestinians against the Israelis, on the side of blacks against whites, on the side of women against men, on the side of the rest of the world against the West (these days being anti-American seems in itself to be treated as a sufficient credential for being 'left-wing'), on the side of homosexuals against heterosexuals, on the side of the registered disabled against those who are not registered disabled, on the side of Muslims against the kufr, and so on. The ideologically correct cannot take a political position without also taking a side. This is infantile. It crudely divides the world into the 'goodies' and the 'baddies' where the 'goodies' are always right and the 'baddies' are always wrong.

Nowhere is this more true than in the politics of gender. Feminists were the first amongst the politically correct to take sides and it has led to nearly half a century of disastrous error. At the end of the 1960s second wave feminism set the agenda for a political discourse of gender that has been followed ever since, with women as the irreproachable 'goodies' and men as the pantomime villain 'baddies'. Feminists have created a cultural, legal, and political system in which it is held to be true that:

- Women are victims / Men are victimizers

- Women are innocent / Men are guilty

- Women are good / Men are bad

- Women are deserving / Men are undeserving

- Women are entitled / Men are not entitled

- Women have women's rights / Men do not have men's rights

- Women must be protected / Men do not need protection

- Women's social advantages are not seen as privileges / Men are seen as being privileged even when they are not socially advantaged

- Women are not accountable for their own actions / Men are accountable for everyone's else's actions as well as their own

The freedom movement of the 1960s was utterly perverted and betrayed by second wave feminism when that ideology insisted that men were not the *fellow victims* of women in a societal imposition of gender that victimised both sexes but rather that men were the class of oppressors in a *solely misogynist sexism*. This belief, that in the past only women suffered sexism and that it was inflicted upon them by men, warped the principle of sex equality entirely out of shape. Patriarchy theory said that men were the oppressors in power who ruled in a male interest and this single idea made it *impossible* for women to view men as having been their fellow-victims under traditional sexism. Instead of seeking a mutual liberation of both sexes, women and men were cut off from one another by feminist political theory because one half of the victims now *blamed* the other half of the victims.

This perversion and betrayal of *what should have been* is the greatest of all the crimes committed by feminism. How much more sex equality would people of both sexes have had over the last forty years if feminism had not entirely usurped the sex equality agenda and become totally dominant in all discussions about the politics of gender? Might we have achieved a genuine and impartial sex equality by, say, the year 2000? Might we have achieved a society in which women and men were equally respected as child-carers, equally respected as wage-earners, equally respected as sexual partners, equally respected as citizens, and equally respected regardless of what particular life-choices they made as individual human beings? But feminism does not allow *men* to be *respected* equally with women. Men have to be cast in the gender-role of the guilt-objects, the people who are to blame for everything that is wrong with the world. This is what I mean when I say that feminism stopped us from achieving sex equality.

In a traditionally gender-bifurcated society sexism was also bifurcated. But under the corrupting power of feminism women and men were denied their opportunity to see one another as fellow-victims with a shared interest in the abolition of all sexism because the fundamental axiom of feminism was that sexism was a crime committed *by* men *against* women; that sexism was something that *men* did *to* women; that men were the guilty perpetrators and women were the innocent victims. How can women unite with men against misandry if they have

133

been taught to believe that misandry doesn't exist? https://www.youtube.com/watch?v=7qstExhvr2g

Feminism has always been fighting a dreadful sex-war of men against women and women against men. This is why feminists are so implacably hostile to Men's Rights Activists (MRAs) in the present day. They view any attempt to defend men from sexism as an attack upon women. This view is the very antithesis, the total opposite, of a true movement for sex equality where women support men in opposing misandry and men support women in opposing misogyny. Impartial sex equality is not about equality *of* the sexes, it is about equality *for* the sexes. It is not a set of scales in which the social benefits accrued by one side is balanced against the social benefits accrued by the other side (equality *of* the sexes), it is about removing artificial and unnecessary gender restrictions and thereby giving equal freedom to everyone (equality *for* the sexes).

But feminism is not about equality, it is a gender-supremacist ideology waging a war on behalf of one sex against the other sex. Consequently, it has robbed us of the sex-equalitarianism that *ought to* have developed out of the 1960s, the liberation of both women and men as they progressed together to overcome both the misogynist sexism and the misandrist sexism of traditional society. Yet anyone should be able to see that a *one-sided equality* is a contradiction in terms. If you believe in sex equality but *only for women*, then you do *not* believe in sex equality at all. If when discussing the politics of gender you use the phrase 'equality for women' as if that *meant the same thing* as sex equality, then you don't even know what sex equality means.

Equal But Different - A Hypocrites Charter

If we wanted an axiom for impartial sex equality it would be rational to devise something along the lines of 'both or neither'. Men should not be treated adversely compared to women and women should not be treated adversely compared to men. Like the old saying 'what's good for the goose is good for the gander' sex equality requires an axiom of impartiality. If something is currently permissible for one sex but forbidden to the other sex, then it must either become permissible for both or forbidden to both. Either both are free to do it or neither are free to do it. Then, either way, the sexes have equality. If one sex currently has a certain civil right but the other sex does not, then either both must have this civil right or neither must have this civil right. *The suffragettes demanded the vote on this basis;* that it was wrong for one sex to have the vote but the other sex to not have the vote. This is why the suffragettes cry of 'Votes for Women!' has always struck people as symbolic of sex equality, precisely because it employs a principle of both or neither. As a lifelong supporter of impartial sex equality this is the principle I have always endorsed myself: both or neither.

Consequently, either both women and men are entitled to occupy a certain job or neither of them are (gender should not be an employment criteria, so no affirmative action). Either both women and men should receive the specific rate of pay for a particular job or neither of them should (either everyone is paid the same rate of pay or individuals are paid at different rates of pay regardless of gender). Either both women and men should receive paid parental leave from their employer or neither of them should (e.g. if men aren't entitled to six months paid paternity leave, then women aren't entitled to six months paid maternity leave either or both should get three months paid leave, etc.). Either both women and men should be expected to accept the risks entailed in their job or neither of them should (female construction workers, female firefighters, female police officers, etc, should have the same risk of death and injury as their male colleagues). Either both women and men have the freedom to make the life-choice to be the primary child-carer or neither of them do (so an end to gender-supremacist attitudes about motherhood and an end to public disrespect toward husbands who are financially dependent upon their wage-earning wives). Either both women and men have a complete set of parental rights or neither of them do (so no female privilege where child custody is concerned). Either both women and men have a duty of financial obligation for their children or neither of them do (if the father gets custody of the children, the mother must pay child support). Either both women and men can be conscripted for national military service or neither of them can (if governments want to declare war, they must sacrifice their daughters as well as their sons). And so on.

'Both or neither' is a straightforward principle that women and men should have equal entitlements, equal accountability, equal liberties, equal constraints, equal life-choices, equal opportunities, equal treatment. If women and men *then* tend to make different life-choices we'll be better placed to recognise this as a result of evolutionary psychology rather than a socially imposed sexism because they will have made their choice from a position of equality. 'Both or neither' rejects the privileging of either sex. It does not seek to advantage or disadvantage either sex in comparison with the other. It is non-partisan. No one can say that a wife ought to do the washing up because that's woman's work. No one can say that ex-husbands must pay alimony but ex-wives don't have to because men have a financial responsibility to women but women have no such financial responsibility to men. Either a right, an opportunity, a freedom, an obligation, etc., holds good for *both* sexes or it holds good for *neither*. Under this principle, men are equal with women and women are equal with men.

However, despite having used this principle in the 'first wave' when demanding votes for women, second wave feminism came up with a maxim that is *almost the opposite* of this principle of equality. The maxim of second wave feminism is 'equal but different'. This phrase typifies the feminist political agenda more than any other. It is the phrase most associated with feminism. It is, both in its conception and very obviously in its practice, a demand for female privilege. It does indeed typify feminism in that it reinterprets the concept of 'sex equality' as meaning 'advantaging women and disadvantaging men'.

'Equal but different' combines two principles, a *principle of equality* and a *principle of difference*. Men have been made to give up all their traditional advantages on a principle of equality; that women must be equal with men. But women have not been made to give up their traditional advantages because of the principle of difference; that the 'difference' between the sexes means that 'vulnerable' women are entitled to special consideration because of their gender.

It is a hypocrite's charter. Women are recognised as having a right to everything that men have, but men are not recognised as having a right to everything that women have. Women are equal with men but men are not equal with women. It is a one-sided equality and a one-sided equality is a contradiction in terms. The habitual practice of constantly addressing any and all misogyny whilst entirely ignoring any and all misandry has led inevitably to the crudest inequalities. Let's clarify this with a few examples from various areas of life.

The Military: Women in the military must have equal pay and equal promotion but not equal risk of death and injury. The British armed forces do not put women into combat. Women's traditional advantage of being the protected sex and men's traditional disadvantage of being the expendable sex are both still in operation. The sexist double-standard about the value of human life persists because of a principle of gender 'difference'.

This example is powerfully reinforced by society's attitude to violence generally. There is a constant stream of well-funded research about violence against women. There's very much less research about violence against men. Yet it is men who suffer the greater amount of violence in society. So why does the great majority of research focus specifically upon women? It is because there is a much greater concern to protect women. The cry goes up 'look at this research, something must be done!' Violence against women is seen as being a much more important issue than violence against those other people whose pain counts for less. The huge quantity of research about violence against women does not reflect a society in which women are *more at risk* than men, it reflects a society which is more concerned to *protect* women at risk than it is to protect men at risk. The sexist double-standard about human pain persists because of a principle of gender 'difference'.

The Workplace: The principle of equality was used to argue that women must have equal pay for equal work but the principle of difference was used to argue that mothers were entitled to six months paid maternity leave whilst fathers were not. (So it's not, in fact, equal work, is it?) Men's former financial advantage must be surrendered but women's former child-care advantage is retained.

This example reminds us of the way that the origins of feminism have affected the way people think about gender privilege. Feminism was created by middle-class women, especially amongst cloistered academics, who were irate because they wanted what middle-class men had and they didn't. They wanted to be high-flying super-achievers, they wanted to be professors, they wanted to smash the glass ceiling. They saw work as a self-fulfilling career rather than as an irksome chore which men were forced to do to earn a living. As a result, the advantages that women had were excluded from this perspective. *Female privileges were not seen as privileges.* They still aren't. But if you are an ordinary working man, you might much prefer to spend your days bonding with your newborn baby instead of having to spend your days at some boring job in an estate agents office or suffering the frustration of driving a bus through heavy traffic with the passengers giving you ear-ache, and only getting to see your new baby for a few hours each evening.

Ask yourself the question, reader: which is more important to you, your job or your child? Which do you value most? Would you prefer to be bonding with your baby or tediously filling out invoice dockets? Being the sex that has much greater access to your own children is a privilege that women have had, based upon traditional gender roles. This is what I mean by the phrase 'women's child-care advantage'. In the UK this advantage was legislated as the law of the land. Liberal Democrats in the current coalition government have plans to change this (in 2015) and give fathers and mothers a shared parental leave. http://www.theguardian.com/money/2013/nov/29/jo-swinson-conflict-jobs-family-life Hopefully the law will be changed but *if* it is, then the change will have come much later than it should have, and that delay was caused by the maxim of 'equal but different'.

Family Life: For decades the legal system has been treating fathers as being intrinsically inferior to mothers; a bald-faced example of gender-supremacism. Consequently, mothers have been given custody of the children in divorce cases as a matter of routine as if they had a greater claim on their children than do fathers. In the UK over 80% of children of separated parents live exclusively or mainly with their mother [Hunt & Roberts, Child contact with non-resident parents 2004]. The 2011 UK census is worse, reporting around 90% of lone parent households with dependent children being female lone parents. The usual excuse offered for this is by appeal to the old-fashioned assumption that 'a child needs their mother' because maternal love is 'different' to paternal love. The principle of difference is applied to parenthood as if women and children are an inseparable unit, unlike men and children.

The unchallengeable mantra that 'the interests of the children must come first' means that the children must remain safely at home, not cast out into the streets like orphans in a Victorian melodrama. But as the mother is routinely given custody of the children this means *she also* keeps her home, and it is the father who is required by law to leave. This is why so many more divorces have been filed by women than by men. Divorce means the woman keeps everything she wants and loses only that which she wants to get rid of: the man. But fathers lose everything; they lose their children and their home, and thereafter they have to finance two households. Women have everything to gain and nothing to lose. Men had everything to lose and nothing to gain.

This blatant inequality has been perpetrated by deceiving the public into believing that *excluded* fathers are really 'absent' fathers who are so selfish that they irresponsibly walk out on their own children. I'm *not* saying that there aren't absent parents, simply that the phrase 'absent fathers' and 'deadbeat dads' are habitually used whilst the phrase 'excluded fathers' is

139

seldom if ever heard. Yet for decades everyone has heard the endless public comments about *irrelevant* fathers, *disposable* fathers, *redundant* fathers, just as everyone has heard fathers being blamed for children's fatherlessness. Now where could society have gotten that misandrist attitude from? This degradation of fatherhood has been going on for so long that even people outside of Men's Rights Activism are now speaking up about it. (For example, Karen Woodall's blog at http://karenwoodall.wordpress.com/2013/06/11/the-bad-men-project-on-the-devaluation-and-disposal-of-fatherhood/)

Social Clubs: Early second wave feminism complained about 'gentlemen's clubs' and golf clubs that did not accept female members. Any environment that was largely or exclusively male was sneered at derisively as a 'boy's club'. But this did not inhibit those same vagina-gazing feminists from organising women-only groups in all manner of things from assertiveness classes to women-only times at the swimming baths. This mind-set created a conventional acceptance of the double-standard, so that, for example, girls are entitled to join the Boy Scouts but boys are not allowed to join the Girl Guides. The refusal to permit male-only spaces whilst endorsing the permissibility of women-only spaces is standardly excused on the spurious grounds that females need 'safe spaces'. This is motivated by feminism's fear of men, it's negative gender-stereotype of all men as a threat to all women, and it trades upon the old sexist caricatures of 'shrinking violet' women and boorishly overbearing men. In complete contrast, the reality of feminist society is that men are probably more in need of safe spaces than are women since society is always on women's side against men in feminism's sex-war and it is the disrespected guilt-objects who need a safe place to hide.

Sport: In the past the grand slam tennis tournaments paid male players more in prize money than it paid female players. It also required male players to play matches that were the best of five sets (i.e. a minimum of three sets if the same player won the first three) whereas female players only had to play matches that were the best of three sets (i.e. a minimum of two sets if the same player won the first two). After much protest that it was sexist for men to be paid more than women, grand slam tennis introduced equal prize money for male and female players. But it did not change the gender disparity in the number of sets each sex had to play. Men still have to play the best of five sets to the women's best of three. So men have to work harder than women to earn the same amount of prize money.

Why was the length of tennis matches not equalised *at the same time* that the prize money was equalised? Because feminism only recognised misogyny, it was blind to misandry. Feminism seeks to remove any and all disadvantages to women, it does not seek equality for women and men. So it wasn't an issue for feminism that male players have to work harder than female players to earn the same prize money. Or is someone going to claim that poor weak little girlies couldn't possibly have the stamina to play five sets and therefore female players are entitled to the same money for less work on a principle of 'equal but different'?

Those five examples are diverse enough to suggest how the double-standard is insidious and pervasive but to appreciate the full hypocrisy of 'equal but different' we have to ask another question: when has the principle of difference ever been used to favour men? After all, if 'equal but different' were to be taken seriously, shouldn't it apply to men being advantaged because of their 'difference'? Not in feminist society. Here are a couple of examples.

Insurance: Sometimes 'different' treatment by gender is defended statistically. For example, until the EU court declared otherwise, young women paid less than young men for their car insurance because insurance companies said that statistically young men had more car accidents. But at the same time car insurance companies offered *lone female priority* roadside assistance. This means that the companies treat call-outs by lone females for roadside assistance as being priority cases because of the perceived threat to lone females of attack by the hordes of salivating male predators roaming the streets. But statistically the people most likely to suffer attack in the streets are young men. On the statistics the insurance company should have been *prioritising lone men* in their call-outs for roadside assistance.

Pensions: For a very long time politicians simply ignored the blatant injustice of men being required to work in paid employment later in life than women, despite women on average living longer. Shouldn't this gender 'difference' in longevity have been applied to the retirement age? Shouldn't women have retired *later* in life than men, not earlier, since they lived longer? Instead politicians continued to expect men to fulfil their traditional gendered social role and work longer than women. Now, the UK government is finally raising the female retirement age. But are they doing so on a principle of equality? No, the reform is *not for equalitarian reasons*, it is simply *for economic reasons* because of the pensions crisis. They aren't equalling out retirement age in order to give men equality with women, merely as a part of raising the retirement age for both sexes as they try to cut the overall cost of a state pension which is no longer affordable.

The double-standards built-in to the twin principles of 'equal but different' are never put forward when women are being advantaged and men disadvantaged. It is a gendered prerogative. 'Equal but different' is unequivocally a straightforward claim of sexist privilege for women. That such a claim of privilege has been presented to the world as being what 'sex equality' means is the crudest kind of hypocrisy. That female privilege has been maintained on the grounds of gender 'difference' is further proof that those who have advocated this were *never* supporters of equality, they were interested only in the advantaging of women and the disadvantaging of men; a project in which they were wholly successful.

But another question remains to be raised in connection with 'equal but different'. As feminist society endorses the idea that women are so 'vulnerable' and in need of special 'protection' because of their gender difference that women-only 'safe spaces' are required and priority roadside assistance should be provided and privileged dispensation must be given to female

142

soldiers so that they don't have to go into combat, and all the rest of it, does this mean that feminists view women as being *less able* to deal with the hardships and harsh realities of life than men? Does feminism view women as the delicate flowers that traditional sexism presented them as being? After all, as we shall see in chapter 4, feminist society habitually speaks of women as being better than men. How can it, at the same time, take this outrageously misogynist position of viewing women as the 'weaker sex'?

This misogyny seems to be especially true of professional feminists as a result, ironically, of their wish to perpetuate the traditional misandry that panders to feminine 'weakness' and expects stoical fortitude from men. Anthropologist Peggy Reeves Sanday (at the 2nd World Congress on Matriarchal Studies) speaks approvingly of the Minangkabau of Indonesia when she says:

"The Minangkabau are aware of the father's biological role, but chose to ignore it in favor of the social well-being of the mother-child bond. They think that males can fend for themselves, but mothers and their children need social support. As Pak Hakimy told me: Here we elevate the weak instead of the strong. Women *must* be given rights *because* they are weak. Young men *must* be sent away from the village to prove their manhood so that there will be no competition between them and their sisters." [original emphasis]
http://www.second-congress-matriarchal-studies.com/sanday.html

Reeves Sanday presents this as a contrary and better cultural custom to those of western societies and she seems to be bizarrely blind to the obvious *parallel* with the old western maxim 'He's a man, he can take care of himself' which specifically and deliberately denied support or assistance to men in western cultures.

Apparently, she is also wholly unaware of the obvious parallel with the old western custom of men protecting women because they are (allegedly) weak, a custom that has been around for many millennia in the West. And as for boys being expected to

143

prove their manhood, well, it sounds like the Minangkabau have an awful lot in common with the traditional customs of the West.

But my point in quoting this passage is not merely to note the similarity between the culture of the Minangkabau and the cultures of the west, a similarity which Reeves Sanday appears to have missed. I quote this as one example among very many of the way in which feminists view *the privileging of women over men* as being a position of sex equality *because of women's supposed weakness*. This is the attitude of a middle-class Victorian 'lady' who can't be expected to cope on her own without the assistance of 'gentlemen' because her corsets are too constrictive and her petticoats get in the way.

The idea that women and men should be treated equally and just left to get on with their lives as best they can on the basis of their own individual capacities seems to be utterly alien to the feminist mind-set. They want women to be the CEOs of corporations, they want women elected as Presidents and Prime Ministers, they want women to edit newspapers and manage television companies, *but they also want* women to receive the special gendered protection and support that women have traditionally received *as well* because the 'weak' people have to be accorded rights that the 'strong' people don't need. This is the feminist view of what 'equality' means.

In the UK women are the majority of the population (2011 census) and the majority of the electorate, yet feminists habitually speak of women as a 'vulnerable' minority group in need of assistance. Feminists are guilty of shamefully exploiting old fashioned misogynist ideas about how 'at risk' and defenceless women are because this has always been their chief weapon of political persuasion when demanding privileged treatment for women. This is what the hypocrites charter of 'equal but different' really means.

Feminist Society Endorses Traditional Sexism

Have you ever heard the phrase 'man-flu'? Of course you have, it's a part of the culture. It's also a typical imposition of traditional sexism by people who *think* that they're *opposed* to traditional sexism. In the past the gendered role of men required them to be butch macho-types who were stoical in the face of pain and far too 'manly' to give in to mere illness. So expressing how woeful and miserable you feel when sick with the flu was traditionally unmanly. A 'proper' man was supposed to just shrug it off and march off to work to earn money for the wife and kids, not laze around feeling sorry for himself.

Feminist society still employs this traditional misandry to treat male illness as being nothing more than weakness. A man who is laughed at for having 'man-flu' is being treated as if he were not ill really, but was just a weakling committing a failure of masculinity. The implication is that only women have *real* flu where they're *genuinely* ill. This attitude expresses the traditional sexism which allowed women to be weak, it even encouraged women to be weak. But men, never! Men had to be strong in all circumstances. So the contemporary man is accused of not having real flu, only 'man-flu'. The ridiculous weaklings.

I mention this minor example of misandry simply because it is so ubiquitous, but feminist society readily perpetuates traditional gender roles in very significant ways whenever it serves a misandrist political agenda. The UK government's Child Support Agency exists to enforce the traditional gendered social role of the father as financial provider. The CSA has no concern to give father's equal custody rights with mothers and it has no interest in a father's relationship with his children, *they just want the money* because that is what the government created them to do.

In 2011 the UK government's 'Family Justice Review' recommended that fathers *should continue to be denied equal custody rights with mothers*. But it's still a man's duty to pay. For two generations of excluded fathers, society has treated them as the inferior parent whilst continuing to make them fulfil the old-fashioned gender role of man-as-wallet. These oppressed men are put in the position of having responsibilities without rights.

In the past rights and responsibilities were two sides of the same coin. Men had a right of greater access to paid employment than women *precisely because* men also had a gendered obligation to financially support their wives and families; an obligation that was not part of the 'feminine' social role. (I'm not saying that women didn't work in paid employment, I'm saying that it wasn't part of their gendered social role.) For men to fulfil the role society allocated to them, they had to have access to paid employment. So the *right* and the *obligation* went together. That's why ex-husband's were also expected to pay alimony after a divorce. Alimony was an expression of male financial responsibility for females even after the marriage was over.

Another example, is men having a legal authority over women in marriage. Husbands were held legally responsible for what their wives did. If a wife took out a loan, her husband was responsible for paying it back (but *not* vice versa). That's why wives needed their husband's permission to take out a loan. She couldn't take out a loan without his signature on the document. If he is held responsible for any loan she takes out, then he must have control over any such actions on her part. Those who were given the responsibility were also given the necessary authority to fulfill that responsibility.

To offer a modern parallel: in the UK in 2010 nearly 12,000 parents were prosecuted and 25 parents were sent to prison because of their children's truancy from school. http://www.theguardian.com/education/2011/nov/08/truancy-parents-12000-prosecutions The child is persistently truant and the parent is punished for it. This law holds that parents have a legal authority over their children and that parents can therefore be punished, including being sent to prison, for failing to exercise a proper control over their children. If a parent says 'but I can't control my kid, she never does anything I say', this is not an excuse. Parents have a legal authority over their children and are responsible for their children's actions. In the past, the law applied this to husbands and wives.

Now, we can all agree that it was misogynist to treat women as if they were children, just as it was misandrist to give men a gendered social role of responsibility for an adult who ought to be personally accountable for her own actions, but the point here is to understand the legal relationship between *authority* (exercising a legal control over someone) and *responsibility* (being accountable for that person's actions).

If we are to understand traditional society *as it actually was* we must recognise that it imposed advantages and disadvantages on both sexes. Women didn't have the same access to the workplace that men had, but they didn't have the same financial obligations that men had. Women didn't have the same legal autonomy that men had, but they didn't have the same accountability for another person's actions that men had. Women were put in a position of dependency upon their husbands but men were put in a position of carrying the weight of that dependent. Traditional sexism advantaged and disadvantaged both sexes in different ways.

In modern feminist society everything about traditional society is seen from the perspective of the female, in terms of the ways in which men were advantaged and women were disadvantaged. Ever since feminism was adopted as the political and cultural orthodoxy, nothing has been said about the ways in which *women* were advantaged and *men* were disadvantaged. This is why feminist society has spent decades habitually speaking of women 'shouldering the burden of child-care' and how lazy irresponsible men must be encouraged to do their share. It speaks of child-care *as a burden* when it could speak of child-care as a rewarding and self-fulfilling area of life from which men continue to be much more excluded than women; where society continues to advantage women and disadvantage men. But that perspective wouldn't portray women as the eternal victims, would it? Feminist society doesn't speak of men 'shouldering the burden of financial provision' and how lazy parasitic women must be encouraged to do their share. Instead men's gendered disadvantage of having financial responsibility for others is presented in terms of women being denied access to the workplace or from particular types of jobs in the workplace. Feminism's sex-war requires it to hugely emphasize all the disadvantages women had whilst entirely ignoring all the disadvantages men had.

So when it comes to the rights and obligations which men had in traditional society, feminism, with its hypocrite's charter of 'equal but different', *takes away* the rights that men had but *maintains* the obligations men had. This is why the CSA hounds fathers to fulfil their traditional gendered obligation of child support but has no concern at all whether the modern feminised workplace permits fathers the access to paid employment that is necessary to fulfil that obligation. Men have to fulfil their traditional obligation even though they no longer have the traditional right which allowed them to do so.

And when they fail? Fathers are sent to prison for failing to comply with the demands of the Child Support Agency in its enforcement of this traditional social construct of gender. Predictably, the media do not object to this policy on the grounds that it is misandrist, their only concern over the policy is that fathers who are sent to prison are therefore not in a position to earn money and fulfil their obligations. http://www.independent.co.uk/news/uk/crime/more-fathers-jailed-over-child-support-2265787.html

Did you ever find this 21st century version of debtor's prison strange? These days, no one is sent to prison for owing money to another person in other circumstances, are they? If you are bankrupt and can't pay your creditors, you don't go to prison for the debt. If you refuse to pay your rent, the landlord can try to get you evicted but you won't be sent to prison. It's the same with the bank if you don't pay your mortgage, they can take your house back but they can't send you to prison. Fail to pay back your credit cards and there's no going to prison for the money you owe. The *only* people who are sent to prison for owing money are people who owe money to the state, like those who don't pay their taxes. Oh, and fathers who owe money to mothers. And this is the excuse the law makes. It says that the father is not sent to prison for owing the money to the mother, he is sent to prison for *defying the court order* that ordered him to pay the money.

Yes, that's right; not paying his ex-wife is the same as not paying the authorities. She has all the power of the state at her command, just like the taxman. But the same does not apply the other way around when it's a question of a father's access to his children. If the mother *defies a court order* by not allowing the father access to his children, *she* is not sent to prison. Why not? Oh, because if she were sent to prison her children would suffer and we must put the interests of the children first. So she can defy court orders with impunity but he is sent to prison.

In America this persecution of fathers has reached insane levels where men are even made to pay for children who are not their own. Joe Vandusen of Davenport Iowa had a demand for child support in regard of a child born to his long-estranged wife despite their having had "no contact whatsoever in 16 or 17 years". There is no doubt that the child is *not* his, but he is legally required to pay because he is still legally married to the woman. He is the legal husband therefore he is financially responsible for his wife's children, regardless of who the father is, and regardless of how many years it has been since he last saw his "wife". There could hardly be a clearer case of the law's imposition of the traditional gender-role that males must accept financial responsibility for females: *you married her, you pay for her.* http://wqad.com/2016/03/23/davenport-man-protesting-law-that-requires-him-to-pay-for-another-mans-child/

Joe Vandusen is very far from being the only man who's expected to pay for other people's children. You can find many such cases online. For example, here is one from Houston https://www.youtube.com/watch?v=NxemLKqIOPI and one from Memphis https://www.youtube.com/watch?v=S26wVc437Is and one from South Georgia https://www.youtube.com/watch?v=drl1YdbTSx8 and from Florida https://www.youtube.com/watch?v=q1nQH8sfV3Q&list=PL5541959C74E02D40

It will be interesting to see how women react to changes in alimony and child-support law now that an increasing number of women earn higher salaries than their male spouses and may find *themselves* paying alimony and child support. For generations men have been expected to shut up and pay up (i.e. to 'be a man' about it) but is it likely that women, who are so accustomed to both the protection of traditional sexism and to feminism's female-entitlement culture, will be so accommodating when the law requires *them* to pay up? http://ideas.time.com/2013/05/16/the-de-gendering-of-divorce-wives-pay-ex-husbands-alimony-too/ Amongst those who are fighting a sex-war on behalf of women, a certain amount of panic is setting in already over the beginnings of reforms to the alimony law so that it better reflects today's society.

This sting in feminism's tail is something which women have begun to be confronted with only recently, but it derives from *the foundational lie* of feminism. For as long as it has existed feminism has claimed to be seeking to achieve sex equality. Despite the rather obvious fact that it has actually pursued an agenda of advantaging women and disadvantaging men, feminism has always presented itself to the public as the advocate of sex equality. As a result, now that women are increasingly advantaged and men are increasingly disadvantaged, some voices are being raised even amongst the establishment that maybe a few of the ways in which traditional society benefited women are now out of date, so that a man shouldn't have to pay alimony just because he's male, or that a woman should have to pay alimony even though she's female, or that alimony is culturally redundant and should cease to exist for either sex. That such developments come as a *surprise* to some people shows just how entrenched was the popular feminist misrepresentation that *advantaging women over men* was *the same thing as sex equality*.

Even so, these early gestures in the direction of a genuinely impartial sex equality have a very long road to travel. Feminism's endorsement of traditional misandry is systemic in modern society. The misandrist double-standard about the value of human life was the grossest sexism there has ever

150

been (at least, so far), yet feminism continually reinforces this misandry with it's gender-stereotypes of victimized women in peril living in a society of male predators, where all concern and sympathy is extended to *the sex which society values* and is denied to the sex which society views as mere guilt-objects. Similarly with the misandrist double-standard about human pain, which is deliberately exaggerated by feminism's constant propagandising of 'rape culture' and of domestic violence as a 'male crime', where male victims are marginalised to invisibility and women are classified as victims simply for having been born female.

I say that this endorsement of traditional misandry is systemic in feminist society because you can see the attitude of *prioritising the protection of women* everywhere. Men, it is assumed, need no such protection. It's the same old story of people saying dismissively 'he's a man, he can take care of himself', where each man is on his own, and can neither ask for help nor accept any help. A good example of the way that contemporary feminist society perpetuates this old prejudice is the lack of concern it exhibits over the gender inequality amongst the homeless and destitute.

The Men's Health Forum quotes a figure from back in 1999 that 90% of rough sleepers were men and 70% of single homeless people were men. http://www.menshealthforum.org.uk/22612-men-and-mental-health-stats Since then there's been an economic recession and the near-crash of 2008 and things have gotten even tougher in the jobs market. So what are the figures now?

I mean, if approximately three quarters of the homeless population were women, do you think that the society you live in would be shy about saying so? Or would the statistic be bellowed from every media outlet as proof of how women suffer so much more than men? In fact, the vast majority of the homeless *are men* yet if you want to know what the actual statistic is, it can be a little tricky trying to find out. After all, men are *supposed* to be able to take care of themselves, aren't they? They're *supposed* to not need any help but to make their own way in the world by means of their own endeavours. This is what traditional misandry has always told us. Men aren't 'vulnerable' like women.

Crisis, a national charity for single homeless people in the UK, tells us that 88% of people sleeping rough *in London* are male, and over 80% of people sleeping rough *in Scotland* are male. But the site says that there is no national UK figure for homelessness. The Crisis website also has a page giving details about "Homelessness among different groups". http://www.crisis.org.uk/pages/homeless-diff-groups.html There are two sections on the page. The first is about *women* and the second is . . . yes, that's right, the second is about "Migrants, refugees and asylum seekers". Is there a group missing here? Could that missing group possibly be the group which makes up the majority of single homeless people in the UK?

Crisis is a charity specifically for *single* homeless people. The section about women *actually states* that "In the single homeless population, women are in the minority. In England, women make up 26 per cent of clients of homelessness services." So they have a section devoted to the 26% but they don't have one devoted to the 74%? Crisis also provides research publications about the single homeless. These include *twelve reports* that feature the issue of 'female homelessness'. But where are their reports on 'male homelessness'? http://www.crisis.org.uk/publications-search.php?topic=6

I'm not trying to pick on this one charity, here. On the contrary, I'm citing them as typical. I'm using their website as a way of making the point that society has a mind-set of being habitually neglectful of men *as men*. Even when men are the large majority of the victims of a particular social evil, and even when the informed professionals involved in alleviating that social evil are caring and compassionate people, there is still a very strong inclination to care far more about women than about men. This is a reflection of traditional misandry *amplified by* contemporary feminist misandry. The men are not a recognised 'vulnerable group' like women, or like migrants, refugees and asylum seekers. Aren't men lucky to be so invulnerable.

152

According to Crisis, on average homeless people die at the age of just 47 years old. Surely that must mean that *all the homeless* qualify as vulnerable, doesn't it? Including the men. But who are the prioritised groups? You don't need me to tell you, you can guess. Shelter, another major homeless charity in the UK, lists those in *priority need* as:

- Pregnant women (and the people who live with them)
- People responsible for dependent children
- People made homeless by fire, flood, or other disaster
- Certain people aged 16 or 17, or 18 to 20 year-olds previously in care
- Victims of domestic violence or harassment
- Those who have fled their homes due to a threat of violence
- Those vulnerable due to time spent in care, custody or the armed forces
- Vulnerable people with mental illness or disabilities
- People under the age of 25 who are vulnerable because they have slept on the streets in the past or have problems with drugs or alcohol.
- Older people

http://england.shelter.org.uk/get_advice/homelessness/help_from_the_council_when_h
omeless/priority_need#other_people_who_are_particularly_vulnerable

This might sound reasonable. After all, doesn't it mention the people who live with pregnant women as well as pregnant women; doesn't it include veterans of the armed forces and older people; doesn't it thereby include males as well? But when you look at these priorities in more detail you repeatedly find phrases being used like 'although women are the minority of the homeless, there are high levels of vulnerability within the female homeless population . . .' which then proceed to prioritise care and concern on the basis of the special needs and special vulnerability of women. My point here is not that charities shouldn't be concerned for these groups, it's simply that men shouldn't suffer neglect due to their supposed lack of vulnerability. Men feel hunger and cold, too, not just women. But whenever you see the word 'vulnerable' you know that men have just been put at the back of the queue again.

So what percentage of the homeless are men? We still don't have an authoritative overall figure. The homeless charity St Mungo's has some clear statistics. In 2013 they reported that 73% of their clients were male and 23% of their clients were female. But these are the homeless who used St Mungo's services, they're not the national statistics.
http://www.mungos.org/homelessness/facts/homelessness_statistics

Still, the government must know, right? They may know but are they telling? In a UK government statistical release document "Rough Sleeping Statistics England - Autumn 2012" *men are not actually mentioned at all* because, although there are ethnic breakdowns, there are no gender breakdowns. So we are told, for example, that 11% of rough sleepers in London were Polish but not how many were men. Do you get the idea that maybe no one in a position of authority in society wants to actually tell us the size of the male majority of the homeless?

It's not that I don't appreciate that reliable figures for the homeless will be difficult to get because of the transient character of the homeless population. But there are nonetheless plenty of available statistics about the homeless; there are statistics on homeless households, on the ethnicity of the homeless, on women and children who are homeless, on how many of the homeless are drug users or alcoholics, on how many are suffering mental illness. There are plenty of statistics available. It's just that the figure on how many of the homeless are male is kind of hard to find. Yet everyone agrees that they are the majority of the homeless.

This is unlikely to change. In recent years the number of homeless families with children has increased, so now the focus of public concern is even further removed from men.

And it's not just a matter of the government's apparent reluctance to give us an overall figure for male homelessness. Both the family who are living in temporary bed & breakfast accommodation and the destitute man who is sleeping rough in a shop doorway can be classified as 'homeless', but their circumstances are not really the same, are they? That's why the statistics I quoted for those 'sleeping rough' are so significant (88% male in London, 80% male in Scotland). There's also the question of whether men comprise of larger percentage of the chronic homeless (the long term homeless or those who suffer repeated episodes of homelessness). An American report "Single Males: the Homeless Majority" (2001) said "Men comprise 77% of single homeless adults, but only 16% of adults in homeless families. Single adults are more likely than homeless families to have experienced multiple homeless episodes, of longer duration." http://www.nhchc.org/wp-content/uploads/2012/03/June2001HealingHands.pdf

The basic issue I'm highlighting here is the way that feminism's privileging of women is an endorsement of, and a continuation of, what they themselves call 'patriarchal' attitudes. Traditionally women were the 'weaker sex' and according to feminism women are the 'vulnerable' sex. Hence the automatic focus on homeless women rather than homeless men, regardless of whether those sleeping rough are actually in a position of greater vulnerability than those living in temporary bed & breakfast accommodation. If around three quarters of the homeless population were women, we would be told by the powers-that-be that homelessness was a 'women's issue'. So why don't those in political power consider it a 'men's issue'? Oh, yes, I remember. Men are not officially classified as a 'vulnerable' group by those in positions of authority because both traditional sexism and feminist sexism agree that 'he's a man, he can take care of himself'.

When considering issues like child-support and male homelessness, or indeed issues like domestic violence and rape which I shall come to later in this book, it is very important to realise how often feminism makes use of traditional misandry. The title of this book is "Feminism is Sexism". I do not mean that feminism is 'reverse sexism', as it is sometimes called. I mean that it is *the same sexism as traditional sexism.* Feminism *is* sexism. The phrase 'reverse sexism' implies that feminism is a counter-sexism which goes in the opposite direction from traditional sexism. I am not arguing that, I am arguing that feminism goes in the same direction as traditional sexism; it is *the same* sexism. Feminism's misandry *is* traditional misandry.

As we shall see later, feminism clings to the idea that rape is a crime perpetrated with an erect penis, an idea which is so old-fashioned that it might be thought quaint, with it's assumption of the sexually 'active' male and the sexually 'passive' female. When feminist society prioritises the protection of women and ignores the protection of men, this perpetuates the idea of women as 'weak' and men as 'strong'. When feminist government refuses equal parental rights to fathers, it reinforces the old idea that women and children belong together whilst men belong in paid employment. Feminism may have added greatly to the amount of misandrist sexism in society but it is the same old misandry. Feminism is, at least in many cases, based solidly on beliefs found in traditional sexism.

Take this example. Islamic cultures have a custom of hijab where women wear the burqa. It is often pointed out that feminists are surprisingly quiet in their lack of protest against this misogynist practice, and their unaccustomed silence is usually put down to multiculturalism and the fear of saying anything that might bring an accusation of racism. This is a part of the story but it not the whole of the story.

One reason put forward in Islamic cultures for women to wear hijab is that it 'protects' women from sexual harassment and sexual assault. (It doesn't actually protect them, the rationale is complete nonsense, but this is one argument that is put forward in defence of hijab.) Muslim women start wearing hijab at puberty. This is the age when they start to become responsible for their own behaviour and it is the age when they start to develop as women and therefore begin to become sexually desirable. So how does this Muslim practice connect with feminism? The connection is in *its view of men*. Hijab is (supposedly) protection from men because men can't be relied upon to restrain themselves from assaulting a woman if they see her hair, her elbows, her kneecaps. Men are so sexually predatory that no woman could be safe from them unless she is wearing a full-body face mask. The rationale that wearing hijab is necessary to protect women from sexual assault by men paints a picture of men as being innately sexually rapacious. *This is exactly the gender-stereotype of men that feminism has been propagandising for as long as feminism has existed.*

Implicit in the traditional sexism of hijab is a misandrist caricature of men that feminism endorses and practices. A man is presented as someone who will sexually violate any woman, any time, anywhere, if he is not externally restrained. In this case, the external restraint is that the woman's sex-appeal has been obscured by her hijab and therefore nullified. The misogyny of this custom lies in making a woman responsible for protecting herself from assault to such an extreme extent that it leads to a belief that if she is not wearing hijab she is therefore to blame for being assaulted. This is a genuine case of *blaming the victim*. Simultaneously, the misandry of this custom lies in the way that it crudely stereotypes men as being predatory sex criminals who have no control over themselves, so that women everywhere are in constant need of protection from them.

In fact, in the western world, a woman can lay on a beach in a bikini, or even go topless, without being raped or molested. All the men on the beach don't suddenly become unhinged with lust when they see a woman go topless. (They might actually be thinking what ugly breasts she has. The idea that all men find all women sexually desirable is utterly ludicrous. Most women are no more sexually desirable than most men.) The belief that society must have a special and systemic protection for women in the form of the burqa because men are all sex-crazed beasts *is the same misandry* as feminism's systemic anti-male domestic violence and rape laws to 'protect' women.

When a man meets a woman in a burqa she has, by the way in which she is dressed, told him that he is a sexually predatory male from whom she must protect herself. *Her burqa is a misandrist insult.* This is a point that is never mentioned in public discussions about the sexism of the burqa. But in this sexist caricature of men-as-rapists the 'patriarchs' of Islam are in accord with the 'matriarchs' of feminism. The latter's gender-stereotype of men as inherently dangerous sex-criminals is very much in keeping with traditional sexism. It is not a reversal of it, feminism is just the same old sexism.

Another example of the traditional character of feminism's misandry can be found in its acceptance of the benefits (to women) of chivalry. It's noticeable that *male feminists* are especially prone to adopting the gendered social role of the hero protecting women from harm. (The type of male feminist that MRAs call 'white knights'.) This is in spite of the fact that these male feminists believe themselves to be completely committed to putting an end to traditional 'masculinity'. Contrary to their own professed belief, male feminists very often seem to still view men as having a duty to personally intervene to protect women from possible danger instead of just letting her handle it herself. In his charmingly entitled essay "Why talking about 'healthy masculinity' is like talking about 'healthy cancer'" John Stoltenberg advocates male intervention to protect females in terms of bystander-intervention:

"Basically bystander-intervention training is a program to equip penised people with communication skills, empathy, emotional intelligence, relational tactics, and a sense of personal agency to intervene when they see another penised person about to commit a sexual assault. Bystander-intervention training is widely regarded as one of the most effective means of primary sexual-assault prevention in social situations such as bars and parties where there are likely to be observers."

http://feministcurrent.com/7868/why-talking-about-healthy-masculinity-is-like-talking-about-healthy-cancer/

In case you were wondering, yes "penised people" is his phrase for men. Apparently, Stoltenberg requires men to fulfil the manly duty of coming to the rescue of a damsel in distress despite that fact that he doesn't even use the word 'man' in describing those people who are doing their manly duty. They mustn't be 'men' but they still ought to act chivalrously toward the fair sex. If a woman is being pestered by a penised person in a bar, then the other penised persons should rush to her side to protect her. Stoltenberg may not used *the phrase* 'manly duty' to describe this bystander-intervention, instead he uses the phrase "a sense of personal agency to intervene", but since he's advocating this only for "penised people" this is mere semantics. It still ends up being the man's gendered social role. He says nothing about women putting themselves at risk by intervening to protect a penised person.

Notice, too, how penised people have to receive a program of training in order to acquire their "communication skills, empathy, emotional intelligence". They couldn't possibly have these qualities already as male human beings. Do women have these qualities *naturally*, whilst penised people have to be taught these things?

This is relevant because Stoltenberg is keen to avoid any such bystander-intervention descending into physical conflict (what he calls a "cockfight"). The penised people are supposed to use their training in communication skills, empathy, and emotional intelligence to diffuse the situation. But if women were by nature blessed with these qualities, shouldn't *they* be the ones to intervene? After all, muscle-power is not going to be needed because the situation is going to be diffused, not end in physical conflict. So women could intervene just as well, or even better, than penised people. Especially in a situation where the bystander is intervening to prevent an assault occurring by one penised person upon another penised person because the two men (if you'll pardon the word) might not have been through a program of training in communication skills, empathy, and emotional intelligence, so the intervention of a woman would be all the more necessary.

I'm not mentioning this article merely to make fun of the verbal absurdities of feminism. I'm making the serious point that, regardless of how it is dressed up in feminised language, Stoltenberg is advocating the same old traditional gendered role for men to intervene to protect women when they are perceived to be in danger. A feminist is a person who will spend their life propagandizing a grotesquely negative gender-stereotype of 'toxic masculinity', of men as predators who force women to live under siege from male violence, but then that same feminist will turn around and tell men that they should put themselves personally at risk to protect a woman *as if a woman's safety was more important to a man than his own*. As if the lives of women were more valuable than the lives of men. As if male pain counted for less than female pain. These are the same double-standards about human life and human pain that were at the heart of traditional misandry. Feminists will endorse misandrist chivalry because they will endorse anything that benefits women, including traditional sexism.

To put the final nail in this coffin, we can look at the kind of personal attacks commonly made by feminists (on message boards and on blogs and in You Tube videos and in real life, etc) against anyone who argues in favour of equality for men and an end to misandry. Nowhere is the old-fashioned traditional character of feminist sexism more egregious than when feminists are using *classic shaming tactics* to try to coerce Men's Rights Activists and MGTOWs (Men Going Their Own Way who reject marriage or cohabitation with women) back into the traditionally masculine gender role of protecting and providing for women. The typical knee-jerk comments made by feminists in trying to silence MRAs and MGTOWs are the clearest possible imposition of a macho gender-identity upon men. Let's consider the kind of male-shaming comments that we could expect to find in a typical top ten, and then clarify what's actually being said:

1. "Men have nothing to complain about."

Translation: Men aren't allowed to complain because real men don't admit to having problems, they solve them.

2. "You're just afraid of women."

Translation: No real man would be afraid of a female because men have to be courageous and heroic, not a coward who's frightened of a girly.

3. "Don't be such a crybaby; be a man."

Translation: Be a man = be a real man.

4. "I bet you live with your mother."

Translation: A man mustn't be a "mummy's boy".

5. "The only reason you're an MRA / MGTOW is because you can't get laid."

Translation: Men who fail to 'score' with women are failed men. You are a failed man.

6. "You're never going to get laid."

Translation: You are a failed man and you'll always be a failed man.

7. "You're such a loser."

Translation: Men must be achievers and winners, not losers.

8. "Are you gay?"

Translation: Any man who doesn't want to have as much sex with women as possible, and any man who isn't willing to do whatever is necessary to have as much sex with women as possible, must secretly be homosexual. And you don't want me to think that you're homosexual, do you? (Notice how homophobia is embedded in misandry.)

9. "You hate women."

Translation: Men have a gendered social role to protect women, not be hostile to them.

10. "You're threatening me."

Translation: You're making a woman feel afraid, so you have failed in your gendered social role to protect women, you big bully.

161

Check this out for yourself on feminist sites on the Internet. When you hear feminists saying these things, how can you seriously deny that feminism endorses traditional sexism?

Chapter 4

Feminism is a Gender-Supremacist ideology

"I believe that women have a capacity for understanding and compassion which a man structurally does not have, does not have it because he cannot have it. He's just incapable of it." [Barbara Jordan, US Congresswoman from 1972-1978]

"Women and men are distinct species or races . . . men are biologically inferior to women; male violence is a biological inevitability; to eliminate it, one must eliminate the species/race itself . . . in eliminating the biologically inferior species/race Man, the new Ubermensch Womon . . . will have the earthly dominion that is her true biological destiny." [Quoted *disapprovingly* by Andrea Dworkin, of a feminist *even more extreme than herself*, in "Letters From a War Zone", p110]

"In considering male intellectual and scientific argumentation in conjunction with male history, one is forced to conclude that men as a class are moral cretins." [Andrea Dworkin herself, four pages later in the same 1977 essay in "Letters From a War Zone", p114]

Identifying Gender-Supremacism

It is the long-standing practice of cultures that they gratuitously gender human character traits and then *attach values* to the traits they gender. For example, traditional society gendered rationality as 'masculine' and emotionality as 'feminine', and the alleged emotionality of women was considered a reason to exclude them from political office (emotionality being seen as a *negative* value in political decision-making). Feminist society genders rationality and emotionality in exactly the same way, except that now the values attached to the two traits have been reversed so that the alleged emotionality of women is considered a *positive* asset in political office and one reason to introduce women-only shortlists in order to feminise parliament, improving it by making it a more compassionate, caring environment through the increased presence of feminine emotionality (emotionality seen as a positive value in political decision-making). This gendering of humanity is frequently done so crudely that you will hear idiots say that if women held political power in parliament there would be no wars (as a positive effect of emotionality).

If we wish to know whether any given culture is gender-supremacist, the most clear and direct way of finding out is to look at *what that culture believes and says about men and women*, to examine what human attributes it genders female and male, and what values it places upon those gendered attributes.

This approach makes much more sense than the conventional feminist method of identifying gender-supremacism, which is to ask: what is the sex of the people who occupy the highest paying jobs and hold political office? Not only did feminists do this in the 1960s and 70s, they continue to do this today, claiming that society is still a male-supremacist 'patriarchy' because most politicians and senior corporate business executives are male. Feminism uses this method of identifying gender-supremacism by means of the sex of those who occupy the senior ranks in the social hierarchy (regardless of how many people of the same sex *do not* hold those ranks) because it is the method which generates the answer that serves feminism's ideological agenda. It generates the answer that society was, and is, male-supremacist and portrays men as the advantaged sex.

People accept the feminist version of male-supremacism because intuitively it sounds plausible to them to say that if all the people in the government and high up in the economy were men, then this must mean that men were in charge. (Although, as we saw in chapter 1, the fact that this tiny minority of men were completely unrepresentative of men as a class of persons, and did not rule in the interests of men, shows that the intuitive plausibility of this version of male-supremacism is entirely mistaken.) People also find it intuitively plausible because men of all economic classes had more access to the workplace to earn a living and thereby had more personal autonomy. (Although we have seen that this, too, is a mistaken intuition because it is not *being the mule who makes the money* that matters, what counts is upon whom *the money is spent*.) This intuition has been reinforced by years of feminist action focusing heavily on women having equal access to the workplace.

But let's set intuition aside and employ some common sense. Women's exclusion from much of the workplace was derived from a long historical process: (a) in prehistory there was a gendered division of labour resulting from evolution itself where the repeatedly pregnant child-bearers occupied roles consistent with being repeatedly pregnant, and the other sex occupied roles that the child-bearers were less suited to occupy; (b) certain *beliefs about gender* arose from those evolutionary gendered roles of male hunters, builders, fighters, farmers, etc., and female domesticity; (c) with the advent of 'civilisation' those gendered roles were formalised to serve societal needs, with men being assigned a greater diversity of public roles *in keeping with the belief* in their greater/broader capability compared to the repeatedly pregnant child-bearers. From this history we can see that if traditional society was male-supremacist, then the supremacism lies in *those beliefs*.

Traditional society was generally male-supremacist because *society believed men to be more capable than women,* which was reflected in their much wider diversity of occupations (many of which required physical strength) and public roles. The character of this male-supremacist attitude was *paternalistic*, it gave men a duty of care toward women (both a cultural and legal obligation) in the belief that the more capable people should take care of the less capable people. This is why men were given the gendered role of protecting women, where women were held in a kind of protective custody, because society believed women to be less capable of taking care of themselves in a hostile world and therefore in need of men's protection. This method of identifying gender-supremacism also explains why traditional society did have *female-supremacist* beliefs, too, but only in regard of things like child-rearing and medical nursing where society's beliefs about women as natural 'carers' viewed them as the people of superior capacity in those roles.

It is *beliefs* of this sort which constitute gender-supremacism. If a society's political structures are gender-supremacist it is because they *reflect and embody* such beliefs. But, on the feminist model, traditional gender-supremacism resides in the political structures themselves, simply in the male occupation of the senior ranks of hierarchies. This is a mistaken model. It also *leaves open* the question of how these political structures came into being, and this is why you'll hear feminists trying to explain those political structures by saying brainlessly stupid things like 'men hate women' or attributing the existence of those political structures to 'male violence'.

But, properly understood, the gender-supremacism of traditional society was not found in the fact that women were not allowed to be pilots, it was found in *the belief that women were not capable of being pilots*. Thus, when women like Amy Johnson proved that women could be excellent pilots, society had to start changing its attitude about women's capacities. The gender-supremacism of traditional society was not found in the fact that women were largely excluded from being scientists, it was found in *the belief that women were not capable of being scientists*. Thus, when women like Marie Curie proved that women could be excellent scientists, society had to start changing its attitude about women's capacities.

This is why it was so significant that women occupied a lot of traditionally male workplace occupations during World War 1 and World War 2 when the male workers had been conscripted into the armed forces to fight those wars. Society had no choice but to employ women in the roles of munitions workers and truck drivers and all sorts of 'men's' jobs because there were not enough men left to do them, and *this proved that women were capable of doing them*. Take women out of their corsets and petticoats, put them into overalls and boots, and they could do those jobs as well as men. Women in the workplace during the two world wars refuted the old belief that women were less capable than men. This was hugely undermining of the traditional male-supremacist attitude so, when the contraceptive revolution (1960s and 70s) and the technological revolution (1980s and 90s) came along in the second half of the twentieth century, society was ready for the gender revolution which duly occurred. These days, society's beliefs/values about gender have changed enormously in many ways and so have the political structures which reflect and embody society's gender beliefs.

Once this is understood, then the peculiar nature of gender-supremacism is more visible. We can see, for example, that it does not necessarily serve the individual interest of a member of the 'superior' gender. Traditionally, most men spent their hard-earned money on financially supporting women and children as the family breadwinner, and they might often have felt themselves to be the family workhorse carrying everyone else on their back. But society's belief that men were more capable than women (a male-supremacist belief) is one of the things which made it easier for a man to accept the role of having to break his back to provide financially for the wife and kids because, not only does it appeal to his humanity in asking him to support those who are less able, but the supremacism *flatters him* into feeling good about fulfilling his 'manhood'. (There could be other reasons, of course, not least his loving his wife and kids.) This same male-supremacist attitude lay behind society's belief that it was *appropriate* for an ex-wife to receive alimony from her divorced ex-husband, something that was clearly beneficial to women, not to men. It was thought justified because of female 'incapacity'. Not only were the same jobs not available to her, but she also *couldn't be expected to cope* without his support. When he married her, he took on a financial obligation to her for life, even if their marriage ended. It was *not in his interest* to go on supporting her but a male-supremacist attitude in society told him that it was right for him to do so, and made it a legal requirement that he do so.

So to establish whether a society is gender-supremacist or not, we should not make the mistake that feminism has made in thinking that employment practices and hierarchical political structures identify supremacism. It would far more realistic and accurate to examine what beliefs about women and men a society has, addressing both the positive and negative values that it imposes upon each sex, and the way that these beliefs and values are reflected in cultural norms, political priorities, government legislation, judicial practices, and so on. *Gender-supremacism consists in a societal set of beliefs, attitudes, and values which hold people of one sex to be inherently superior to people of the other sex.* How the sexes are treated within that society is secondary to the belief that it is 'appropriate' to treat them that way. If one sex is valued more highly than the other, if one sex is believed to have a greater degree of virtue than the other, then *that* is gender-supremacism.

This clear and direct approach to identifying supremacism in a society is strongly reinforced if we consider a couple of historical examples of white-supremacism. We can be confident in asserting that 18th century England was a white-supremacist culture. But this was not because black people were excluded from employment opportunities and excluded from the senior ranks of the political and commercial hierarchy. There were almost no black people in the country at the time. The percentage of the population of England that was black would have been too microscopic to measure in a census. What made 18th century England a white-supremacist culture was what it *believed* about white people and what it *believed* about black people. The 'inferior' people were not even physically present in any meaningful sense, but the attitude toward black people *elsewhere in the world* was white-supremacist.

Similarly, there would not have been very many black people in Nazi Germany but Nazi culture is the embodiment of white-supremacism. Why? Because it believed that white people were innately superior, both intellectually and physically, to black people. This is why it was so glorious that Jesse Owens was so successful in the 1936 Olympics. Jesse Owens demonstrably disproved the supremacist beliefs of the Nazis. Every gold medal he won was a refutation of their belief in white superiority. But Owens' victories on the track *didn't make any difference at all* to how many black Germans were employed, or in what jobs. Owens' Olympic triumphs *didn't change the political and commercial hierarchies of German society* in any way at all. Nor, we might remember, did they have any effect upon the social hierarchy back home in America either. But they did strike at the very heart of Nazi white-supremacism.

The same thing happened again when Joe Louis defeated Max Schmeling for the heavyweight boxing championship in 1938. Schmeling had been exploited by the Nazis as an example of the Aryan master race (this was nothing to do with Schmeling himself who was, if anything, an anti-Nazi and even had a Jewish manager) so when Schmeling was knocked out dramatically in the first round of the fight his defeat exposed the lies of the German supremacist propaganda very effectively. Yet Joe Louis' victory made no difference to the political and commercial hierarchy of Germany or to black employment under the Third Reich. That's not what supremacism is. Black Americans were dancing in the streets in jubilant, euphoric celebration of Louis' win. But it didn't change employment practices in America any more than Owens' victories had.

As with race-supremacism, so too with gender-supremacism. It is found in society's beliefs and values, not its employment practices or political structures. Supremacist beliefs might be *reflected in* those things but, crucially, it is not those things themselves which *identify* whether a society is supremacist or not. So we now have our method to identify gender-supremacism. It consists in the societal judgement that people of one sex are intrinsically better human beings, are more virtuous and of superior value, to people of the other sex.

If we apply this method to contemporary society, the answer is emphatic. Over the last forty years society has gendered human traits in accordance with the extreme misandry of feminism. Nothing has been more central to the prevailing gender attitudes and beliefs of mainstream society than feminism. If we wish to know how present-day society values women and men, what it considers the 'appropriate' treatment of women and men, then we must look at what it believes about women and men. We must look at how it *genders* human character traits and how it *values* those traits. If we make two lists of these, they will look like the lists below. You, the readers of this book, have surely heard these predicates being culturally assigned to women and to men thousands of times throughout the last few decades, so this should all be very familiar.

Feminism's Gender Stereotypes

Human traits gendered Feminine	Human traits gendered Masculine
Nurturant (value – positive)	Violent (value – negative)
Conciliatory (value – positive)	Combative (value – negative)
Co-operative (value – positive)	Competitive (value – negative)
Mature (value – positive)	Immature (value – negative)
Self-sacrificing (value – positive)	Selfish (value – negative)
Considerate (value – positive)	Inconsiderate (value – negative)
Sexually loving (value – positive)	Sexually predatory (negative)
Appeasing (value - positive)	Aggressive (value – negative)
Domestically competent (value – positive)	Domestically incompetent (value – negative)
Emotionally open (positive)	Emotionally shut-off (negative)
Communicative (positive)	Uncommunicative (negative)
Interested in people (positive)	Interested in games (negative)
Spiritual (value – positive)	Material (value – negative)
Innocent (value – positive)	Guilty (value – negative)

And so on. If you have lived in contemporary western society, you will have heard men and women being described in these terms more times than you can count. You might want to add a few more traits to the lists yourself. The point, however, is already clear. Whenever someone is talking about 'typical' men its always a bad thing, never a good thing. Generalisations about men are always negative, just as generalisations about women are always positive.

If you want to deny this, then test yourself: try to think of a *positive generalisation* about men that you've heard somebody say in mainstream society. Something said about men as a sex *that is to their credit*. If you can't think of one, then you'll have to concede the point. If you're still reluctant, then instead of trying to think of a positive generalisation about men that you've actually heard, just try to think of one yourself now. A generalised statement about men that shows them in a virtuous light. How long did it take you to think of one? Did you manage to think of one at all?

In contemporary society women are presented to us as intelligent, maternal, altruistic, carers and sharers, while men are presented to us as irresponsible, selfish, unreliable, foolish, and violent. Men are said to be little boys who never grow up; boys with toys. Women are held to be best at everything that really matters in life, and what do men get to be best at? Reading maps.

If you have the intellectual honesty to admit that you, reader, live in a society in which negative generalisations about men are routinely made every day and are considered to be socially acceptable (whereas any negative generalisation about women would be heavily criticised as misogyny), then you really have no choice but to acknowledge that you are living in a female-supremacist society. Commonplace generalisations about a group of people express society's prevailing attitude toward that group of people. If you live in a society that commonly expresses anti-Semitic generalisations, then you know that you're living in an anti-Semitic society. It's the same for any other group.

Disparaging, disrespectful comments are made about men in western society on a daily basis, and over the last four decades these remarks have been met with amused chuckles and general agreement. When feminists started popularising negative generalisations about men back in the early 1970s they presented these sexist generalisations as a way of counteracting what they said was the prevailing male-supremacist attitudes of the time. But after more than forty years, who can possibly pretend that the constant denigration of men that we all hear every day is intended to *counteract* anything? I was a child in the early 1970s and today I am a grey-haired old man in my fifties. I have heard these negative generalisations about men (and therefore about myself) throughout the whole of my adult life. Derogatory comments about men are an expression of the society in which I have lived my one and only life. Feminism is not a *counter*-culture, feminism *is* the culture. Feminism's misandry *is* the sexism of mainstream society.

If you can admit to yourself that you have heard the gendered traits in the two lists above being used to describe females and males all *your* life, too, then you'll have to face the fact that you live in a female-supremacist culture which believes women to be intrinsically *better human beings than men* and that this is attributed crudely to the femaleness of women and the maleness of men. Look at the two lists again. Can you seriously deny that these are the gender values of the mainstream culture all around you? (If you are gritting your teeth and adamantly denying it, then skip ahead to read the section on The Demonisation of Men in Mainstream Popular Culture in chapter 6 before continuing with this chapter.)

Expressions of female-supremacism are commonplace and yet people seem not to recognise them as such. For example, notice how in the present culture people often advocate that a man should 'get in touch with his feminine side', as if this will make him a better person, but a reconstruction of gender is *only* recommended *for men*. No one ever advocates that women should 'get in touch with their masculine side'. This is because the masculine side is presumed to be the bad aspects of humanity (aggression, violence, being sexually predatory, etc.) so that for a woman to get in touch with the masculine side of her nature would be a *downgrading* of her status as a person, making her a worse person, not a better person. It is assumed that men will be *improved* by becoming more 'feminine' but that women would be *degraded* by becoming more 'masculine'. We see this confirmed in the popular criticisms made of 'ladettes' who are thought to be behaving like lads; behaving in a male fashion.

Moreover, every time you hear someone advocate that a man 'get in touch with his feminine side' the person who is saying this probably thinks that they are liberating the man to experience the human attributes that traditional social constructs of gender have forbidden to him. But by calling those attributes 'feminine' they are actually reinforcing the old idea that a certain range of thoughts and feelings are *female* in character. They are telling him to behave in a less-male and more-female manner. In doing so they are continuing his alienation from thoughts are feelings that are as much *his* as they are anyone else's; as much *male* as they are female because they are *human* thoughts and feelings. The emotions he experiences that society calls his 'feminine side' as much *his* thoughts and feelings as any other thoughts and feelings he may have. For as long as people talk of a 'feminine side' those old social constructs of gender are still doing their insidious work. In fact, those feelings are his *as a man*, they are his male feelings. All such feelings are found in people of both sexes. There is no such thing as a sex-specific feeling.

In the musical "My Fair Lady" Professor Higgins sings "Why can't a woman be more like a man? Men are so honest, so thoroughly square, eternally noble, historically fair. Who, when you win, will always give your back a pat. Why can't a woman be like that? etc." [Lyrics by Alan Jay Lerner] We can immediately tell that this is a comedy song because no one would for a moment take his sentiments seriously, not even in 1963. But feminism has actually been playing a gender-reversal Professor Higgins *in real life* and without humour for forty years, endlessly exhorting men to try their best to be more like women, to 'get in touch with their feminine side'. How can anyone mistake this for anything other than what it is: gender supremacism?

Another commonplace example is the 'feminization' of societal structures, laws, culture, politics, business, education, and anything else that can be feminized. It is always taken for granted that greater female participation in any area of life will improve that area of life. More women in the workplace improves the workplace, more women in parliament improves parliament, more women in the civil service improves the civil service, and so on. The excuse given for this is that the inclusion of women into formerly 'male' areas of life increases the amount of available talent and will therefore necessarily improve performance.

This is a clever excuse because it masquerades as a perfectly reasonable principle that is almost certainly true: that *the inclusion of people who were formerly arbitrarily excluded will increase the available talent and thereby improve performance.* This is an impartial principle that we should all be able to endorse. But notice that this is not what feminists and politicians actually say. They speak of the inclusion *of women*. They say nothing about the inclusion of men. An impartial gender-neutral principle would mean, not only that feminizing formerly 'male' areas of life necessarily improves them, but also that masculinizing formerly 'female' areas of life would necessarily improve them. To apply the principle impartially, it would also have to be taken for granted that greater male participation in any area of life from which they were formerly arbitrarily excluded will improve that area of life.

But have you ever heard a feminist saying that the increasing the number of male midwives will necessarily improve the quality of midwifery? Have you ever heard a feminist saying that the increasing the number of male secretarial staff in business will necessarily improve business administration? Have you ever heard a feminist saying that increasing the number of male nurses will necessarily improve nursing standards? Have you ever heard a feminist saying that more

174

male involvement in child-rearing will necessarily improve the way that children are raised? A feminist would cut her tongue out before admitting such a thing because it might be thought to imply that men had talents or virtues which women don't have.

The politicians who say that the inclusion of women into formerly 'male' areas of life increases the amount of available talent and will therefore necessarily improve those areas of life *mean exactly what they say*. They do not apply an impartial principle, where the inclusion of women and men in the areas of life from which each were formerly excluded increases the amount of available talent and will therefore necessarily improve performance. They mean the inclusion *of women*, not the inclusion of men. It's politically acceptable to believe that women have a special feminine capacity which will enrich an area of life, but it is not politically acceptable to believe that men have a special masculine capacity which will enrich an area of life. This is a gender-supremacist attitude.

You don't believe me? Okay, imagine that someone who gendered men and women as masculine and feminine were to say that the increased inclusion of men into child-rearing would necessarily improve the way in which children are raised because fathers are less self-indulgent with their children than are mothers, and this is why fathers are better able to instil self-discipline into their children. So children would commit fewer anti-social crimes if more men were included in child-rearing. Do you think that the average feminist television pundit would agree with this and endorse it? Or do you think she would protest that this was an outrageous thing for anyone to say because it was nothing more than *blaming single-mothers* for the criminal anti-social behaviour of their children by suggesting that mothers can't instil self-discipline equally well as fathers? Which of these two responses would you expect to hear?

I, for one, am perfectly happy with the idea that the inclusion of people into an area of activity from which they have traditionally been arbitrarily excluded can improve that activity. But this is not to say that the inclusion of women *as women* will improve anything. The principle simply states that if you draw from a larger pool of people, then more talent will be available. The inclusion of bright and resourceful women in business will improve business if they replace staff who were dim and lacklustre in their jobs. The inclusion of committed and hard-working women into parliament will improve the quality of parliament if they replace politicians who were apathetic and lazy in their jobs. But the improvement will come from these individual women being bright and resourceful and committed and hard-working, it will not come from their being *female*. The improvement could equally well have come from men who had these same positive qualities. There is nothing about women *as women* that entails improvement. The idea that it is 'feminization', a process of making an area of life increasingly female, that brings improvement to everything it touches is a gender-supremacist idea. It implies that women have certain qualities of excellence that could not be found in men; qualities that would be absent if women were excluded.

How often have you heard some fool claiming that women are better at multitasking than men? No one seems to feel shy about making this claim since it is culturally understood that this is a *female trait*. Multitasking is accordingly seen as having positive value and women are constantly being complimented on their ability to multitask while men are sneered at for being no good at multitasking. No one would dream of suggesting an alternative reading of the situation: that people who are good at multitasking lack focus; that they are less good at concentrating on a single task. Would anyone compliment men for having the ability to focus on a particular task whilst sneering at women for their inability to focus? No one would dare. Under feminization, it has to be multitasking that is positively valued and therefore men who are disparaged for their deficiency. It is always men who are defined in negative terms.

This assertion of the uniquely female character of certain qualities of excellence reminds us of how much feminism is heavily invested in a belief in natural biological gender. Moreover, the idea of the 'feminine' which is used is often strongly traditional. For example, the way that feminism speaks of the feminization of the workplace includes changes in what is considered 'appropriate' and 'inappropriate' *conduct* in the workplace. It is understood that greater female participation in a working environment brings with it the requirement that *staff behaviour must conform to feminine gendered norms*. As a result, off-colour humour is no longer funny and 'bad language' must be silenced. There is a greater concern over sexual relationships developing between colleagues because 'vulnerable' women must be protected from predatory men of senior rank who might take advantage of women who are junior to them. There is a much greater concern over the issue of workplace bullying because competitive and combative men are supposedly so lacking in the conciliatory and cooperative social skills that women have.

Nobody cared about workplace bullying when it was *men* who were being bullied, but as soon as women arrived bullying became an important issue because *women must be protected*. The workplace must change out of respect for the delicate sensibilities of women. In short, the workplace must become *more ladylike*. Think about that. Feminization brings changes to working practices which reflect the traditional gendering of women as 'ladies'.

These changes are, of course, seen as improvements. Feminized rules of conduct are taken to be superior because feminism holds the female to be closer to the ideal human norm. The character traits it classifies as feminine are seen as *what human beings ought to be*; the best of humanity. Look again at the two lists above of traits that feminism genders male and female, and then tell me 'feminization' has no such implication. The way that feminists speak about women and men makes it obvious that they hold to an idealised female human norm. It follows from this that males will be viewed as necessarily inferior because they are insufficiently female. Men fail to accord with the human norm. Men are insufficiently human. This is why so many people believe that having more women participating in something *always* improves it; civilizes it; humanizes it.

177

Let's be clear on what I'm saying. I am *not* suggesting that the old working practices were better. The best form of working practices is a subject for debate between the bosses and the workers (in which my political sympathies are with the workers). *Nor* do I object to the idea that the workplace might be improved by its becoming a more compassionate, more caring environment. What I *do* object to is the belief that the workplace will become more compassionate and caring due to the presence of women, an idea which is entirely in keeping with the traditionally gendered idea of women being the 'gentle sex'. This insults both men and women. It perpetuates a traditional social construct of femininity and treats men as being intrinsically less caring and compassionate than women. What I *am* saying is that feminization is a political programme that presupposes two separate and distinct genders, which favours the feminine as being better than the masculine, and which is therefore gender-supremacist.

Feminization has long since reached the point where anything associated with the 'feminine' tends to be seen in a positive light and anything associated with the 'masculine' tends to be seen in a negative light. For example, we used to have a Police *Force* to protect us from dangerous criminals, but now we have a Police *Service* to help people live together peacefully. *Force* is seen as a 'masculine' trait and therefore negative, whereas *service* is seen as 'feminine' and therefore positive. The doughty man in a police uniform who stood in harm's way to protect the public has been replaced by the police community liaison officer who engages in diversity awareness events.

Even justice itself has been feminized. In the past we had justice on a principle of *retribution*; the criminal had violated one of their fellow citizens and, having done wrong, he/she deserved to be punished for it. Now we have *restorative justice* where the criminal is brought face-to-face with their victim so that the victim can express the pain they felt at being violated and the criminal, in sincere repentance, can understand the error of his/her ways. The tears of the victim will rehabilitate the misguided person who committed the violation. This is the Oprah Winfrey/Jerry Springer school of justice, where it's all

178

about expressing your feelings and displaying your emotional wounds.

Again, to be clear, I am *not* saying that 'force' is necessarily superior to 'service'. *Nor* am I saying that the principle of restorative justice has no place in the legal system. I am merely pointing out the way in which these feminized revisions to the state's approach to law and order are assumed to be an improvement upon the supposedly 'masculine' things that they replaced. There is an assumption that feminization is *always and necessarily* an improvement. This is the mind-set of feminist society.

Feminism is, and always has been, a female-supremacist ideology. *That is why* it has produced a culture with female-supremacist beliefs. It was never a sex-equalitarian ideology. That is why it has *not* produced a culture with sex-equalitarian beliefs. Mainstream society's positive gender-stereotype of women and its negative gender-stereotype of men have not come about by accident, they are the direct result of what feminists have been saying for the last half-century. And gender-supremacism is the *absolute opposite* of sex equality. So get this straight: feminism is *not opposed* to sexism, feminism *is* sexism.

I said earlier that the contraceptive revolution of the 1960s and the technology revolution of the 1980s were the changes in the material circumstances under which people lived that gave society its opportunity to achieve a genuine impartial sex equality. For the first time in human history society could have begun to do away with the traditional bifurcation of the species. Gendered identities could increasingly have been consigned to the past and all human traits could have been recognised as being precisely that; *traits common to humanity*. Social constructs of gender which held certain traits to be feminine or masculine could have been set aside as anachronisms. Instead, *feminism went in completely the opposite direction*. It has gendered human traits with all its political strength in order to present women as superior to men; as intrinsically better human beings. All the bad human traits have been gendered male, all the good human traits have been gendered female. This propagandizing of female virtue and male vice is the heart and soul of feminism's betrayal of sex equality.

Once a person opens their eyes to it (or rather opens their mind) the female-supremacist attitudes of contemporary society are not difficult to find. Sexuality in women is spoken of in a positive way, as 'making love'. Sexuality in men is spoken of in a negative way, as 'fucking'. The implication is always that making love is superior to fucking. In reality, women have a huge diversity of sexualities and men have a huge diversity of sexualities, and all these human sexualities can be found in people of both sexes. But feminism believes in *gendered sexuality*, in a 'good' female sexuality and a 'bad' male sexuality, because you can't be a gender-supremacist unless you believe in biological gender.

Examples abound. When a woman sexually propositions a man she's seen as being self-assured and confident. But when a man propositions a woman he's seen as being guilty of sexual objectification and of having a one-track mind. When a women is aggressive toward a man she's seen as being a feisty, sassy woman asserting herself in girl-power. But when a man is aggressive toward a woman he is seen as being a bully and a thug. Have you ever heard of a *man* being described as feisty or sassy? When a woman is domestically abused by a man it is seen as irrefutable proof of men's innate violence and their hatred of women. But when a man is domestically abused by a woman he can even find himself being blamed for the abuse he suffers because of the commonplace belief that he must have brought that violence upon himself by some wrongdoing on his part (as if female violence can be assumed to be justified). https://www.youtube.com/watch?v=LIFAd4YdQks

Feminists are the biggest hypocrites who ever lived. They have spent half a century demanding that women must be equal with men, but they've spent not a single day demanding that men must be equal with women. Feminism is a female-aggrandising, male-degrading, gender-supremacist ideology, and it's been a victorious roaring runaway triumph.

180

Just how far have feminists taken their obsession with female self-aggrandisement? As an example of the narcissism of the Feminist Ego, consider this comment from Charlene Spretnak about the motivation behind 'patriarchal' cultures:

". . . in such cultures the elemental power of the female body (the capacity to bleed in rhythm with the moon, to grow both females and males from our flesh, and to transform food into milk for the very young) is regarded with fear, envy, and resentment." [Spretnak, (1992) "Treating the Symptoms, Ignoring the Cause", Women Respond to the Men's Movement, p174]

In addition to womb-envy we now have lactation-envy and, incredibly, *menstrual-envy*. Not to mention men's fear and resentment toward all three. The first time I read this, many years ago, I thought it must be a joke, making fun of the similarly absurd Freudian notion of penis-envy. Okay, I could maybe imagine womb-envy as a possibility for some men. It's at least imaginable. Lactation-envy in males is apparently taken seriously by some psychologists, although I would have thought it much more likely to be an issue for mothers who discover that they are not able to breastfeed. Lactation-envy may also be more of a problem in lesbian relationships. American celebrity Rosie O'Donnell has admitted publicly to being so jealous of her partner Kelli Carpenter breastfeeding their daughter that she put a stop to it.
https://www.lifesitenews.com/news/jealous-rosie-odonnell-orders-lesbian-partner-to-stop-nursing-her-child

But as for menstrual envy?! Men are covetous of genital bleeding? What else could that be but a joke? Who says feminists are humorless? But Spretnak isn't trying to be funny. She means it. She thinks that men envy women because men don't regularly bleed from their genitals. And notice that menstruation is spoken of as a "capacity", as if it were a talent or a skill rather than an involuntary biological function. To Spretnak it's a spiritual capacity because they "bleed in rhythm with the moon", the lunar goddess.

There is, you may or may not be surprised to learn, quite a lot of feminist anthropology devoted to the curious pursuit of menstruation-aggrandizement and its 'blood magic'. Spretnak is not alone. Judy Grahn is another leading figure (see "Blood, Bread and Roses: How Menstruation Created the World" http://bailiwick.lib.uiowa.edu/wstudies/grahn/01toc.htm) and it's very popular with eco-feminists http://eve.enviroweb.org/perspectives/issues/menstru.html. Feminist society enjoys sneering contemptuously at something it calls 'the male ego'. I shall leave it up to the reader to decide what they make of the feminist ego.

Feminists are Biological Determinists

Take a moment to look again at the two lists in the previous section of human traits that feminism genders female and male. The ideology which daily describes women and men in those terms and which has taught society to believe in those gender-stereotypes is the very same ideology that has also insisted that ideas of gender are nothing more than social constructs. In which case, we must conclude either (1) feminism *does* believe that gender is nothing more than social constructs and so it has deliberately and cynically sought to politically generate these new social constructs of gender in order to advantage women with a glowingly positive stereotype and disadvantage men with a vilely negative stereotype, or (2) feminism has been lying; it does not believe in a social construct theory of gender but in fact believes women to be *what feminism says they are*, and it believes men to be what feminism says they are.

Feminism *claims* to believe that ideas of gender are social constructs but it *behaves* in accordance with a biological determinist view of gender. When you hear a feminist say that 'men are violent' do you think she is saying that men have suffered the misfortune of having a social construct of gender imposed upon them by society which causes them to behave violently? Or do you think she is saying that men, as male human beings, are violent? When you hear a feminist say that 'men are aggressively competitive' do you think she is saying

182

that men have suffered the misfortune of having a social construct of gender imposed upon them by society which causes them to behave competitively? Or do you think she is saying that men, as male human beings, are aggressively competitive? The clue is in the way that these things are never said sympathetically, as toward someone who has been the unfortunate victim of a societal imposition of a gender, they are always said in condemnation of men *as men*.

The reader's own direct personal experience of feminist society should be sufficient to demonstrate that it is very much the second position, the belief that women and men are *what feminism says they are*, which is feminism's actual ideological position. When a feminist claims that girls mature earlier than boys and that men are so immature they're like little boys who never grow up, she is not attributing male immaturity to some social construct of masculinity, she is expressing a view of what she thinks men are naturally like.

She doesn't attempt to examine multiple definitions and various possibilities of what we might understand 'maturity' to be. She doesn't evaluate the plausibility of different social constructs which offer different understandings of what does or does not constitute maturity. She doesn't even argue that feminism's social construct of maturity is more realistic and accurate than anyone else's social constructs of maturity. Instead she speaks of maturity and immaturity from the perspective of feminism's crude stereotypes of biological gender.

For example, if a woman is reading a romantic novel and a man is watching an action movie, these entertainments are evaluated differently. The action movie is a ludicrous fantasy of male heroism and will be considered proof of how violent and immature men are with their delight in guns and explosions; boys with toys. The equally ludicrous fantasy of a feisty heroine who wins the love of a roguish alpha male and thereby teaches him the true meaning of life will not be considered *equally immature*, rather it will be viewed as being concerned with adult preoccupations like 'relationships'. The writing style of romantic fiction may be thought a bit trashy but the subject matter, being perceived as feminine, is thought to be much more mature than the action movie's car crashes and fist-fights. Yet, in truth, both are absurdly unrealistic fantasies and neither should be taken seriously as a comparative measure of maturity. They only appear to show that men are more immature than women because of a female bias in the concept of 'maturity' that derives from contemporary society's prevailing positive and negative gender-stereotypes.

It is a commonplace in feminist society to hear someone say that men start all the wars because men are so violent, that men commit all the sex-crimes because men are so sexually predatory, that men are to blame for domestic abuse (including that committed by women) because men are so aggressive. How could any of these things be said to be true *of men*, if they were actually only true of a *social construct of 'masculinity'*? These ubiquitous condemnations of men could not be anything else but the expression of a belief in biological gender. Contrary to its public facade, feminism in practice firmly endorses gender as a fact of nature.

But perhaps you're still unconvinced? Okay, imagine a scene where a woman walks into a room in which two other women are loudly arguing in a heated quarrel. She reacts by saying: 'Hey, slow down, what's all this about? Why are you quarrelling?' Now imagine a scene (which you may well have witnessed in real life) where the same woman walks into a room in which two men are loudly arguing in a heated quarrel. She reacts by saying: 'Hey, testosterone-frenzy! There's far too much testosterone in this room.'

The 'explanation' of why the two men are arguing so heatedly is assumed to be *hormonal*. In feminist society biological maleness is considered an adequate explanation of male behaviour. When a man (who is supposedly emotionally uncommunicative) gets upset about something and expresses his wounded feelings, feminist women describe this as male aggression and attribute it to his high testosterone levels. They give a *biological* account of his behaviour and you can't get more of a belief in natural gender than that. It sounds like a zoologist observing two rams butting heads in the wild.

'Explaining' behaviour by reference to testosterone is the feminist equivalent of a man in the previous society 'explaining' female behaviour by assuming it must be 'the wrong time of the month' regardless of where the woman was in her menstrual cycle. For feminists, the maleness of men is always a complete explanation of whatever men do or don't do. They are immature *because* they're men. They are violent *because* they're men. They are selfish *because* they're men.

Men are viewed as being such crude and simple creatures that they can be assumed to act on biological impulse. This is why when a woman commits domestic violence against a man, feminists look for some explanation of her behaviour (i.e. *he* must have provoked her beyond all tolerance, so it's really *his* fault that she hit him) because *female violence is inconsistent with the feminist gender-stereotype of what women are like*. But when a man commits domestic violence no further explanation is sought because male violence is absolutely consistent with the feminist gender-stereotype of what men are like. His very maleness is held to be all the explanation required.

It is also a commonplace to hear men described as 'thinking with their cock'. When a woman is led by her sexual appetites to behave in a way that is contrary to her rational self-interest (e.g. the erotic appeal of 'bad boys' and 'bastards') no one in mainstream culture says that she is thinking with her cunt. No one would dream of disparaging the exalted vagina. But if a man is led by his sexual appetites to behave similarly, he will be sneered at as a 'typical' man with a one-track mind. He will be a 'dickhead', a term that equates stupidity with 'thinking with his cock'. Men are assumed to be hopelessly and helplessly in the grip of their own biology in a way that the superior woman is not.

If you are still thinking, 'no, no, no, this can't be right because I've always been told that feminism is *against* the idea that gender is biologically determined', then you're forgetting that feminists are the biggest hypocrites on the planet. Certainly, feminism will claim to be against biological determinism when it leads to conclusions about women that feminists don't agree with, but they endorse it whenever it suits their agenda.

For example, you will have heard the gender-supremacist and self-aggrandizing cry of 'men make war but women are the peacemakers because we carry life in our wombs; we are the life-givers'. Women have wombs therefore women love peace? Regardless of whether you agree or disagree with this claim, you can hardly divorce it from biological determinism. The link is explicitly stated.

Feminists will endorse anything that enables them to elevate the status of female human beings, just as they will endorse anything which degrades the status of male human beings. This is why mainstream feminism employs a reductionist biological determinism in all its crudest forms (testosterone frenzy, dickheads thinking with their cocks, etc.) whenever it affords them the pleasure of reducing men to male biology and attributing male guilt to the very hormones and chromosomes that constitute maleness.

So we should not be misled by feminism's intermittent use of social construct theory, given their intellectual dishonesty. If someone says that 'nearly all the wars were started by men', then feminism will take an essentialist position and say that this shows conclusively the inherent violence of men; claiming that when women are equally in positions of political power there will be far fewer wars. But if someone says that 'nearly all of the famous scientists have been men', feminism will view this as a matter of contingent political circumstances and say that this is solely the result of women having been excluded from science; that if women had been allowed to be included in scientific endeavour, then they would have achieved just as much.

If we are speaking of something good, then a feminist will tell us that it was only done by men because women were excluded (social construct theory). Yet if we are speaking of something bad, then a feminist will tell us that men did it because it's their male nature to behave that way (biological determinism). So a feminist will confidently say that men start wars *because* they are men, but she would never say that men accomplished the vast majority of scientific achievements *because* they are men. On the contrary, she would be more likely to say that the achievements of science would have been *much better* if they had been accomplished by women because women would not have perverted science for the invention of weapons of war and ecologically damaging machines.

Of course, if she did say that, then she would be taking an *essentialist* position about women, claiming that females are naturally less violent and more peace-loving than men, even whilst arguing a *non-essentialist* position by claiming that the lack of women in the history of science was not the result of their female nature. Feminism will adopt a posture of biological determinism when it pleases, but it will also hold to the belief that gender is nothing more than social constructs when it pleases. It is an ideology that doesn't worry about holding to a principle or being logically consistent, it just believes any damn thing which makes women look good and makes men look bad.

Even so, despite its unprincipled hypocrisy, feminist orthodoxy noticeably inclines more strongly toward biological determinism in practice than toward social construct theory. (In matters of academic feminist theory, the opposite is true.) The biological determinism of feminism is habitually manifested in the way that feminism always *blames* men.

Only those who are responsible and accountable for their actions can be blamed. Clearly, someone who has been coerced into a social construct of gender cannot be blamed for having been coerced. If gender is socially constructed, then men did not create the world into which they were born and in which they were raised, and cannot be blamed for the ways in which they have been coerced into behaving. But whenever feminist society reels off its litany of all the things that are wrong with men, there is always a definite implication that men *are to blame* for their behaviour. There is never any suggestion that an oppressive society has forced men to be the way they are; that men and women have both been constrained and compelled to conform to their respective gender identities by the culture in which they live.

Feminism treats *women* in traditional society as the unfortunate victims of a societal imposition of gender but it doesn't treat men that way. On the contrary, men have always been held blameworthy *as the ones who imposed those social constructs*. The excuse for this is the lame old chestnut that 'men ruled society' therefore they are responsible for what society did; that men have *chosen* to be the way they are whereas women were not given any choice. But we have already seen in chapter one that men did not rule society. So that excuse won't do.

If feminists were to take seriously the claim that gender is socially constructed, then they would be committed to a very different political position from the one taken by mainstream feminism for the last half-century. The argument would have to go like this: Men and women were born into a world they did not create. Men and women were raised in accordance with whatever ideas of gendered social roles society was employing at the time. Little boys did not choose the way they were raised and neither did little girls. Therefore both were the victims of societal constraints and both should be liberated from those constraints. In other words, the idea that gender is socially constructed leads to an endorsement of impartial sex equality, not to an endorsement of partisan feminism.

Feminism only clings to social construct theory by means of the delusion that a social construct of gender was forced upon women but was not forced upon men, so that one sex can be blamed and the other not blamed. And it only clings to that delusion by means of viewing the male role in traditional society as being a bed of roses for privileged men, giving them a reason to accept their social construct without being forced to accept it. But everything said in chapters 1 and 2 demonstrates that men had a hell of a time in traditional society. Men might have been a lot better off *without* traditional social constructs of gender. So the feminist delusion fails.

But no feminist can do otherwise than believe in traditional male privilege because *all feminism* is based upon patriarchy theory; the theory that women were oppressed by men. If there were no privileged male oppressors, the foundation stone of all feminism vanishes in a puff of smoke. A belief in the historical male oppressor is not merely central to feminism, it is *essential to feminism*. The ideology cannot exist without that belief. In the absence of a belief in the male oppressor, the guilt-object who is to blame for everything, feminists would be forced to become sex-equalitarians.

Worse still, for feminists, not only does social construct theory not work for their partisan ideology, neither does a straightforward biological determinism. They need a very particular, and peculiar, type of biological determinism to suit their agenda of treating all men as guilt-objects. After all, it could be argued that if men behave as they do because their biology *makes* them behave that way, then this could be seen as another form of coercion. It would excuse men from blame on the grounds that they couldn't help themselves. If what men do is literally *determined* by their biology, then their natural biology gives them *no choice* in the matter and they cannot be held accountable and blameworthy. If it's believed that a man starts a quarrel because of his testosterone, then he could avoid blame for his quarrelsome behaviour by saying that it's not his fault that he was born with testosterone. This might even lead to a situation in which a rapist says 'nature made me a rapist so it's not my fault'. A biological account of male behaviour which *excuses* all their behaviour is the very opposite of what feminism wants. So how does feminism use biological determinism to practice its blame-game?

The type of biological determinism adopted by feminism is one which holds that men behave oppressively *because* they are men, and ascribes blame to *maleness as such*. In this way each man is guilty, not so much for *acting* as a man but for *being* a man. Guilt is attributed to maleness itself, so every man is guilty regardless of what he does or doesn't so. As *one instance of maleness* each man participates in a collective gender-guilt. In this way, if one individual man commits a rape, this is held to be a manifestation of guilty oppressive maleness. And if one individual man sexually objectifies a woman, this is held to be a manifestation of guilty oppressive maleness. And if one individual man beats up his wife, this is held to be a manifestation of guilty oppressive maleness. And so on. Feminism doesn't just blame the individual rapist for the specific rape, it blames all men *as men* for 'rape culture'. It doesn't just blame the individual husband for the specific domestic assault, it blames all men *as men* for 'violence against women'. It blames maleness as such.

This peculiar version of biological determinism practiced by feminists is inherently politicized, and it allows them to make the status of the male guilt-object irrevocable and inescapable. Any individual man who hasn't committed any offences against women is nonetheless guilty because he is a part of that which is to blame: maleness. If his maleness in itself establishes a man's guilt, then males *by definition* must be blameworthy forever; not just in the past and in the present but forever. So no matter how politically powerful feminism becomes, no matter how massive a feminist bias the law may have, no matter how privileged and advantaged women may be, no matter how powerless and disadvantaged and vulnerable the overwhelming majority of men may be in their actual lives, feminism will still be able to blame men for everything bad in the world because men's guilt is determined by men's biology. Maleness is to blame.

This is, of course, what feminism continually tells us, that society's injustices are all caused by 'masculine systems' and by men as a class of persons. It's really the only basis on which men could be held accountable for what feminism calls 'male oppression'. Feminism's long decades spent in the incessant condemnation of men must be based upon a biologically determined view of gender but it needs to be one *that isn't dependent on the choices made by individual men*. Since men didn't choose their own social constructs and men didn't choose their own biology, it's only by attributing the guilt for oppression to *the very existence of maleness itself* that feminism can make everything men's fault. Men are not guilty of being the way they are because they chose it, they are guilty *simply of being the way they are.*

Regardless of their academic theorising about social constructs, feminists *have to* believe in guilt by biological gender in order to say the things that they say on a routine basis in mainstream society. When feminists speak about women they praise them to the skies as paragons of virtue and when feminists speak about men they denounce them as demonic practitioners of vice. Feminists indulge themselves in crass female-supremacist beliefs and to hold gender-supremacist beliefs it is necessary to believe in gender. So every time a feminist makes a sweeping generalisation about how marvellous women are and how appalling men are, she is declaring herself someone who believes in biological gender. She couldn't make such statements if she wasn't. Women are praised simply for *being* women. Men are blamed simply for *being* men.

Applying its own peculiar version of biological determinism is feminism's excuse for blaming its own victims. Feminists constantly accuse men of "victim-blaming" about rape but, having inflicted a multi-generational onslaught of abuse and slander upon men for which they invariably blame men, feminists are the ultimate victim-blamers.

There is a popular feminist slogan which defines feminism as: "Feminism is the radical notion that women are people". http://www.beverlymcphail.com/feminismradicalnotion.html But, as we've seen, feminism does not treat male human beings as people, it treats them as guilt-objects. It treats them as things to be blamed. It treats them as 'patriarchy'. It treats them as an indiscriminate collective entity called "men". It does not treat each individual man as a person in his own right, it treats him as one instance of maleness. So the truth is the contrary of the feminist slogan. A more accurate definition of feminism is that:

Feminism is the radical notion that *men* are *not* people.

This is the fundamental reason why feminism is an obstacle to achieving genuine impartial gender equality. This is the reason why feminism will never permit society to achieve genuine impartial gender equality. Gender equality requires that men be treated equally with women. But *a guilt-object can never have equality with a person*. A scapegoat, whose social function is to be blamed, can never have equality with the blameless. In this way, *feminism makes gender equality impossible*.

Sometimes the barking mad fringe of radical feminists go beyond the usual level of feminist sexism because attributing the guilt for oppression to *maleness as such* means that the logic of feminism's version of biological determinism is ultimately gender-fascist. It is the logic of the final solution. The essential argument is this:

(1) Men are the reason that women are oppressed; all the problems in the world are caused by men.

(2) The reason for this is intrinsic to their maleness; their biology generates a male psychology that causes men to behave the way they do in oppressing women.

(3) Since the problem of men is biological, it cannot be cured by environmental factors.

(4) Therefore, the only solution to the problem is to get rid of maleness itself.

This kind of gender-fascist feminist thinking leads inevitably to the endorsement of a genetic holocaust to eradicate the Y chromosome through abortion/eugenics, and feminism has indeed produced extremist bigots who have expressed views of an overtly genocidal kind.

"If life is to survive on this planet, there must be a decontamination of the Earth. I think this will be accompanied by an evolutionary process that will result in a drastic reduction

192

of the population of males." [Mary Daly, interviewed in "What Is Enlightenment?" magazine, 1999.]

"The proportion of men must be reduced to and maintained at approximately 10% of the human race." [Sally Miller Gearhart, 1982, "The Future - If There Is One - Is Female".]

For those who enjoy collecting really egregious examples of feminist hypocrisy, it is worth noting that the Miller Gearhart quote comes from a book entitled "Reweaving the Web of Life: Feminism and Nonviolence". Yes, that's right, feminism and *nonviolence*. You see, it's the men who are violent so if we get rid of nearly all of the men, then there won't be any violence any more, right? That's supporting nonviolence, see? It's a kind of *genocidal nonviolence*.

Although I described this sort of feminist position as coming from the barking mad fringe of radical feminists, we should not assume that no one takes these feminists seriously. Miller Gearhart was a professor at San Francisco State University and the University of Oregon has a Sally Miller Gearhart Chair in Lesbian Studies as a part of its Women and Gender Studies program. Daly (who was open about her female-supremacism and her opposition to sex equality) was a feminist theologian at Boston College. So these quotes are from credentialed professional academics.

In addition, the blogosphere has plenty of feminists who write appreciatively, even glowingly, of sentiments like those expressed in these quotes. Both Daly and Miller Gearhart are viewed by many as feminist heroines. Yet, as we all know, feminists accuse *their political opponents* of hate-speech whenever anyone dares to speak out against their ideology in any way at all. A feminist can talk about the slow genocide of billions of men or speak of men as a contamination of the planet and find supporters for her view. Feminism's gender-fascists use man-hatred to inspire their followers, just as the Nazis used Jew-hatred to inspire their followers. Yet a book like the one you're reading now which argues in favour of *impartial sex equality* will be traduced with the false accusation of 'hate-speech'.

The irony of genocidal feminist statements like those above is that they reminds us of how feminism is wholly dependent upon the despised male because without the male there would be no ideological oppressor and without an ideological oppressor there would be no feminism. Feminists need men like fish need water. Without the existence of men in the world feminists would have no one to blame for everything. Without the male guilt-object feminism would have no choice but to hold women accountable for their own actions. They would have to blame women for the injustices of the world. And that would be the death of feminism. Feminism *needs* its male inferiors.

Whenever anyone draws attention to this sort of 'feminazi' feminism, the predictable and complaisant response from the reactionaries of the politically correct establishment is to say that 'this is not true feminism, just ignore it'. Yet this is not the attitude they take about political position with which they disagree. For example, recently when Godfrey Bloom of the UK Independence Party used the phrase "bongo bongo land". http://www.bbc.co.uk/news/uk-politics-23608106 the whole politically correct establishment responded to that comment by saying 'Told you so! This proves that UKIP are a bunch of racists'. And it goes without saying that the establishment concludes that if someone in the English Defence League raises their hand in what looks like a Nazi salute, then this is proof positive that *every* member of the EDL is a Nazi who wears swastika underpants.

But when feminist gender-fascists make genocidal comments about eradicating men from the face of the earth or demand a curfew on men during the hours of darkness to 'take back the night', those same establishment hypocrites never apply the same principle and conclude that this must say something about the true nature of feminism. Instead they just tell us that 'this is not true feminism, ignore it'. Their complacency in the matter is not merely a reflection of their hypocrisy, it reflects their contempt for men. It simply doesn't bother them if someone advocates a genocide of men. (#killallmen) After all, we know what feminism thinks of men, don't we?

And this prompts one last point that might be worth ruminating on. If ideas of gender *are* social constructs, even in part, then *what social constructs of gender are being culturally imposed in present day society?* How are boys and girls being taught to see themselves in feminist culture? For the girls it's a contradictory combination of girl-power entitlement and woman-as-victim. And for the boys? Young males in feminist society are constantly being given negative gender constructs of what men are like. Political discussions perpetually speak of men in terms of date-rapists and domestic abusers and absent fathers (deadbeat dads). Television programmes continually represent men as being childish selfish idiots and game-obsessed frat-boys. This cultural indoctrination continues unabated. Will a popular culture dominated by feminism's negative gender-stereotype of how dreadful men are influence young boys into thinking that *this is who they really are?* That this is who they must inevitably grow up to be? Will it coerce them, as social constructs of gender have always coerced people, into *conforming to* what their society tells them is a true picture of men? If so, then boys will identify with, and become, the social construct of 'masculinity' that female-supremacism has given them. They will become MTV's Jackass.

Perhaps a supporter of feminism might try to excuse this unremitting cultural misandry on the grounds that it is one aspect of feminism's attempt to feminize boys by motivating them to escape this constant avalanche of criticism by becoming what feminism requires them to be, and thereby become more feminine, better human beings. But that won't do as an excuse because we have to ask the question: *what exactly does feminism require men to be?*

The answer, as we've seen, is that feminism requires men to be perpetual guilt-objects. Feminism's peculiar version of biological determinism, in its actual political consequences, creates and imposes a feminist social construct of the 'guilty male' on all men and makes that status irrevocable and

195

inescapable because maleness itself is believed to make all men guilty forever. In other words, the disparaging and disrespectful gender-stereotype of how stupid and selfish and violent and sexually predatory men are *is what feminism requires men to be*. Feminism *needs* that stereotype in order to justify itself, and so that stereotype must go on and on, so that feminism can go on and on. The only role for men within the politics of feminism is the role of a guilt-object. If society admired and respected the male sex, what would be left of feminism?

The Reconstructed Man and the Crisis of Masculinity

This question of what effect the constant negative stereotyping of men will have upon men's characters in the future seems to have been largely ignored in favour of the assumption that men need to be 'made-over' into something that better serves the perceived interests of women. This deliberate reconstruction of the social construct of male-identity has always been viewed by mainstream society as something that was necessary, well-intentioned, and socially improving.

In the 1980s, at exactly the same time as it was condemning the 'patriarchy' for having imposed a traditional social construct of gender upon women, feminist society consciously set about the task of imposing a new social construct of gender upon men. I'm not speaking here of the male guilt-object but rather to the proposed solution to 'the problem of men'. This solution was even given a name, it was called the 'New Man'. The phrase refers to a social construct of gender that was advocated so ubiquitously in the eighties that the term even made it into the Oxford English Dictionary:

"New Man. A man who rejects sexist attitudes and the traditional male role, esp. in the context of domestic responsibilities and childcare, and who is (or is held to be) caring, sensitive, and non-aggressive."
http://www.oed.com/view/Entry/245763?rskey=dV3Sct&result=1&isAdvanced=false#ei d

The 'New Man' was an unambiguous policy of telling men who they ought to be; the gender construct to which they now had to conform. It was a blatant case of the social imposition of a gender-identity, where a set of attitudes and behaviours is demanded of people of one sex and any failure by a person of that sex to conform to this identity is reprimanded. The 'New Man' did the washing up in the kitchen, he changed babies nappies/diapers, he cried when watching romantic films, he rejected the machismo of the traditional 'real man' and behaved much more like the traditional woman. But he was *not liberated* because this reconstruction of his identity was done *for the sake of women*. He wasn't changing nappies/diapers because he had been given equality in childcare, he was changing them because it wasn't fair to expect a woman to 'shoulder the burden of childcare'. He wasn't doing the washing up because he was no longer expected to be the financial provider, he was doing it because she damn well wasn't going to be his bloody servant. The New Man wasn't liberated, he was feminised.

We should not make the mistake of thinking that this new gender construct was a attempt to free men from the old misandry. Remember, this took place within the social context of the rigid feminist belief that all sexism was misogyny. Nobody even used the word 'misandry' in the 1980s. No, the point of the 'New Man' was to make men less oppressive to women. He had been domesticated but this was not done in order to give him equal access to the domestic sphere as a life-choice, it wasn't about removing women's traditional advantage in this area of life, it was done merely to alleviate her 'burden'. Any man who failed to comply with the new gender-identity was held to be a part of that 'burden'. How often have you heard a woman say something like 'I've got three kids and a husband to take care of, so really I've got *four kids* to take care of'. This new social construct of gender wasn't imposed for the benefit of men, it was imposed for the benefit of women.

The idea was supposed to be that the previous gender-construct of the traditional 'real man' could now be re-evaluated (i.e. devalued) as redundant and be discarded. Any man found still conforming to the old gender-identity was therefore reproached for being an 'unreconstructed' male. Inevitably, the 'real man' was presented as being something of which men were *guilty*. This old imposition of gender had been victimising men for countless generations, it had been killing men for centuries, but it was presented by feminism as something for which men were to blame. So if a man continued to display traits of masculinity in accordance with the idea of a 'real man' he was condemned for being an 'unreconstructed' male.

This much-used phrase, the 'unreconstructed' male, is very revealing; it shows that there was a deliberate, pre-meditated social policy of reconstructing men. The phrase publicly declared that men were to be re-made in an image found more acceptable by feminist society. So if feminists were to *deny* that the 1980s 'New Man' was a deliberate imposition of a social construct of gender by feminism, then their own use of the term 'unreconstructed' would reveal them to be liars as well as a hypocrites.

A few years after the introduction of the 'New Man' people started talking about something called 'the crisis of masculinity'. All the many discussions about this crisis were completely futile because, of course, they were all taking place *within a discourse* that presupposed all sexism to be misogyny, and which took it for granted that any problems men had must necessarily be their own fault, because all of the discourse treated feminism as being unchallengeably correct. The crisis had been caused by the sexism of feminism but none of the discussions could acknowledge this (or even comprehend this) because the political orthodoxy said that feminism was the *solution* to sexism, not the *instigator* of it. As a result, a great deal of hot air was expended upon the crisis to no purpose.

Yet the true character of the 'crisis of masculinity' was transparently obvious to anyone who was not wearing the blindfold of political correctness. Despite all the propagandizing in favour of the 'New Man' the traditional societal expectations imposed upon men were still in place. There had been no men's liberation from traditional misandry. Men were still required to be wage-earners and financial providers, they were still required to be 'success-objects', they were still required to exhibit 'masculine' physicality (just think about the proliferation of 1980s tough-guy movies with muscular heroes like Schwarzenegger, Stallone, Willis, and so on), they were still expected and required to be a 'real man' in spite of all the vitriolic feminist abuse thrown at that social construct of gender.

The 'crisis of masculinity' was that men were being told by the culture they lived in *to conform to two contradictory gender-identities at the same time*: the 'real man' and the 'New Man'. These two imposed gender-identities were in total conflict with one another. How could one man be *both* at the same time? Men were being told that they must reject being the 'real man' but still be him. Hence the 'crisis of masculinity'.

The attitude of heterosexual women to this new gender construct was crucial. The 'New Man' was all well and good when it was time to send hubby into the kitchen to wash up, or to upbraid him for daring to collapse exhausted into a chair when he staggered home from work, or to reproach him for not 'shouldering the burden of child-care', but the 'New Man' was of no interest to her *in the bedroom* because *he wasn't sexy*. Too many women didn't find a man doing the vacuuming an object of erotic desire. She wasn't turned on by a man in a kitchen apron. It was the macho man that women wanted to fuck, with his broad shoulders and his dark dangerous eyes. How many women wanted their man to be a 'New Man' in the kitchen but a 'real man' in the bedroom? (Were these the same hypocrites who had complained bitterly about how men wanted their women to be a domestic servant in the kitchen and a whore in the bedroom?)

The 'New Man' wasn't a viable gender-identity because women didn't want to fuck him. It turned out that a great many women were still sexually attracted to the traditional hunk and didn't want to have sex with a man who was feminised. In a society in which the word 'masculinity' is continually criticized as a reprehensible thing, the word 'emasculated' is still used as a *criticism of men*. Hence the 'crisis of masculinity'.

A woman now has lots of culturally sanctioned reasons for despising a man. (a) She can condemn him for being an 'unreconstructed' man who arrives home from work and then spends the whole evening on the couch watching television instead of joining her in harmonious mutuality at the kitchen sink. (b) She can sneer at him for not being a erotically desirable 'real man' who boldly takes the sexual initiative with an assertive and arousing manliness, cave-man style. (c) She can loathe him for being one instance of maleness, the cause of all the evil in the world, because he's a part of the warmongering, child-endangering, domestically violent, misogynist 'rape culture'. (d) She can deride him for his failure of traditional masculinity because he is an immature 'man-boy' who won't 'man-up' and accept his gendered responsibility to support and protect women and children, not that any woman would want to marry such a loser who earns less money than she does.

Men are now told that they must not be guilty of the crimes of 'masculinity' but at the same time they must not be 'emasculated'. The *contradiction* of social constructs to which men are required to conform persists to the present day and, consequently, the 'crisis of masculinity' persists. Men over the last few decades have been like the character played by Kurt Russell in the movie "Soldier" (1998). This film could serve as a metaphor for the male experience.

First, the society he is born into puts him into a social role in which he must harden himself to perform the brutal tasks that society requires of its soldiers. Social institutions censor his tender emotions, impose a requirement of muscular male physicality, and teach him to practice an emotional isolation from others because they are his rivals and his adversaries. They teach him to fight and they teach him to kill.

Then society tells him that *he is a dangerous individual who cannot be trusted around more civilized people* and excludes him from 'inclusion' in that society on the grounds that he presents a danger to other people. "Soldier" would also serve as a metaphor, more explicitly, for the social isolation and frequent homelessness of war veterans whom society trains to be its warriors and then has no place for when they return home from the war zone.

If read *politically*, "Soldier" is a remarkable statement about traditional and contemporary misandry in its depiction of the victimisation (both emotional and physical) entailed in the male experience. It shows the social redundancy of the men who have had this role imposed upon them (e.g. in the movie the soldier is replaced by a new more efficient fighting unit, whereupon he is literally dumped on a waste disposal planet), and society's rejection of the man that society itself had made. Predictably, none the of the film critics saw any of the insights into gender politics that the film contains, and the movie was a box-office flop.

With the imposition upon men of a double and contradictory gender-identity to which they must conform, misandrist sexism has increased under feminism. The most conspicuous example of this is the debasement of fatherhood over the last thirty years. The feminist society which told men to be a 'New Man', sharing in childcare and domestic duties, is the same feminist society that has estranged two generations of children from their male parent. Men have been told that fathers are unnecessary and disposable; an optional extra. It's hard for a man to change his child's nappy/diaper when he's no longer allowed to see his kid for more than one Saturday afternoon every fortnight. In the UK (which has an estimated total population of 63 million) the Centre for Social Justice reported in 2013:

"Around one million children grow up with no contact with their father. Many are in "men deserts" and have no male role model in sight . . . . Lone parent families are increasing at a rate of more than 20,000 a year and will total more than two million by [2015].

. . . . In one neighbourhood in the Riverside ward of Liverpool, there is no father present in 65 per cent of households with dependent children . . . . There are 236 [areas with an average population of 1,614] in England and Wales where more than 50 per cent of households with dependent children are headed by a lone mother . . . . in the Manor Castle ward of Sheffield . . . . among households with dependent children, 75 per cent are headed by a lone parent (most commonly a woman). http://www.centreforsocialjustice.org.uk/UserStorage/pdf/Press%20releases%202013/ CSJ-Press-Release-Lone-Parents.pdf

For any readers who are wondering about that phrase "most commonly a woman", the Office for National Statistics says that in the 2011 UK census the number of lone parent households with dependent children were broken down by gender as: 1,715,025 with a female lone parent, 180,808 with a male lone parent.https://www.ons.gov.uk/peoplepopulationandcommunity/birthsdeathsandmarr iages/families/adhocs/005602numberofmothersandnumberoffatherswithdependentchild reninthehouseholduk1996to2015 This would make lone fathers around 9.5% of lone parents and lone mothers around 90.5% of lone parents (including widowers and widows, presumably). So, roughly speaking, 9 out of 10 lone parents are mothers. Gingerbread, a single parents advice service, says that 26% of households with dependent children in Britain are single parent families, and that three million children (23% of all dependent children) are living in single parent households. That's just over *a quarter of all families* and just under *a quarter of all children*. http://www.gingerbread.org.uk/content/365/Statistics

The Excluded Father

Nobody knows how many fathers have been excluded by feminist oppression from seeing their own children grow up. Hundreds of thousands? More? Nobody seems to care much. But this feminist crime can never be annulled because no one can go back in time and re-live their life. An excluded father who has been deprived of the experience of being present throughout his children's childhood has lost something which can never be recovered. Yet this wasn't enough for feminism. Insult had to be added to injury. Fathers are men, so feminism requires that they must be blamed for their own victimisation. For decades, everywhere in the culture, on all the public media, fathers were endlessly referred to as 'absent' fathers (deadbeat dads), as if it were their own fault that they had been excluded. This is not to deny that there are men who are absent fathers, certainly there are, it is only to point out that *all the excluded fathers were called absent fathers as well.* Their misandrist victimisation was never acknowledged by the feminist establishment. How could it be? It was the feminist establishment that was the perpetrator of this victimisation. They preferred to paint a picture of fathers as wife-battering, child-battering thugs.

The standard approach to concern over fatherless families focuses on (a) its damaging effects upon the children, and (b) its damaging effects upon society. This is then responded to by those who are keen to assert that it's wrong to blame social breakdown on single motherhood, and then the whole debate is suddenly *all about women* again, as usual. But the issue that is seldom if ever raised by those in political authority, the issue that feminist society is massively resistant to even mentioning, is the damage done to fathers and the injustice done to fathers. It's as if men weren't *people.* It's the old double-standard about human pain; men are expected to suffer in silence.

Feminist society had a second reason for presenting excluded fathers as 'absent' fathers, besides its habitual abuse of men as guilt-objects. They also needed to disguise decades of gross misandry by the judiciary in the way than custody courts routinely favoured mothers over fathers in the belief that mothers were more valuable and vital to a child's well-being than fathers. This sexism persists. In 2011 the Family Justice Review (the Norgrove Report) had the opportunity to recommend that fathers should receive equal custody rights with mothers after a divorce. The review declined. This refusal meant that *fathers continue to be denied equal custody rights with mothers* in the UK.

This is an example of legal sexism, where misandry is written into the law of the land. Could anything be more blatantly gender-supremacist than this assertion of the superiority of mothers over fathers? Campaigners have pointed out that the current family justice system fails to satisfy the UN Convention

on the Rights of the Child to maintain meaningful relationships with both parents. They have also condemned the report on the usual grounds that the widespread practice of denying children a father leads to damaging social repercussions, both for the child and for society at large. But what about the *misandry* of the report? Who in contemporary society dares to demand that men should have equality with women, therefore fathers should have equality with mothers?
https://www.youtube.com/watch?v=hLJHR0MpKos

The Government's excuse for the perpetuation of this gender-inequality was the procedural and financial issue of not making custody disputes too time-consuming for the courts and the usual mantra that it was in the best interest of the children. But if the government thinks that it is in the best interests of the children for *one* parent to have *superior* parental rights, how would it be if it was the father who had custody rights and the mother who didn't? This would be dismissed out of hand. But why would it be different to permit superior custody rights to fathers and deny them to mothers, instead of permitting them to mothers and denying them to fathers? Wouldn't it be an equal injustice either way?

There are two customary excuses for favouring mothers. The first is simply a naked assertion of gender-supremacism, that mothers really are by nature intrinsically superior parents to fathers. The people who say this exhibit no shame when they say it because maternal superiority is a commonly held view in society and people treat it as a 'well-known fact'. Child-rearing has traditionally been the woman's gendered social role and traditional social constructs of gender are routinely endorsed by feminist society whenever they advantage women.

The second excuse relies upon the negative gender-stereotype of the male predator. Feminism's forty year campaign to portray men as dangerously violent abusers has established the popular belief that *mothers can be relied upon to keep children safe*, whereas a man *may* be okay but *maybe* he'll turn out to be a child-raping paedophile. The truth, however, is that statistically the people most likely to harm children are their mothers. This is hardly surprising, given that mothers generally have much greater access to their children than do fathers, both in marriage and as lone parents. For example, in America the US Department of Health and Human Services says:

"How do fathers compare to mothers in the perpetration of child maltreatment? As discussed earlier, Federal data derived from CPS reports in 2003 indicate that in 18.8 percent of the substantiated cases, fathers were the sole perpetrators of maltreatment; in 16.9 percent of the cases, the fathers and the mothers were perpetrators; and in 1.1 percent of the cases, the father acted with someone else to abuse or neglect his child. Mothers were the sole perpetrators in 40.8 percent of the cases and acted with someone besides the father in 6.3 percent of the cases. This means that fathers were involved in 36.8 percent of child maltreatment cases and that mothers were involved in 64 percent of child maltreatment cases." [User Manuals, Fatherhood, Chapter 3 https://www.childwelfare.gov]

The presence of single mothers may play a role in this much higher occurrence of child maltreatment by women than by men because the US Department of Health and Human Services also says:

"The rate of child abuse in single parent households is 27.3 children per 1,000, which is nearly twice the rate of child abuse in two parent households (15.5 children per 1,000). An analysis of child abuse cases in a nationally representative sample of 42 counties found that children from single parent families are more likely to be victims of physical and sexual abuse than children who live with both biological parents. Compared to their peers living with both parents, children in single parent homes had:

- 77 percent greater risk of being physically abused

- 87 percent greater risk of being harmed by physical neglect

- 165 percent greater risk of experiencing notable physical neglect

- 74 percent greater risk of suffering from emotional neglect

- 80 percent greater risk of suffering serious injury as a result of abuse

- 120 percent greater risk of experiencing some type of maltreatment overall.

A national survey of nearly 1,000 parents found that 7.4 percent of children who lived with one parent had been sexually abused, compared to only 4.2 percent of children who lived with both biological parents."
https://www.childwelfare.gov/topics/can/factors/contribute/risk/

The point of listing these statistics here is *not* to blame mothers for committing the majority of child abuse and neglect but merely to highlight how an appeal to the feminist gender-stereotype of the violent male is an *excuse* for denying fathers their rights, not a justification. All statistics can be challenged and all statistics should be challenged, so whether you think these figures are proof of anything is up to the judgement of the individual reader. *My* point is simply to draw attention to the fact that when the US government published statistics on the issue of fathers and mothers mistreating their kids, the results were *entirely contrary* to what mainstream feminism has taught the general public to believe. The idea that children are *safe* with women but *at risk* with men is the popular misconception, it isn't the truth. Children can be safe or at risk with either women or men.

Similarly, the popular perception that women have to drag men kicking and screaming into taking a share of the domestic and child-rearing duties is very questionable these days. The Equality and Human Rights Commission reported in 2009:

"Fathers appear to have less traditional views than mothers on some aspects of parenting. For example, they were less likely

(23 per cent) than mothers (34 per cent) to think that childcare is the primary responsibility of the mother, and more likely (55 per cent) than mothers (41 per cent) to believe that the parent who is paid more should stay at work regardless of whether they are male or female." [equalityhumanrights.com, 2009, Fathers Struggling to Balance Work and Family]

There may be a parallel here with a point I mentioned earlier. When a traditional man said 'no wife of mine is going out to work' he was acting against his own interest but did so because his pride was invested in the male-supremacist belief that men were more capable than women and should therefore provide financially for their wives. In the case of childcare the roles are reversed. Are mothers resistant to the idea of equal parenting and instead choosing to take on a larger share of childcare because their pride is invested in the traditional female-supremacist belief that, as women, they are more capable than men? This is plausible in many domestic environments. The woman will reproach the man for not doing enough childcare but, at the same time, she will not trust him to do more because he is only a man whereas she, the mother, is the superior parent. It is her domain. Contrary to the popular perception that men are reluctant to take on the domestic role, might the truth be that women are reluctant to surrender it to them?

This may become increasingly significant in the years to come. The double-standard that favours mothers over fathers in child-custody cases is beginning to break down a little as a few *career women* find themselves in the position that men have been in for so long. This is not due to any admission on the part of the judiciary that fathers have suffered injustice at their hands, it is simply a matter of who is the high-earner and who is the domestic partner in a marriage. The financially dependent partner has much more time for the children and so some *fathers* are now getting custody because *they* were the domestic partner in the marriage. http://www.dailymail.co.uk/femail/article-1024304/Why-more-women-losing-custody-battles-children.html We should remember two things when this happens: (1) a mother's pain is not more serious than a father's pain; (2) if this causes women to re-evaluate the respective roles of breadwinner and child-carer *in favour of the latter*, then this will require them to also re-evaluate decades of feminism which told them that the traditional male role of breadwinner gave men an advantaged position over women. Any woman who decides that raising her children is a more valuable life-choice than going out to work to earn money will have to admit that her own expressed preference proves that feminism has been lying all these years about the so-called male 'privilege' of paid employment.

Fathers, Abortion, and Baby-Making Machines

Politically, abortion is consistently presented as a 'women's issue'. Certainly, the pregnant woman is the person most directly concerned, it being her body in which the foetus is growing. (Although the 'pro-life' lobby would claim that the child is the person most directly concerned, it being his/her life that is at stake.) But, in feminist society, the idea of abortion being a 'women's issue' goes much further than that, it states unequivocally 'my body = my choice', end of story. As if there are no further considerations to be taken into account. Some feminists even assert that men are not entitled to an opinion on the issue of abortion because it is entirely a 'women's issue'. http://blog.talkingphilosophy.com/?p=6005

In the ongoing battle between the advocates of a 'pro-choice' position and the advocates of a 'pro-life' position, those who are pro-choice *prioritize the woman* and those who are pro-life *prioritize the child*. Do you notice who is *not mentioned*? Never mind being prioritized, do you notice who has been entirely excluded from consideration?

Those who argue for the moral permissibility of abortion (of which I am one) generally call themselves 'pro-choice'. But this phrase implicitly excludes men. In law, there is no such thing as 'pro-choice' for men. If the man *wants* the child and the woman *doesn't*, then she can abort the child. If the man *doesn't* want the child but the woman *does*, then she can carry the foetus to term and he will have to pay child support or be sent to prison. This is *not* to say that men cannot be in favour of the 'pro-choice' position politically. They may endorse it on the principle that no one, female or male, should have their body used for the purpose of procreation against their will. A man may therefore endorse the political position of 'a woman's right to choose' rather than the 'pro-life' position, *if these are the only options.* (It is my own position.) But this endorsement does not mean that men have equality with women. Neither of the two available options permits a 'man's right to choose'. She decides and he must accept her decision because it's her body. Even though it's not entirely her foetus.

Moreover, this inequality cannot be rectified by 'a father's right to choose' (not that any such thing will ever be more than a discursive hypothesis) because even if father's had a right in the matter, *they could not exercise that right* since doing so would violate the woman's right over her own body. The woman's right not to be used as a human incubator would always trump the father's right to have a child, and the woman's right not to be forced to have an abortion against her will would always trump the father's right not to have a child without his consent. So any 'father's right to choose' would not be a 'right' worthy of the name. A right is supposed to *guarantee* something to which that person is entitled. A right that can never be exercised would be a sham.

The reader may well be wondering why I would hypothetically speculate on so unimaginable a thing as 'a father's right to choose' in a society which refuses to allow fathers even equal custody rights with mothers. In a society which still routinely speaks of 'women and children' as if they were one group of people, as if those words just naturally went together, we might more pertinently ask the question, do fathers actually have any parental rights at all?

The answer is yes and no. In the UK fathers can acquire legal rights in regard of their children in any of three ways: (a) they are named as the father on the birth certificate; (b) they fill out a 'parental responsibility' form; (c) they are married to the mother. https://www.gov.uk/parental-rights-responsibilities/who-has-parental-

209

responsibility But if fathers can acquire parental rights in these ways, why did I answer the question 'yes and no'? Because you'll notice that the father does *not* acquire parental rights simply by being the father. Mothers do. When a woman becomes a mother she thereby has parental rights. But fathers do not have parental rights *because they are fathers*. They have to complete one of three *legal procedures*. If they don't, then they don't have any rights. This is why the UK government website admits that:

"*All* mothers and *most* fathers have legal rights and responsibilities as a parent - known as 'parental responsibility'." [my italics] https://www.gov.uk/parental-rights-responsibilities/what-is-parental-responsibility

So, in a society in which all mothers have parental rights simply because they are mothers but only most, not all, fathers have parental rights, and that only as a result of having signed a piece of paper, should I be discussing something as unconventional as the idea of 'pro-choice for men' or is this a non-issue? It's worth thinking about because it connects with an important issue of misandry that is, as so often, largely ignored by mainstream discussions on reproductive rights.

It comes back to the question of people (of either sex) not being reduced to their biology by being used as a baby-making machine. This is an issue that has attracted a lot of attention in feminist society ever since Margaret Atwood's dystopian science-fiction novel "The Handmaid's Tale" was first published back in 1985. The book has sold millions of copies, it was made into a Hollywood movie in 1990, and it was even staged as an opera in 2003 by the English National Opera. The phrase 'handmaid's tale' has become a part of the vocabulary of feminists. The story employs the usual clichés of 'male' political violence in a totalitarian and militaristic police state of uniformed men, where a class of women have been reduced to their biology to serve the state's need for procreation and are forcibly impregnated to give birth.

The only interesting thing about this landmark of feminist literature is the way that *it turned reality on its head*. This book was published in the eighties and the film was produced in the nineties. These are the decades when feminist women in significant numbers started deliberately having children without any intention of living with the father. These are the decades when it became socially acceptable for women to decide, as a matter of personal choice, to have a child but not a father to go with it. They decided they wanted the baby but not the man. These women were *using men* as (sometimes voluntary, sometimes involuntary) sperm-donors, as a tool of insemination, as impregnation machines.

Moreover, the eighties and the nineties were the decades when it became the norm for heterosexual couples to rely upon a female oral contraceptive only (because there was no male equivalent) as the primary form of birth control. This meant that married and co-habiting women could use men as involuntary sperm donors by means of a convenient lie. She could claim that the pregnancy was an 'accident' and thereby impregnate herself without his consent if she wanted a child and he didn't. Yet in a society where many married, co-habiting, and single women were all able to exploit men as a tool of insemination, everyone was talking about a science-fiction novel where *men did this to women* and treating *that* as being an allegory for the world we lived in. This is what I mean when I say that "The Handmaid's Tale" turned reality on its head.

In the past there may have been societies which used women as baby-making machines, and Atwood may have dreaded the nightmare of such a thing happening again in a dystopian future, but *at the time when the book and the film appeared and were so influential* society was not doing this to women, women were doing this to men. In real life it was men who were being reduced to their biology as baby-making machines. Yet the entire cultural intelligentsia, the whole educated elite, seemed *not to notice this*. They were blinded by ideology. Their feminist beliefs did not allow them to notice. The use of a person's body for the purpose of procreation against their will has become a common occurrence in contemporary society but the reactionaries of the feminist establishment still affect not to notice.

Anyone who is in favour of the 'pro-choice' position in the abortion debate *on the principle that no one should have their body used for the purpose of procreation against their will*, if they believe in sex equality, must apply this principle to *both* sexes. They must necessarily agree that this principle has been violated where a woman uses a man to impregnate herself without the man's consent because she wants a baby and he hasn't been consulted in the matter.

Which brings us back to 'pro-choice' for men. In *practical terms*, this would mean one of two things. In the best case scenario, it would mean the creation of a male oral contraceptive (available via the NHS or Medicare, etc.) so that the man can at least exercise a negative choice when having sex, the choice not to father a child. There would also need to be standardized DNA testing at the birth of every child so that when a man *does* consent to fatherhood there is confirmation that the child is his, and the injustice of men paying for children who are not their own could be circumvented.

Doubtless, the idea of standardized DNA testing would be condemned by many people on the grounds that it is an unromantic way to bring a child into the world and that it is discourteous (implying that women cannot be trusted in what they say or in their sexual fidelity). But it should be remembered that I am only arguing for standardized DNA testing because of the way that feminist society exploits men in the interests of women. We have to address the situation in which men actually find themselves. *Feminism is the death of romance* and no one in contemporary society seems to have a problem with discourteously implying, or even stating flat out, that men cannot be trusted in what they say or in their sexual fidelity. Sex equality operates on a principle of 'both or neither', so if men are not to be believed then neither are women.

In the absence of a male contraceptive pill, a second-best 'pro-choice' scenario would mean father's having *no financial responsibility* for a child when they have *not chosen* to father that child. The pregnant woman would then have the decision to make whether to have the child or not, and it would be her decision alone ('my body = my choice'), knowing that she will have sole financial responsibility for that child. As an adult, the choice is hers and the consequences of her choice are hers.

I call this a second-best option because, inevitably, it would lead to legal disagreements about whether the man had actually consented to fatherhood or not, and 'consent' would become as much an issue in paternity cases as it currently is in rape cases. Additionally, the women with sole financial responsibility for the children that they had chosen to mother alone would, in many cases, expect financial support from the state. And what government is going to countenance 'pro-choice for men' when it would mean that *the state* would have to pay out the child-support money that men who exercise the choice not to be fathers are no longer paying?

A male oral contraceptive combined with standardized DNA testing would be much the better option but, in feminist society, such a policy would be a complete non-starter because this argument in its favour is an argument based upon a principle of sex equality, and that's not a principle which society endorses at present. 'Pro-choice for men' has never been on the political agenda and never will be for as long as the powers-that-be practice traditional misandry and feminist misandry. Men have always had the gendered social role of protecting and providing for women, and if feminist society continues to have its way men always will. Those who legislate the law of the land will continue to use men as a financial utility to service the interests of women and children by ensuring that men do not have equal fertility rights with women.

And this is what it comes down to. Despite the deceitful feminist claim that men want to control women's fertility, the opposite is actually true. *It is women who control men's fertility.* It is women who decide whether a man becomes a father or not. He cannot impregnate her without her permission (unless by rape) nor force her to carry the child to term against her will.

213

But she can contrive to impregnate herself 'accidentally on purpose' and, although she has used him as an involuntary insemination tool, he is still financially responsible. Alternatively, if she should fall pregnant genuinely by accident, from then on it is her right to choose. She makes the choice to abort or not to abort and he must accept her decision. He is a father *if she says he is*, and he is not a father *if she says he isn't*. The power of decision lies with her from first to last. He doesn't decide whether he is a father or not, she does.

Do you see now why a male oral contraceptive is so urgently needed? Without it, equality will never be achieved in respect of *the most important life decision that anyone can ever make in their lives*: whether or not to become a parent.

Fathers and Paternity Fraud

When the UK government's Child Support Agency DNA-tests to resolve *contested* paternity cases, in 2007/08 almost one in five cases (19%) proved that the alleged father was not in fact the biological father. So the paternity claims made by one in five women in these cases were either deliberately or inadvertently false but, as you would expect, none of the women were prosecuted.
http://www.telegraph.co.uk/news/uknews/2483751/Mothers-wrongly-identifying-fathers-in-Child-Support-Agency-claims.html

There are high levels of disagreement about the prevalence of paternity fraud because, again in keeping with expectation, feminist society is very concerned to protect women at the expense (both financial and emotional) of men. Feminism also has a traditionally sexist attitude about female sexual infidelity; they prefer to believe that it is men who are the sluts that lack commitment. Paternity fraud explodes the myth of female sexual fidelity. It makes women look bad, so naturally feminism is against it. But it is commonplace for paternity tests to show that the man who is named as the father on a child's birth certificate is not actually the biological father.
http://canadiancrc.com/Paternity_Fraud.aspx

214

The Child Support Agency only use DNA testing if they cannot "presume" the parentage of a child. They say:

"By law, we can believe that the person named as the parent of a child is the parent if we have no reason to doubt it. This is called 'presumed parentage'. There are several different ways we can presume parentage . . . We will presume that a person named as the parent of a child is the father if they:

- were married to the child's mother at any time between the date the child was conceived and the date the child was born (if the child has not since been adopted), or

- are named as the father of the child on the child's birth certificate and the child has not been adopted since the birth certificate was issued."

The Child Support Agency will also assume parentage if someone has "been declared the parent in a 'declaration of parentage'."

[What happens when someone denies they are the parent of a child?", The Child Maintenance Service, 2012.]
https://www.gov.uk/government/publications/what-happens-when-someone-denies-they-are-the-parent-of-a-child

The significance of this becomes apparent when we remember that in the UK a man can only acquire *legal rights as a father* if (a) he is named as the father on the birth certificate; (b) he fills out a 'parental responsibility' form; (c) he is married to the mother. So the three ways in which a man can acquire legal rights as a father are also three ways in which the Child Support Agency will "presume" parentage.

In other words, when a woman tells a man that he is going to be a father and he believes her, *if he wants to acquire his rights* as a father he must take one of the three steps which will cause the Child Support Agency to "presume" he is the father. Which means that if he should subsequently come to believe that he is *not the father after all* (e.g. because he and the mother both have black hair and the child is very blonde or because one night the mother drunkenly admits he isn't the father but then retracts her confession the next day or whatever), he has already been classified as a legally responsible parent by the Child Support Agency. Or put another way, if a man initially suspects that he is not the father and doesn't wish to be *presumed* to be the father by the Child Support Agency (and therefore have to pay child support) he must not seek any legal rights regarding the child. Which means that if he is subsequently found to genuinely be the biological father he will have *forfeited his rights*. He will have the financial responsibility but no rights to accompany his responsibility.

As with everything else relating to families, the system is designed to favour women at every turn. The excuse which is invariably given for this is that the system is designed to favour the interests of the children, but the 'interests of the children' seem always to turn out in practice to coincide with the interests of the mother. This is why it is no surprise to discover that the Child Support Agency only use DNA tests if both the alleged father and the mother *agree* to take the test. The 'parent with care' (usually the mother) will also need to agree that the child can take the test, unless the child is 16 or over when they can decide for themselves.

What this amounts to is that during the child's entire childhood (i.e. up to their 16th birthday), a man needs *the mother's permission* for a paternity test from the Child Support Agency. And if she knows she lied to him about his being the father, how likely is she to agree to take the test? His only recourse is to go to law.

Men are made to pay maintenance from the moment a woman names them as the father of her child. The mothers don't even have to pay for the DNA tests when their paternity claim is discovered to be false. If the man turns out to actually be the father, then he pays. If he turns out not to be the father then the state (i.e. taxpayer) pays. But paternity fraud is not just about the financial exploitation of men. The emotional costs may be even higher than the financial costs.

Imagine loving your child for years and then discovering that she/he is not actually your biological child; that you have, in effect, adopted somebody else's child without knowing it because you were lied to by the woman who supposedly loves you. This is why some *men* prefer not to have paternity tests; they know that they couldn't bear the agonising pain of finding out that the child they love is not biologically their own.

When paternity fraud happens within families medical practitioners who discover it (as a result of other medical tests, e.g. a genetic test for cystic fibrosis) keep quiet about it. In Canada, Cheryl Shuman, the director of genetic counselling at the Hospital for Sick Children, was reported as saying:

"Over the years, the hospital has relied on the advice of lawyers and ethicists to develop policies for handling the situation" . . . When a test disqualifies a father, "most women do express some surprise, but then there is a resignation, or an acceptance that they were kind of half anticipating this was going to happen. But then all this is followed very quickly by panic and questions as to whether or not we will betray their confidentiality." If the case involves an expectant mother, Ms. Shuman explained, the hospital's legal obligation is clear: "the developing baby is considered part of the mother and the results of the tests therefore belong to her. After birth, the course of action is less clear, she said, but lawyers advise that the child is to be considered the patient, whose needs trump those of the parents. Since telling the father could trigger a break-up and leave the child without proper support, the hospital keeps the secret."
http://www.canadiancrc.com/newspaper_articles/Globe_and_Mail_Moms_Little_secret_14DEC02.aspx

This means, of course, that in the interests of the child (that it continue to receive "proper support" from *the man who is not the father*) medical practitioners collude with the mother in a fraud perpetrated upon that man. But who gives a stuff about him? This, let's remember, is the advice of "lawyers and ethicists".

Unlike rape, unlike domestic violence, paternity fraud *is* a genuinely sex-specific gendered crime. Women commit it against men, men do not commit it against women. Therefore we can be entirely certain that feminists will do everything they possibly can to downplay and sideline the issue, and they will do everything they can to ensure that women are not prosecuted for it, or if they are prosecuted, that they pay no penalty for it.

Why Do Men Permit Their Own Victimisation?

After everything that I've said in this book so far, the reader might be wondering 'if all of this is true, why on earth have men put up with such shabby treatment for so long? Why do men tolerate this injustice?' A full answer to this would probably require a book in itself but, for the sake of brevity, let's condense the answer to what are probably the four major reasons:

(1) Evolution and traditional sexism strongly inclines men to want to protect women when they appeal for help. Feminism has exploited this relentlessly.

(2) Most men supported sex equality and feminism deceitfully used *the language of sex equality* to pursue a female-supremacist agenda. Most men were naïvely fooled by this.

(3) People are culturally conditioned and they are strongly inclined to accept society's orthodox beliefs, whatever those beliefs happen to be at the time. Most people, most of the time, believe whatever they hear most often.

(4) We live under *government by acquiescence*, not government by consent. People go along with things because they don't feel they have the power to change anything.

218

Now let's clarify these four reasons.

(1) Evolution has given men a genetic predisposition to protect women because it was those communities who protected the people with wombs that were best able to survive to the next generation. The cultural norms of society then reinforced this genetic inheritance over many centuries in which men were raised to believe that they had a duty to protect women. There are endless examples, from medieval romances about Sir Galahad to Hollywood movies in the twentieth century.

Men's gendered social role to value women and children above themselves is so strict that it has been used to emotionally coerce men into volunteering for war, as with the poster "Men of Britain! Will you stand this?" (1915) http://lowres-picturecabinet.com.s3-eu-west-1.amazonaws.com/109/main/1/378943.jpg This poster specifically mentions in large text that "78 women and children were killed and 228 women and children were wounded" in a German air raid. This is followed by the imperative: "ENLIST NOW". The gendered imperative could hardly be any clearer, men must die to protect the lives of women and children.

Feminism has ruthlessly exploited this traditional sexism by appealing for an *ever larger societal provision* for the protection of women because of their 'special needs'. Double-standards about sexual consent? It's for women's protection. Double-standards about domestic violence? It's for women's protection. Double-standards about maternity and paternity leave? It's because women have special needs. Double-standards about personal accountability? It's because women have special needs. It's the oldest trick in the book and it's still devastatingly effective.

This is why feminists constantly exaggerate male physical strength, male physical violence, and male lack of emotionality. Actual men are painfully aware of their own physical and emotional vulnerability but feminism, which is so wilfully ignorant about men, seems to view all men as a mixture of Mike Tyson and Genghis Khan. Feminism constantly casts womankind in the role of the damsel in distress, squealing in terror at the menacing males that surround her. She is easily bruised, forever on the verge of tears, incessantly appealing to politicians and social institutions to protect her from the predatory dominant male. This takes a traditional woman's weapon for manipulating men and orchestrates it into an extensive political strategy and, sadly, men seem to fall for the old routine every time.

(2) Feminism has always made cynical and hypocritical use of the language of sex equality. Many of the claims for greater sex equality made by women in the 1960s and 1970s were perfectly legitimate and recognised as such by fair-minded men who endorsed sex equality. Traditional society had a great deal of misogyny in it and men acknowledged this, favouring equality for the sexes. When someone said there should be equal pay for equal work, fair-minded pro-equality men answered yes of course there should. When someone said if both husband and wife went out to work to earn money, then both of them should share the domestic chores, fair-minded pro-equality men answered yes of course they should. There were plenty of demands made about the justice of women having equality with men to which fair-minded pro-equality men answered yes.

So why was feminism's use of the language of sex equality cynical and hypocritical? Because what was missing from all this, of course, was any consideration of *men having equality with women*. It had already been so long established in people minds (from the suffragette movement in the Edwardian period) that the issue of sex equality was all about *women's* liberation and *women's* equality with men, that feminism gave no thought to *men's* liberation and *men's* equality with women. No feminists were saying that a single-sex military conscription was a clear case of misandry. No feminists were saying that men shouldn't have to shoulder the burden of financial responsibility and should have equal access to the domestic sphere as house-husbands because to deny them this was misandry. No feminists were saying that the rape laws should be revised so that rape wasn't defined in terms of penetration by a penis (and therefore defined as a male crime) but should instead cover all acts of coerced sex including those perpetrated by female rapists. No feminists were saying that it was every bit as serious a crime for a woman to hit a man as it was for a man to hit a woman. Nor were they acknowledging that women can be just as violent as men. The word 'misandry' was never used.

But the phrase 'sex equality' was used over and over, and it garnered the support of all those fair-minded pro-equality men who were misled into believing that feminism was actually about sex equality because that's what feminists kept *saying* it was about. By the end of the 1970s the terms 'women's liberation' and 'feminism' and 'sex equality' had all become synonymous in the public mind. Men supported feminism because, foolishly and mistakenly, they thought that by doing so they were supporting sex equality.

(3) People like to think of themselves as having a certain level of sophistication in their thinking. They hold to the fond belief that their opinions are the result of evidence and argument. They like to feel that they have a mind of their own and that, when presented with the available evidence and the available arguments, they decide for themselves what they think. It would be wonderful if people really did have this kind of independence of mind and really did insist upon arguing their own evidence-based opinions. But if this were as true of people as they like to believe it is of themselves, wouldn't there be much less conformity of opinion and much more cultural dissent?

In reality, how many people believe what other people believe *because other people believe it?* How many people believe whatever their friends believe, whatever their co-workers believe, whatever the television tells them to believe? People are social creatures and they want to be popular, they want to fit in, they want to belong. If a hundred years ago most men believed that a woman's place was in the home, wasn't this because those men lived in a society in which the people around them believed it? If most men today believe that the

221

idea of a woman's place being in the home is an act of misogynist oppression, isn't this because these men live in a society in which the people around them believe it? People's beliefs and values are culturally conditioned. They are drawn toward conformism.

Cultural orthodoxy has a much more powerful Press Agent than non-conformity. It's a matter of repetition. If a person hears *the same point of view* expressed repeatedly over time from numerous different sources (television, radio, movies, books, magazines, newspapers, politicians, academics, co-workers, etc.) then it's very difficult for them to resist believing it. They hear it everywhere so surely it must be true. The sad truth is that most people's opinions are *not* the result of bringing their own independent thinking to bear on the available evidence and argument. Instead, *they believe on the basis of repetition*. The more something is repeated, and the greater the number of sources from which it is heard, the more seemingly plausible it becomes. This is what I mean when I say that most people, most of the time, believe whatever they hear most often.

Men today have lived their entire lives under the incessant propaganda machine of feminism. For example, patriarchy *theory* is believed as if it were *factual history,* not merely one interpretation of history. If you asked a thousand people, did men historically oppress women? How many would treat the idea of male oppression as anything other than an indisputable fact? But if you challenged them with the arguments and counter-evidence in the first two chapters of this book, how many of those thousand people would be in a position to rationally defend patriarchy theory against the arguments and counter-evidence? How many would bother to try? Instead, they would simply ignore everything said in those two chapters and respond by parroting what they have been taught to believe, with all the usual assumptions and presuppositions in place. They would go on thinking what they have been told to think. Patriarchy theory is believed on the basis of its being 'received wisdom'. It's thought of as being something that 'everybody knows'.

The conventional response to this is to say to the non-conformist 'what arrogance, how can you think that you are right and everyone else is wrong?' But this response merely confirms the point I'm making. The person who responds in this way is treating what 'everyone else' thinks as being true simply because 'everyone else' thinks it. As if the conformist position can't possibly be wrong. The man in the past who thought that a woman's place was in the home would have defended *that* opinion in exactly the same way.

A great many men submit to their own victimisation in contemporary society on this basis. They don't defend themselves against feminist oppression because *they believe what their culture tells them to believe*, and that excludes even acknowledging the existence of feminist oppression. So, instead of defending themselves, instead of standing up and answering back, they live on their knees and believe that as 'men' everything is their fault and they are very, very sorry.

(4) Another fond belief held by many people is that we in the West live under a system of democracy. 'Democracy' means the rule of the people, where the people themselves are sovereign and directly exercise political power. Unfortunately, 'democracy' is popularly and incorrectly conflated with the practice of having regular elections. Yet, as we know from long experience, all that elections do is to give the electorate a choice between which of two or three largely indistinguishable professional political parties are going to rule over them and make their decisions for them. This is a long way distant from genuine democracy. But what can the average person do about it? Nothing. So people go along with the system because they're stuck with it. This is *government by acquiescence*.

This means that if both or all of the political parties that are in a position to get elected endorse the same ideology (as, in fact, they all do in the case of feminism), then people acquiesce to that ideology. If they vote at all, then by default they vote for that ideology because all the parties endorse it. In the UK feminism is so entrenched in the establishment that the national government doesn't have a Minister for Equality, it has a "Minister for Women and Equalities". The very title of the minister with special responsibility for equality *implies the exclusion of men and issues of misandry*. The ministry understands sex equality in these terms:

"The Minister for Women and Equalities has overall responsibility for policy on women, sexual orientation and transgender equality and is responsible for cross-government equality strategy and legislation."
https://www.gov.uk/government/ministers/minister-for-women-and-equalities--2

So all women, gay men, and transgender men are included. But those heterosexual male bastards are excluded. This is the *government* telling us this. And this is supposed to be democracy? Well, *some* of the people are represented. Just not those heterosexual male ones. And you know why not, don't you, it's because of the feminist belief that there are no equality issues for heterosexual men. They're officially classified as the privileged, advantaged ones. This is *patriarchy theory enthroned in the state*. When men permit government by acquiescence, they permit their own exclusion. So why don't they complain? In fact, some men do complain (e.g. A Voice For Men http://www.avoiceformen.com/) but they are invariably and vehemently dismissed as lunatic fringe MRA women-haters. Who dismisses them thus? Feminism does.

Most men acquiesce in their own exclusion and victimisation because they are *not allowed* to complain about it. Feminism is a licence to bitch, in contrast to the silenced male. Constant complaint is now held to be a woman's prerogative; her right. But complaint is forbidden to men by both traditional sexism and feminist sexism. The former forbids it on the grounds that men complaining is a sign of weakness and a 'real' man should be the strong silent type, stoically enduring life's travails. The latter forbids it on the grounds that only women suffer sexist oppression, therefore men have nothing to complain about. A man who protests about misandrist victimisation will be insulted as a puny wimp by the traditionally sexist and as a self-deceiving fool by sexist feminists. The reviews of this book will no doubt provide some evidence of this double misandry.

The Male Feminist

It is easy for a woman to be a feminist if she has been socially conditioned by the culture she lives in to be thoughtless and uncaring toward men as a sex. All she needs is to be conceited enough to *believe* feminism's absurdly flattering positive gender-stereotype of herself, and sufficiently ignorant of men to *believe* feminism's negative gender-stereotype of the men in her life. But what about male feminists? Surely they must know from their own direct mental experience of themselves as male human beings that feminism lies about men. Why, we might ask, would anyone sign up for a lifetime of self-loathing? I would suggest two reasons for this.

The first we have already touched upon. People are strongly inclined toward conformity. No matter how ridiculous their society's beliefs and values, people will adopt those beliefs and values in order to fit in and belong. A couple of hundred years ago there were white people in America who held to the view that black people weren't people at all but animals. Deranged as this view may appear from outside of that culture, when people are inside a culture they are highly susceptible to internalizing its beliefs and values. And just as a white slave-owner could be *having a conversation* with their black slave whilst simultaneously conforming to the belief that the person they were *in conversation with* wasn't really a person, male feminists have internalized feminism's demonisation of men to such an extent that they can ignore all the actual realities about themselves and about other men which contradict feminist beliefs.

How does the male feminist rationalize his personal and ideological contradictions? True, he has never personally committed domestic violence but, hang on, he has shouted at his wife and that kind of aggressive bullying counts as domestic violence if men do it, so he is guilty after all.

True, he has never personally raped anyone but, hang on, can he be absolutely sure that every time he had sex with his wife she definitely consented? His own consent is not an issue, of course, but if he can't be absolutely sure that his wife hasn't in the past had sex with him when she'd really rather not have, well then, he's a rapist. Besides, he was erotically aroused by those scantily clad female dancers on the television last night which proves that he has a 'male sexuality' and is therefore a potential rapist.

True, he is himself a pacifist but everyone knows that its always men who start all the wars because he's heard that a hundred thousand times, so his own pacifism does not excuse 'men' of this charge. Nor does it make any difference if women are amongst the power-players in political administrations that take their countries into war, like Margaret Thatcher or Condoleezza Rice, because these women are trapped within 'masculine systems' and the 'masculine' is by definition warmongering even though he himself is a pacifist.

All observations of reality which contradict feminist theory can be rationalized away by the male feminist. Culturally orthodox beliefs take precedence over evidence where conformism is concerned and we should not underestimate the astonishing power of conformism.

There is a famous old adage, usually attributed to either Abraham Lincoln or PT Barnum (probably apocryphally in both cases), that: 'You can fool all of the people some of the time, and you can fool some of the people all of the time, but you can't fool all of the people all of the time'. When this is quoted the emphasis is generally on the last contention, the optimistic one, that you can't fool all of the people all of the time. But when it comes to contemporary politics we should remember that the two earlier contentions are also importantly true. *You can fool all of the people some of the time, and you can fool some of the people all of the time.* Over the last forty years feminism has, on a daily basis, proven this to be true. In particular, the male feminist is one of the people who can be fooled all of the time.

But there is another reason that motivates male feminism which is just as strong as the need to conform. Whenever you meet a male feminist he always seems to speak of 'men' as if he himself weren't male in quite the same way that they are. And this is the clue. The whole point of being a male feminist is to *disassociate oneself* from the male guilt-object.

It's not that difficult to understand. Imagine if you lived in a society which blamed liberals for everything bad that ever happens. You might be quick to condemn liberals at every opportunity in order to let everyone know that you are not a liberal. The more frequently you condemn liberals and all their works, the more you emphasize *how far removed* from liberals you are yourself.

Or take an example that requires no imagination. If you are a student on a contemporary American university campus, you are living in an academic environment that is obsessive-compulsive in its anti-Americanism. You are immersed in an academia which blames America for all the woes of the world. Islamic terrorism? That's the fault of US foreign policy. Famine in Africa? That's the fault of American corporate capitalism. Riots in Egypt? That's the fault of American imperialism. And so on. But you are yourself an American. So you make damn sure that you are quick to condemn America at every opportunity, you are loud in your denouncements of all things American and make sure that everyone knows that you are not a part of all these American crimes but rather a vocal opponent of them. This is why American students are so often more anti-American than anyone else. They must put distance between themselves and the object they have been taught to hate.

It's the same with male feminists. They have been born the guilty sex. They are personally tainted by testosterone and the Y chromosome. They may even have been born heterosexual and are therefore guilty of having sexual feelings toward women, with all the vile sexual objectification that this entails. They were born guilty of the male gaze and male subjectivity.

What to do? They must disassociate themselves from all this wickedness, they must get as far away from being what feminism says men are as they possibly can. But, unless they

227

are psychologically transsexual, there is only one way they can do this. They must make sure that they are the first to denounce men. They must make it clear to everyone that, although they have had the bad taste to have been born male, they have nonetheless overcome this bad start in life and are now eager to condemn and reject all things male. They must be zealous in their feminism in order to demonstrate just how different they are from those guilty unreconstructed men.

Male feminists are psychologically very damaged. These 'Uncle Tom' sycophants have embraced a belief in their own inferiority because they think that it is the only way that they can exorcise the demon of maleness from themselves. Male feminists want to degrade themselves and all other men as a way of apologising for having been born male. It is pitiable.

Chapter 5

Wielding the Big Stick

For those of us who have lived through feminism since the 1970s, it's been noticeable how the primary feminist obsessions have changed over the years. There was a time when feminists used to talk about how 'phallocentric' everything was; tall buildings, streetlights, pens standing upright in pen-holders, more or less anything vertical. They had cock on the brain and used to see phalluses everywhere.

That was replaced by feminist activities which gloried in being gynocentric and the word phallocentric dropped off the radar. Once upon a time the workplace was the major battleground of feminist struggle and later pornography seemed to be the issue of overriding importance.

But these days there are two issues which are so prominent in feminist activism that they deserve a chapter all to themselves. Together they constitute the big stick with which contemporary feminism constantly beats men. They are extremely sensitive issues, which makes it enormously difficult for anyone to argue against feminism on these topics without being viewed as some sort of immoral monster of bad-taste.

Feminists are accustomed to pushing against an open door because it has always been their claim that anyone who argues against their ideology is thereby attacking women, and we live in a society in which nobody wants to be seen as attacking women. But that attitude goes double for these two issues. That's what makes them so valuable to feminism as a political weapon. That's what makes them the big stick.

They are domestic violence and rape.

Domestic Violence

Before we get to grips with this issue, there is a point that deserves to made first. As I explained at the very beginning of this book (in the section "What is Sexism?"), in opposing sexism we are addressing those injustices which are created by and/or enforced by society's constructs of gender. Sexism is the societal imposition of gendered identities and social roles, where cultural norms psychologically condition women and men to see themselves in a certain way and constrain the social roles which women and men can occupy.

But feminism's quite different project of pursuing a sex-war means that they treat *any female suffering* at male hands to be sexism. So if personal violence between two individuals involves violence by the male against the female, then feminism counts this *as sexism*. But it isn't. It's a personal conflict between individuals. Not all suffering experienced by women is misogyny. It's only sexism if it's created or enforced by society. This is why feminism has to fantasise about a systemic 'male *culture*' of violence against women and fantasize about the systemic oppression of women through 'rape *culture*', in an attempt to classify any and all female suffering as misogyny.

When men die as combat soldiers in a war, there is no question that this is the result of a socially enforced gendered social role, especially if they are conscripts, so there is also no question that it is misandry. But if a married couple have a quarrel and fight? Why classify *that* as sexism? Men hitting women isn't a socially enforced gender role, on the contrary, as I shall show in what follows it has always been *socially disapproved of* in the strongest terms. It is an issue of criminal law, it is not intrinsically an issue of sexism. Yet feminism has convinced people to believe that a personal quarrel between a man and a woman *is* sexism, but that men having a manly duty to sign up as a soldier or be held in societal contempt as a unmanly coward somehow *isn't* sexism.

Nor does feminism classify domestic violence as sexism if it is perpetrated by a violent woman against a male victim. Feminism cannot even apply *it's own attribution of sexism to domestic violence* both ways, female on male as well as male on female. After all, fairness and impartiality are not the way to win a sex-war. So it is worth remembering, as I now discuss the issue of domestic violence from a sex-equalitarian perspective, that we should not make the mistake of thinking that *the violence* itself is sexism. The chief element of sexism in this issue is the feminist social construct of gender which categorises domestic violence as a 'male crime'.

Traditional society viewed what is now called 'domestic violence' solely in terms of the crime of 'wife-beating'. It's a very old-fashioned phrase that reflects the perennial concern to protect women. This view of domestic violence was inevitable given the gender stereotypes used in traditional society. Women were the 'gentle sex' and the 'weaker sex'; they were delicate little flowers. Men, in contrast, were butch two-fisted tough guys. So the traditional assumption regarding domestic violence was that no dainty girly could possibly assault a big strong man, and even if she did it couldn't possibly hurt him. The only public *concern* over domestic violence was concern *for women*.

Moreover, under traditional sexism, men who assaulted women were vilified for their failure to be a 'proper' man. Men had a duty to protect the 'little woman'. The man who had so far failed to protect a woman as to commit violence against her was pilloried and scorned as a cad and a bounder, he was a coward and a bully despised by all. He would be told to 'pick on someone his own size'. His crime was thought disgraceful, as it would have been if an adult had assaulted a child. The stereotypes of the physically 'strong' man and the physically 'weak' woman, regardless of the actual physical capacities of the two people involved, classified male violence against females as *dishonourable*. This traditional attitude (which is still around today, especially amongst 'unreconstructed' men) held to the belief that any man who hit a woman had broken the rules of manhood. He was a failed man.

Feminism, of course, claims the total opposite of this. It likes to portray traditional society as a place which condoned wife-beating and where men were regularly encouraged to beat their womenfolk. In order to maintain this misrepresentation feminism has to ignore the actual reality of how most domestic violence occurs, where heated and messy domestic quarrels spill over into physical violence. Instead, feminism paints a picture of some middle-class Victorian patriarch imperiously thrashing his wife with a rattan cane every Sunday afternoon after church, or of some working-class man who gets drunk every evening and when he arrives home punches hell out of his wife before going to bed. Feminism trades in sexist clichés.

But the claim that traditional society endorsed and approved of domestic violence against women is instantly disproved if we simply recognise how the term 'wife-beater' was not used as a compliment, it was used *in condemnation* of the 'wife-beater'. Traditional society's true attitude is expressed in the disapprobation carried in the phrase.

Something else that feminism has to do, if its theory of traditional violence is to be maintained, is to separate (allegedly) legally sanctioned domestic violence from any other kinds of legally sanctioned violence. It has to do this in order to ignore the huge quantities of legally sanctioned violence that men suffered. For example, Anthony Trollope begins his novel "The Bertrams" (1859) with:

"A man who beats his wife is shocking to us, and a colonel who cannot manage his soldiers without having them beaten is nearly equally so."
https://ebooks.adelaide.edu.au/t/trollope/anthony/bertrams/chapter1.html

Men who lived their lives, not in the domestic home, but in the army barracks suffered officially sanctioned and legal floggings that were hideously brutal, sometimes resulting in their deaths. There are numerous accounts from the early 19th century of men sufferings hundreds of lashes in a public flogging http://www.napoleon-series.org/military/organization/c_murder.html#floggings and these were not hole-in-the-corner beatings hidden away behind closed doors, these were performed in front of a parade ground of soldiers as a deterrent, to terrify the other men into obedience. Such punishments were not rare. In the British army 894 men were officially recorded as having been flogged in the year 1838, the following year 843 men were flogged, the year after that 874 men were flogged, the year after that 925 men were flogged, the year after that 862 men were flogged. These punishments were for breaches of discipline of a relatively trivial nature like theft and insubordination (soldiers were hanged for serious crimes) and the severity of the flogging might depend largely upon the personality of the officer in charge.

By the middle of the 19th century there were calls for the abolition of corporal punishment for soldiers because it was so barbaric. In response, in 1846 Lord Russell spoke in parliament on a reduction to the number of lashes that could be legally inflicted upon soldiers. His Lordship said:

"The House should know what is the existing regulation with respect to corporal punishment in the army. By the articles of war, no offender convicted before a general court-martial is liable to be sentenced to any corporal punishment exceeding 200 lashes; the punishment of an offender convicted before a district or garrison court-martial cannot exceed 150 lashes; and if convicted before a regimental court-martial the punishment cannot exceed 100 lashes. Now the Duke of Wellington, in taking this subject into consideration, has given directions to the officers to whom the duty appertains of ordering such courts-martial, that by no court-martial whatever, whether general, district, garrison, or regimental, shall any greater punishment be inflicted than fifty lashes. This is a very considerable diminution, and this the Commander-in-Chief has ordered to be carried into effect throughout the army."
http://hansard.millbanksystems.com/commons/1846/aug/07/flogging-in-the-army

In the eight years preceding Lord Russell's speech 6,339 soldiers had been officially recorded as having been flogged (I say 'officially recorded' because who knows how many men suffered impromptu beatings unofficially and unrecorded).

These were the conditions of life for many men, but this is not the kind of history that feminism is ever interested in. Historical facts of this sort do not promote the idea of woman-as-victim, so they are worthless to the feminist agenda and are ignored. But it is worth remembering what corporal punishment has meant for *men* in the past when you hear a feminist speaking of how society used to sanction the corporal punishment of women.

Feminists go to great lengths to find anecdotal evidence for 'legal' wife-beating. There is a website called "British Women's Emancipation since the Renaissance" (BWER) which, to be fair, is far better than most feminist websites in that the author, Helena Wojtczak, is clearly making an effort to compile legitimate evidence for the history of British women that she wishes to present. She is not just relying on the usual repetition of feminist mythology.

Yet, even here, the contradiction in feminism's claims about legally sanctioned wife-beating is apparent. BWER has a page of 19th century press cuttings of men being prosecuted in the law courts and being sent off to prison for the crime of beating their wife. http://www.historyofwomen.org/wifebeatcuttings.html These are presumably offered as evidence of how commonplace it was for men to beat their wives. But let's not overlook the fact that these are press reports of men being *prosecuted and sent to prison*. So wife-beating was *not* legally sanctioned. As BWER admits, people often believed it to be the 'common law' that men could beat their wives, but it was not the actual law, *as her own evidence proves*.

Wojtczak also has the honesty to acknowledge the traditional rationale behind the 'common law' sanction of men punishing their wives, that as husbands were held legally responsible for what their wives did, they were also given the necessary authority to fulfill that responsibility. As she says: "the 'old law' was applicable for 'correction' of someone who has misbehaved in such a way that the man in question has to answer for it publicly". http://www.historyofwomen.org/wifebeatingthumb.html

So when taking an historical perspective on domestic violence we should not gullibly believe feminism's usual re-writing of history. We should remember that (a) there was a strong disapproval expressed toward 'wife-beating'; (b) when it was culturally condoned by some people, this was more by custom than by law, and it was a consequence of the husband being held accountable for his wife's actions; (c) the legally sanctioned violence done to men in the past would often far exceed the violence done to women (e.g. compare a wife living under the tyranny of her husband to a seaman in the navy living under the tyranny of his ship's captain). Feminism is guilty of perpetuating the traditional *sexist double-standard about human pain* in the way that it focuses concern *solely* on women's pain, and in the way that it is only interested in 'gendered' violence (i.e. violence done by men to women).

There is one more consideration that we should not overlook: women's domestic violence committed against men. Here the double-standard is very conspicuous. Not only did traditional society despise the man who was a 'wife-beater' for his breach of the social construct of 'masculinity' in failing to protect women, men were also held to be to blame for domestic violence of which *they were the victim*. A man who was beaten by a woman was in a situation that was utterly contrary to everything that men were required to be. The idea of a man tolerating violent abuse from a women was seen as such an unforgivable failure of 'masculinity' that there wasn't even a name for it. Husbands were supposed to have authority over their wives, so a man who permitted his wife to abuse him had, once again, failed as a man. Any man in this situation couldn't possibly admit to it. If he was being 'beaten up by a girl' then it was considered to be his fault for not being a 'real man'. The shame and the blame were his for allowing it.

The classic example of this was the 'Skimington ride' https://en.wikipedia.org/wiki/Skimmington or 'Skimington riding' which was a noisy parade conducted by the whole community (e.g. a rural village) with lots of shouting and banging on pots and pans as a ritual expression of the community's censure and denunciation of a married couple. It was intended to humiliate the miscreants with ridicule. It was seen as having a moral purpose in that it upbraided the married couple for their bad example to the young and punished them for their disturbance of good social order. So what had the married couple done to deserve this procession of collective censure by the whole community? They were guilty of an act(s) of being quarrelsome or disputatious in a struggle for domestic ascendancy where the man had adopted a submissive or acquiescent role. The "History of Lyme Regis" (Roberts, 1834) gives three specific reasons. http://www.darkdorset.co.uk/skimmington_riding It says that:

"The following are the principal causes for riding the Skimmington:

(i) When a man and his wife quarrel and he gives up to her.

(ii) When a woman is unfaithful to her husband, and he patiently submits without resenting her conduct.

(iii) Any grossly licentious conduct on the part of married persons."

In short, this was the public shaming of a married couple where the husband had not exercised control over his wife but had permitted her to dominate him. There is a wall frieze in Montacute House in Somerset, England, depicting a Skimmington ride. It depicts a hen-pecked husband whose wife catches him drinking when he's supposed to be minding the baby, so she hits him on the head with a shoe. The scene is witnessed by a neighbour and the abused man is punished by the community with the Skimmington ride. The man is paraded around the village on a pole while being made to play a flute. [For more on the Skimmington ride see "Skimmington Revisited", Dr MJ George, Dewar Research]
http://www.dewar4research.org/docs/skim-revisited.pdf

The Skimmington (also called charivaris, from the French) was used for other infractions of domestic custom as well, and these included the offence of a man beating his wife. Yes, that's right, not only could a husband be publicly shamed for being the *victim* of domestic violence, he could also be publicly shamed for being the *perpetrator* of domestic violence. Bryan Palmer offers two examples of this in his academic paper "Discordant Music: Charivaris and Whitecapping in nineteenth century North America" p.11. (1978) and he recounts the derogatory songs sung by those performing this 'rough justice'. http://journals.hil.unb.ca/index.php/LLT/article/view/2381/2785 One of the songs goes:

"There is a man in this place
Has beat his wife!! (*forte*. A pause)
Has beat his wife!! (*fortissimo*)
It is a very great shame and disgrace
To all who live in this place
It is indeed upon my life!!"

Men who were the victims of female domestic violence in the past had to keep it a secret (just as many men don't report their victimisation these days) because if they admitted to being bullied by the 'weaker sex', traditional misandry would punish them with ridicule. This cultural derision toward male victims of domestic violence, the idea that a man being beaten by a woman is 'funny', was typified in the type of popular humour that would laugh at a puny husband being menaced by a powerful wife, usually with a kitchen rolling pin in her hand. (e.g. this clip https://www.youtube.com/watch?v=1hAIKSLKTjg from a Harold Lloyd silent movie) The weakling male who is smashed over the head with a rolling pin is an object of humour. It serves him right for not being a proper man, the weakling. People laughed out loud.

Male subservience to women was never viewed sympathetically. He was the butt of the joke. (e.g. this http://sullydish.files.wordpress.com/2013/02/vinegar_henpecked.jpg Edwardian picture postcard.) You can see the same thing in Benny Hill sketches from the 1970s and 1980s where the cowed and browbeaten 'henpecked' husband is menaced and thumped by his harridan wife. Men being hit by women has always been considered a socially acceptable source of comedy. What's even more unforgivable, is that *it still is*. (e.g. this contemporary cartoon of two politicians in Australia, a husband and wife, who made the news for an incident of violence) http://www.sauer-thompson.com/archives/opinion/2008/06/17/Neale%2BDellaBossa.jpg

Even today people sneer at men for being 'pussywhipped'. The 'pussywhipped' male is modern society's version of the 'henpecked' husband. Nor has the misandrist double-standard about domestic violence really changed where popular entertainment is concerned. For example, the Hollywood movie "My Super Ex-Girlfriend" is a comedy in which Uma Thurman is a superhero with super-strength, etc., who repeatedly uses violence against her human boyfriend when he wants to break-up with her. It was a fairly successful mainstream movie. But what if Lois Lane wanted to break-up with Superman and was too terrified to do so because he would beat her up if she tried it? Would that be funny? Would that be a suitable subject for a comedy movie?

It's important to understand the real double-standard about domestic violence in traditional society, because feminism has always shared and exploited the traditionally sexist position. It has spent decades propagandizing the social constructs of the violent male and the non-violent female, presenting all domestic violence as one-way traffic. It, too, treats women's violence against men as something for which men are to blame. Back in the early 1990s I used to have discussions on domestic violence with feminists at university in which the dialogue would follow a definite pattern. It would always go this way:

Me: Women's domestic violence against men should be treated equally with men's domestic violence against women.

Feminist: Rubbish! Women don't commit domestic violence, it's a male crime.

Me: Are you saying that no women ever commit violence of any kind against their domestic partners?

Feminist: Perhaps there might be a tiny, tiny minority of cases

238

where women are violent but that's nothing compared to the huge amount of violence men commit against women.

Me: But in a case where the woman is violent against the man, would you condemn her equally with a man who committed the same crime?

Feminist: Ah, but *what did he do to provoke her?!*

If we'd been speaking of a man hitting a woman, no feminist would ever have asked: what did *she* do to provoke *him*? The question would have been considered so unspeakably misogynist as to be, well, unspeakable. And no feminist would have seen any need for such a question. For feminism his *being male* is a sufficient explanation of his violence. His maleness explains why he was violent because 'that's what men are like'. No further explanation is needed because biological determinism will do. Men are just naturally violent, that's why he hit her.

But when a woman hits a man this is entirely contrary to feminism's positive gender-stereotype of women. Nurturant, compassionate, emotionally caring people do not commit violence. Therefore an explanation of *why* she hit him is required. Fortunately, an explanation is readily to hand: he must have provoked her beyond endurance, he must have *made* her do it. So *her* violence is *his* fault. To make domestic violence consistent with feminist social constructs of gender all that is necessary is for them to blame the guilt-object. Make all the violence his fault, regardless of who actually commits it. So if *he* hits *her*, it's his fault and if *she* hits *him*, it's his fault.

Erin Pizzey started the first women's refuge in the UK in 1971 which has since grown into a national organisation called Refuge. She has spent her life in the cause of protecting battered women. So shouldn't she be hailed as a champion of the women's movement? But, when Pizzey spoke openly about most domestic violence being reciprocal and how women are equally as capable of violence as men, Pizzey became a hate-figure for feminists. It didn't matter what she personally had

done for women, she was *ideologically unsound*. She did not endorse the feminist line.
http://www.dailymail.co.uk/home/search.html?s=&authornamef=Erin+Pizzey

She received death threats from feminists. She was thrown out of the organisation that she had started. If you type "Erin Pizzey" into the search engine of the Refuge website, it produces "No Results". She isn't even mentioned on their "History" page which states (under a list of bullet points dubiously called "Facts") that *"Refuge* opened the world's first women's refuge in 1971". [my italics] Not *Erin Pizzey* opened it. She has been airbrushed out of the picture. For feminists, it's not the truth that matters, it's the ideology.

The presumption of male guilt is so routine that it is generally taken for granted even by the police. In Oklahoma City on 15th February 2014, a mother and daughter had a fight outside a movie theatre. Nair Rodriguez slapped her 19 year old daughter and someone phoned the police. In response to the domestic violence call, the police arrived and promptly *arrested the husband/father*, Luis Rodriguez. He had not been involved in the violent argument between the two women but he was, unfortunately, the man. Five officers restrained him on the ground and pepper-sprayed his face. Due to a heart condition, Mr Rodriguez died. http://edition.cnn.com/2014/02/26/justice/oklahoma-arrest-death-video/ In the media reports of his death, no one mentioned the sexism of *assuming that the man must be the criminal*. Mr Rodriguez could reasonably be said to have been murdered by misandry.

The traditional misandrist double-standard over domestic violence has grown much worse now that it has sexist feminism to endorse and reinforce it. In the UK an experiment set up by the Mankind Initiative demonstrated that people passing by will intervene to protect a woman being violently abused by a man but they smile and laugh at a man being violently abused by a woman. The bigotry and hypocrisy of feminism is written all over their grinning faces. https://www.youtube.com/watch?v=u3PgH86OyEM

It is the same in the USA. This ABC "What Would You Do?

video https://www.youtube.com/watch?v=LIFAd4YdQks shows a woman abusing a man in public. Some people in the video *approve* of women being violent to men. They take it for granted that if a man is violently abused by a woman, then *he must have done something to deserve it.*

In Russia feminists have tried to prove their social construct of gendered male violence with a video showing men getting frustrated by a vending machine that doesn't dispense its product. When the man hits the machine to try to dislodge the product that he has just paid for, the machine plays a filmed recording of a woman weeping. The video begins ominously with the text: "Every seventh murder on our planet occurs within families. And in most cases its all men's fault. How hard is it to drive a man wild? Well, not hard at all." It then shows men getting frustrated with the faulty vending machine. https://www.youtube.com/watch?v=Bfsq9X9C5rY

The entirely natural reaction that *both women and men* might respond with, of hitting the vending machine to knock loose the item which wasn't dispensed, is apparently taken as being proof of inherent male violence against women. (In fact, when hitting the machine produces a filmed image on the machine's screen of a woman cowering in fear, the men stop and look bewildered.)

I don't mention this solely to show the sheer duplicity of a feminist's idea of experimental research, in trying to link murder with vending machine frustration, but also to show how far they will go in their constant propagandising of their negative gender-stereotype of the 'violent male'. Yet perhaps what is most revealing about this video is the way that the female pedestrians passing by *react* to the filmed recording of the woman cowering in fear on the machine's screen *as if she were a real woman* rather than a recording; as if the men slapping the vending machine were actually *slapping the woman* on the screen. Feminist beliefs about 'violence against women' are so entrenched in contemporary society that people have become entirely divorced from reality.

But so much research has been emerging recently to show that women can be as violent in their relationships as men that a few feminist's at least are slowly being forced to revise their view of domestic violence by acknowledging male victims and female perpetrators. Even so, feminists have not changed their *political position* on domestic violence. They can't. Patriarchy theory doesn't permit them to. The theory requires that gender violence be (mis)understood as a part of the systemic male oppression of women. Evidence to the contrary notwithstanding. http://www.batteredmen.com/index.htm

As long ago as 1999 research by the UK government Home Office "found relatively high levels of male victimisation, to the extent that men appear to be at equal risk to women of domestic assault (4.2% of both sexes reported an assault in the last year)" although they qualified this finding by saying that women were more likely to suffer "serious assault" or "be repeatedly assaulted". [Mirrlees-Black, 1999, "Domestic Violence: Findings from a new British Crime Survey self-completion questionnaire", Home Office Research Study 19.]

In 2004 the government Home office quoted the British Crime Survey: "The BCS estimates that one in four (26%) women and 17 per cent of men aged 16 to 59 have experienced at least one incident of non-sexual domestic abuse, threat or force since they were 16." They also said: "Thirty-one per cent of female victims and 63 per cent of male victims had not told anyone other than the survey about the worst incident of domestic violence that they had suffered during the last year." [Walby & Allen, "Domestic violence, sexual assault and stalking: Findings from the British Crime Survey" Home Office Research Study 276.]

As more research began to take male victims and female perpetrators into account, the statistics increasingly reflected the truth about domestic violence as being something which both women and men commit, and both women and men suffer. By 2010 even the arch-establishment newspaper The Guardian was reporting that government statistics and the British Crime Survey were admitting that men made up about

40% of domestic violence victims between 2004 and 2009, and were as high as 45% of victims in 2007-08. Yet feminists had been claiming for decades that this was an exclusively 'male crime' perpetrated against females, which was therefore a 'women's issue'.

If even The Guardian http://www.theguardian.com/society/2010/sep/05/men-victims-domestic-violence has become aware that female domestic violence perpetrated against male victims is roughly equal to male domestic violence perpetrated against female victims, you might think that *everyone* was aware of it. But the mainstream feminist position still clings desperately to patriarchy theory by fudging the issue with comments like 'although men can be abused too, in most cases it is women who are abused by men' or words to that effect. Truth and justice have no place in feminism.

The Crime Survey of England and Wales 2011/2012 revealed that 1.2 million victims of domestic violence were women and 800,000 were men. What would the real figures be if it was adjusted for male under-reporting? But after more than forty years of feminist hypocrisy men are finally beginning to speak up for themselves. Even in a bastion of traditional masculinity like Northern Ireland, men are finally speaking out. In December 2013 the Belfast Telegraph wrote of the increase in domestic violence reports by men:

"Domestic violence against men in Northern Ireland has increased by more than 40% in nine years – and that's just reported incidents. PSNI figures reveal that the figure reached a record of 2,525 male victims in 2012/13, up 259 cases on the year before. Police started recording the statistics nine years ago. They also show that in one year alone (2011/12) the level of reported incidents jumped 25% (from 1,833 to 2,266). But this may be only a fraction of the true figure due to the reluctance of many men to come forward because of embarrassment and shame." [Claire McNeilly, Belfast Telegraph 29/10/2013 http://www.belfasttelegraph.co.uk/news/local-national/northern-ireland/domestic-violence-against-men-at-its-highest-level-in-northern-ireland-since-police-began-recording-statistics-29707051.html]

243

So are things improving? Are people ceasing to misrepresent domestic violence by portraying it as a male crime?

The National Centre for Domestic Violence (NCDV) describes itself as "one of the only national charities who helps both men and women" and they even had a "Male Domestic Violence Awareness week". Hooray, you might be thinking. But don't get too excited. In 2012 the NCDV launched an interactive billboard campaign at Euston Station in London. Passers-by could use their mobile phones to interact with an electronic billboard to drag a violently gesticulating domestic abuser away from a passive victim. What was their campaign called? It was called "Drag Him Away". Yes, you read that correctly, drag *him* away. http://www.youtube.com/watch?v=EEKC-Yu-LeQ

Any chance of a "drag her away" campaign any time soon? No, I thought not. How about a gender-neutral campaign, or is that too much to ask for?

The White Ribbon Campaign is a fairly typical example of the current state of activism on domestic violence. Their website http://www.whiteribboncampaign.co.uk does indeed have one page on male victims of domestic violence. But look at everything else on every other page of their website. Their slogan is "Men working to end violence against women". Their "About Us" page begins "Violence against women happens more than you think. It's mostly committed by men. We won't stand for it. We're a group of men who know that there's never an excuse for violence against women." Their white ribbon day, 25th November, encourages people to "say NO to violence against women." They can scarcely use the word 'violence' without appending the words 'against women'. Their whole site, apart from that one page, promotes the *feminist orthodoxy* that domestic violence is a male crime perpetrated against females.

And yet nearly half of all reported victims are male. Thanks for that one page, guys.

New UK definition of Domestic Violence

In the campaign prior to the UK general election in 2010 the New Labour party (which has been a fanatically feminist party since its creation in the mid-1990s following the death of the Labour party) made it known that, if re-elected they would introduce lessons into schools that would teach children about how domestic violence was a crime committed *by men against women and girls*. I heard it announced myself on the BBC's flagship radio news programme 'Today'.

Anyone with a functioning brain knows that domestic violence is perpetrated by all sorts of people against all sorts of people. Domestic violence is committed by women against men and by men against women; it is committed by women against women and by men against men; it is committed by adults against children and by children against adults. It's even committed by children against children. But the New Labour party announced their intention, if elected, to *teach schoolchildren* that domestic violence is a crime perpetrated by men against women and girls.

That they would intend to teach this sexist lie to children too young to defend themselves is appalling enough, but notice that they voiced this intention immediately prior to a general election. They must have thought that it was a *vote winner*. They were appealing to the misandrist bigot constituency. They apparently believed that so many voters would share their disgusting sexism against men that the electorate would want to vote for a party that intended to teach children that domestic violence was committed only by men and suffered only by women and children.

But don't get the idea that any of the other mainstream UK political parties are any better. They're all the same. From 31st March 2013 the Conservative/Liberal Democrat coalition government defined domestic abuse as:

"any incident or pattern of incidents of controlling, coercive, threatening behaviour, violence or abuse between those aged

16 or over who are, or have been, intimate partners or family members regardless of gender or sexuality."
https://www.gov.uk/domestic-violence-and-abuse#domestic-violence-and-abuse-new-definition

Notice the phrase "regardless of gender"? Don't be fooled. This new definition is part of a government policy called . . . . wait for it . . . . "Ending Violence Against Women and Girls in the UK" which has an action plan entitled "Call to End Violence Against Women and Girls" and a newsletter called the "Violence Against Women and Girls Newsletter."

This government policy describes the issue that it is designed to address thus:

"Issue: In 2012 around 1.2 million *women* suffered domestic abuse, over 400,000 *women* were sexually assaulted, 70,000 *women* were raped and thousands more were stalked. These crimes are often hidden away behind closed doors, with the victim suffering in silence. Fewer than 1 in 4 people who suffer abuse at the hands of their partner - and only around 1 in 10 *women* who experience serious sexual assault - report it to the police. We are determined to support victims in reporting these crimes, and to make sure perpetrators are brought to justice. We all need to do more to prevent violence against *women and girls* happening at all." [my italics]
https://www.gov.uk/government/policies/ending-violence-against-women-and-girls-in-the-uk

Regardless of gender? What liars. There is no mention of men and boys in the issue statement. The policy makers are fully aware that the government's own Home Office statistics are reporting over 40% of victims to be male and the issue statement quotes the figure of 1.2 million female victims. But it neglects to mention the 800,000 male victims. Is this because those 800,000 victims are an inconvenience in a policy entitled "Ending Violence Against Women and Girls in the UK"?

If the reader doubts that feminism is a part of the reactionary establishment, then I would invite you to explain how a Conservative-led government has decided upon an ideologically feminist definition of domestic violence? Progressive counter-culture, anyone? You can also see in this legislation how a nominally right-wing government with lots of white males in the cabinet legislates *not* in a male interest (patriarchy) but in an *anti-male* interest.

This definition of domestic violence would mean that shouting in a threatening manner constitutes an act of domestic violence but the title of the policy document tells us that this judgment *will only be applied* if the victims are women or girls. If it were applied impartially to both sexes, then it's likely that all the women reading this book would have been guilty of domestic violence at one time or another. But they don't have to worry because feminist hypocrisy means that the definition of domestic violence will *not* be applied impartially, it will be applied in accordance with the feminist gender-stereotypes of 'what men are like' and 'what women are like'.

The government draws attention to their consultation process for this policy, which took place between October 2011 and September 2012. Do you think that there was *anybody* involved in the consultation process who *wasn't* a feminist or who wasn't willing to submit their own judgement to that of the feminists involved? Everything about the policy reeks of feminist misandry.

Remember, this isn't a policy by the avowedly feminist New Labour party, this is a policy by the Conservative party and the Liberal Democrat party. *All of the mainstream parties in the UK are misandrist parties*, leaving a supporter of genuine impartial sex equality with nobody to vote for. You can vote for Feminist Party A or Feminist Party B or Feminist Party C. But there aren't any parties who support sex equality.

The new definition is typically feminist in its hugely sweeping broad brush-strokes. The phrase "any incident or pattern of incidents of controlling, coercive, threatening behaviour" enables feminism to claim that *almost anything* is domestic violence if a women claims that it is. If she feels her partner's demeanour is threatening, then he's guilty. If she feels coerced by him, then he's guilty. Feminism won't require her to prove threats or coercion because for feminism a woman's feelings are all the evidence she needs. But you can bet your life that it won't work the other way around. If a man feels threatened, he'll be told not to be such a wimp. If a man feels coerced, he'll be told to 'man up'. Feminism loves legislation that is wide open to the broadest possible interpretation because then they can claim that it means whatever they want it to mean.

This kind of law leaves men with only one rational position to take; they must not share a domestic space with women and girls. Under such a law a man cannot afford to marry or cohabit with the privileged sex because he will be living under the hammer of imprisonment on a woman's say-so. Feminist legislation systematizes male disadvantage. Feminist laws are to sex equality what the Jim Crow laws were to racial equality.

But what about those men who already cohabit with women? The White Ribbon Campaign offers some examples of what 'controlling' or 'coercive' behaviour might be in practice. They list:

- Preventing someone from seeing their family and friends
- Preventing someone from managing their own finances
- Preventing someone from using their phone
- Removing someone's independence and making them reliant on the perpetrator
- Humiliating someone in front of their friends

If these were applied in a gender-neutral fashion (there's no chance that they will be, but let's just suppose), then women might be convicted of domestic violence far more often than men. It has long been a male complaint about married life that newly-wed wives start curtailing their husbands time spent with 'the boys'. That's the first bullet point. Women are as likely to control the family finances as men, perhaps more likely, so that's bullet point two. The third and fourth points are so broad as to apply to either sex and some men would describe bullet point five as a female speciality. Men's Rights Activists would also be interested to know if the first bullet point "preventing someone from seeing their family and friends" would include women who refuse ex-husband's access *to see their children*. On this new definition of domestic violence, a woman denying a father access to his kids would legally be guilty of domestic violence.

But we all know that the systemic misandry in the law will not permit men to have anything like equality in the application of this new definition. It has been written by feminists for the further disadvantaging of men by making it even easier for men to be falsely accused and convicted of crimes they haven't committed.

Rape

One of the most notorious maxims attributed to feminism is the slogan 'all men are rapists'. This may have originated in Marilyn French's internationally bestselling novel "The Women's Room" in 1977 where one of the characters says "All men are rapists and that's all they are." French has publicly d*enied* that this is what she herself believes and has pointed out that these words are spoken by a fictional character in a novel. But the phrase has been used so often in discussions about rape and feminism that it is viewed by many as the feminist position.

So, does feminism assert that 'all men are rapists'? The answer, I would argue, is: as good as. Most feminists would probably want to disown the phrase because, of course, it makes them look like a bunch of extremist sexist pigs, but when we look at feminist texts they repeatedly assert things which might be concisely paraphrased or summarised as 'all men are rapists'. If so, then we might conclude that feminism *does* believe this and does, in effect, *say* this but that it wishes to maintain *plausible deniability*. How plausible that deniability is, the reader must decide for themselves.

"From prehistoric times to the present, I believe, rape has played a critical function. It is nothing more or less than a conscious process of intimidation by which all men keep all women in a state of fear." [Susan Brownmiller, "Against Our Will: Men, Women and Rape", 1975.]

"I claim that rape exists any time sexual intercourse occurs when it has not been initiated by the woman, out of her own genuine affection and desire." [Robin Morgan, "The Demon Lover" NY: Norton & Co., 1989.]

"Politically, I call it rape whenever a woman has sex and feels violated." [Catherine MacKinnon, "Feminism Unmodified: Discourses on Life and Law" (1987) A Rally Against Rape (1981), p.82]

Do these three well-known and influential statements add up to treating all men as rapists? The three quotes approach the allegation of societally systemic rape slightly differently in each case (social history, jurisprudence, and psychology, respectively) so they give us a range of feminist claims about the all-pervasiveness of rape to examine.

Brownmiller speaks unequivocally of "all men" and "all women". She puts forward an historical thesis about rape that is not about individual criminals committing the rape of individual victims, but instead asserts that rape is a political weapon employed systemically by *all* men against *all* women. Nor is the use of this weapon the result of cultural forces outside of the control of ordinary men because the use of it is described as a "conscious process of intimidation". It is a deliberate, even premeditated, act of terrorism conducted by all men to "keep all women in a state of fear". All men are guilty of this, so the guilt for all the rapes which are committed attaches to all men *including those* who haven't actually committed an act of rape personally. Brownmiller's position is a way of saying that all men are guilty of rape, without saying that every single man in the world has committed the act. The reader must decide if the assertion that 'all men are guilty of rape' is effectively equivalent to 'all men are rapists'.

Morgan's position focuses on the issue of a woman's consent to sex. If what Morgan says is true, then it is impossible for a man to *initiate* sex with a woman without thereby being a rapist. *All* non-criminal sexual encounters between women and men would have to be initiated by the woman. Not only that, but if a woman initiates sex *for any reason other than* "her own genuine affection and desire", then she has been raped.

This would mean, for example, that if a woman initiated sex with another man as an act of revenge against her boyfriend who had cheated on her, then the other man that she had taken to her bed to use him for this purpose would be a rapist. It would mean that if a woman was in the mood for sex and fucked some guy she didn't know because he was a good-looking hunk, then he would either *be a rapist* because she felt no genuine affection for him, or he would *not be a rapist* because although she felt no affection for him she did at least desire him. Morgan's position means that women are free to *use men* for sex as they please to indulge their sexual appetites, but if men were to so much as take the first step in initiating a sexual encounter, then it's rape. So, in Morgan's case, 'all men who initiate sex are rapists' rather than 'all men are rapists'.

MacKinnon is defining rape on the basis of *how a woman feels*. If she *feels* violated, then she *has been* violated. Although the quote is prefixed with "Politically, I call it . . ." we should remember that Mackinnon is a lawyer and her position is consistent with the orthodox feminist attitude toward rape trials, in that mainstream feminism treats all accusations of rape made by women against men as being true. It is not a matter of evidence, it is not a matter of facts, it is a matter of how the woman feels. If, in her view, she has been raped, then she has been. Hence, the feminist outrage if an accused man is found not guilty. How dare a jury fail to believe a woman?

MacKinnon's position, in the role of 'prosecutor', is the equivalent of defending counsel saying 'politically, I call it a false accusation of rape whenever a man is accused and *feels himself to be innocent'*. On MacKinnon's account rape has little or nothing to do with what the man actually *does*, it's simply a matter of how the woman *feels*. The total absence of any concern with sex equality is conspicuous in MacKinnon's assertion. Only the woman matters. The man doesn't matter and the truth of what actually happened doesn't matter. So, from the MacKinnon quote, we must conclude that 'all men accused of rape are guilty' rather than 'all men are rapists'.

Whenever quotes like this are put forward as evidence of the ultra-sexist bigotry of feminism, the usual response is what has become known by the acronym NAFALT: Not All Feminists Are Like That. We're supposed to believe that such quotes come from *radical extremists and fringe loonies* who do not in any way represent true feminism.

But Catherine MacKinnon is a feminist of international renown. She's a Professor of Law at the University of Michigan and has been a Visiting Professor of Law at various other American universities, including Harvard Law School. Her writing has influenced, among others, the Supreme Court of Canada. She is praised and acclaimed by feminists all over the world. So stop kidding yourself about NAFALT. If Catherine MacKinnon is a loony, she is definitely not a *fringe* loony, she is mainstream and credentialed. The radicals and loonies have been the foremost spokeswomen of feminism for the last half-century. If you look up the biographies of feminists who are routinely quoted for their extreme misandry, you'll find that lots of them are professional academics in US universities. Indeed, the university campus in America is a radical feminist environment. The 'radicals' *are* the mainstream. There is nothing fringe about this lunacy.

The crucial element in feminist theory about rape is to present it, *not* as a crime committed by individuals against individuals, but as a *systemic oppression* of one sex by the other sex. Patriarchy theory bifurcates society into two classes of persons

252

by gender, the victimizers and the victims, each of which is co-extensive with males and females respectively. Anyone who didn't view rape in this light (e.g. some of the members of the jury in a rape trial, perhaps) would not be employing a feminist interpretation of the world and everything that happens within it. Feminism *needs* rape to be viewed systemically, as an act of political oppression, in order to deploy it as a big stick in their sex-war. By describing rape in terms of *a weapon men use politically against women*, feminism is thereby able to *use rape as a political weapon against men*. That's why they speak of 'rape culture' and why some feminists view consensual heterosexual sex as being very closely akin to rape with very little, if any, dividing line between the two.

"Rape represents an extreme behaviour, but one that is on a continuum with normal male behaviour within the culture." [Mary Koss, Professor of Psychology, Kent State University, 1982.]

"And if the professional rapist is to be separated from the average dominant heterosexual [male], it may be mainly a quantitative difference." [Susan Griffin, "Rape: The All-American Crime", 1971.]

"Heterosexuality is a die-hard custom through which male-supremacist institutions insure their own perpetuity and control over us. Women are kept, maintained and contained through terror, violence, and spray of semen." [Cheryl Clarke, "Words of Fire", 1995.]

It is being made very clear in these quotes that the crime of rape is not to be seen as an aberration from the way that men normally have sex with women, but rather a mere amplification or exaggeration of it. Heterosexual sex is presented as being *qualitatively* the same as rape. But what about the women involved in these sexual encounters with men? Surely these women are mature adults who know their own minds and can make their own decisions? Surely these women are not being raped without their even realising it? Apparently, they are. How is this possible? Back in the 1980s a feminist agenda called 'political lesbianism' gave the answer to this question. Women engaged in consensual heterosexual sex are being raped but they don't realise that it's rape because of their lack of feminist consciousness.

The premise behind this outrageous (and profoundly misogynist) feminist idea is that humanity has not yet achieved the enlightened equal power-relations between women and men that would make consensual sex between the two possible. In the present circumstances, with women being so terribly oppressed, the inequality between men (powerful) and women (powerless) means that all heterosexual sex takes place within a context of societal misogynistic coercion and must therefore be attributed the status of rape. But as not all women have yet been awakened to the way that society systemically subordinates all women, some of them may mistakenly think that they are having uncoerced sex when really they're being coerced.

This idea gave rise to the agenda of 'political lesbianism', women who did not have sex with men as a matter of political principle. There was also the suggestion that, rather than do without the comfort of intimacy, and rather than sleep with the enemy, heterosexual women could look for this intimacy *with other women*, although this was not compulsory. They would not be lesbians, they would be 'political lesbians' who had rejected heterosexuality. The world-view of the 'political lesbian' can be discerned in the following three quotes from "Love Your Enemy? The Debate Between Heterosexual Feminism and Political Lesbianism" (1981) which argues the case against hetero-sex and for political lesbianism:

[The function of penetration by a penis] "is the punishment and control of women. It is not just rape which serves this function but every act of penetration, even that which is euphemistically described as 'making love'."

"Men are the enemy. Heterosexual women are collaborators with the enemy."

"If you engage in any form of sexual activity with a man you are reinforcing his class power."

http://www.scribd.com/doc/82867540/Love-Your-Enemy-The-Debate-Between-Heterosexual-Feminism-and-Political-Lesbianism

And, in case you were wondering, yes the idea of 'political lesbianism' is still around among some lesbian feminists, as with this 2009 article in The Guardian by the notorious Julie Bindel. http://www.theguardian.com/lifeandstyle/2009/jan/30/women-gayrights

'Political lesbianism' was (is) the logical consequence of the claim that all men in society systemically use rape as a weapon to oppress women and that heterosexual sex is qualitatively the same as rape. It is often said, quite rightly, that feminism's absurdist excesses actually belittle the genuine suffering of women *who have actually been raped* because feminism treats its ideological constructs as if they were of equivalent seriousness with *real women's real suffering*. Consider two real-life examples of organised rape gangs committing multiple rapes systematically:

(a) Serbian rape camps in the Balkan war in the 1990s, and (b) Muslim rape gangs in the UK.

The first thing we notice about these examples is the central importance of *a factor other than gender*. The Serbian military didn't rape Serbian women, they raped the women of the enemy as a tool of ethnic cleansing. The systematic use of rape as a weapon of war wasn't put to the goal of oppressing females in the interest of males, it was used for *ethnic and nationalist* reasons. The same is true of Muslim rape gangs. They don't groom and rape Muslim girls, they groom and rape kufr infidel girls whom the rapists see, for *ethnic and religious* reasons, as being nothing but whores. Unfortunately for feminism, these examples help to disprove patriarchy theory, not support it, by showing how when a group of men really do turn rape into an organised weapon, it is not for reasons of fighting a universal gender war.

255

But, on top of that, it is an appalling insult to the women and girls who suffered multiple rapes in the Balkan war or from Muslim rape gangs for feminists to treat women's ordinary experience of heterosexual sex as being qualitatively equivalent to the suffering of genuine rape victims; to treat both of these experiences as a part of the same systemic rape. Normally the cruel callousness of feminism is directed at men but sometimes, as in this case, it is also directed at women.

Of course, not all feminists are so extreme as to endorse the idea that heterosexual sex is rape. But *they still have to convince themselves that rape is sufficiently systemic for them to continue believing in patriarchy theory*; with the claim that rape is a part of the oppression of all women. So to do this they are forced to invent ever-broader definitions of what constitutes rape, an ever-widening circle of types of behaviour included under the appellation 'rape', until the circle is so wide that it includes the behaviour of enough men for feminism to fabricate the appearance of a 'rape culture'.

A few years ago when the New Labour party were in government they wanted to pass a law in which if a woman woke up in bed with a man after having been so drunk the night before that she couldn't remember whether or not she had consented to sex, then the man was to be classified as a rapist. So this would have meant that if two people on an evening out together both get so drunk that they can't remember how they ended up in bed together the next morning, *he* would be a criminal but *she* would not.

But why isn't *she* also a rapist, since he cannot remember whether or not he consented to sex? Because New Labour endorses traditional sexist gender-stereotypes. They take male consent *as a given*. No one asks if *he* consented because it is simply presupposed that any man consents to any sex at any time with anyone. (The misandry which says 'men are all sluts', as discussed in chapter 1.) New Labour's proposed law was based upon the crudest of gender caricatures, that of the ever-ready sex-obsessed fuck-anything male, combined with that of the woman-as-child who is not to be held responsible for her own actions, or for her own consumption of alcohol, when she drunkenly decides to fuck some guy.

This proposed extension of the definition of rape didn't actually make it into law. So what is the law on rape in the UK? How is the crime defined? Section 1 of the Sexual Offences Act 2003 defines the offence of rape on the criteria of three main points which must be proven beyond reasonable doubt for a conviction of rape. http://www.legislation.gov.uk/ukpga/2003/42/contents

"A person (A) commits an offence if:

- he intentionally penetrates the vagina, anus or mouth of another person (B) with his penis
- B does not consent to the penetration, and
- A does not reasonably believe that B consents."

Notice that rape is defined in terms of penetration with a penis. It is not defined in terms of a person being coerced into sex against their will or a person having sexual acts forced upon them without their consent. It is not defined in a gender-neutral manner to include all the possible perpetrators and all the possible victims. Instead, it is defined in terms of penetration with a penis.

The first of these three criteria is what makes rape a 'male crime' in the eyes of the law. The law is deliberately and unequivocally misandrist in the way that it *excludes women* from being classified as rapists. Rape is not a male crime because only men commit it, rape is made a male crime by being defined in such a way that only men can commit it, insofar as rape is defined in terms of penetration by a penis. It is the law itself which makes rape a male crime.

But surely penetration could also apply to fisting? What if a woman forcibly penetrates another adult person sexually with her fist against their will? The law tells us that such an act would be "Assault by penetration".

"A person (A) commits an offence if:

- he intentionally penetrates the vagina or anus of another person (B) with a part of his body or anything else,
- the penetration is sexual,
- B does not consent to the penetration, and
- A does not reasonably believe that B consents."

Other offences classified as rape follow this phraseology to make 'rape' distinct from 'assault', so that "Rape of a child under 13" is defined with specific reference to the penis as "A person commits an offence if:

- he intentionally penetrates the vagina, anus or mouth of another person with his penis, and
- the other person is under 13."

Could the definition possibly be any more clearly gendered? Penis = rape. No penis = assault. This, needless to say, is a hangover from the antiquated notions of traditional gender-relations where men were seen as the seducers and women were seen as the seduced. Traditional society didn't include the sexually predatory woman amongst it's sexist clichés. But surely contemporary society can now face facts and acknowledge the existence of the sexually predatory woman amongst its citizens?

So why hasn't the law been re-written to something more in keeping with modern sexual relations? Why isn't rape defined in a sex-equalitarian way, such as *coercing someone into an invasive sexual act without their consent* (where 'invasive' is understood to include taking the penis into one's own body without the consent of the man, as well as inserting the penis into someone's else's body)? If the word 'penetration' is to be used, why can't the definition also include 'being *made to* penetrate' so that it clearly covers the rape of men by female perpetrators?

You know perfectly well, without me telling you, why the law hasn't been re-written to make it gender-neutral. It would not be in the interest of feminism. A gender-neutral definition would mean that, in law as well as in reality, rape would cease to be a male-only crime. And that would undermine feminism's use of rape as a political weapon.

This failure by government is all the more glaring in that Section 1 of the Sexual Offences Act 2003 does include a definition that could be employed as a definition of rape except that it is applied to something called "Causing a person to engage in sexual activity without consent". This is defined as:

"A person (A) commits an offence if:

- he intentionally causes another person (B) to engage in an activity,

- the activity is sexual,

- B does not consent to engaging in the activity, and

- A does not reasonably believe that B consents."

What is the perceived difference between this offence and the offence of rape? Ask a lawyer if you think you can get a straight answer from one. But it hardly matters anyway since the law against "causing a person to engage in sexual activity without consent" goes on to state "A person is guilty of an offence under this section, if the activity caused involved:

- penetration of B's anus or vagina,

- penetration of B's mouth with a person's penis,

- penetration of a person's anus or vagina with a part of B's body or by B with anything else, or

- penetration of a person's mouth with B's penis"

Did you notice? Penetration, penetration, penis, penis. Yes, that again. So if a bullying wife coerces her husband into performing cunnilingus against his will, this won't count as either "rape" or "assault by penetration" or "causing a person to engage in sexual activity without consent" because she merely sat on his face and forced him to lick out her vagina with his tongue. No penetration by a penis involved, although *she* could charge *him* with "assault by penetration" if he was forcing her to submit to cunnilingus against her will.

And as for her coercing him into vaginal sex when she wants it and he doesn't, well, that's not going to be proscribed by any UK law. The bullying wife would presumably have to force her husband to submit to sodomy using a strap-on dildo against his will before she could be charged with "assault by penetration", and even then I wouldn't give much for his chances in a court of law.

In America there was a change to the Federal law's definition of rape in 2012. The archaic definition from 1927 of 'the carnal knowledge of a female, forcibly and against her will' was finally replaced with:

"The penetration, no matter how slight, of the vagina or anus with any body part or object, or oral penetration by a sex organ of another person, without the consent of the victim."

The Department of Justice website says, quite correctly, that the old definition "included only forcible male penile penetration of a female vagina and excluded oral and anal penetration; rape of males; penetration of the vagina and anus with an object or body part other than the penis; rape of females by females; and, non-forcible rape".
http://www.justice.gov/opa/pr/2012/January/12-ag-018.html

The *implication* is that the new definition *will* include these things. If so, then it's a *big* improvement, especially the recognition of penetration by something other than a penis. The phrase "any body part or object" would include, for example, non-consensual anal fisting as rape. On the other hand, the phrase "no matter how slight" means that a single fingertip up the anus would also be rape, so people had best not get carried away in the throes of passion.

What's noticeable by it's absence is that, despite the usual focus on penetration, there is no mention of 'being made to penetrate' which may be the crucial phrase when it comes to the legal recognition of the rape of men by female perpetrators, acknowledging both the victim who is forced to suffer being penetrated and the victim who is forced to penetrate their rapist for their rapist's pleasure. (I'll return to this point later.)

Rape: Feminist Research

The figure you will hear incessantly repeated in every bastion of political orthodoxy is that '1 in 4' women will be raped during their lifetime. This has been presented as fact over and over until everyone has heard it and repeats it. Yet only anti-establishment speakers ever mention that the 1985 'research' conducted by Mary Koss that gave rise to this figure has been discredited.

Professor Neil Gilbert of the University of California at Berkeley, investigated the methodology used in the Koss survey. The general public would be shocked if they were aware of how the bogus 1 in 4 statistic was actually generated and, even though many people have tried to draw attention to this, the 1 in 4 figure is still routinely quoted by people who don't care about the legitimacy or illegitimacy of research methods. For example, Gilbert points out that 73% of the women categorized as rape victims by Koss *did not themselves define their experience as rape*, it was Koss who classified their experience as rape. In other words, the women didn't tell Koss they'd been raped, *she* told *them*.
http://www.d.umn.edu/cla/faculty/jhamlin/3925/MythsGilbert.htm

The Koss-method of 'research' is very popular with feminist researchers. At the time of writing (March 2014) the findings of a massive Europe-wide study into gendered violence against women has just been released, conducted by the European Union Agency for Fundamental Rights. (It is concerned *only* with violence against women, not with violence against men, nor with violence perpetrated by the women who were surveyed.) The study questioned over 40 thousand women between the ages of 18 and 74. The technical report which explains the methodology of this interview-based research states that:

"Drafting the questionnaire, it was important to avoid terms such as 'rape', 'violence' or 'stalking', because different women might have different preconceived ideas on the types of violence usually associated with these terms, and the types of perpetrators involved. Following the example of numerous national surveys on violence against women, the FRA survey also asked about women's experiences of violence by describing various acts of violence in as concrete terms as possible. Therefore, the survey asked women whether or not they had experienced any of these acts, instead of asking if they had generally experienced 'violence' or 'rape'."
http://fra.europa.eu/en/publication/2014/vaw-survey-technical-report

Yet the findings of this study are full of shock-horror headline statistics about how "one in 10 women has experienced some form of sexual violence since the age of 15, and one in 20 women has been raped since the age of 15" and "one in five women have experienced some form of stalking since the age of 15, with 5% having experienced it in the 12 months preceding the survey".

So who ascertained that these rapes and stalkings have occurred? The researchers are reporting that these crimes *have* taken place but, on their own admission, they could not have been told this by the women interviewed because the respondents were specifically *not asked* questions including the words 'rape', 'violence' or 'stalking'. If it wasn't the women interviewed who identified themselves as having been raped or stalked, then there's only one other possibility: it was *the researchers themselves* who decided whether or not a particular woman had been raped or stalked.

But we might think, okay, no problem, the questions asked must have made it clear what type of offence had been committed against these women, right? But when we look at the questionnaire we find that *various* types of actions are all defined by the researchers as constituting a particular crime based upon a *feminist conception* of that crime.

For example, actions classified as "sexual harassment" include "Sexually suggestive comments or jokes that made you feel offended; Inappropriate invitations to go out on dates; Intrusive questions about your private life that made you feel offended." At the same time, sexual harassment also includes "Somebody indecently exposing themselves to you." Now, would the average person consider an *inappropriate invitation to go out on date* as being the same offence as *indecent exposure?* But they're both sexual harassment according to this study.

So when the research findings reveal alarming figures of "Between 74% and 75% of women in a professional capacity or in top management jobs have experienced sexual harassment in their lifetime", what does this actually mean? That they've been asked out on dates by "inappropriate" people or that their male colleagues have indecently exposed themselves in the boardroom?

The questions on "Experiences with the Current Partner" begins with questions asking, does the partner "Try to keep you from seeing your friends?" or "Insist on knowing where you are in a way that goes beyond general concern?" But then the questions move through a series of "experiences" of ever-increasing severity such as, has your partner "Belittled or humiliated you in front of other people" or "Done things to scare or intimidate you on purpose, for example by yelling and smashing things?" Eventually the questions reach acts of violence like, has your partner "Burned you?" or "Tried to suffocate you or strangle you?" or "Cut or stabbed you, or shot at you?"

Isn't it duplicitous to classify *all* of these things as "violence", including someone trying to "keep you from seeing your friends" and someone trying to strangle you or stab you? But if the feminist definition of violence includes all these very different things, then as with the Koss research it may be *the researchers who are telling the women* that they have suffered violence rather than *the women who are telling the researchers*.

Similarly with questions relating to sexual offences, the question "Your current partner has forced you into sexual intercourse by holding you down or hurting you in some way" is included alongside the question "Or have you consented to sexual activity because you were afraid of what your current partner might do if you refused?" To a non-feminist these two circumstances might seem to be somewhat different (depending upon how we are to understand the word "afraid"; for example, what if she was afraid that he would sulk for the next few days so it's easier just to have sex than to put up with his sulking, or if she were afraid that if they don't have sex regularly he might look for sex elsewhere and be unfaithful) but to an orthodox feminist researcher they are both equally rape.

Don't misunderstand me, I'm not objecting to the asking of detailed questions, not at all. My point is that we should notice how the shock-horror headline statistics which were broadcast by mainstream media all over Europe *were not presented in these detailed terms*. Instead they made sweeping statements like "Of women who are currently in a relationship, 7% have experienced four or more different forms of psychological violence". But what types of psychological violence were these? Were they things like "insist[ing] on knowing where you are in a way that goes beyond general concern"?

When the research study tells us that "of those women who experienced violence by a previous partner and were pregnant during this relationship, 42% experienced violence by this partner while pregnant" this sounds horrifying. 42% suffered violence while they were pregnant! But then we have to remember that this is 42% of those women who were pregnant during a previous relationship. So how many of the 40 thousand women surveyed would fall into that category? Is it a large or small category? And then we have to remember that the survey includes many levels of "violence" that range from being "belittled" to being "stabbed". So when they say that 42% experienced violence, what does "violence" actually mean in this statement? In fact, what solid information does this figure of 42% really give us once you get passed the shock-horror impression it creates on the mind of those who hear it?

I'm not suggesting that there is nothing to be learned from this research, only to point out that the way feminists formulate and present their data to serve their political agenda is more likely to mislead and confuse than it is to enlighten. Feminist research methodology is corrupted by their ideology so we have to be very wary of their findings which are publicised in the mainstream media. Feminist research is always looking for the most headline-grabbing statistics it can find on female victimhood because they want to influence policy-makers and legislators. (It's also another reason why they don't like to make comparisons with male victimhood).

And don't they grab the headlines! Yes they do. Let's look at an online CNN report about rape on college campuses in America. CNN tells us that:

"10.8% of men surveyed at two universities reported committing at least one rape from age 14 through the end of college" and that "7.7% of men surveyed said they committed rape during college". [CNN, July 14th 2015
http://edition.cnn.com/2015/07/14/health/campus-serial-rapist-assumption/index.html]

Are we seriously supposed to believe that so many male college students actually confessed to the crime of rape just because a feminist researcher asked them the question: *have you committed rape?* Are we seriously supposed to believe that these college students sat across a table from a feminist researcher in an interview room and cheerfully admitted "Oh, yes, I've committed rape. More than once. It's a normalised part of my culture. Certainly, I've committed rape. What's your problem?"

265

In America, as elsewhere, rape is considered a very serious crime which carries a hefty prison sentence. Actual rapists refuse to confess their crimes even when being vigorously interrogated by the police, so is it plausible that they would freely confess to rape during an academic interview?

Since this scenario is too ludicrous for any sensible person to believe, we have to ask ourselves what it means when CNN states quite boldly that *men reported* committing rape and *men said* that they committed rape. Is the reality that the men did not say any such thing? In fact, were they asked some innocuous interview questions which to them sounded quite innocent but their answers were then *classified by the feminist researchers* as being rape?

For example, were they asked a question like 'Have you ever had sex with a woman whilst she was under the influence of drugs or alcohol?' and the male interviewee, who has indeed had sex with a woman while they were both drinking alcohol, answers honestly 'yes'. What he is actually reporting is that he has had sex with a woman whilst she was under the influence of alcohol because the two of them were drinking together before they had consensual sex together. But the feminist researcher can then enter this answer into their 'research' findings as an admission of rape because they classify a woman who is under the influence of alcohol as being incapable of giving her consent, so a man having sex with her in that condition has thereby committed an act of rape.

This is what we might call the 'Koss method'. The rape is being reported *by the feminist researcher*. It is *not* being reported by the male interviewee. He is not saying that he committed rape, the feminist researcher is saying that he committed rape *on the feminist's own definition* of what constitutes rape. We might ask: was the word 'rape' actually mentioned in any of the interview questions?

The 'Koss method' allows the feminist researcher to ask questions which (to the person being interviewed) are not about rape but which are then reported as rapes in the feminist's 'research' findings. These findings are then disseminated to the mainstream media, like CNN, who report the 'news' that "10.8% of *men reported* committing at least one rape" and "7.7% of men surveyed said they committed rape during college". [My italics]

But if someone really wants to believe research of this sort, then they have another question to answer. If these college men actually confessed to rape during the interviews, then why does the CNN report make no mention of the researchers passing on these confessions to the police? Why is there no mention of subsequent prosecutions? Did the feminist researchers agree to protect the rapists by keeping their confessions of rape confidential? That wouldn't be very feminist, would it?

Dishonest research findings are ubiquitous. Another example is the EU research which says that "8% of women have experienced physical and/or sexual violence in the last 12 months before the survey interview, and one in three women has experienced some form of physical and/or sexual assault since the age of 15."
http://fra.europa.eu/en/publication/2014/violence-against-women-eu-wide-survey-main-results-report

One in three women! Wow, that's a lot of women suffering sexual violence, right?

But, hang on a second, it says "physical *and/or* sexual violence". Why are these offences combined together? Is it to generate the scary "one in three" figure? Yet, consider, if you were to ask the same question *of men*, would anyone be surprised if *nearly all men* had experienced "some form of physical and/or sexual assault since the age of 15"? Would the statistic for men be 1 in 2 or something like that? How many men *haven't* been punched, slapped, or pushed over at one time or another? It's such a common experience for men.

What should give us pause when we hear the shock-horror headline statistics is that, so often, the usual bias of feminist

267

research is present in the methodology. This bias may include but is not limited to:

(a) How women *feel* is taken as being proof that an offence has occurred; e.g. if she *felt* offended by what he said, it was therefore sexual harassment. There is no requirement to explore whether her feelings were objectively justified in the particular circumstances.

(b) What women *say* is taken as being *true* simply because they say it; e.g. she said *his purpose* in yelling was to scare and intimidate her, therefore that *was* his purpose, it *wasn't* an expression of frustration or an exasperated response to the way that she was yelling at him.

(c) Since what the respondents say might not produce the answers that the researchers are looking for, the women are not to be allowed to judge for themselves whether they were raped or suffered violence or whatever, instead it is left up to the feminist researchers to decide what the woman's answers actually mean in terms of whether she was raped or not, whether she suffered violence or not, etc. Feminist definitions of these offences are to be imposed upon the respondents' answers.

(d) Women are always assumed to be the *passive recipients* of violence and sexual violence, their own perpetration of these offences is discounted; e.g. if male and female cohabitees have a fight and slap one another, the only relevant data is that *she* was slapped, the context is considered irrelevant.

(e) No one ever asks if the situation is even worse for men.

Feminist research is sometimes called 'advocacy research' to highlight the important point that the researchers are *not* making an impartial and objective evidence-based enquiry seeking to discover the truth whatever it might turn out to be (i.e. even if it is contrary to their expectations or to their own political beliefs), but are instead trying to find evidence *to prove something that they already believe*. Advocacy research seeks evidence which supports the political position the researcher advocates. This is a very polite term to be attributed to a great deal of feminist 'research' where, given the ideology of the researchers, you can expect conclusions to precede enquiry, where the selection of evidence (often just personal testimony) is designed to generate the desired research results, and where language can be re-defined to make it mean whatever they want it to mean.

For example, you might be listening to the news on the radio or on the television and you'll hear some statistic quoted about how 80% of female university undergraduates report having been sexually molested or something of that sort, and since you're hearing this via the mainstream media you may assume the statistic is legitimate. But there are a few basic questions about research methodology that you should want answered before you trust the research findings. You might wonder:

(a) Did the research consist solely of *self-selecting* research subjects? When all the data is provided by people who are motivated to volunteer to participate in the research (i.e. self-selecting) they may not be a random cross-section of the relevant population, so any findings from such research should not misrepresent their answers as being representative of the population as a whole.

(b) Were the respondents asked loaded questions? How a question is phrased can significantly affect the answers given (as any commercial market surveyor will tell you), so to evaluate the answers accurately, *you need to know what the questions were*. For example, the question 'did you ever regret having sex with a man after he got you drunk?' does not mean the same thing as the question 'did you ever regret having sex with a man because you were drunk?'.

(c) What relevant questions were not asked? If the research is about sexual molestation, for example, then were the respondents asked whether *they themselves had ever committed* the same kind of acts upon a man as those they were reporting having suffered as molestation? Were men also

269

asked about their experience of being molested by women? Were identical questions used for both genders?

(d) Are all the respondents actually talking about the same type of experience? For example, what constitutes 'sexual molestation'? If a hundred women are surveyed, they may have a wide range of different understandings of what does or does not count as 'sexual molestation', so *they are not all talking about the same thing*. If the researcher treats their answers as referring to one type of experience, this is misleading. But the alternative can be worse, where the researcher imposes her own understanding of the term' sexual molestation' upon the respondents answers when the respondents may not agree that this is how their answers should be interpreted.

(e) Is the research evidence solely testimony evidence? If so, then it involves a subjective perspective, and this should be made clear in the findings. There is a difference between saying 'last year 80% of female university undergraduates were sexually molested' and saying 'last year 80% of female university undergraduates expressed the view that they had been sexually molested'. A perception should not be reported as a fact, since people's perceptions of what happened may vary. Research requires intellectual rigour to be exercised.

I'll give you an example of subjective perspective from my own experience. Back in 1993 I conducted a small research survey into domestic violence as an appendix to an M.A, dissertation. One of the respondents was a female friend of mine who reported that she had never committed domestic violence. But she had previously told me, in a purely casual conversation, about an incident where she had poured steaming hot gravy over her boyfriend's lap when she was upset with him. When I later reminded her of this incident, her answer was very revealing. She said: "Oh, does that count?" It was *not* that she was lying when she reported never having committed domestic violence, it was simply that a woman scalding a man's genitals with gravy wasn't what *she understood* the phrase 'domestic violence' to mean. She was thinking about men punching women, not a woman attacking a man with a gravy boat. The subjectivity of respondents answers needs to be taken into account when conducting research using testimony evidence.

Unfortunately, the news media seem much more interested in trumpeting sensational headlines than in scrutinizing research methods to see if the research findings are justified. For their part, the general public is often deferential toward anything referred to as 'research' because they associate the word with *scientific* legitimacy. But anyone who has worked in university research in the social sciences will know that the social sciences can be very unscientific at times. Feminist research is not given academic legitimacy on the basis of its intellectual rigour. *It doesn't have any intellectual rigour.* It's accorded academic legitimacy simply because academics are almost uniformly committed feminists and universities are totally dominated by feminist ideology. If you look at the shelves of books on the politics of gender in any university library, you will find that all the books are written from a feminist perspective. They consider themselves to be the only people who have any legitimacy. But these days we have to make a distinction between *academic* legitimacy and *intellectual* legitimacy.

So, if the news media are not questioning the sensational headline research findings, and the general public are according scientific legitimacy to 'research' which may be far from scientific, and the academic community closes ranks as a professional group which is supportive of its ideological colleagues, then the accuracy of feminist research is not something which can be credulously relied upon. I'm not saying that all feminist research is *necessarily* bogus, merely that the legitimacy of any piece of research is dependent upon the methodology employed. So the question becomes, do you think that researchers who are committed to an ideology like feminism can be trusted to be impartial and objective in their methodology?

If you want to find out more about the way particular feminist researchers have interpreted and even fabricated their 'evidence' you could read Christina Hoff Sommers book "Who

Stole Feminism?" which includes numerous specific examples, but perhaps the quickest way of evaluating decades of feminist research *as a body of work* is to look at the kind of mind-set that lies behind it.

How do feminist academics view the concept of the 'truth'? This is an epistemological question (epistemology is the study of how humans acquire knowledge). On what basis can we say that we know something to be true? One example of *feminist epistemology* is called 'standpoint theory' which allows feminists to claim a privileged status for feminist 'knowledge'. (See numerous online sources, http://plato.stanford.edu/entries/feminism-epistemology/ or http://www.iep.utm.edu/fem-stan/ etc.)

The political purpose of the feminist version of standpoint theory is to convince other people that they are in a position to speak *with authority*. After all, why should anyone accept feminism's presumption that it can speak on behalf of all womankind if it's just some feminist's personal opinion? Having an authoritative opinion means you are the *informed and knowledgeable* person who gets to talk down to the ignorant people who disagree with you, and you can tell them what to think because you're the person *who knows best*. You speak from a position of knowledge; you speak with authority on the subject. (If you imagine a feminist reading this book, she'll be dismissing everything I write as the ravings of one demented male whose arguments count for nothing because he speaks with no authority, but merely from his own prejudiced opinion. Observation, rational argument, and common sense don't count as 'authoritative' for postmodern academics.)

Feminists want people to believe that their ideological interpretations of society and of history are something more than just the illogical hate-mongering of misandrist bigots. They want to be seen as the people *who know*; who can speak with authority. Standpoint theory, as one example of feminist epistemology, supposedly offers a justification for this.

To have a 'standpoint' you need to be part of a collective identity which develops a collective point of view (e.g. 'a woman's point of view') with a special insight into the world that is available only to the members of that collective identity living in their particular social circumstances. This is called 'situated' knowledge. The collective identities of 'marginalized' and 'victimized' groups are the most instructive kind because they reveal things about society that the dominant standpoint ignores. Feminism, of course, sees 'patriarchy' as the dominant standpoint and women as a marginalized group. (You know - the people who for years have been supported by political campaigns and advantaged by affirmative action; the people on whose behalf government legislates; the people who are the majority in higher education; the people whose status as a parent is held to be legally superior; the people with 'well-woman clinics' and well-funded breast cancer research; the people that the whole of society is constantly talking about because of the dominance of feminism in all aspects of mainstream culture – you know, the *marginalized* people.)

But in addition to being marginalized you also need to be engaged in political 'struggle' in order to be able to see beneath the surface of an unjust social order to understand its iniquitous mechanisms. (e.g. feminists self-portrait of their opposition to the 'patriarchy'). This collective point of view and this political struggle combine to make a person's opinion authoritative when they speak about the ways in which society treats the people in their collective identity because it is the opinion of someone who is in the best position *to know*. By being women and having 'feminist consciousness' they have achieved a 'feminist standpoint'. They then tell the rest of us, who lack this standpoint, the truth about the world we live in.

So what this seems to amount to is: feminist 'knowledge' = the 'truth about women' because it is the distilled perspective of a marginalized group in struggle. This is in keeping with the way that feminists in the 1970s dismissed 'logic' because it was an allegedly 'masculine' mode of thinking. Feminists wanted a type of specifically 'women's knowledge'.

The great benefit of standpoint theory is that it means that if any critic points out a self-contradiction in a feminist's 'authoritative' contention about the plight of women or presents any contrary evidence to disprove it, this still doesn't invalidate the feminist's contention, it merely means that the critic has failed to understand the truth in what the feminist has said because the critic occupies a different place in society with a different standpoint. The feminist 'knowledge' is still true. Moreover it is more valuable than the critic's churlish disputations because it speaks from a women's standpoint; it is authoritative. Consequently, it would appear to be impossible that feminism could ever be held to be *wrong* about anything that it says about women. It makes feminism unfalsifiable.

Standpoint theory is presented as being an epistemological theory. It isn't. It's a way of giving your own ideological opinion a vaguely academic-sounding name as if that bestowed upon it some sort of special authority which makes you right even when you're wrong. It's a way of saying 'when I make a statement, it isn't just an assertion based upon my chosen ideology's interpretation of the world, it's knowledge of the truth even if you have the evidence to disprove it'. And, amazingly, this kind of thing is taken seriously by professional academics. What a bunch of babies. But it is on the 'philosophical' basis of such 'epistemology' as this that feminist research is undertaken and it's this kind of underlying mind-set that enables them to feel entitled to conduct their 'research' in a way that *produces results to suit the ideology they advocate*. They supposedly have a special insight which validates whatever it is that they want to believe.

Perhaps the reader will think that I am unfairly lampooning or parodying feminist research in the way that I have described it? Again, judge for yourself. In "Feminist Research" Debbie Kralik and Antonia van Loon explore feminist methodology in the context of nursing research. They begin with an account of feminist theory and feminist epistemology (situated knowledge) and then go on to say:

". . . understanding personal experiences of a phenomenon is assisted by first person accounts about the lived experience of the phenomenon under study. The researcher may only know these states by interpreting signs and features, or obtaining descriptions of the study subject from the person experiencing the phenomenon. Such knowledge relies on how the person represents their experience and the emotions, values, attitudes and interests the phenomenon holds for that person. In many instances this knowledge is tacit, unspoken and highly intuitive." [Kralik and van Loon, 2008, Nursing research: designs and methods, pp. 35-43]

Notice that the person who is the subject of the research 'assists' the researcher's understanding and that the researcher "may only know" by "interpreting" what the research subject says. This knowledge may in many instances be "tacit, unspoken and highly intuitive". In plain everyday language, this means that the researcher makes an *interpretation* of what the research subject is saying and their interpretation can extend to things that *the research subject hasn't said* but which the interpreter intuitively understands are unspoken but tacit. This is not a rational inference based upon evidence, this is an intuitive inference based upon . . . what? Feminist ideology? Well, yes. Kralik and van Loon inform us that:

"The researcher's epistemology is shaped by the life experiences she or he brings to the research as well as the influences of the many voices and conversations within feminism. As researchers, our assumptions and values underpin the research process." [Kralik and van Loon, 2008]

This is a confession of ideological bias. It admits that what the researcher believes that they know about the research they've conducted has been influenced from the outset by feminist discourse and the assumptions and values which that discourse has given them. It's a straightforward confession that ideological preconceptions govern the way that feminist 'research' operates. As Kralik and van Loon tell us next:

"Feminist research is not an intellectual exercise guided by theory, but is passionate, political, participatory and personal. Feminist principles are intimately connected to our lives; hence *knowing our world through a feminist lens* has implications for

275

how we live and work . . ." (my italics) [Kralik and van Loon, 2008]

What feminists claim to know is known "through a feminist lens". There is also the problem that 'situated knowledge' gives feminist researchers an excuse to treat anything said by a woman as being the truth; that whatever women say is therefore true. Kralik and van Loon conducted research into women who had been sexually abused as children, and admit that in their research: "We took the perspective that *every woman was the expert of her experience* . . . We believed and accepted that each woman's story was true and sought to *validate her experiences. . .*" [original italics]

So get this clear. Feminist research is a part of feminist political action. It's purpose is to pursue the feminist agenda. If you, reader, had the quaint old-fashioned idea that 'research' was an impartial enquiry which seeks to discover what is objectively the case, then you've had entirely the wrong idea about what feminist research is and what it's for. Whenever the public are presented with the results of a piece of advocacy research they should be careful not to credulously believe those results but instead find out something about the research methods employed. Just because something is said to be 'research' and it comes from a university, that doesn't necessarily make it honest or accurate.

The use of feminist epistemology in research into rape and other sex-crimes is not something that should be indulged or pandered to because it clouds and confuses an enormously important issue. The public needs reliable and accurate information on the amount of sexual crime which occurs in society. But because so much of the research conducted into sexual crime is conducted by feminist or feminist-influenced researchers, this results in the public being presented with a plethora of different statistics that are both unreliable and conflicting. Consequently, the public is left unsure as to what they ought to believe when yet another statistic is circulated in the media about how many people are raped, how many molested, how many abused in childhood, etc. For example, what is *your* response to the following statistics?

- 1 out of every 6 American women has been the victim of rape or attempted rape in her lifetime.

- 1 in 33 of American men (about 3% of all American men) have been the victim of rape or attempted rape in their lifetime.

- In America in 2003, 1 in every ten rape victims were male. (Men were one tenth of all victims.)

- The lifetime rate of rape/attempted rape is 17.6% for American women as a whole but is much higher at 34.1% for American Indian/Alaskan women.

- 2.78 million men in the U.S. have been victims of sexual assault or rape.

Do you believe all of these statistics? Do you believe some of them but not others? Do some seem more plausible than others? The thing is, all of these statistics are on the same web page and are taken from various US government sources. http://www.rainn.org/get-information/statistics/sexual-assault-victims What about the following statistics from WOAR (Women Organised Against Rape) http://www.woar.org/resources/sexual-assault-statistics.php who quote a variety of sources:

- 1 in 3 American women will be sexually abused during their lifetime.

- 1 in 4 women and 1 in 6 men will be sexually assaulted before the age of 18.

- 247,730 people were raped/sexually assaulted in the US in 2002.

- 54% of rapes and sexual assaults were reported to the police in 2002.

- Every 2 minutes someone somewhere in America is sexually violated.

When reading these statistics, do you think that you have a clear idea of what the differences are between 'rape' and 'sexually abused' and 'sexually assaulted' and 'sexually violated'? Can you understand these statistics if you don't know the difference? And who do you believe when one statistic conflicts with another from a different research study? The 2010 National Intimate Partner and Sexual Violence Survey http://www.cdc.gov/violenceprevention/nisvs/state_tables.html tells us, among many other things, that:

- "Nearly 1 in 5 women (18.3%) and 1 in 71 men (1.4%) in the United States have been raped at some time in their lives.

- More than half (51.1%) of female victims of rape reported being raped by an intimate partner and 40.8% by an acquaintance; for male victims, more than half (52.4%) reported being raped by an acquaintance and 15.1% by a stranger."

And what do you make of this statistic from the 2010 survey? "Approximately 1 in 21 men (4.8%) reported that they were *made to penetrate someone else* during their lifetime." [my italics] This would appear to describe the situation of a man being forced to have penetrative sex without his consent. So is this a recognition that *women rape men*, after all the years of people denying that this ever happens or could ever happen? Will it now finally be acknowledged that there are female rapists who rape men? Or are we supposed to assume that all the men who reported this are gay?

Rape: The Presumption of Guilt

When a politician says, as they often do, that the conviction rate for men accused of rape is too low, she is taking it for granted that some or all of those men found not guilty in a court of law were in fact guilty. How does she know? She doesn't. It is a *presumption of guilt*. Of course, we might say that on the law of averages some of them might have been guilty but it

278

couldn't be proved. But this would also apply to every other type of crime. Yet you don't hear any politicians saying that the conviction rate for people accused of burglary is too low or that the conviction rate for people accused of car theft is too low. Why not? Because the politicians do not have a presumption of guilt for burglary and car theft, they only have a presumption of guilt when men are accused of sex crimes by women. Rape, as ever, is treated as a special case.

If those politicians are demanding a higher conviction rate for rape, it means that the ordinary people on juries are *defying* the politicians. Apparently, juries are *not* applying a presumption of guilt to rape cases and the politicians are angry about it. Worse still, from the perspective of the politicians, the majority of alleged rapes don't even result in a court case and, because they have a presumption of guilt, this must mean that large numbers of rapists are getting away with it.

It is not difficult to see why so many politicians have this crime-specific presumption of guilt. The media's presentation of rape also takes it for granted that an alleged rape is the same thing as a rape. For example, the Telegraph newspaper tells us that:

"Around 78,000 victims are raped each year, but just 1,070 rapists are convicted, each guilty of an average of 2.3 attacks, figures published by the Office for National Statistics (ONS) showed. At least four in five rapes are not even reported to the police, and less than one in six of those which are lead to a conviction." http://www.telegraph.co.uk/news/politics/9793210/Fewer-than-one-in-30-rapes-lead-to-a-conviction-figures-show.html

The figure of 78,000 may be taken from ONS research but this is not a figure for rapes, it is a figure (or an estimated figure) for people *who said* they had been raped. Yet there is no suggestion in the Telegraph article that there is any doubt whether these are actually cases of rape or not, it is simply presumed that all of the accused must be guilty. If research estimates that 78,000 rapes *were said* to have occurred, then the newspaper reports that "Around 78,000 victims *are raped* each year". [my italics]

My point here is *not* to suggest that people reporting rapes should be viewed with suspicion, I'm merely trying to highlight how readily journalists and others employ a presumption of guilt regarding rape, perhaps without even realising it. By way of comparison, the following is taken from the Gov.uk website quoting ONS statistics on sexual offences:

"Based on aggregated data from the 'Crime Survey for England and Wales' in 2009/10, 2010/11 and 2011/12, on average, 2.5 per cent of females and 0.4 per cent of males said that they had been a victim of a sexual offence (including attempts) in the previous 12 months. This represents around 473,000 adults being victims of sexual offences (around 404,000 females and 72,000 males) on average per year. These experiences span the full spectrum of sexual offences, ranging from the most serious offences of rape and sexual assault, to other sexual offences like indecent exposure and unwanted touching. The vast majority of incidents reported by respondents to the survey fell into the other sexual offences category.

It is estimated that 0.5 per cent of females report being a victim of the most serious offences of rape or sexual assault by penetration in the previous 12 months, equivalent to around 85,000 victims on average per year. Among males, less than 0.1 per cent (around 12,000) report being a victim of the same types of offences in the previous 12 months."
https://www.gov.uk/government/publications/an-overview-of-sexual-offending-in-england-and-wales

Here, at least, statistics for men as well as for women are mentioned and it specifies that these figures are for people who "said that they had been a victim". I don't think it's pedantic to want the distinction between (a) allegations and (b) crimes to be preserved. After all, we're talking about an extremely serious crime, here, and one where innocence or guilt can be difficult to prove. It's not something that journalists and politicians should be slapdash about when discussing the topic. For the same reason, the casual exclusion of males from consideration is not a trivial matter because it perpetuates the misconception that only females are raped.

But, of course, traditional misandry views women as being entitled to a level of concern and protection that men are not entitled to, and this long-established sexism is fervently endorsed by feminism. We can see this endorsement in the way that feminists frequently and persistently tell us that, with a very few exceptions, women do not lie about rape. Thereby implying that the men who have been accused of rape *are* lying about it. This is an unequivocally gender-supremacist position. It relies upon a belief in the moral superiority of women; the belief that a man would commit a crime against a woman (rape) but a woman would not commit a crime against a man (slander and perjury). Not only is this a forthright rejection of sex equality, it is refuted by those women who subsequently admit to having lied or are proven to have lied. (For example, see http://latimesblogs.latimes.com/lanow/2012/06/brian-banks-accuser-money-wanetta-gibson.html and http://nypost.com/2009/12/07/woman-confesses-to-lying-about-rape-story-that-sent-man-to-prison/ and http://www.nydailynews.com/new-york/woman-accused-father-raping-lied-article-1.1430957 and http://www.cotwa.info/ and etc.)

It need surprise no one that feminism has a presumption of guilt for men accused of sex-crimes, nor that they use the traditional social imperative to 'protect women!' as their political banner, and it's not difficult for feminism to exert pressure on mainstream culture to sanction their presumption of guilt. Accusations of rape, since they revolve around the issue of mutual consent, are inevitably ambiguous unless there is definite physical evidence to support them and even then the evidence might be far from conclusive. Feminism trades on this ambiguity.

If a woman does not make a report of rape to the police, feminists can claim that she *was* raped but the legal system is so traumatic for rape victims that she would rather not pursue a legal case because it means being 'raped' all over again in the witness box. If a woman makes a charge of rape and then withdraws it, feminists can claim that she withdrew the charge out of fear for the way in which she would be treated by the judicial system. If a woman admits that she lied about being raped, feminists can claim that she must have been pressured into making her recantation. It is always possible to *speculate* on possible reasons why a genuine victim might recant her previous testimony, so there is always elbow room for feminists to not believe that a woman had lied. Even if a women is shown to have a history of false accusations of rape, feminists can claim that this is a sign of mental disorder and sexual trauma brought on by her living under the oppression of a 'rape culture'. The ambiguity about what really happened in any particular incident and thereafter gives feminism its excuse to continue to believe that all accusations of rape made by women against men are true.

This is why feminists persist in calling someone a 'victim' or a 'survivor' even if nothing has been proven and no one has been found guilty of anything. It is why feminists prefer an ambiguous use of the word 'rape' rather than a properly precise definition.

"To use the word [rape] carefully would be to be careful for the sake of the violator, and the survivors don't care a hoot about him." [Catherine Comins, Assistant Dean at Vassar College, quoted by Nancy Gibbs, Time Magazine]
http://content.time.com/time/magazine/article/0,9171,157165,00.html

For feminism, the issue to be addressed is not one of *justice in individual cases*, it is one of *justice for women as a class of persons* under the oppression of a 'rape culture'. The issue for feminism is political. This is why a feminist is capable of being so atrociously immoral as to argue that she might prefer to not spare men the experience of being unjustly accused of rape because the experience may improve their attitudes toward women:

"They [the men falsely accused of rape] have a lot of pain, but it is not a pain that I would necessarily have spared them. I think it ideally initiates a process of self-exploration. 'How do I see women?' 'If I didn't violate her, could I have?' 'Do I have the potential to do to her what they say I did?' Those are good questions." [Catherine Comins, Time Magazine, June 1991]

282

It is clear from this that Comins is concerned with a larger issue than the individual false accusation and justice for the individual innocent man. She is addressing the feminist issue of *reconstructing male human beings* so that they think the way that feminism wants them to think; so that they see themselves as potential rapists; so that they believe the feminist gender-stereotype of 'what men are like'; so that they internalize the feminist version of male gender-identity.

But a man falsely accused of rape is the victim of an appalling crime. Who speaks for the victim? As long ago as 1996 in an American study examining DNA evidence to prove cases of men falsely convicted of rape, "Convicted by Juries, Exonerated by Science: Case Studies in the Use of DNA Evidence to Establish Innocence After Trial", the study found:

"The 19 laboratories reported that, since they began testing, they had received evidence in 21,621 cases for DNA analysis . . . . In about 23 percent of the 21,621 cases, DNA test results excluded suspects, according to respondents."
https://www.ncjrs.gov/App/Publications/AlphaList.aspx?alpha=C&Agency=All

23% is nearly a quarter of all the cases they examined. A quarter of these rape convictions were scientifically proven to be miscarriages of justice by DNA evidence? Shouldn't this be drawing someone's attention to the current state of the rape laws?

If you don't think so, then take a look at the Innocence Project, a non-profit legal clinic in America that is dedicated to overturning wrongful convictions (for any crime, not just rape) which also uses DNA evidence to prove the innocence of the wrongfully convicted. If you read their page of profiles http://www.innocenceproject.org/all-cases/#exonerated-by-dna you'll find that they're nearly all men and a very large number of them were falsely convicted of sex-crimes. Maybe someone should be asking if, with as many as 23% of men accused of rape being proven innocent by DNA testing, whether this is the *real* '1 in 4' statistic?

Rape: Perjury with Impunity

The attitude of feminist society toward rape manifestly derives very directly from the age-old social imperative to protect women, no matter what the cost to men. This is why, under the UK legal system, women bringing a charge of rape have the protection of *anonymity* and the accused men do not. (This looks like a positive encouragement to women to bring malicious false charges.) The principle of sex equality, 'both or neither', would insist that either both the accuser and the accused should have anonymity or neither of them should have it. Whichever of these were chosen, it is clear that for the accuser to be protected by a shield of anonymity whilst the accused is publicly vilified even before any evidence has been heard is a blatant case of gender inequality. But, extreme though this sexism is, the relative immunity given to those who make false allegations of rape extends society's traditional bias even further.

It's so rare for someone to be prosecuted for a false accusation of rape that it's not likely to happen unless their crime is difficult for the authorities to disregard, as when someone has made false rape allegations repeatedly and eventually the law decides that something must be done about them.
http://www.express.co.uk/news/uk/380458/Jailed-woman-who-lied-about-rape-11-times

Significantly, when women are prosecuted for making false allegations of rape, the charge may actually be one of 'wasting police time' or 'perverting the course of justice'. Apparently, it is *the state* who is the victim in these cases, not the men against whom the false allegations were made.
http://www.dailymail.co.uk/news/article-2595891/Law-student-cried-rape-11-times-university-exams-court-hears.html

In 2013 http://www.cps.gov.uk/news/latest_news/under_the_spotlight/ the UK Crown Prosecution Service admitted that only around two people per month were being prosecuted for making false allegations of rape. It's important to understand what this means. It means that where a rape allegation has been shown to be false *and* there was enough evidence to prosecute the person who had lied *and* it was considered to be in the public interest to prosecute them, then the CPS went ahead with the prosecution at a rate of two prosecutions per month. This does *not* mean that all the other rape allegations were true or that this is the total amount of false rape allegations. It's merely the very low number who were *prosecuted*.

We should remember that some of the rape allegations in which the police or the CPS do not undertake a prosecution of the alleged rapist (e.g. that were dropped because of a total lack of evidence) may have actually been false allegations. But none of these cases will feature in the CPS statistics about people being *prosecuted for making false allegations* because the false accuser was not prosecuted.

But do the authorities take this into account? No. Instead, all allegations that are not specifically proven to be false are presumed to be actual rapes (prior to the court case) because of the *presumption of guilt*. This is why, when you hear the much-repeated statistic that 'only 6% of rapes result in conviction', that's actually 6% of all allegations of rape recorded by the police, it is not 6% of actual rapes. The presumption of guilt means that they are treating all *allegations* as being *rapes*. In fact, the Stern Review 2010 (an independent review into how rape complaints are handled by public authorities in England and Wales) reported that the conviction rate for people who are actually *charged* with rape is 58%.
https://fullfact.org/factchecks/rape_conviction_rates_deserve_careful_explanation-28408

In the same dishonest way that the authorities perform this sleight of hand of quoting statistics about rape allegations as if they were statistics about rape, they also fool the public in regard of the number of false rape allegations. Here is a quote from the Stern Review 2010:

"How common are false allegations? It is not possible to establish an exact figure and the research that is available gives a wide range of suggested percentages. Some research suggests that a figure of eight to ten per cent of reported rapes could well be false reports. However, those we spoke to in the system felt that there were very few. A Crown Prosecution Service (CPS) lawyer told us, 'They are extremely rare. I have been prosecuting for 20 years, and have prosecuted for a false allegation once.' The judges we talked to said these cases occur very infrequently. An experienced police officer had come across two such cases in 15 years." [The Stern Review, 2010, Government Equalities Office, page 40.]

Did you notice the way that, within the same paragraph, they went from speaking about the number of "false allegations" and "false reports" to speaking about the very different matter of the number of *prosecutions* for making a false allegation? I'm sure *prosecutions* of false allegations are very rare but that says nothing about whether *false allegations* are rare. It may just mean that women aren't being prosecuted for it. (We will come to the reason why they aren't in a moment.)

The Crown Prosecution Service performed this same sleight of hand when they released their 2013 report which announced that only two people per month were being prosecuted for this crime. Rather than acknowledging how this low rate of prosecution reflects society's endorsement of the feminist belief that 'women don't tell lies', the CPS actually had the audacity to cite this low prosecution rate *in support of that belief* by declaring that the low number of prosecutions proved that false rape allegations are rare.

The argument is: if the number of prosecutions is low, then the number of offences must be low. But how would the CPS react to *exactly the same argument* being applied to rape itself; that if the number of rape prosecutions is low (as we're continually told it is), then the number of offences must low? The argument is absurd and they themselves would reject the argument if it were applied to rape, yet they shamefully assert that absurd argument in regard of false accusations.

In fact, the truth about the number of false rape allegations is unknown. Various figures are quoted but none of them are definitive. (e.g. http://www.foxnews.com/story/2006/05/02/false-rape-accusations-

286

may-be-more-common-than-thought/ which cites variously that 25%, or 20%, or 41% of rape allegations are false, and http://www.slate.com/articles/news_and_politics/jurisprudence/2009/10/how_often_do_women_falsely_cry_rape.html which favours 8% to 10%).

But it's no wonder that nobody knows what the real number of false allegations is when those in authority don't want to know, they just want to go on believing that 'women don't tell lies'.

The conventional practice is that women who make false rape accusations are not prosecuted for their crime. This practice is so well-established that it can be said to be the general rule. The culturally and politically orthodox position on false rape allegations taken by the authorities is that if women are prosecuted for lying about having been raped, then this might create the impression in the mind of the general public that women who make rape allegations are not believed. This in turn might mean that women who have genuinely suffered rape might not report the crime for fear that they won't be believed. Therefore, women who make false accusations of rape must not be prosecuted for their perjury in case this makes the victims of genuine rapes less likely to report them.

Notice, firstly, that this position does not speak of any *necessary consequence* between prosecuting perjurers and inducing a fear in others that they will not be believed. The position doesn't say that if a liar is exposed as a liar, this will inevitably lead to genuine victims thinking that no one will believe them. It merely claims that prosecuting the perjurer who has lied *might* cause genuine victims to fear they will not be believed. Maybe it will, maybe it won't.

Notice, secondly, that this does not speak of any *necessary consequence* between genuine victims fearing that they will not be believed and their not reporting the crime. The position merely claims that the genuine victims *might* not report the crime they've suffered if they fear that they won't be believed. Maybe they will, maybe they won't. Anyone who has been the victim of any crime that they cannot immediately prove might fear that they will not be believed. It doesn't mean that they won't report it.

Yet, despite the extreme seriousness of false accusations of rape, the accepted position adopted by the political establishment is that prosecuting the perjurer might stop genuine victims from coming forward for fear that they will not be believed and might cause them to worry that if they lose their court case, then they might be thought to have perjured themselves and so be prosecuted, too. Therefore women who make false accusations of rape should not be prosecuted for it. This is the reason why there are so few prosecutions and why the number of prosecutions tells us nothing about the actual number of false allegations (regardless of what the CPS may duplicitously claim).

This shows to just what an extent rape is treated as being different from all other crimes. No one would treat other perjurers in the way that rape-perjurers are treated. For example, no one would say that if a man falsely accused another man of physically assaulting him and was prosecuted for perjury, this might discourage genuine victims of assault from reporting it to the police, therefore we should not prosecute the perjurer who had falsely accused a man of assault. No one would say that if someone makes a false insurance claim and is prosecuted for it, this might discourage people with genuine insurance claims from making them, therefore we should not prosecute the person who made the false insurance claim.

What makes rape different? Is it simply the seriousness of rape that makes it a special case or is it because most of the victims are *women* (and until very recently it was believed that *all* of the victims were women)? Certainly, feminism focuses all it's attention on the *femaleness* of the victim in their constant assertions that women cannot trust the judicial system because society is prejudiced against women and is just looking for any excuse not to believe rape victims; that juries and judges and police officers are all part of the same woman-hating system of despotic male power.

But, in the absence of feminist fantasies about systemic male oppression, the situation can be seen for what it really is: an endorsement of the old fashioned belief that men should put the interests of women ahead of their own interests; that if anyone is going to suffer, then it is better that *men* should suffer rather than women.

Remember, the orthodox position is that prosecuting women for lying about having been raped might mean that women who have genuinely suffered rape will not report the crime for fear that they won't be believed, so this might mean that victimised innocent women would have to suffer in silence without receiving justice from the law. In order to avoid this, women who make false accusations must not be prosecuted. This means that justice is *denied* to victimised innocent men (the falsely accused) who must suffer in silence without receiving justice from the law. If *one of the two sexes* is going to suffer in silence and receive no justice, then as usual traditional sexism says that it is men who must accept this role. The innocent men must have no justice because otherwise the innocent women might have no justice. The law prefers a situation where the men *must* suffer to a situation where the women *might* suffer.

As we have already discussed at some length, the traditional social constructs of gender lay a heavy emphasis on male self-sacrifice *in the defence and protection of women*. Whenever there is a choice between protecting men and protecting women, the former is always forfeited in favour of the latter. Men are expected to 'man up' and 'take it on the chin'. The injustice to men is perfectly clear but men are expected to accept it because it is their gendered social role to put women's physical security ahead of their own; that if a man must suffer in order to spare a woman suffering, then it is his 'manly duty' to do so.

The refusal to prosecute rape-perjurers does not treat women and men as being *equal before the law*, it gives priority to women over men. They matter more. This is a gender-supremacist position. Yet those who endorse this position would no doubt inform us that they support sex equality. They might even be so hypocritical as to claim that their position furthers the cause of sex equality. But it is impossible that it could. Gender-supremacism is *the opposite* of sex equality and a rule which says that innocent people of one sex should be sacrificed for the sake of innocent people of the other sex can never support sex *equality*. No one in feminist society is going to suggest that women should take their chances in a hostile world equally with men. But a sex-equalitarian *would* suggest this. In fact, a sex-equalitarian would demand it.

The excuse that is likely to be offered in defence of the gender-supremacist position on false rape accusations is that a woman's suffering as a result of being raped is far greater than a man's suffering as a result of being falsely accused of rape. But is it? The innocent man may have his life destroyed as a consequence. He will be branded a sex-criminal. He will be sent to prison on remand. He may be violently attacked (perhaps raped) by other prisoners who share society's presumption of guilt regarding men accused of sex-crimes. His name and face will be dragged through the media. His family will be publicly shamed. He may lose his job and his friends. And, *if he is not convicted of a crime he didn't commit*, even after he has been cleared of the false charge, he may be left wondering for the rest of his life just how many people actually believe him to have really been guilty. All those feminists who claim that 'women never lie' about rape will certainly continue to believe him guilty.

Is a women's suffering as a result of being raped so much greater than a man's suffering as a result of being falsely accused of rape that it justifies the gender-supremacist principle that justice for innocent men should always be sacrificed for the sake of justice for innocent women? No one doubts the torturous suffering of the rape victim, but we know that feminists treat the suffering of the falsely accused astonishingly lightly (as with the vile quote from Catherine Comins above, suggesting that men might find false accusation a useful learning experience). The test might come when men start falsely accusing women of rape. Will the falsely accused woman be told that she has no recourse in law because her suffering must be discounted on the grounds that the suffering of the man she raped must take priority? Or will the law treat those cases differently? If so, then we'll know that the assertion that a woman's suffering from having been raped is greater than a man's suffering from having been falsely accused is just an excuse, and what we're really dealing with here is the traditional sexist belief that *male pain counts for less than female pain.*

The Female Rapist / The Male Victim

If you were told that 35 year old Robin Mowery repeatedly 'had sex' with a 15 year old and was now in court for it, what would you think? Would it be something like: That's rape! Lock him up, the bastard! Our children must be protected! If you were then told that Robin was female and the 15 year old was male, would that alter your judgement?
http://sentencing.typepad.com/sentencing_law_and_policy/2008/12/an-honest-and-honorable-gendered-sentencing-in-adultteen-sex-case.html

In the Mowery court case the woman was given a 2 to 4 years prison sentence for sexual assault. Notice that phrase, sexual assault. Not rape. The general public is still very resistant to the idea that women commit rape because of the traditional belief that a 'weak' woman can't force a 'strong' man and that, anyway, all men are sluts; a prejudice that apparently extends to underage boys. People with a traditionally misandrist mind-set are inclined to say that when a man has sex with female 'jailbait' that's *different* from when a woman has sex with male 'jailbait'. They usually have an idea that fourteen year old boys who get laid are lucky. But if there is one type of female sex-crime that the general public may already be inclined to acknowledge as 'rape', it is the rape committed by a woman who has sex with someone who is underage. For example, Sarah Beth Hopkins, the 35 year old Oregon woman who repeatedly raped a 12 year old boy over a period of eight months. http://www.dailymail.co.uk/news/article-2540373/Woman-35-admits-raping-friends-12-year-old-boy-multiple-times.html

291

There are plenty of similar examples where the perpetrators of child-rapes were women, like Amanda Brausey, a school bus driver who was sentenced to 30 days in jail for 'having sex' with a 14 year old boy on her bus. http://www.dispatch.com/content/stories/local/2014/02/06/former-driver-sentenced-for-having-sex-with-teen.html

Or 34 year old Keri Gonzalez, who was caught 'having sex' with a 15 year old boy in the boy's own bedroom and was charged with 'sexual misconduct with a minor'. http://www.dailymail.co.uk/news/article-2557220/Naked-woman-34-breaks-ankle-jumping-15-year-old-boys-bedroom-window-mother-catches-2am-tryst.html

Or Loren Morris, who was sent to prison for two years (although she would probably only serve one year) for 'having sex' more than fifty times with a boy when he was between 8 and 10 years old. http://www.dailymail.co.uk/news/article-2583647/Female-paedophile-21-jailed-two-years-sex-eight-year-old-boy-50-times-starting-16.html

The apparent inability of the law to sentence these women to the kind of punishments that men would have received in their place is a measure of how society is still struggling to come to terms with the idea of the female rapist. Joy Morsi, a 39 year old female schoolteacher (and mother of four children), 'had sex' with two of her underage male school students and was charged with 3rd degree rape. But in this television report commenting on the case https://www.youtube.com/watch?v=6tZ1P-Uef1c the television pundits are solely concerned with the effect that this may have on the male students *future attitude and behaviour toward women*. The pundits are concerned that by being the victims of rape by their schoolteacher the boys may have been taught to *sexually objectify women*. For feminists, it is the possibility of harm to women in the future that is the issue of concern. When a female schoolteacher rapes her male students, the cause for worry is the need to protect women from sexual objectification. It seems that there are no limits to the sexist injustice of feminism's 'woman-centredness'.

And, incredibly, it gets worse. In this television discussion https://www.youtube.com/watch?v=hjl4T_-oM0g about a 20 year old woman who repeatedly "had sex" with a 13 year old boy, there is no mention of rape. The show focuses on whether the boy is the father of the woman's new-born baby. It's a *paternity* issue. How is it that the woman is not in prison for raping a child of thirteen, but instead is on a television show asking for financial help from the boy and his family in raising her baby? (As it turns out, DNA testing shows that the boy is *not* the father of the baby.)

Of course, female rapists have nothing to do with what feminism calls 'rape culture'. For feminism rape is very much a 'male crime'. Yet on the very day that I was writing this (13/02/14) the UK government announced a new initiative to support male *victims* of rape. The amount of money being spent is paltry, but it is a significant development that the issue is being addressed at all:

"The Government has committed £500,000 over the next financial year to provide services, like advice and counselling, to help male victims who previously have not been able to receive such support and encourage them to come forward after experiencing such a crime . . . . We believe around twelve per cent of rapes are against men. Yet many choose not to come forward, either to report the crime or seek the support they need. I am determined to help break the silence on a subject still seen as taboo . . . . Latest figures show there were 2,164 rape and sexual assaults against males aged 13 or over recorded by the police in the year ending September 2013."
https://www.gov.uk/government/news/500000-to-help-break-the-silence-for-male-rape-victims

But we should remember that there are actually two issues to be addressed, two cultural taboos that need to be broken. The first is that men, not just underage males but *adult men*, are raped in their thousands every year. The second is that *the perpetrators are women* as well as other men. Society is beginning to understand the truth of the first of these statements (as evidenced by the government's pledge of money) but the second statement is a harder nut to crack. Yet it shouldn't be.

There are basically four reasons why traditionally-minded people refuse to believe that women rape men. None of these objections stands up to scrutiny but they are all very much a part of the traditional gender-stereotypes that mainstream feminism endorses (because the misandrist character of these stereotypes advantage women) and that is why they are still popularly believed. Let's consider each objection in turn. Some people believe that it is impossible for a woman to rape a man because:

(1) All men are sluts who always want sex all the time with anyone. It's impossible to rape a slut because they're always 'up for it'.

This is the most vulgarly offensive of the four objections. As this gross piece of popular misandry has already been dealt with in chapter 1, I won't repeat my argument here. The reader can either re-read that section in chapter 1 or move straight on to the second objection. The only thing I'll add here is an observation on feminism's 'no means no' and 'what part of no don't you understand?' campaign. You could read this http://crunkfeministcollective.wordpress.com/2012/07/02/asking-for-sex-what-do-you-do-when-the-guy-says-no/ article to see how a feminist reacts when *she* asks for sex and a *man* says no. This particular feminist decides that his sexual rejection of her is a ploy by which men seek to exercise male power. (Not that anyone would suggest that women have said no to sex as a way of exercising power over men, gracious no.) Rather than assuming that *no means no*, and that he doesn't want to sleep with her because he doesn't find her attractive or because he just isn't in the mood, she decides that it's another patriarchal plot by which to exert male control over women. What else could a feminist conclude when everyone knows what sluts men are and how they always want sex?

(2) Erection = consent.

This is the most simple-minded of the four objections. The claim being made is that if a man has an erection then this is proof that he consents to sex; that he must have wanted sex because he was physically aroused. It is a measure of how unliberated in their thinking some people are that they would take this objection seriously. It is the equivalent of saying that if a woman's vagina lubricates during a rape as a result of the physical stimulation, that lubrication constitutes consent. No it doesn't. It's an involuntary physical response. The same applies to erections. An erection can be induced purely physically. If a woman is wanking a man's cock, this stimulation may induce an involuntary erection, but that doesn't mean that he has freely given his consent, it's just a physical response to a physical stimulus. It's the same as when a male victim of anal rape gets an involuntary erection as a result of the physical stimulation to his anus. How could anyone mistake this for consent?

In addition, we should not pander to the old misandrist definition of 'rape' as 'penetration by a penis'. Not all non-consensual sex requires an erect penis. For example, forced cunnilingus. If someone has his face forced into a woman's vagina and is made to lick out her insides when he doesn't want to, then this is as much rape as examples of non-consensual sex that include penetration. An erection is irrelevant to this act of forced sex without consent.

(3) Women have no desire to rape because they have a gendered sexuality which only desires romantic love and the coming together of twin-souls in a physical union which is an expression of that love. Women don't 'fuck' they 'make love', therefore raping someone is not a part of feminine sexuality.

This is the most comical of the four objections. Firstly, there is a whole world of evidence from people's personal lives that women have every kind of sexuality under the sun. For this objection to be true, then all the millions of women who have so-called 'deviant' sexualities would either have to *not exist* or, in an ultra-conservative manner, be considered sexually dysfunctional. This would have to extend to all those women who use a vibrator for their physical pleasure because a person cannot seriously be said to have a mutually loving romantic relationship with a shaft of vibrating plastic. Gendered sexuality is a ludicrous idea, given all the women and men whose actual sexualities contradict it. When feminists insist that erotic relations should be limited to strictly equal-power sexual activities they are trying to impose a single sexuality upon everybody, especially women.

Secondly, feminism itself has had a lot of internal disagreement (and very spiteful it was too) between the Victorian-style feminist prudes and the 'pro-sex feminists'. In the late 1970s and the 1980s there were the notorious 'feminist sex wars', with BDSM lesbians being particularly resistant to the imposition of a construct of politically 'correct' sexuality. (See http://www.outhistory.org/exhibits/show/lesbians-20th-century/sex-wars) One of the few things in life that has managed to defy the almighty power of feminism has been women's desire for all sorts of different sexual pleasures. Not even authoritarian feminism has been able to crush sexual variety in women, female consumption of pornography, role-playing and sex-toys, and all manner of erotic diversification. To claim that sexuality in women cannot include a desire to rape is no different from denying that sexuality in women cannot include the desire to dominate and inflict pain or the desire to submit and suffer pain or the desire to wear erotic clothes and sexually objectify herself. Women have all of the sexualities found in humans, just like men do.

And how bizarre that after decades of feminism telling us that 'rape is not about sex, it's about power and domination', that people in feminist society should still be saying that women have a gendered sexuality that precludes their being rapists. Hey, I thought you said that rape was about *power and domination?* Well, women do that too.

(4) Delicate little women are not physically strong enough to rape a great big man.

This is the most clichéd of the four objections. It views rape in terms of the menacing assailant who emerges out of a dark alleyway to pounce upon a passer-by, wrestling them to the ground by brute force. This is a perverse objection for anyone,

296

especially a feminist, to make against the idea that women rape men, given that feminism has argued so vociferously that rape is not merely a matter of men using *physical* force to rape women because it's implicit in all unequal power-relations.

Feminism has insisted that if the power-relations between a man and a woman are unequal, then sex between them is not consensual because the person in the weaker position is covertly pressured into sex by the inequality in the power-relation. On this basis they have claimed that if an employer has sex with his employee, this is a covert use of force; if a university lecturer has sex with his student, this is a covert use of force, and so on. Some feminists, as we have seen, have even applied this to *women as a class of persons* under 'patriarchy' to argue that all heterosexual sex is rape.

Feminists, of course, only ever apply this argument about unequal power-relations to situations where the *woman* is in the weaker position; where the employer is male and the employee is female; where the lecturer is male and the student is female. But, although feminism has made use of this idea solely to pursue its sex-war against men, the basic idea that there are *many different types of force* which can be brought to bear to coerce a person into sex is, in itself, entirely reasonable. Naturally, it should be applied to *both* sexes, not just to women. Ask yourself:

(a) If a woman is in a senior position over a man in his employment and she makes it clear that there will be very unfortunate repercussions for his career if he doesn't agree to have sex with her whenever she wants it, even if he doesn't want it, does that count as coercion?

(b) If a man is living with a woman and the woman has a pronounced psychological ascendancy over him in their relationship, where he has grown accustomed to giving in to her demands and letting her have her own way all the time so that when she wants sex and he does not, he doesn't voice his objections but meekly acquiesces, does that count as psychological coercion?

(c) If a woman verbally browbeats and bullies a man into having sex when she wants it and he doesn't, using ridicule and humiliation, impugning his manhood by saying that he can't 'get it up', calling him a 'cockless eunuch' and a 'limp dick' and suchlike, does her bullying count as coercion?

(d) If, in addition to verbal insults, a woman physically bullies a man with slaps and pushes (and she is able to do so because he believes that *a man should never hit a woman*, so he cannot defend himself by hitting her back) until he agrees to have sex when she wants it and he doesn't, does her bullying count as coercion?

(e) If a woman expects sex-on-demand under the threat that she will divorce her husband and not let him see his children any more unless he complies, does the threat of him losing his children constitute coercion? If a woman threatens a man that *she will accuse him of rape* if he doesn't service her sexually, does that constitute coercion?

The last two involve physical violence and threats, and must surely count as coercion. But it's reasonable to say that all five of these scenarios, as described, would count as coercion. However, let's be clear on what I'm saying; I'm *not* suggesting that whenever a person of senior rank at work has sex with a person of junior rank at work, that it's *necessarily* coercion, or that if one person has a psychological ascendancy over their partner then all sex within that relationship is *necessarily* rape, or that any form of verbal abuse prior to sex means that the sex was rape (I'm not taking a feminist position), I'm merely saying that in a particular set of circumstances *it can be* rape, and that *this applies equally to both sexes*. It would also apply to the rape of a woman by another woman. But traditional misandrists are still thinking of the 'force' used in rape in terms of who has got the biggest muscles.

At one and the same time, mainstream feminist society is relying heavily on traditional notions of 'weak and delicate' candy-floss femininity in refusing to acknowledge the existence of female rapists, whilst feminist activists are busily expanding the range of what constitutes a male 'rapist' to include sex where there is no coercion present, such as classifying as 'rape' situations where a woman has a few alcoholic drinks with a man before sleeping with him or where a man is encouraging a woman to have sex with him too persistently.

Staunch feminists are determined to hang on to the word 'rape' as being applicable to male perpetrators *only*. It's such a powerfully emotive word that they are doggedly resolved to restrict its use solely to male rapists because this serves the feminist political agenda. (What would happen to the concept of 'rape culture' if it had to acknowledge the male victims of female rapists?) Do you know what term the feminist researcher and specialist on rape, Mary Koss, has come up with to describe rape when a women rapes a man? She calls it "unwanted sexual intercourse". Does that sound like rape to you? No, it's not supposed to. Koss holds that:

"Although consideration of male victims is within the scope of the legal statutes, it is important to restrict the term rape to instances where male victims were penetrated by offenders. It is inappropriate to consider as a rape victim a man who engages in unwanted sexual intercourse with a woman." [Mary Koss, "Detecting the Scope of Rape", Journal of Interpersonal Violence, 1993, p206.]

When researching the prevalence of sexual offences including rape committed against men, by means of questionnaires or interviews with men, she advises:

"Clarification is necessary to ensure that male respondents realize that the situations of interest are those in which they were penetrated forcibly and against their will by another person, and not situations where they felt pressure or coercion to have sexual relations with a woman partner." [Mary Koss, "Detecting the Scope of Rape", Journal of Interpersonal Violence, 1993, p208.]

Koss, you will notice, takes the concept of forcible *penetration* to be definitive of rape, just as the UK law did when I quoted it earlier. It is an extremely traditional approach, going way back into what feminists like Koss call patriarchal society. Yet Koss endorses it. Why? Well, if penetration implies penetration by a penis, then it defines rape in a way that limits the crime to male perpetrators, doesn't it? It means that men can only be raped by other men.

But what about Koss' assertion that "situations where they felt pressure or coercion" do not constitute rape? Does this mean that Koss must necessarily *reject* the feminist position that male bosses who sleep with their female secretaries and male professors who sleep with their female students have not committed rape? Actually it doesn't. Notice that the "they" she is referring to are "male respondents" and she specifically mentions their being pressured or coerced "to have sexual relations with a *woman* partner". This provides her with a handy get-out clause, where she could take the position that if a *female* boss coerced her *male* secretary into sex, or a *female* professor coerced her *male* student into sex, it would not count as rape because the female boss and female professor would not have *penetrated* their victim. Whereas a male boss who coerced his *female* secretary into sex and a male professor who coerced his *female* student into sex would have penetrated their victim, so it could be classified as rape. Convenient, eh?

Feminists like to *smear* any man who argues against feminist misandry with the false accusation that he is a 'rape apologist'. But look at that second quote again. This is what being a 'rape apologist' really means. She is describing "coercion to have sexual relations" as being *something other than rape*. On her definition, a woman can coerce a man into sex against his will *without* raping him. This is why Koss has been described by some as a "feminist rape apologist".
http://www.avoiceformen.com/feminism/male-disposability-and-mary-p-koss/

A duplicitous gendered use of the term 'coercion' features elsewhere in feminism, too. Feminists on American university campuses punish male students for a crime called 'sexual

300

coercion' where one person pressures another person into sex by persistently coaxing or nagging or cajoling them into consent. http://www.cotwa.info/2012/03/legal-infirmities-to-punishing-sexual.html Does this mean that those feminists acknowledge how women coerce men into sex? No, of course not, because feminists only apply the offence of 'sexual coercion' to male students. They see it as a part of liberating female students from the oppression of a male 'rape culture' on campus. But there is nothing in the concept of sexual coercion that limits it to males. The assumption that this is something that men do to women but not something that women do to men is based upon the traditional sexism which views men as the 'active' agent pursuing the woman whilst the woman is a 'passive' object being pursued. As so often, feminist sexism is merely an extension or elaboration of traditional sexism.

Feminism's double-standard regarding sex-crimes is evident in their contempt for, and neglect of, the male victim. Entrenched feminist gender-stereotypes compel them to view men as perpetrators. For example, there is a website called Feminist Majority Foundation. On it's sexual assault resources page it includes something called "Resources for Men". http://www.feminist.org/911/resources_male.html An encouraging sign, you might think? A feminist website concerned to provide resources for male victims of sexual assault? Not a bit of it. These are resources for male feminists directed at the reconstruction of male identity to prevent violence *against women*. They include groups like the National Organisation for Men Against Sexism (i.e. against misogyny, not against misandry) who are committed to "ending men's violence". The reality of women's violence against men and the existence of female perpetrators of sexual violence simply doesn't register on the political agenda of anyone who employs crude feminist gender-stereotypes.

'Rape Culture' and 'Victim-Blaming'

The political enforcement of the theory of 'rape culture' is most prevalent on university campuses in America and Canada

301

where it very much embodies the current establishment's obsession with socially engineering people minds to have them conform to ideologically 'correct' rules of conduct, abide by speech-codes, and not commit thought-crimes. There is a great deal of concern about 'attitudes' and conjecture about the consequences of those attitudes by the judgemental and illiberal guardians of public decency who typify a modern university.

In this form, the concept of 'rape culture' is a priggish rejection of sexual liberation in favour of a return to Victorian values with its emphasis on the constant need to protect the delicate sensibilities of the feminine gender from the boorishness of the masculine gender. This antique notion, lifted straight out of the traditional sexism of a book of etiquette for swooning genteel maidens, is employed in the cause of female empowerment over men where a woman's feelings are prioritised over the freedom of men to speak openly about sexual matters in an ideologically 'incorrect' way, *even amongst themselves*. This theory of 'rape culture' will include the condemnation of, and possible prosecution of, any behaviour by men that is coarse or vulgar about sex, such as sexual humour or sexual innuendo or sexual boasting or any kind of hostility expressed in sexual terms, in public or in private, which either hurts a woman's feelings or *might* hurt a woman's feelings *if* she were made aware of it. http://www.cbc.ca/news/canada/ottawa/anne-marie-roy-uottawa-student-leader-subject-of-explicit-online-chat-1.2556948

All of this is classified as sexual violence. So, too, is anything in society at large which sexually objectifies women in movies, television programmes, music videos, lingerie adverts, etc., on the grounds that this 'normalizes' an attitude of tolerance toward rape. 'Rape culture' on campus is seen as being a microcosm of the broader 'rape culture' that is modern day 'patriarchal' society. The theory of 'rape culture' goes far beyond the issue of rape as an act/crime, to make copious unsubstantiated assumptions about *what causes rape* but it therefore also implies that rape is endemic amongst university students, since they are immersed in this culture every day. It follows that if the culture causes acts of rape and the students are submerged in that culture, then innumerable acts of rape must be taking place.

Unfortunately, all of the solutions for 'rape culture' are presented in terms of (a) feminists exercising thought-control over men and (b) feminists removing the offending cultural items.

The former is spoken of in terms of 'educating' men not to be such beasts so that they don't experience the wrong kinds of thoughts and feelings in regard of women but think of them only with feelings of polite respect and quiet admiration. This will be women's entitlement *as women*, it will not be contingent on their own behaviour. No matter how badly they might behave themselves, men's thoughts and feelings toward them must be impeccably gentlemanly. Perhaps some courteous sex might occasionally be permitted, although only if initiated by the woman and with it clearly understood that the fortunate male must be ever-mindful of his partner's civil rights so that he is ready to desist at any moment should she decide to change her mind and withdraw her consent.

The latter would presumably mean the total removal from society of anything that is contrary to feminism's positive gender-stereotype of women. There would have to be no images or representations of women that might be thought to be erotically charged, as these would sexually objectify women. There would have to be no sex scenes in Hollywood movies (a return to the Hays Code of the 1930s?), no sexual imagery in music videos (sorry Beyoncé, it's time to retire), no sexily dressed women on television (exit the cheerleader from Heroes), no lingerie at all (let alone adverts for the deplorable garments) because all of this disgusting eroticism 'normalizes' an attitude of tolerance toward rape. This would just be the beginning of the feminist cultural veto. Lady Chatterley's Lover would probably have to be banned all over again because of its gratuitous use of the words 'fuck' and 'cunt'.

What it comes down to is that *sexual liberation* has had the consequence of there being all sorts of sexual representations and sexualised behaviour in society that feminist ideology vehemently disapproves of, but with their habitual hypocrisy feminists want the guarantee of their own sexual liberation without having to tolerate anybody else's. So they will (quite rightly) condemn homophobia whilst (quite wrongly) practicing their own version of heterophobia with their condemnation of sexual objectification by hetero males and their fear of man as the universal rapist.

Ironically, the 'rape culture' feminists may have far more in common than they realise with the evangelical Christian 'purity culture' that produced young people pledging themselves to abstinence and wearing 'purity rings' to disassociate themselves from the sexually liberated hedonists of conventional youth culture. The idea of 'purity culture' was a complete rejection of the sordid and sexualised society of mainstream America, as is the theory of 'rape culture'. The motivations and agendas of the two ideologies may be very different but the *practical consequences* for society that result from their shared view of sex (i.e. the need to impose constraints upon unbridled male lust) might be remarkably similar.

For example, this article "How the purity culture made me afraid of men" on a *feminist* website could as easily have been written about the effects of the theory of 'rape culture' as the effects of the 'purity culture' movement.
http://www.patheos.com/blogs/lovejoyfeminism/2012/03/how-the-purity-culture-made-me-afraid-of-men.html

A prominent feature of the theory of 'rape culture' is the concept of victim-blaming; the idea that society is full of people determined to blame the female victim of rape for having been raped (e.g. because she was wearing a short skirt, etc). Given the gigantic influence of feminism in promoting the belief that women are never to blame for anything because everything is men's fault, the phrase 'victim-blaming' is revealing either of the very high degree of feminism's ideological paranoia or of its willingness to use the stereotype of woman-as-victim in a cynical power-play.

As an example of paranoia, we might look at feminism's application of the term 'victim-blaming' to any safety guidance that advises women to take personal responsibility for their own protection; that as the world is a dangerous place for everyone, a woman should be aware of how her own behaviour might put her at risk. (e.g. it's safer to go out for the evening with friends than on your own; avoid travelling home alone at night; don't loiter in isolated places; don't get staggering drunk with strangers, etc.) This kind of safety guidance is considered to be 'victim-blaming' because it is seen as putting the *onus on women to avoid being raped* instead of putting the *onus on men to not rape.* Surely, says feminism, it is the behaviour of the potential rapist that must be addressed and modified, not the behaviour of the potential victim. This might almost sound reasonable until you realise the infantile abdication of personal responsibility which it entails.

Feminism, because it is fighting a sex-war, sees the situation as a *choice* between putting the onus *either* upon women *or* upon men. Whereas a sensible grown-up person would not see these two things as being a choice at all, they would want to pursue *both* of these courses of action. But feminism is entrenched in the belief that 'men are the problem'. So instead of endorsing a policy that women should take responsibility for their own safety *and* that men should be careful not to assume any implied consent from the woman's behaviour, feminism insists upon the latter *only;* that men alone must be held accountable. As a result, any advice about taking sensible precautions, like not flashing your tits in public, is declared to be 'victim-blaming'. If a woman is swilling down alcohol until she drinks herself insensible and passes out unconsciousness, to suggest that this is a contributing factor to her loss of personal safety is condemned as 'victim-blaming'. The concept of 'victim-blaming' does not allow the woman to be accountable under any circumstances and, as with traditional sexism, men are made responsible for the safety of women.

(As an example, https://www.youtube.com/watch?v=9IZ7XfC612k in this video a very drunk young woman gets into the car of two male strangers and invites them to take her home for sex. She says

"I'll fuck the shit out of you" and "take advantage of me". Fortunately for her, they decline. The men take responsibility for the safety of the woman.)

Once again, let's be clear on what I *am* saying and what I'm *not* saying. I am *not* in any way excusing, or taking responsibility away from, a rapist for their crime. If, for example, a man were to rape a woman while she is unconscious from alcohol, then that is unequivocally rape and should be punished accordingly. The rapist is to blame for the rape, no question about it. But this does not mean that if a woman recklessly puts herself at risk, that she is nonetheless in no way responsible for having put herself at risk. In the real world where the grown-ups live, her actions may have contributed to the circumstances under which a rape may occur and, as an adult, she should be aware of this and take responsibility for herself. To expect this of her is definitely *not* blaming the victim.

Remember, it is not a choice between blaming *him* or blaming *her*. Feminists only see it that way because they see everything that way. He is accountable for what he did, which is why he is guilty of rape. She is accountable for what she did, which is why her best friend might say 'what the hell did you think you were doing getting rolling drunk with strangers?!'

To take an alternative example. If a drunk in a bar flashes a bankroll of cash around when ordering his drinks, then slumps in an unconscious stupor on a chair leaving his wallet on the table in front of him, then it is not surprising if an opportunist thief steals his wallet. The thief is unequivocally to blame for the act of theft but the drunk is reprehensibly negligent in the way that he virtually invited the theft. The drunk is *not to blame* for the theft but he is negligent in failing to take responsibility for himself in an adult manner. Which is why, when he discovers the theft, he may curse himself for being such a fool.

But in the matter of rape, the feminist position is that because the victim is not to blame for the rape, she is therefore not responsible in any way, not even for any actions of hers which might have put her at much greater risk of the crime occurring.

306

This conflates two different things, *his* actions and *her* actions, and it reduces the concept of responsibility to being crudely synonymous with blame so that to hold her responsible for her own actions is treated as *being the same thing* as blaming her for his actions in raping her.

The feminist concept of 'victim-blaming' is a crude misreading of the true situation. Whilst the word 'responsibility' can sometimes be used to mean 'blame', in this instance it more properly means the "ability to act independently and take decisions" (taking responsibility for one's own decisions) or "having a duty to deal with something or of having control over someone" (i.e. being responsible for having control over one's own dealings with the world; Oxford English Dictionary). The consequence of the feminist view is that it becomes *the duty of everybody else in the world* (and more specifically, of men) to make sure that women never come to any harm, regardless of the risks women take in the way that they behave.

The most notorious example of this ideological paranoia that for a woman to be expected to take some responsibility for her own safety is to *blame women for rape* occurred during a talk about personal safety on a Canadian university campus. It was the comment made by an obscure Toronto police officer, Constable Michael Sanguinetti, who suggested that "women should avoid dressing like sluts in order not to be victimized". This single comment provoked an international response in the form of the highly publicised Slutwalk campaigns of 2011 which took place in several countries around the world.
http://en.wikipedia.org/wiki/SlutWalk

The police constable instantly became the global poster boy for 'victim-blaming'. But, however indelicately phrased, notice that the quote from Sanguinetti does not actually blame the victims; that was a *feminist interpretation* of what he said. His actual intention might have been quite different. But his comment was treated by the mainstream media as being *equivalent to* blaming the victims because the feminist interpretation was simply accepted as being the truth.

A report on the Sanguinetti incident in the Mail Online http://www.dailymail.co.uk/news/article-1358453/Police-officer-tells-student-avoid-sexual-assaults-dressing-like-sluts.html contains a truly astonishing quote from Toronto police spokeswoman Meaghan Gray who said that:

"Cautioning women on their state of dress is not part of any police training. In fact, this is completely contradictory to what officers are taught, she said. They are taught that nothing a woman does contributes to a sexual assault."

Can the police in Toronto really be so feminised that they are taught that *nothing a woman does contributes to a sexual assault?* Nothing at all? Can that be meant literally? It looks like it is. If so, then this is the feminist concept of 'victim-blaming' in its purest form. The official position of the Toronto police is that women are not accountable for their own personal safety in any way whatsoever. (Hey, she could dance naked through the men's locker room with a dildo up her ass singing 'I wanna be fucked by you . . .' and that would have contributed nothing to any assault that took place because she always has the option of changing her mind.)

Anyone who doesn't understand what an *infantile abdication of personal responsibility* this is can only have failed to understand because they are themselves an infant. If what spokeswoman Meaghan Gray is reported to have said is meant to be understood literally, then her comment is far more extreme that what Constable Michael Sanguinetti said. I wonder if the Toronto police do not hold *men* to be in any way accountable for their own personal safety either? I mean, if a male stripper were dancing naked in front of an over-enthusiastic sexually aroused woman who reached out, grabbed his balls, and inflicted a testicular rupture, would she be prosecuted for criminal assault because *nothing a man does contributes to a sexual assault?* After all, he hadn't given her his consent to rupture his balls, had he?

Advocates of the theory of 'rape culture' also apply 'victim-blaming' to the way that cases of alleged rape are handled within the legal system. However, their main target is not, as might make sense, the Sharia law of Islamic cultures where genuine rape victims can indeed be blamed if they don't have a sufficient number of male witnesses to support their testimony. No, instead, feminist concern over 'victim-blaming' within the legal system mainly targets the police and judiciary of western cultures. I wonder why that is, when police in the West are apparently being taught that nothing a woman does contributes to a sexual assault, whereas in March 2013 a Norwegian woman reported to the police in Dubai that she had been raped, and as a result she was sent to prison for sixteen months for the crime of having illicit sex outside of marriage. http://www.dailymail.co.uk/news/article-2367152/Norwegian-woman-reported-raped-Dubai-jailed-16-months.html This is an example of *real* victim-blaming and you can see how utterly different it is to the feminist version.

Ordinary people here in the 'patriarchal' West seem a little more resistant to establishment feminist orthodoxy than the highly feminised mainstream media or the Toronto police department. The 2010 "Wake Up To Rape" research commissioned by The Havens (sexual assault referral centres in London) said in its summary report:

"There are many situations in which some people feel that a person should take responsibility for being raped. Over half (56%) of those surveyed think that there are some circumstances where a person should accept responsibility. Of those people the circumstances are:

- Performing another sexual act on them (73%)
- Getting into bed with a person (66%)
- Drinking to excess / blackout (64%)
- Going back to theirs for a drink (29%)
- Dressing provocatively (28%)
- Dancing in a sexy way with a man at a night club or bar (22%)

- Acting flirtatiously (21%)

- Kissing them (14%)

- Accepting a drink and engaging in a conversation at a bar (13%)"

http://www.vawpreventionscotland.org.uk/resources/research-and-reports/wake-rape

Feminism might want to cite this as evidence in support for their concept of 'victim-blaming' except for the fact that this research also reported that *women* were more inclined toward 'victim-blaming' than *men*. (I began this book by saying that the words 'feminists' and 'women' are not synonymous; this example shows how different they can be.) On these figures, feminism should apparently be attributing a culture of 'victim-blaming' more to women's attitudes than to men's:

"Women are less forgiving than men. They are more likely to think that a person should accept responsibility when:

- Performing another sexual act on them (75% vs. 70%)

- Getting into bed with a person (71% vs. 57%)

- Going back to theirs for a drink (35% vs. 19%)

- Dressing provocatively (31% vs. 23%)

- Dancing in a sexy way with a man at a night club or bar (23% vs. 19%)

- Accepting a drink and engaging in a conversation at a bar (15% vs. 11%)"

Not only that but, along with 27% of men, 14% of *women* agreed with the statement "most claims of rape are probably not true". London, of course, is a comprehensively multicultural city so a great many of the respondents in this survey might have come from non-western cultures. These days London may bear a certain resemblance to Dubai. But even so, it would appear that some women take a very different view of whether women are, or are not, responsible for their own actions and personal safety from that propounded in the theory of 'rape culture'.

Regardless of what *women* may or may not think about it, rape is very definitely one of *feminism's* two favourite subjects, along with domestic violence. In recent years these two campaign rallying cries have loomed so large in feminist activism as to almost eclipse the rest of feminism's ideological obsessions. The public face of contemporary feminism has almost become a 'rape culture' and 'culture of domestic violence' ideology.

This is because feminism is about *power*. It is about the exercising of political and cultural power over people in society, to persuade them to think and behave in the way that feminism wants them to think and behave. The power to indoctrinate children in school. The power to indoctrinate students at university (noticeably more so in America than in the UK). The power to have a feminist bias in the media, where dishonest feminist 'research' is treated as scientific fact. The power to influence government policy. The power to push through legislation. Like any other ideology, feminism acts in pursuit of *its own ever greater power* and the twin issues of rape and domestic violence serve this pursuit better than any other issues. Consequently, the feminist interpretation of rape and domestic violence have become as central to contemporary feminism as women's suffrage was to the suffragettes.

This political strategy works. It's easy to see why. Take a society in which (a) men have an evolutionary psychological predisposition to protect women from harm and (b) traditional sexism has taught men that it is their chivalrous 'manly duty' to protect women. Then combine that with (c) the truly horrific nature of genuine rapes and genuine instances of domestic violence (where the victim happens to be female and the perpetrator happens to be male, but ignoring all the instances of male victims and female perpetrators). If you combine those three things, what do you get?

You get a political weapon of immense power. The more that feminism can convince the public that 1 in 4 women are raped during their lives, and the more that feminism can convince the public that husbands and boyfriends are battering their wives and girlfriends three times a week and twice on Saturday, and the more that feminism can convince the public that hordes of men go out for the evening armed with their date-rape drugs to spike women's drinks, then the *less resistance* there will be to feminist legislation and feminist cultural norms.

The emotive power of rape and domestic violence are the two big sticks that feminism can wield to get their own way whenever political or cultural decisions are being made. The more feminism plays the role of victim, the stronger its political position becomes. For feminism, *victimhood is empowerment*.

Those few brave anti-establishment speakers who dare to challenge feminism's 'rape culture' mythology will be instantly denounced as 'rape apologists'. Who would want to be smeared with that obscene slander? That's why anti-establishment speakers require courage; they know that smears and slanders will be heaped upon them. Meanwhile, feminism goes on exercising its irresponsible power and getting its own way.

Chapter 6

Where We Are Now and The Future

Traditional Joke: "Women have their faults, men have only two: everything they say and everything they do."

Feminist Joke: "Billions of men, why animal test?"

The Psychological Effects of Feminism Upon Men and Boys

Let me put it to you directly, reader, that *your own life* is the evidence for the truth of what I'm saying in this book. How many times in your own experience have you heard ordinary people make gross misandrist generalizations quite casually in everyday conversation? When you've heard someone saying that 'men need women to civilize them' or 'men commit all the crime' or 'men lack commitment' or 'men never grow up' and so on, was the response to this overt bigotry a sage-like nod of agreement or perhaps a peal of convivial laughter? It has long been considered socially acceptable to insult and denigrate men in the crudest fashion. The millions of people who do so expect to receive, and have received, *social approbation* for their gross sexism. Ask yourself honestly, reader, haven't you been witness to this any number of times?

After all, you live in a society in which supposedly educated academics and media pundits use phrases like 'toxic masculinity' in an attempt to lend a spurious intellectual legitimacy to comments expressing extreme misandrist sexism about the need to extirpate 'male pathology'. You live in a society in which the establishment elites speak of 'women-centered' policies as if they promoted sex equality rather than being a *negation* of it. You live in a society which talks incessantly about what should be done for women and

313

constantly takes political action on behalf of women because women are 'marginalized', but which doesn't give a damn about those *other people* whom nobody lifts a finger to help because those *unmentioned other people* are not 'marginalized'.

You live in a society in which inferior males are encouraged to emulate superior females by 'getting in touch with their feminine side'. You live in a society in which feminist women have spent decades calling all men chauvinist pigs (1960s), sexist pigs (1970s), misogynist pigs (1980s), and have smeared all men with a collective guilt for the crimes of rape and domestic violence, but if any man today criticizes feminism or defends men he will be falsely accused of 'hate-speech' against women. You live in a society in which feminists use twitter to 'humorously' express their desire to #killallmen. https://www.youtube.com/watch?v=pZcTG2yFcBE You live in a society in which a mainstream newspaper can include a glowingly positive book review entitled: "How to train your husband like a dog! Hilarious book reveals that you čan keep him on a tight leash." http://www.dailymail.co.uk/femail/article-1257089/How-train-husband-like-dog-An-hilarious-book-reveals-really-tight-leash.html

You live in a society which is obsessively concerned to increase the number and strength of 'women's rights' but treats the very idea of 'men's rights' as a not-very-funny joke. You live in a society in which all discussions of rape are concerned solely with the woman's consent and the woman's vulnerability, never with male consent or male vulnerability because everybody knows that men are all sexually predatory sluts. You live in a society in which males are more likely to suffer violence than women but in which all the campaigns against violence *specifically state that their concern* is about 'violence against women'. You live in a society in which women have been given control over their own fertility while men do *not* have control over *their* own fertility, in which women in fact exercise control over men's fertility, but where men are nonetheless condemned for their alleged despotic desire to exercise control over women's bodies.

You live in a society in which schools in Scotland decided that children should not make father's day cards (although they do make mother's day cards) because 1 in 4 children in Britain are from lone parent families and it would be insensitive to the children's feelings to make father's day cards when a quarter of their pupils don't have a father. You live in a society in which the Munk Debates (who say they are Canada's premier public policy forum) can debate a resolution in front of an audience of 3,000 rich people (tickets cost from $25 to $90 each) about "Gender in the 21st Century: *Be it resolved, men are obsolete*" http://www.munkdebates.com/debates/the-end-of-men during which the votes in favour of the motion increased from 16% before the debate to 44% after the debate. By the end of the debate nearly half of the audience were convinced that men are indeed obsolete. (See also Karen Straughan's excellent response at https://www.youtube.com/watch?v=gaO3THnOHhA)

The effect that decades of this torrential rain of misandrist abuse has had upon men should come as no surprise. Some of them have sought to weather the storm by bowing their heads and accepting their own inferior status, smiling good-naturedly when they are insulted to their faces, feeling that they cannot defend themselves against women because they have a duty to defend women and put women's interests ahead of their own.

But some men have not done this. Instead, they have given up on a society that has no respect for them, wanting to have as little to do with it as possible. In the teeth of that torrential rainstorm of dogmatic invective and crude male-bashing they have been driven into an attitude of self-defence and a desire to seek shelter. They are turning their backs upon a culture that offers them no other gender-identity than that of a guilt-object. And there are some men who cannot help blaming women for so readily embracing a position of privilege and for their widespread endorsement of so much of feminism's misandry. These men feel totally betrayed. They are so heartily sick and tired of a lifetime of being insulted and disrespected that it has led them to feel a total loss of sympathy for women. The bigotry of toxic feminism has poisoned gender relations.

It is only to be expected that many of the men who have lived through feminist oppression have been taught by that experience to never trust women again. After decades of women's disloyalty toward their fellow human beings, this withdrawal of trust is no more than any reasonable person would have anticipated. Yet some people now seem taken aback by the psychological effects that decades of feminist bigotry have had upon men. The gynocentric *concentration of concern* upon women's wants and needs *only*, and the traditional belief that men can stoically endure any amount of pain without coming to harm because they are 'men', seems to have misled some people into thinking that men would simply be reconstructed to meet women's requirements and then society would move forward into the feminist utopia. It doesn't seem to have occurred to them that men might be irreparably damaged. That men might eventually begin to formulate *their own* agenda.

Whenever feminism's 'achievements' are celebrated, it is always in terms of the marvellous advances made by women. In this final chapter I want to look at what feminism has done, not *for* women, but *to* men. But the damage done to the men who have lived through feminism is only half of the story.

The more significant question to ask is: what about those male children and youngsters who have been born and raised under feminist oppression? Have you ever paused to wonder what effect *the unrelenting disparagement of all things male* has had upon boys? What deep psychological scars has feminism inflicted upon them? They are being raised in a society which tells them that they are doomed to grow up into a cross between Jackass and Jack the Ripper. What does it do to a young boy's mind to constantly be told that people of his biological type grow up either into a fool or a villain, or both? What effects do these feminist social constructs of gender have upon a growing boy's sense of self and his aspirations for the future?

In a 1961 film, "Conspiracy of Hearts", set in Europe during world war two, a nun is encouraging a little Jewish girl to speak because the child has so far been completely silent. The nun asks: "Won't you even tell me your name?" The little girl looks at the nun and replies: "Jew-dog. My name is Jew-dog." It is an emotionally shattering moment in the film because the audience understands that this is what the child has repeatedly been told is her name.

Most people, at least, would feel a surge of overpowering sympathy for that little Jewish girl. But how much sympathy do people feel for the little boys in UK schools who are taught by their schoolteachers that men are domestic abusers and sexual exploiters and violent rapists and the historical oppressors of women? Nothing will be said in the classroom about the virtues of men, only what feminists believe to be their vices and their crimes against women. Those little boys know perfectly well that they are male, that they will grow into men, and their schoolteachers have already told them what *men* are.

It is even worse for little white boys, who are told that the history of white people from the UK (and, more particularly, the white men) is a narrative of black slavery and militaristic imperialism and the economic rape of defenceless foreign countries and shameful racism against immigrants. Every culture has both its proud achievements and its guilty crimes but the schoolteachers of multiculturalism only speak of the guilty crimes, not the proud achievements, just as the schoolteachers of feminism only speak of male vices, never of male virtues. So little white boys sitting in their classrooms are identified with guilt and shame and crime both by their biological sex and the colour of their skin.

Does anyone ever exhibit any concern or worry about what this heavily politicised education system is doing to these boys? Give a dog a bad name. "Jew-dog. *My name* is Jew-dog."

Is it any wonder that boys are falling so far behind girls at school? Is it any wonder that working class white boys are at the bottom of the educational heap and are growing up into a generation of unaspirational unemployables?

317

Feminised Education

One of the most high-profile issues of gender inequality today is education. But it is rarely reported as an issue of *institutional sexism*. Why? Because it has been perpetrated by the very same people who get to decide whether something is sexist or not. The institutionalised gender inequality in education is misandrist, therefore the profoundly feminist educational establishment seeks desperately for *some other explanation* of why boys are falling further and further behind girls in all levels of education. The pig-headed belief that all issues of gender inequality must necessarily be issues of misogyny is so deeply entrenched amongst the cultural elite that even when faced with overwhelming evidence to the contrary they try to shield their minds from the obvious truth.

The Higher Education Funding Council for England (HEFCE) cannot escape their own statistics, yet they would cut their tongues out rather than admit that feminist pedagogy and feminist society is responsible for what those statistics reveal:

"Young women have been more likely to enter higher education than young men for every cohort in this analysis. Currently 40 per cent of young women enter higher education compared to 32 per cent of young men. The participation rate of young men now trails that of young women by a decade and over the past 15 years around 270,000 fewer young men than young women have entered higher education as a result of their lower participation rate. In the mid-2000s young women were +25 per cent more likely to enter higher education than young men, rising to +44 per cent more likely in disadvantaged areas."
http://www.hefce.ac.uk/pubs/year/2010/201003/

The gender inequality in UK universities is so glaring that even establishment newspapers like the Guardian express concern: "There are now one third more female than male students applying for university. Women are now more likely to be accepted for higher education than men are even to apply."
http://www.theguardian.com/commentisfree/2012/dec/13/education-leaving-boys-behind

Notice that all those feminists who have been saying for years and years that affirmative action programmes are a necessary measure to combat gender inequality would now, *if they were principled people*, be committed to demanding affirmative action to get more men into higher education. But have you heard any feminists demanding affirmative action for men? No, neither have I. This is because feminists are not principled people, they do not act upon a principle of sex equality, they act to *benefit women*. Affirmative action was never about sex equality, it was only ever about benefiting women. That's why the ideology is called feminism.

The gender inequality is not limited to higher education, it is present throughout the entire state education system in the UK. The feminisation of education disadvantages boys *systemically*. Here are two more newspaper reports that encapsulate the seriousness of the problem.

"This week began with the news that four out of 10 children are virtually illiterate and innumerate when they leave primary school; it ends with the revelation that more than a quarter of boys did not gain a single good GCSE last year. Both situations are a disgrace. Neither is exactly surprising - but the second statistic usefully points us towards a major (and sometimes overlooked) element of the crisis in British schools: the failure to educate boys. The primary school and GCSE statistics come from different sources and so are not directly comparable. But what seems beyond doubt is that, in the case of boys, the handicap of a mediocre primary school education is made worse by a secondary school curriculum that plays to the strengths of girls." http://www.telegraph.co.uk/comment/telegraph-view/3641881/Feminising-education-is-of-benefit-to-no-one.html

"Building on a trend that began more than a decade ago, girls are outperforming boys at every level in education. They get more and better GCSEs and A-levels, win more places at top universities and gain better degrees. Although poor attainment is concentrated in the lower income groups, the gender gap persists to the detriment of boys across all social classes and ethnic groups. And as this week's dismal primary school test results reveal, boys are sinking farther and farther behind. A depressing 40 per cent of boys will begin secondary school unable to write fluently and correctly, compared with 25 per cent of girls." http://www.dailymail.co.uk/femail/article-1205106/The-REAL-gender-gap-scandal-Why-boys-true-victims-discrimination.html

One issue that is sometimes raised is the conspicuous lack of male teachers in primary school education. Boys begin their experience of education with a visual demonstration that education is a 'female' pursuit. If all the teachers are women, then that sends a clear message that education is something that women do. In 2013 the Centre for Social Justice reported:

"Across England one in four state primary schools have no full-time qualified male teacher, and 80 per cent of state-educated boys are in primary schools with three or fewer full-time qualified male teachers." [Centre for Social Justice, 2013 press-release.]

So, once again, can we expect the feminists who have spent their lives demanding affirmative action programmes in the name of gender diversity to now start demanding affirmative action programmes that favour employing male primary school teachers over female ones? Can we expect men-only shortlists for primary school posts? Don't hold your breath. Yet the lack of men in primary (elementary) school education, and in education overall, is an international problem and it's getting worse, not better. https://www.youtube.com/watch?v=_uCaM8ULr6M

But, whilst there should definitely be far more male teachers in schools, the problem of gender inequality in education actually goes very much deeper than just the lack of male role-models in a boy's early experience of education. The fundamental issue is the feminist pedagogy which has long been endorsed and practiced by those in control of state education.

If you've been following this issue over the last dozen or so years you will have heard repeatedly the two phrases that are constantly being used to describe the disadvantage that boys suffer in the state education system. The two phrases are used routinely *both in academic discussions and in most of the media reporting* on this topic. The first is: 'girls are outperforming boys'. Notice how the phrase does not treat the issue as being one of gender inequality or sexist advantage? The phrase does not admit that feminist pedagogy is advantaging girls and disadvantaging boys. Instead, the phrase makes it sound as if the girls are simply more intelligent. They do better *because* they're girls. The phrase 'girls are outperforming boys' is used because it is consistent with feminist gender-supremacism; it suggests that the girls are just smarter, that's all.

The second phrase you hear is: 'boys are failing'. Again, notice how this blames the boys. They are failing *because* they're boys. Feminist gender beliefs have so indoctrinated the concept of the male guilt-object into people's minds that if *boys are being failed by the education system* it must be the boys own fault. They're male aren't they? It's their own fault because they won't sit still. It's because they're *boys.*

The two phrases are used to deftly sidestep any acknowledgement that the real blame lies with the deliberate sexist bias of feminist pedagogy. In reality, it is the feminist pedagogues who are failing boys. Feminists are very skilled at influencing what people think by the subtle use of deceitful language. To say that boys are being failed by the education system lays the blame where it truly belongs, with the education system. To say that 'boys are failing' blames the victims. The pedagogues can never blame themselves because it is always males who must take the blame. Feminists find it inconceivable that they themselves could be at fault, that they themselves are the guilty ones, so instead it must be that 'girls are outperforming boys' and 'boys are failing'.

Despite all the feeble excuses to the contrary, this gender inequality is the direct result of feminised education. To deny this you would have to claim that the hugely advantaged position of girls over boys had occurred at the same time as the introduction of feminist pedagogy in education (from the 1980s to the present) but that this was *nothing more than sheer coincidence*. Only someone with a feminist academic's utter lack of intellectual integrity could have the bare-faced cheek to make such a claim.

For a hardcore gender-supremacist feminist, perhaps the denial would be even more extreme. She might claim that girls had *always been smarter than boys* but that girls had previously been held back by 'masculine' systems of education, and now that those old 'masculine' systems have been discarded the objective superiority of the female over the male has been revealed. Some feminists seem to imply this when they profess not to understand what the phrase 'feminised education' even means, as if contemporary education were conducted in an environment of gender-neutrality (because, of course, they don't count misandry as being sexism). But this is mere deceit on their part because feminists themselves offer definitions of feminist pedagogy and feminised education is simply the practice of feminist pedagogy.

A standard dictionary definition of 'pedagogy' would be something like 'the principles, methods and practice of teaching, especially as an academic subject or in a formal learning environment'. In "What is Feminist Pedagogy?" Carolyn Shrewsbury says that:

"Feminist pedagogy begins with a vision of what education might be like but frequently is not. This is a vision of the classroom as a liberatory environment in which we, teacher-student and student-teacher, act as subjects, not objects. Feminist pedagogy is engaged teaching/learning – engaged with self in a continuing reflective process; engaged actively with the material being studied; engaged with others in a struggle to get beyond our sexism and racism and classism and homophobia and other destructive hatreds and to work together to enhance our knowledge; engaged with the community, with traditional organizations, and with movements for social change."

http://www.jstor.org/discover/10.2307/40003432?uid=3738032&uid=2129&uid=2&uid=70&uid=4&sid=21103242176611

There are certain things we might observe in this straight away. Feminist teaching methods are overtly political, hence the explicit reference to "our sexism and racism and classism and homophobia" and to "movements for social change". (All of these terms will be given rigidly 'politically correct' definitions.) This politicization of the education system is why feminist pedagogy practices something called 'transformative learning' where students are transformed from being the recipients of knowledge to being the agents of societal change.

We can also see from Shrewsbury's account that feminist teaching methods are overtly communal; the liberation envisioned is a liberation from a focus upon the individual, where each student is individually concerned with their own acquisition of knowledge and their own academic success. Instead feminist pedagogy is a collective enterprise where "our" knowledge is enhanced in an atmosphere of caring and sharing. This is why feminised education has always frowned upon a spirit of *competition* in which boys might flourish and advocated a spirit of *cooperation* which favours girls. Shrewsbury asserts:

"A classroom characterized as persons connected in a net of relationships with people who care about each other's learning as well as their own is very different from a classroom that is seen as comprised of teacher and students."

In pursuit of this communality of learning, traditional teaching methods, *where someone who has knowledge of a subject passes that knowledge on to someone who doesn't know it*, is rejected. It is generally dismissed by pedagogues on the grounds that it is 'didactic', which is considered a terrible sin in contemporary education because the word suggests a hierarchical relationship (and is therefore deplorably 'masculine') where the knowledgeable teacher conveys information down to the student who lacks this knowledge.

This is why Shrewsbury refers to the "teacher-student and the student-teacher" rather than to the teacher and the student. Feminist pedagogy claims to support a learning environment in which *everyone is learning from everyone*. This claim is a colossal falsehood, of course, because feminist pedagogues are unshakably convinced that they are the people who know best and that anyone who disagrees with them must therefore be ignorant and wrong. Contemporary education is actually *extremely didactic* in its insistence upon what is ideologically 'correct' and 'incorrect', as would be immediately evident if any student in the classroom ever dared to disagree with feminism or multiculturalism, or to criticize any aspects of Islam (Islamophobia!) or anything like that.

The didacticism of the ideologically 'correct' pedagogue is ever present and they are not slow to abuse their position of power in the face of disagreement. The strongest evidence for the inflexibly dogmatic character of feminist teaching methods is probably found in the way that feminist students on American and Canadian university campuses mindlessly parrot the propaganda of feminist orthodoxy whenever anyone tries to discuss any other point of view. Feminist pedagogy has reduced the 'education' of these students to the level of outright indoctrination. They can only think the 'correct' thoughts that their indoctrination has put into their heads, which they then regurgitate through their mouths.
https://www.youtube.com/watch?v=CRWff4gCwTw

The bigotry and intolerance of feminist academia is now so extreme in America that students who still wish to learn in an environment of intellectual diversity and freedom of speech are having to organize nationally to defend themselves against ideological correctness, for example the Foundation for Individual Rights in Education (FIRE). http://www.thefire.org/

Although the intrinsic hypocrisy of feminism renders feminist pedagogy effectively illegitimate because they are themselves more guilty of the offences that they condemn in traditional pedagogy than traditional pedagogy was (e.g. sexism, top-down hierarchical indoctrination, educational elitism, refusal to listen to alternative opinions, etc.) feminists are, as always, blithely unaware of their own hypocrisy. Feminist pedagogy remains dominant at all levels of education, so we had better continue to explore *what it perceives itself to be*. We can see the same doctrinal beliefs that Shrewsbury is employing in the definitions offered by other feminist pedagogues. The Gender and Education Association tell us that:

"Definitions of feminist pedagogy vary widely, but there is common agreement on these three key tenets:

Resisting hierarchy: In the learning environment, the teacher figure and students work against the creation of a hierarchy of authority between teacher and student; the students also deliver 'content' and influence the design of the class.

Using experience as a resource: As well as using traditional sources of information, such as academic journals and books, the students' and teachers' own experiences are used as 'learning materials'. The purpose of using experience as a resource is twofold: firstly, experiences which have not been documented in academic work are brought into discussion, and secondly the class participants experience transformative learning.

Transformative learning: Feminist pedagogy aims for the class participants (students *and* teachers) not just to acquire new knowledge, but for their thinking to shift in new directions. This may involve the realisation that personal interpretations of experience or of social phenomena can be re-read and validated in new, critical ways."
http://www.genderandeducation.com/resources/pedagogies/feminist-pedagogy/

In the first of these key tenets we can see, again, the refusal to recognise the teacher as being senior (because more knowledgeable) to the student on the grounds that such an attitude would be hierarchical. There are two points to be aware of here, the first of which I would argue is extremely important.

(a) The ways in which boys were taught in the past (which produced the levels of scientific, industrial and technological benefits enjoyed in the modern world) were all hierarchical.

325

They were father teaching son, craftsman teaching apprentice, tutor teaching student. Does that mean that hierarchical teaching is 'masculine' and must therefore be rejected? No, it means that *hierarchical education worked very successfully for boys*. The junior was encouraged to respect the knowledgeable senior, and acquire the skills/knowledge by which the junior would grow to *earn respect* for himself. I said earlier that 'respect' has been for men what 'love' has been for women. Most men are strongly motivated by the acquisition of respect. So, if you want boys to learn, you should make learning a source of respect for them. But this is impossible under feminist pedagogy because feminism requires that everything 'masculine' be systemically *disrespected* (for these are the traits of the 'oppressor') and hierarchical learning itself is rejected on the grounds that it is masculine.

(b) In complete contradiction of their alleged rejection of hierarchy, feminist lecturers and professors in American universities reserve the right *for themselves* to ride roughshod over all dissenting opinion on the grounds that their own ideological point of view *is the knowledgeable and authoritative position*. The feminist educational establishment itself employs a hierarchical approach to knowledge when they are dismissing any contrary opinion as ill-informed and ignorant, feeling themselves entitled to take this high-handed position because they are the educated elite who know best, even though this attitude of dismissal is in direct violation of their own professed pedagogy. You can hear this attitude echoes in a phrase parroted by the indoctrinated students who, in the most *condescending* of tones, say to their opponents 'we invite you to educate yourself'.

In the third of these key tenets we can also see, again, the overtly political character of this pedagogy. Education is not just for students "to acquire new knowledge", their thinking is to "shift in new directions". The plural is dishonest. We all know in which *specific direction* the students thinking is required to shift. Feminist pedagogy is intended to make students into feminists; into reactionary establishment drones. And it succeeds at this, that's why it produces so many bigoted and

326

intolerant students. 'Transformative learning' is *a deliberate imposition of a political programme upon the state education system*. It is thought control. If you don't believe so, then take a look at Evan Maloney's excellent documentary "Indoctrinate U".
https://www.youtube.com/watch?v=WHyvRHrYYBA

The communal character of the pedagogy is also apparent in these three key tenets. They show the strong emphasis feminist education has on the expression of personal feelings and the validation of "personal interpretations of experience or of social phenomena". This is *exactly the same* attitude that we saw in chapter 5 when discussing feminist research, where the subjective perspective of the woman being interviewed was taken as being the truth. What a woman *says* is therefore *true*.

Readers will be long familiar with this attitude in any debate about gender in which a woman begins her contribution to the discussion with the words 'Speaking as a woman . . .' and then relates her feelings on the subject under debate. The old fashioned gender-stereotype of how female human beings are primarily concerned with their feelings is a misogynist caricature that is thriving under feminism because feminism believes in *validation by feelings alone*. The second key tenet states that "the students' and teachers' own experiences are used as 'learning materials'". Learning materials? This means that these experiences are to be treated as being a form of academically legitimate evidence.

For example, if one of the female students doesn't feel safe on campus, then this is evidence that 'rape culture' is real. What a woman *feels* is therefore *true*. This will only apply, of course, where the personal experience being related conforms to feminist theory. Personal feelings *contrary* to feminism would not be considered valid. (So the feelings of a Sarah Palin or an Ann Coulter won't count even though they're women.)

Nor, it need hardly be said, will this apply to men's feelings. The book you are reading at the moment draws upon my own (and the reader's) personal experience of living under feminism for the last four decades but do you think that any feminist

327

would want to validate *my* personal experience as being academically legitimate evidence?

So, if this is feminist pedagogy, how does this approach to teaching affect the education of society's children in the contemporary classroom all the way from primary school education to university? The most straightforward way to describe this approach in school classrooms might be as follows.

There was a time when boys were expected to conform to 'good boy' behaviour and girls were expected to conform to 'good girl' behaviour. The boys had to be boisterous, energetic, brave little sportsmen and girls had to be sweet, gentle, obedient little angels. But, *now that there is no such thing as 'good' maleness*, the idea of 'good boy' behaviour has become redundant and both sexes are expected to conform to 'good girl' behaviour. Both sexes have to be sweet, gentle, obedient little angels. And, guess what, *the boys find it harder to be good girls than the girls do*. What a surprise.

But their matriarchal teachers seem undaunted by this. They persist in giving the boys this golden opportunity of rejecting their degraded maleness and trying instead to become honourary girls. Some of the boys can manage it, or at least they can fake it, but some of the boys take the opposite direction. Rejecting the status of honourary 'good girls', they deliberately indulge everything that their teachers say is wrong with them; they live down to their reputation; they embrace their otherness. They misbehave. https://www.youtube.com/watch?v=ofT6j1oj8dl

Feminist pedagogy operates with a female human norm. This is inevitable because of its ideological foundation. Gender-supremacist feminism itself has a female human norm, where males are seen as deficient because they are insufficiently female. This adherence to a female human norm is so blatant in the school system that people are now talking about it openly:

328

"Being a boy can be a serious liability in today's classroom. As a group, boys are noisy, rowdy and hard to manage. Many are messy, disorganized and won't sit still. Young male rambunctiousness, according to a recent study, leads teachers to underestimate their intellectual and academic abilities. 'Girl behavior is the gold standard in schools,' says psychologist Michael Thompson. 'Boys are treated like defective girls'."
http://ideas.time.com/2013/10/28/what-schools-can-do-to-help-boys-succeed/#comments

To say that "boys are treated like defective girls" is exactly what it means to have a female human norm. Teachers treat girls as being *what children ought to be*, and boys are treated as inferior specimens because they fail to be female. This is most noticeable in matters of disobedient and unruly behaviour. So what is to be done with those boys who fail to conform and obey? The ones who reject the status of 'good girls'. How are the 'behavioural problems' of these children to be dealt with?

Feminism has never been able or willing to take criticism or to deal with anyone who answers back. That's why feminist teachers introduced the politically correct term 'challenging' for children's naughty or disruptive behaviour. Did you ever ask yourself *what is it that is being challenged?* It's the authority of the feminist teacher. And how does this matriarch deal with 'challenging' behaviour? She diagnoses it as an illness: Attention Deficit Hyperactivity Disorder (ADHD).

"ADHD is much more common among males than females. It is estimated that boys are two to three times more likely to have ADHD than girls. They are up to nine times more likely than girls to be referred for evaluation and treatment. The difference in referral rates between ADHD boys and girls is likely due to ADHD boys having more behavior problems than ADHD girls. Studies have found that ADHD girls tend to have more internalizing behaviors such as anxiety, social withdrawal, and depression. Most girls diagnosed with ADHD, tend to cluster in the inattentive subtype. Because they are not a behavior problem, their difficulties are often overlooked. Boys diagnosed with ADHD are usually clinic-referred because of oppositional, aggressive, and conduct behaviors. They tend to be very disruptive in the classroom, drawing the attention of their teachers." [Lesley Jamison, 2000, "Gender Differences in ADHD Children"] http://cpancf.com/articles_files/art_57attached_file.asp

"There is a "discrepancy in the male-to-female ratio between clinic-referred (10 to 1) and community (3 to 1) samples of children with attention deficit hyperactivity disorder (ADHD) . . . . although girls with ADHD were at significantly greater risk for disruptive behavior disorders (conduct and oppositional defiant disorder) than girls without ADHD, disruptive behavior disorders were clearly less prevalent in girls, regardless of ADHD status." [Biederman et al., 2002, American Journal of Psychiatry, "Influence of Gender on Attention Deficit Hyperactivity Disorder in Children Referred to a Psychiatric Clinic".]

Notice that diagnosis and treatment of ADHD is gendered in accordance with traditional ideas of gendered behaviour seen through a feminist lens. ADHD in girls is said to make them quiet and withdrawn, whilst ADHD in boys is said to make them unruly and unmanageable. What is being diagnosed as ADHD is behaviour which exaggerates the respective failings of the male and the female on the feminist model, that the girls are too quiet and undemanding while the boys are too loud and demanding. The words used to describe the boys "disorder" are all traits that feminism has trouble coping with and is therefore frightened of; males who are "oppositional" and "aggressive" and "defiant". 'Pathological maleness' might be the feminist term for it. It wouldn't be the first time that feminism had diagnosed maleness as pathological; as a disease.

ADHD is a psychotherapists label for a combination of types of behaviour which they consider to be an illness. I'm not suggesting that there no such thing as ADHD, merely that it may well be vastly over-diagnosed as a result of feminist educators not being able to deal with the behavioural consequences of feminised education. Is it a *coincidence* that apparently an epidemic of ADHD suddenly erupted among the children of the western world at just the same time as education became feminised? Or could much (not all) of the diagnosis of ADHD be a clinical 'explanation' that feminised education can use to rationalize the behavioural problems and educational failure that its own pedagogy creates?

What types of behaviour are we actually talking about? Here is a checklist for the *diagnosis of ADHD*. It's a fairly typical example. http://www.cdc.gov/ncbddd/adhd/checklist.html

- "Often does not give close attention to details or makes careless mistakes in schoolwork, work, or other activities.

- Often has trouble keeping attention on tasks or play activities.

- Often does not seem to listen when spoken to directly.

- Often does not follow through on instructions and fails to finish schoolwork, chores, or duties in the workplace (loses focus, gets sidetracked).

- Often has trouble organizing activities.

- Often avoids, dislikes, or doesn't want to do things that take a lot of mental effort for a long period of time (such as schoolwork or homework).

- Often loses things needed for tasks and activities (e.g. toys, school assignments, pencils, books, or tools).

- Is often easily distracted.

- Is often forgetful in daily activities.

- Often fidgets with hands or feet or squirms in seat when sitting still is expected.

- Often gets up from seat when remaining in seat is expected.

- Often excessively runs about or climbs when and where it is not appropriate (adolescents or adults may feel very restless).

- Often has trouble playing or doing leisure activities quietly.

- Is often "on the go" or often acts as if "driven by a motor".

- Often talks excessively.

- Often blurts out answers before questions have been finished.

- Often has trouble waiting one's turn.

- Often interrupts or intrudes on others (e.g., butts into conversations or games)."

If you put young boys into a classroom where the methods of teaching have been designed for girls, where everyone is expected to behave like sweet little sugary angels, where the approach to teaching is mind-numbingly dull because it's so lacking in anything which might get a boy enthusiastic about learning, and at the same time you remove traditional ideas of discipline and any respect for masculinity, isn't this checklist of ADHD behaviour exactly what you would expect from a great many boys? A non-feminist interpretation of this checklist of behaviour would be that it describes the fidgeting and indiscipline which results from *boredom due to bad or inappropriate teaching methods*.

Some of the indicators of a behavioural "disorder" on this checklist can scarcely be believed. A schoolboy who "often fidgets with his hands or feet, or squirms in his seat when sitting still is expected"? That describes *generations* of bored, uninspired schoolboys, doesn't it? A schoolboy who "often has trouble keeping attention on tasks or play activities"? Doesn't that describe any schoolboy who has been given something to do that he has no interest in? A *schoolboy* who is "often easily distracted" and who often "has trouble playing or doing leisure activities quietly"? Are you kidding me?!

The drug-pushers who compiled this list should be made to sit down (if they can keep still long enough without fidgeting) and be made to read the "Just William" novels by Richmal Crompton. Their checklist of a behavioural "disorder" exactly describes William's behaviour, and his personality is one that generations of children have *delighted in*. A boy who is often "on the go" or who acts as if "driven by a motor"? That *is* William Brown. It's also the kind of restless energy that created generations of explorers and inventors and creative artists in the past; the kind of people who moved society forward.

What was once seen as a sign of a vigorous spirit and good physical health is now classified as a form of illness because these dynamically active personalities can't sit still. Maybe what the teachers and the psychotherapists are really objecting to is *childhood* itself. Being a boy is now a psychological disorder. It is treated with psychotropic drugs that affect a person's mind, their emotions, and their behaviour. They alter the body's natural chemical levels and ratios, altering the brain's chemical composition to modify behaviour. Feminised education (and feminist society's medical practice) is drugging boys into submission to enforce 'good girl' behaviour; it's trying to sedate boys into becoming 'good girls'. (But the list of ADHD behaviour is so absurdly broad and imprecise that it means that a number of the girls are also caught in the net.)

Ask yourself this question: is feminist pedagogy employing science to address its deficiencies? Are Ritalin and other psychotropic drugs being used to sedate the children who can't conform to the imprudent behavioural constraints of feminist pedagogy? The full consequences of this policy are as yet unknown. A documentary like "The Drugging of Our Children" https://www.youtube.com/watch?v=26e5PqrCePk suggests how disturbing these consequences might actually be.

The simple non-medical way of dealing with ill-disciplined children is to discipline them. But feminism views 'discipline', especially physical discipline, as a 'masculine' exercise of patriarchal control. If it is masculine it must therefore be a bad thing. Therefore discipline must not be used. Certainly not physical discipline. It has long been 'unacceptable' to cuff a child round the ear. The present culture holds to the maxim that there is never an excuse for hitting a child, just as it holds to the maxim that there is never an excuse for hitting a woman. In fact we're told that there is never an excuse for shouting at a child or shouting at a woman. Any form of intimidation is culturally taboo for those who are classified as 'vulnerable' and in need of society's protection.

But the obvious problem with this is that the child may remain ill-disciplined. Therefore it is necessary to drug the child to make him behave nicely and obey instructions. This is feminism's idea of progress. This is presented to us as the moral high ground. But what is it really? It's a decision to keep children medicated rather than face up to the adult responsibility of exercising a necessary level of *unmedicated* control over them. Increasingly, feminist society has no control over its children other than by keeping them drugged.

If feminised education says that the majority (nearly two thirds) of children diagnosed with learning disabilities are boys http://www.learningdisabilities.org.uk/help-information/Learning-Disability-Statistics-/187687/, is this because boys just naturally have more learning disabilities than girls, or is it because the diagnosis is based upon a female norm in a feminised education system? Is the most significant learning *disability* that boys have actually *the education system* in which they're required to learn?

It doesn't seem likely that the current feminist educational establishment will be seriously addressing these questions any time soon. They cannot permit themselves to take the blame for boys doing increasingly badly at school because nothing that is 'feminist' can ever be admitted to be at fault. Feminisation is believed to be the cure for problems, not the cause of problems. So instead of blaming themselves, feminist pedagogues find an alternative explanation. The children must be the problem; the children must have ADHD and learning disabilities.

Society normally targets its medical provision mostly at women because of the traditionally sexist belief that women are more entitled to the provision of support and protection than men are. But it is very different in the area of drugging children into obedience. Here it is boys who are the main target of this 'medical' treatment. But would you trust feminist society to diagnose correctly? Are all of these boys actually ill? Or are they just part of feminism's 'problem' with boys? The boys who don't obey and conform. The boys who are diagnosed as being ill because feminist society *doesn't know what else to do with them*. So sedate them with drugs and then get back to celebrating how well the girls are doing.

The irony of this situation is that feminised education is obsessed with children's sense of well-being and children's sense of self-esteem. This is something it prioritizes. But it never seems to occur to the pedagogues that feminised education could hardly be more effectively designed to undermine a boy's self-esteem.

The types of learning that boys used to be good at (e.g. problem solving, definite right and wrong answers, competitive individual achievement, hierarchical learning) have been dropped in favour of the types of learning that girls do better in (e.g. greater emphasis on coursework, modular learning, group learning, *agreed* answers rather than *right or wrong* answers). Boys enter the education system in primary schools in which nearly all (often all) of the teachers are female. Boys are taught in a school environment in which everyone *expects* them to do worse than the girls academically; the teachers expect it, the girls expect it, and the boys expect it. Boys are taught in a school environment in which there is no real authority or discipline and in which there is an expectation that they will be more of a problem than the girls. And yet this is supposed to be an education system which is greatly concerned with children's sense of self-esteem?

Nor is it solely a matter of a school environment which is uniformly matriarchal in its personnel and politically feminised in its beliefs, values, and educational methods. Boys are not immune to the wider society in which they live. Boys are raised in a culture in which the male stereotypes presented to them in popular culture are of losers and inadequates. Boys live in a society in which men are seen as the problem and women are seen as the solution. They have few role-models in school and *negative* role-models in society. Yet the feminised education system keeps paying lip-service to its concern for children's self-esteem.

The wider society makes working class white boys bear an even greater burden under economic deprivation and the combined political prejudices of multiculturalism and feminism. Poor white boys, those most likely to be living in multicultural locations, fail more and more as the years go by. In 2013 the Centre for Social Justice reported:

"White working-class British boys are falling further behind other groups of children at GCSE, despite a string of initiatives designed to boost the performance of disadvantaged pupils. A major new study of the roots of educational failure in England finds that over the period 2007-2012 the gap in performance between poor white boys and the average for all pupils actually widened. The report from the Centre for Social Justice (CSJ) – which also highlights how many children are shockingly unprepared to start school – says the attainment gap between poor white British pupils and their better off counterparts is "startling"." [Centre for Social Justice, 2013 press release.]

Did you notice the "string of initiatives"? These initiatives were carried out by *the same politically correct ideologues who caused the problem in the first place*, so they're scarcely likely to come up with a solution, are they? The situation continues to grow worse despite their "string of initiatives". This is because their initiatives need to target the people who are actually causing the problem: themselves. To do anything effective they'd have to start re-evaluating their pedagogy and re-evaluating their politics. They are not prepared to do either.

So boys continue to do worse than girls in nearly every subject from primary education upwards. At university female undergraduates have outnumbered male undergraduates for years and the gap between the women and the men is widening rather than narrowing. Yet no one in the education system can admit that it is feminism that has *caused* this gender-inequality because education professionals have always been at the forefront of *advocating* feminism. They can't admit that they were wrong. After all, they are the educated elite; they are the people who know best.

On American university campuses feminist academics are as passionately concerned with gender issues as ever. So are they addressing the gender-inequality that boys suffer in education? No, they are doing the opposite, they are deliberately *adding to it*. With their theory of 'rape culture' they are making the position of male students on US campuses even more difficult by increasing the level of misandrist persecution. The Violence Against Women Reauthorization Act of 2013 amends the Violence Against Women Act of 1994 to add or expand what types of behaviour are covered by the act to further constrain the assumed sexual rapacity of male students. There is also the Campus Sexual Violence Elimination Act, a bill to amend the Higher Education Act of 1965 to "improve education and prevention related to campus sexual violence, domestic violence, dating violence, and stalking". http://www.campussaveact.org All of this is directed solely at male students on the basis of the feminist gender-stereotyping of men as rape-minded sexual predators.

The current victimisation of male students at American universities due to the *institutionalised* use of the feminist theory of 'rape culture' is truly appalling and shows just how far no-limits feminist hypocrisy is eager and willing to go. For a convenient source of information about the systemic degradation of male students on American campuses, take a look at the series of Misandry in Education video essays by Jonathan Taylor, including Rape Hysteria by Students https://www.youtube.com/watch?v=e5HokWxhG8A and Rape Hysteria by Faculty and Administrators https://www.youtube.com/watch?v=ZTc5s6v0xwl and the Death of Due Process for Male Students https://www.youtube.com/watch?v=0GC_QVIgGPA .Taylor is also addressing the injustices of the notorious Title 9 on American campuses at http://www.titleixforall.com . But to encapsulate the situation we can hardly do better than to quote in full a piece published in the Wall Street Journal that was written by a feminist, Judith Grossman, *when her own son* fell foul of the feminist theory of 'rape culture' as practiced and enforced by American academia:

"I am a feminist. I have marched at the barricades, subscribed to Ms. magazine, and knocked on many a door in support of progressive candidates committed to women's rights. Until a month ago, I would have expressed unqualified support for Title IX and for the Violence Against Women Act.

But that was before my son, a senior at a small liberal-arts college in New England, was charged - by an ex-girlfriend - with alleged acts of "non-consensual sex" that supposedly occurred during the course of their relationship a few years earlier. What followed was a nightmare - a fall through Alice's looking-glass into a world that I could not possibly have believed existed, least of all behind the ivy-covered walls thought to protect an ostensible dedication to enlightenment and intellectual betterment.

It began with a text of desperation. 'CALL ME. URGENT. NOW.' That was how my son informed me that not only had charges been brought against him but that he was ordered to appear to answer these allegations in a matter of days. There was no preliminary inquiry on the part of anyone at the school into these accusations about behavior alleged to have taken place a few years earlier, no consideration of the possibility that jealousy or revenge might be motivating a spurned young ex-lover to lash out. Worst of all, my son would not be afforded a presumption of innocence.

In fact, Title IX, that so-called guarantor of equality between the sexes on college campuses, and as applied by a recent directive from the Department of Education's Office for Civil Rights, has obliterated the presumption of innocence that is so foundational to our traditions of justice. On today's college campuses, neither 'beyond a reasonable doubt,' nor even the lesser 'by clear and convincing evidence' standard of proof is required to establish guilt of sexual misconduct. These safeguards of due process have, by order of the federal government, been replaced by what is known as 'a preponderance of the evidence.' What this means, in plain English, is that all my son's accuser needed to establish before a campus tribunal is that the allegations were 'more likely than not' to have occurred by a margin of proof that can be as slim as 50.1% to 49.9%.

How does this campus tribunal proceed to evaluate the accusations? Upon what evidence is it able to make a judgment? The frightening answer is that like the proverbial 800-pound gorilla, the tribunal does pretty much whatever it wants, showing scant regard for fundamental fairness, due process of law, and the well-established rules and procedures that have evolved under the Constitution for citizens' protection. Who knew that American college students are required to surrender the Bill of Rights at the campus gates?

My son was given written notice of the charges against him, in the form of a letter from the campus Title IX officer. But instead of affording him the right to be fully informed, the separately listed allegations were a barrage of vague statements, rendering any defense virtually impossible. The letter lacked even the most basic information about the acts alleged to have happened years before. Nor were the allegations supported by any evidence other than the word of the ex-girlfriend.

The hearing itself was a two-hour ordeal of unabated grilling by the school's committee, during which, my son later reported, he was expressly denied his request to be represented by counsel or even to have an attorney outside the door of the room. The questioning, he said, ran far afield even from the vaguely stated allegations contained in the so-called notice. Questions from the distant past, even about unrelated matters, were flung at him with no opportunity for him to give thoughtful answers.

The many pages of written documentation that my son had put together - which were directly on point about his relationship with his accuser during the time period of his alleged wrongful conduct - were dismissed as somehow not relevant. What was relevant, however, according to the committee, was the unsworn testimony of 'witnesses' deemed to have observable knowledge about the long-ago relationship between my son and his accuser.

That the recollections of these young people (made under intense peer pressure and with none of the safeguards consistent with fundamental fairness) were relevant - while records of the accuser's email and social media postings were not - made a mockery of the very term. While my son was instructed by the committee not to 'discuss this matter' with any potential witnesses, these witnesses against him were not identified to him, nor was he allowed to confront or question either them or his accuser.

Thankfully, I happen to be an attorney and had the resources to provide the necessary professional assistance to my son. The charges against him were ultimately dismissed but not before he and our family had to suffer through this ordeal. I am of course relieved and most grateful for this outcome. Yet I am also keenly aware not only of how easily this all could have gone the other way - with life-altering consequences - but how all too often it does.

Across the country and with increasing frequency, innocent victims of impossible-to-substantiate charges are afforded scant rights to fundamental fairness and find themselves entrapped in a widening web of this latest surge in political correctness. Few have a lawyer for a mother, and many may not know about the Foundation for Individual Rights in Education, which assisted me in my research.

There are very real and horrifying instances of sexual misconduct and abuse on college campuses and elsewhere. That these offenses should be investigated and prosecuted where appropriate is not open to question. What does remain a question is how we can make the process fair for everyone.

I fear that in the current climate the goal of 'women's rights,' with the compliance of politically motivated government policy and the tacit complicity of college administrators, runs the risk of grounding our most cherished institutions in a veritable snake pit of injustice - not unlike the very injustices the movement itself has for so long sought to correct. Unbridled feminist orthodoxy is no more the answer than are attitudes and policies that victimize the victim."

[Judith Grossman, Wall Street Journal, April 16th 2013
http://online.wsj.com/news/articles/SB100014241278873246007045784052802110435
10]

When her own son was falsely accused, it was a wake-up call for this feminist. But what if she had been the mother only of daughters? What if it had been someone else's son, as it so often has been?

I have quoted this piece at length because it touches upon so many of the issues: (a) the blatant sexist hypocrisy of feminists in power who are willing (and probably proud) to commit acts of manifest injustice in their sex-war, (b) the way that feminists themselves are astonishingly blind to their own sexism, (c) the lack of concern mainstream society has for misandry, ignoring it or denying that it even exists until it affects them personally, (d) the identification of "unbridled feminist orthodoxy" as the source of the injustice, and (e) the way that feminism, in theory and in practice, is *directly opposed* to genuine impartial sex equality.

So what future is there for male students in the American higher education system? Now that the feminist Obama administration has effectively abandoned due legal process for male students, riding roughshod over their constitutional rights, and the education establishment is introducing the concept of "affirmative consent", how many potential university students will decide that the US academic campus is no longer a safe place for a male to reside? http://fff.org/explore-freedom/article/making-men-rapists/

Authoritarian feminist academics will preach endlessly about creating a safe and respectful environment for students but then teach courses in which men are spoken of as domestically abusive predatory sex-criminals who have politically orchestrated a 'rape culture' to force women to live in terror. Is this a safe and respectful environment for male students? Or have the feminist academics grown so accustomed to female-majority classrooms that the male minority can be blithely disregarded in favour of being 'women-centered'?

Equality in the Workplace

For many people equality in paid employment is the paradigm case of sex equality. But, as popularly perceived, this is a feminist paradigm. It is spoken of solely in terms of male concessions to female advances. This is not a true picture of workplace equality. The popular perception comes closer to genuine equality when it takes into account husbands and father's having more access to the domestic sphere because, properly understood, equality in the workplace is not only about equal *access to* paid employment but also about equal *responsibility for* paid employment.

Under feminism, the issues of concern have been for women to have the life-choice of a career when they wanted it, but time off for other life-choices (e.g. family) when it suited them, and then a return to career without loss of promotion opportunities. Alongside this has been the option of state-funded parenthood for women, financial support from ex-husbands and partners, or even (in the view of some feminists at least) the traditional option of being entirely supported by a husband/partner. Feminism has demanded equal access, equal pay and equal seniority but never equal responsibility. What feminism

342

demands for women is something *that men have never had*, multiple life-choices in and outside of paid employment.

Historically, men were *expected and required* to fulfil a role in paid employment. If they wanted promotion, they were on their own in trying to achieve it. The idea of taking time out to raise a family was unthought-of; when men became fathers they applied for extra overtime to earn more money to meet their expanding family commitments. It was considered shameful for a man to live off of a woman's financial income (the 'kept man') and for a man to be the primary child-carer was an idea which society would have laughed at in disbelief. No, for the vast majority of men, life was no choice at all. Paid employment was either a necessity, a duty, or both.

In the 1970s and 80s feminists, and women too, used to frequently complain that when a woman of child-bearing age applied for a job the employment panel would ask her if she was planning to have a child, but they would never ask such a question of a man. The reason for this, though it never seemed to occur to them, was screamingly obvious. If the woman were to become a mother, she would very probably take time off work or leave the job entirely, but if a man were to become a father, he would just carry on working to fulfil his financial responsibilities. Employment panels didn't ask men about parenthood because they knew there was no possibility that the new father would suddenly quit his job. So, clearly, what feminism demands for women is not *equality* with what men formerly had, but something *far beyond* what men formerly had; to be financially independent, or not; to pursue a career, or not; to be a full-time parent, or not; or to do all of the above at different times in her life.

True equality in the workplace can only be achieved *in conjunction with* equality in the domestic sphere. This means that men must have *equal opportunity* and *equal entitlement* to be house-spouse and primary child-carer, and to not have any specifically gendered responsibility as a financial provider. Or, to put it another way, women must accept equal responsibility for fulfilling the role of financial provider.

Let's be clear, I am not saying that women should have the opportunity to accept this responsibility if they choose to or to reject this responsibility if they don't want it (and then rely either on a man or the state to support them). I am speaking of a *responsibility* here. I'm saying that men and women should have an equal responsibility to be the financial provider, so that if a cohabiting couple have a child there will *not* be any female privilege in deciding whether she wants to continue in paid employment or leave it, whilst the man must simply accept her decision.

She will have an *equal responsibility* with him for financial provision and he will have an *equal entitlement* with her to leave paid employment and become the primary child-carer. This would also apply to couples without children if one of them is working and the other isn't. Equality is not just about women's choices, it's also about men's choices. Equal choice and equal access for *both* partners to both the workplace and the domestic sphere. For as long as society gives men a *responsibility* for paid employment whilst giving women the *opportunity* for paid employment should she choose it, there will be no equality in the workplace.

If, as seems likely, feminised education results in an *increasing* number of women in high-income jobs, and a *decreasing* number of men in high-income jobs, then this equal access and entitlement to the domestic sphere may become a necessity for some couples. These women will, in practical financial terms, have *no choice* but to continue in paid employment while their male partner becomes the primary child-carer because he will simply not be earning enough money in his job for them to be able to afford for her to give up her higher income. She will have to *fulfil her responsibility* as the financial provider, whether she wants to or not. It will be a practical necessity.

Once true equality in the workplace is understood, it should be very clear to the reader how completely contrary this is to the feminist agenda. The suggestion that women should have equal responsibility with men and that men should have equal entitlement with women would set the average feminist hypocrite screaming and seething with rage. Feminism seeks to put women in an advantaged position and it has done so. It has worked hard to give choices and entitlements to women that men are denied. And it has insisted, from first to last, that the interests of women must come first.

For example, formerly male-dominated workplaces have been required to change in order to accommodate the greater presence of women. But have you ever heard of formerly female-dominated workplaces being required to change in order to accommodate a greater presence of men? Has nursing, for example, been forced to alter its working practices to make them more male-friendly for male nurses? Primary school education is massively female-dominated, so shouldn't working practices in primary education be drastically changed to enable more male teachers to find employment there? Lest we forget, feminism is *not* about sex equality, it is about advantaging and privileging women. So any men who might squeeze in through the cracks and find employment in female-dominated workplaces will be expected to conform to feminism's idea of what is female-friendly. On the feminist agenda, only men must make concessions, never women.

But as an advocate of impartial sex equality, surely I must approve of the greater opportunities for women in employment that have taken place over the last half-century? Yes, I entirely endorse women having exactly equal opportunities to paid employment and financial independence with men, of course I do. (That should go without saying, but as feminists tell such lies about their critics it's probably best to explicitly state it.) What I do not endorse is gender inequality in favour of women *masquerading* as equality (e.g. paid maternity leave but no equal paid paternity leave, women-only shortlists, etc.) nor do I endorse *women's absence* from so many of the traditionally male jobs that feminism never takes any interest in because they are not the kinds of jobs that most people want to do. Both of these things are contrary to sex equality. The former is self-evident and quite often spoken about. The latter, however, is frequently overlooked, so let's consider it now.

Ask yourself this question: what is the statistic for gender inequality amongst underground sewage workers? Don't know? It's hardly a surprise that you don't because what middle-class feminist academic would do the research to answer such a question? This bastion of male privilege in which privileged men get to wade through shit for a living is not the kind of thing we ever get to hear about in feminist society because, hey guess what, women don't particularly want to wade through shit for a living. If they don't, then *let the men do it*. Let men wade through shit, *that's a man's job*.

What is the statistic for gender inequality amongst refuse collectors (garbage men/dustmen) or people who work outside in all weathers (e.g. road maintenance) or people who do dangerous jobs (e.g. construction workers)? Don't know that either? These bastions of male privilege in which privileged men get to handle other people's rubbish or drill tarmac in the freezing cold or fall to their deaths from a steel girder are also of no interest to middle-class feminist academics. Let the men do all the cold, filthy and dangerous jobs whilst women sit in a clean, warm office employed as their administrative line-managers. After all, men have always been the expendable, disposable sex.

But when it comes to all the *good* jobs, all the hygienic and well-paid high-status jobs, like university professors, the CEOs of major business concerns, television presenters, cabinet ministers, human resource managers, or publishing executives, *then* feminists can reel off any amount of research statistics. Feminism has always been about women getting a larger share of the good things in men's traditional gendered social role and *only* the good things. But impartial sex equality means that women must take up an equal share of the burden of all the *bad things* about men's traditional gendered social role. Someone has to do the dirty and dangerous jobs. Women should have as much *responsibility* for these as men. A true sex-equalitarian will demand that society gets more women down the sewers wading through shit and more women working outdoors in the cold and wet, not to mention women taking their equal share of deaths in the workplace.

Is there any chance of that happening, do you think? We've already noted that the UK government's statistics for fatalities in the workplace 2012/13 http://www.hse.gov.uk/statistics/fatals.htm doesn't even mention that men suffer the overwhelming majority of deaths in the workplace, so I wouldn't hold your breath.

Sex equality in the workplace doesn't just mean equality at the top of the tree in the clean and comfortable, high-paid high-status jobs. Feminism is quick to complain about women being employed in lower paid part-time jobs like waitressing or shop-work, but it never seems to complain about women being kept out of the kind of jobs that it is essential for *somebody* to do (to keep society in operation) even though they are unpleasant occupations, which many men are lumbered with because they need the money, and which they put up with because of their financial obligations.

A classic example of this was the Bevin Boys. During world war two when men were being forcibly conscripted into the armed forces there was, as a result, a shortage of coal miners. Young women were also conscripted during world war two, into the jobs that had been left vacant by the men who'd been called up into the military (e.g. the land army girls who replaced agricultural labourers). So the British government should have replaced the missing coal miners with female conscripts, right?

Wrong. Instead, the government redeployed some of the men who were being conscripted into the armed forces into these filthy arduous jobs underground. It sounds crazy, doesn't it? Having conscripted the male coal miners *into* the armed forces, they then replaced those miners with other male conscripts *from* the armed forces who weren't even coal miners by trade.

Why didn't they replace the missing miners with female conscripts? For the usual reason, that women weren't physically strong enough. (There were a few women who went down the pits but they didn't do the heavy work.) This is the same old excuse given even today for not putting women in the army into combat, that they are too weak to carry their guns

347

because they don't have the necessary upper body strength. But is this merely an excuse to mask the real reason?

Consider this: my father had very traditional ideas about gender and he was sincerely amazed when, in the 1980s, women started running marathons in athletics competitions. He had assumed that women simply lacked the physical strength and stamina to run twenty-six miles. He was even more astonished in the 1990s when fun-running became popular and very ordinary women who were not elite athletes would run twenty-six miles in events like the London marathon.

This revelation of how physically strong and tough women actually are is something that feminism celebrates because running a marathon is an admirable thing which shows female capacity in a triumphant light. But the same celebratory attitude is never applied to women being physically strong enough to do the hard graft at grueling manual labour or to go into combat and get killed. No, no, when it comes to punishingly arduous and unglamorous toil, *then* women are just weak little girlies who couldn't possibly be expected to do a *man's* job.

When the idea of female physical weakness is used to stop women from doing something that they *want* to do, like long-distance running, then it is a feminist issue to oppose the idea. But when the idea of female physical weakness is used to *excuse* women from having to do the hard and dangerous tasks that are required of men, then it is not a feminist issue. Is anyone surprised? No, I thought not.

What made things even worse for the undervalued and unglamorous Bevin boys who were conscripted against their will to serve their country down the coal mines is that they were subjected to verbal abuse from the general public for being *young men who were not in uniform* (enforcing the imposition of a gendered social role upon men to be soldiers) and it was popularly believed that the Bevin Boys included a lot of conscientious objectors, and so they were also subjected to abuse for being 'conchies'.

Greater sex equality in the dangerous areas of employment is unlikely to find favour with the management class. Employers know that they cannot oppose anything as powerful as feminism but they are generally more resistant to initiatives for workplace equality if those initiatives address misandry.

For example, up to now they have seemed fairly confident when refusing any demands for equal paid paternity leave or when pressuring men to not exercise any options they may have for more flexible working hours. Employers are accustomed to treating men as work-units who are expected to put their jobs ahead of other considerations. So the employers in industries where men risk serious injury and even risk their lives might be less than pleased about greater sex equality in *their* workplaces because the presence of more women would very likely require those workplaces to be made safer. The sexist double-standard about the value of human life would mean that more women in dangerous occupations would kick-start the customary imperative to 'protect women!' by imposing additional safety measures. To take the construction industry, for example:

"Although the construction industry accounts for only about 5% of the employees in Britain, it still accounts for 22% of fatal injuries to employees and 10% of reported major injuries. Construction had the highest level of workplace deaths of any industrial sector in 2012/13; 39 people were killed at work in the year to March 2013." http://www.leighday.co.uk/Illness-and-injury/Accident-and-personal-injury/Construction-industry-accident-claims

If half of those 39 deaths were the deaths of *women* (and again the next year, and again the following year, and so on), do you think that it would make a difference *politically?* Would employers in the construction industry have a reason to worry that legislation might be introduced to increase the level (and therefore the expense) of safety procedures because female construction workers were dying?

By the way, if you're wondering what the actual gender-inequality in workplace fatalities is in hard numbers, then the

"Census of Fatal Occupational Injuries Summary 2012" http://www.bls.gov/news.release/cfoi.nr0.htm from the US Bureau of Labor Statistics tells us (you have to read it carefully because the gender breakdown is hidden amongst a mass of other data) that 4,383 fatal work injuries were recorded in the United States in 2012. Of these 4,045 were men and 338 were women. Approximately 92% men and 8% women.

Would women in general be pleased at the increased sex equality brought about by their participating to a much greater extent in the dirty, cold, wet, dangerous jobs? And, if not, should they be expected to do these jobs anyway as a part of their civic responsibility to society?

Perhaps this brings up a larger question: now that women have so much greater access to paid employment, are they therefore much happier than they used to be? After all, we've been told innumerable times that in the past access to paid employment was one of the *privileges* men enjoyed that made their lives so much easier and more powerful than the lives of women. Are women living happier lives now that they are sharing in this formerly male social role? There seem to be frequent studies showing that women are now less happy than they were decades ago. For example, "The Paradox of Declining Female Happiness" (Stevenson & Wolfers, 2009):

"We will show in this paper that women's happiness has fallen both absolutely and relative to men's in a pervasive way among groups, such that women no longer report being happier than men and, in many instances, now report happiness that is below that of men. Moreover, we show that this shift has occurred through much of the industrialized world."
http://www.nber.org/papers/w14969

It is quite comical to see how this report twists and turns in its efforts to explain, in a way that does not contradict feminism, *why* women are less happy. I don't know if women really are less happy than they used to be because I don't know how on earth something as intangible as happiness could be realistically quantified. But *if* it is true, then this would again

350

highlight the falsehood of patriarchy theory. The theory says that personal independence through paid employment advantaged men. Now that women have that same independence they can spend their lives working and paying and working and paying just like the men always did. But, apparently, now that women are doing what men used to do, women are less happy than they used to be. It seems that the more women occupy the traditional male role, the unhappier they get. Shouldn't this have suggested to the happiness researchers that, in reality, men were *not* privileged and did *not* have an easier life than women?

The Demonisation of Men in Mainstream Popular Culture

When sex-equalitarians complain that misandry is all around us on a daily basis in feminist society, those people who have not yet understood what sex equality actually is (because it has been so misrepresented by the double-standards of feminism) have a tendency to look baffled by the complaint. It makes no sense to them. Surely, they reply, the issue of sexism in mainstream culture is all about skinny supermodels in women's magazines because 'fat is a feminist issue'. They remind us for the umpteenth time that sexism in mainstream culture is found in the lyrics of hip-hop songs which indulge and normalize the sexual objectification of women. Everybody knows, they insist, that sexism in mainstream culture is typified in the way that female characters in computer games are all young and pretty and have large breasts.

The sex-equalitarians, for their part, are just as baffled by the way that anyone can be blind to the egregious and consistent misandry in popular culture when it is so glaringly conspicuous. They are as aware as everyone else of the endlessly repeated examples of sexual objectification quoted by feminists but they are *also* aware of the huge amount of relentless misandry being pumped out by mainstream culture, and of how the misandry is treated as being far more *socially acceptable* in feminist society and is consequently far more corrosive and damaging to its victims. As sex-equalitarians, they find it difficult to understand how people can be so closed-minded as to be unaware (or so sexist as to pretend to be unaware) of such a strikingly prominent aspect of the culture. The sex-equalitarian asks: how is it possible that so much in-your-face misandrist sexism can be invisible to the people who stubbornly deny that misandry even exists?

Perhaps there are even readers of this book who have found it strange that I have repeatedly referred to the way that men are routinely insulted in contemporary society, and that I have voiced concern over the psychological damage that this must be doing to boys and young men. So, for the sake of those who haven't already seen it for themselves, let's try to make the misandry in popular culture more explicit by listing half a dozen very well-known examples of the kind of thing sex-equalitarians are talking about when they speak of the habitual widespread misandry in everyday life.

(1) The television programme "The Simpsons" is undeniably mainstream and successful. It is popular all over the world and has been around for years on endless re-runs. Look at the gender-typing in that programme. It isn't just that Homer suffers endless physical pain while Marge suffers none, and that all Homer's sufferings are seen to be his own fault because he's a stupid selfish male slob. It isn't just that the childish Homer is presented as being a vastly inferior parent to the capable Marge, and that Bart is the 'problem child' whilst Lisa is the high-achieving 'good girl' concerned with the humanitarian issues of the day. All of that would be sufficient to make the show the embodiment of mainstream culture's gender-stereotypes of females and males. But "The Simpsons" actually went further than that. It included a storyline which encapsulates feminist society's misandry in a nutshell.

In the episode "Lisa the Simpson" the story is about the Simpson gene; about how *male* Simpsons become idiots as they grow older. The defective gene only exists on the Y chromosome, so only the males are affected. Female Simpsons are unaffected by this hereditary trait because of their XX chromosomes, so women and girls (and small male

352

children) are fine. The girls all grow up to be intelligent and emotionally mature women. It's only adolescent and adult Simpson males who are genetically imbecilic; who are idiots by nature. So Homer Simpson is not so much a *stupid* man as a stupid *man*. http://simpsons.wikia.com/wiki/Lisa_the_Simpson

Could anything possibly be a more concise depiction of feminist society's view of what-men-are-like? It is a succinct encapsulation of the overtly gender-supremacist feminist stereotype of biologically determined male inferiority. And, of course, it's a thirty minute summary of the content of *all the other episodes* of "The Simpsons" each of which has Homer foolishly embarrassing himself and hurting himself due to his deficiencies of character; level-headed Marge patiently holding the family together despite her husbands idiocy and failure; Bart misbehaving himself at every opportunity whilst never taking responsibility for his boisterous wrongdoings; Lisa coming top of the class in school and planning her golden future of personal success and charitable good works.

It's important to understand that what matters is not just a single misandrist episode, it's the unrelenting repetition of the misandry. "The Simpsons" repeats its culturally orthodox gender-stereotypes in every episode, season after season after season. (So far, over five hundred episodes have been broadcast.) And it's embedded in a wider culture in which large numbers of other television series full of inept husbands and super-competent wives are also endlessly repeating these same 'inferior-male / superior-female' stereotypes *ad nauseam*. There's nothing more ubiquitous. It's a matter of attrition over time. Mainstream culture is a ceaseless erosion and elimination of any kind of respect for men; the constant grinding down of male self-esteem.

This type of formulaic gender-supremacism is not some fringe opinion expressed a few extreme feminazis. "The Simpsons" is a totally mainstream piece of television viewed by hundreds of millions of people who watch it over and over. It is the longest-running American sitcom and the longest-running American primetime scripted television series. There has also been a feature-length film that grossed over $527 million. Time Magazine named it the 20th century's best television series and it was awarded a star on the Hollywood Walk of Fame, as well as 28 Primetime Emmy Awards and numerous other awards. http://en.wikipedia.org/wiki/The_Simpsons

Before moving on, let's deal with the predictable cop-out response: 'It's a *parody*, dummy. The show isn't *endorsing* these stereotypes, it's making fun of them. It's a *satirical* comedy, it's not meant to be taken seriously.'

This is no different from saying that magazines full of photos of naked women are 'ironic' because they're making fun of sexual objectification. Is anyone convinced by that argument? "The Simpsons" certainly *does* endorse the stereotypes it depicts because of *who the audience are laughing at*. The conventional we-all-know-men-are-inferior attitude has to be in place for the audience to be laughing *at Homer*. If it were a parody, the audience would be laughing at anyone who thought that men really were inferior, or laughing at the female characters in the show for thinking that they are superior. (Compare it to the movie "Blazing Saddles" where the film uses racism *to laugh at the racists*, not to laugh at the black characters. That is parody. That is satire.) But the joke is not on those who believe in male inferiority, the joke is on *Homer*. "The Simpsons" trades in the comedy of gender-stereotypes every bit as much as the "Benny Hill Show" did. The people who refuse to see this are the people who themselves endorse those stereotypes.

(2) A tee-shirt company called "David & Goliath" has made millions of dollars from misandrist tee-shirts with slogans that insult male children. They began with "Boys are smelly" shirts but they hit the big time when they produced their "Boys are stupid throw rocks at them" tee-shirts.
http://data.whicdn.com/images/63222260/large.jpg

These were so commercially successful that they were followed by the "Boys are stupid throw rocks at them" book http://farm3.staticflickr.com/2624/4058616425_8f71f4418d_o.jpg and the "Throw rocks at boys" game http://www.blugah.com/48/boys_are_stupid (which you can play online if you follow the link). The clothing company also produced tee-shirts with the slogan "Boys tell lies, poke them in the eyes" and their "The stupid factory, where boys are made" tee-shirts.

The point here is *not:* shouldn't we have a sense of humour about this kind of thing? The point is actually twofold. Firstly, would anyone have *thought* to make money out of misogyny directed at little girls? Would anyone have made a "Throw rocks at girls" game? And secondly, if anyone had, would their products have been so massively popular that their multi-million dollar company would have produced lots of spin-off products on the same theme? The issue here is about *societal attitudes* toward males and females. The commercial success of the "Boys are stupid throw rocks at them" franchise is an expression of the same widespread cultural contempt and hostility toward males (and of how socially acceptable it is) that is evident in the popular "Billions of men, why animal test?" tee shirts. http://xa7.xanga.com/e7cf5b27d0633253218974/z201195419.jpg

(3) "Men Behaving Badly" is a British television comedy show that ran for six years and which the BBC website describes as "the defining sitcom of the 1990s".
http://www.bbc.co.uk/comedy/menbehavingbadly/

It has a reasonable claim to being the most deliberately sexist television sitcom ever made. The central joke is that the "men" are imbecilically immature and grossly slobbish. Their lives are spent in rambling conversations of sheer idiocy whilst sitting in an apartment full of empty pizza boxes, empty crisp packets, and empty lager cans.

To make sure that everyone gets the message, the two main women in the series are intelligent, mature, sensible adult human beings who are, unaccountably, drawn toward these sub-human male specimens and who, despite the men's constant displays of personal inadequacy, somehow manage to feel some affection for them. I find myself in the unusual position of being in agreement with the BBC in one respect, I think these crude gender-stereotypes of how inferior men are and how superior women are probably was "the defining sitcom of the 1990s". The staggering misandry of the show, summarised in its title, probably was *definitive* of society's attitudes toward men and women in the 1990s. What an incredibly sexist decade.

(4) A guy called Vinny Mac in the USA was so sick and tired of misandrist television commercials with their endless repetition of male incompetence and male imbecility, which laugh at male pain, and which have slogans like "so easy, a man can do it", whilst presenting women as the capable and responsible grown-ups who order men around, that he decided to make a You Tube video compilation of such commercials called "Misandry in the Media".

But there were so many misandrist commercials on American television that he had to make a second compilation, and then a third, and . . . at the time of writing Vinny Mac is up to compilation number *twenty* in his "Misandry in the Media" series. American television commercials are so sexist against men that he could probably go on making compilations indefinitely.

If you want to see the kind of gratuitous and ubiquitous sexism that he's rightly complaining about, I would recommend that you watch the entire series. Here are a few examples on the usual contemporary themes:

Men are all stupid
http://www.youtube.com/watch?v=9rasnBGmTrA

http://www.youtube.com/watch?v=VLi1s0vzOrk

Men are all irresponsible childish slobs
http://www.youtube.com/watch?v=-RZ-y50lFzc

Men in pain can be laughed at (gender double-standard)
http://www.youtube.com/watch?v=OVGaq6fxuMl

Blatant female gender-supremacism
http://www.youtube.com/watch?v=9Ok3N7xmsvE

If you watch *one* of these commercials, you might think: so what, it's not a big deal? But you'd be missing the point. The reason these commercials tell you something about the extreme sexism of the society you live in is (a) the sheer number of them, and (b) the fact that it's all one-way traffic. What counts here is the inexorable *accumulation* of commercials on the same misandrist themes. It's not about one commercial, it's about one after another after another after another. That's why you should watch several of Vinny Mac's compilations, so that you can appreciate how relentless the misandry is.

(5) I said that "Men Behaving Badly" was a candidate for the most deliberately sexist sitcom ever made. But the prize for the most deliberately sexist Reality TV show ever made has a clear winner. In 2008 a UK television company called Channel 4 broadcast a show called "When Women Rule the World".

Eight women and ten men were taken to a tropical island where they had to build a society. The woman were the masters and the men were the slaves. The show's humour consisted of the women barking orders at the men and the men having to obey their every command. The women were authorized to inflict punishments on the men to increase their humiliation. Each week the women voted one man off the island. The man who survived to be last won £30,000.
http://www.channel4.com/programmes/when-women-rule-the-world/episode-guide

Not only did this vile Reality TV show make society's routine practice of male-bashing the *entirety* of the 'entertainment' it provided, but take note of the absence of consent in the way that the men were invited on to the show. Prior to their arrival on the island the men who were to be the slaves *did not know* that this was the premise of the show. If Channel 4 had taken a bunch of women to a Reality TV island *without telling them* that they were to be the slaves of men, do you think that the television company might have been legally prosecuted for this? Moreover, such is the disparity between the levels of human dignity accorded to women in society and accorded to men in society, we might think it likely that no *women* would have agreed to participate in the show after they were told of their role as slaves. But men? They're accustomed to being treated like shit so why wouldn't they just shrug their shoulders and participate?

It is revealing how, when two of the female participants and two of the male participants were interviewed later on the "Richard and Judy" talk show https://www.youtube.com/watch?v=ZJu_6Ri2NEY, the two women behaved with exactly the same air of arrogance and entitlement that they'd displayed on "When Women Rule the World". The excuse given for the show was that it was supposed to be gender role-reversal but, of course, this claim relies upon the blatant falsehood that in real life men have all the power and boss women around as their personal servants. Who but the feminists in charge of Channel 4 (and every other television station) could believe that?

"When Women Rule the World" would be better described as an exaggeration of the position that men occupy in mainstream culture. The fact that the show was *actually made and broadcast* (when a genuine role-reversal with women as the slaves would never be permitted to appear on television screens) surely goes some way to proving this.

(6) At the height of their fame in 1997 The Spice Girls, the pop group whose slogan was 'girl power', did a television show called "An Audience with The Spice Girls". The show had an all-female audience, including various female celebrities. But included were five male celebrities who were present solely to be humiliated. The form this humiliation took was very revealing because it was *very traditionally sexist*. The five men were required to dress up *in drag* and dance on stage so that the female audience could howl with laughter at the sight of men dressed as women. The level of hostile ridicule from the audience was truly grotesque.

The pop group also led an audience chant of 'girl power' and later explained the philosophy of 'girl power': they shouted "Boys are smelly!" The whole evening was peppered with comments about how "girls and better than boys" and similar childishness. The Spice Girls were, let's remember, the biggest pop stars in the world at the time.

https://www.youtube.com/watch?v=zoR7funqvMw

I have said elsewhere in this book that feminism infantilizes women and infantilizes society, but the astonishing level of sexist immaturity displayed on "An Evening with The Spice Girls" was simply jaw-dropping. It was not so much the crass misandry of the group themselves (whose main audience demographic was presumably ten year old girls, and who could therefore be expected to be puerile), it was the astonishing *delight* that the audience took in the crudest possible sexism. Rather than being embarrassed and ashamed of their pathetically juvenile behaviour, they were celebrating it. The more the pop group shouted out misandrist insults, the more the audience cheered. Could that audience have existed before the decades of systemic feminist bigotry?

These half a dozen examples are just the tip of the iceberg of the incessant endorsement of misandry found in the society in which men must live and in which boys are being raised today. Once you wake up to this reality, you will begin to see this all around you and you will wonder how on earth you never noticed it before. People who conform to cultural orthodoxy have been taught to view the world they live in through a feminist lens. This gives them a closed mind on the subject of gender.

To recover (or acquire) their independence of mind people need to learn to start reading the world without this feminist bias. For example, you will hear about young men going on killing sprees in America where they have access to guns. The two routine comments made about this social phenomenon that you will certainly be familiar with because you will have heard them so frequently are (a) this is proof that men are intrinsically violent, and (b) this is proof that gun control is needed because men are intrinsically violent. But, having read this book, there are a couple of questions that might occur to you the next time that you hear about a young American male who goes on a death spree.

Firstly, had that young man been put on mind-altering drugs as a result of having been diagnosed with something like ADHD or depression? If so, that might be relevant information, especially if the prevalence of such diagnoses is increasing.
http://www.cchrint.org/school-shooters/

Secondly, since a lot of these spree killers also kill themselves, could this social phenomenon be closely related to the high male suicide rate? If these young men are a part of the community of the society despised, if they have no future and are ready to die, and if the reasons for this are such as to make them *very angry*, then might these death sprees actually be a form of male suicide where they want to take a bunch of other people with them when they go?

I'm not saying that this is the truth about American spree killers (e.g. I can't know if they went crazy because they were prescribed drugs or if they were prescribed drugs because they were crazy), I'm just making the point that when you *stop* thinking with a feminist bias, these questions *start* to occur to you. But these questions would never occur to the closed mind of a feminist because she already has her explanation: it's just what-men-are-like.

Romantic-Comedy

Having looked briefly at half a dozen examples of misandry in contemporary popular culture, now let's consider another example in more depth: the romantic-comedy movie. This is worth exploring because these are films that are produced with the assumption that women will be their primary audience; they are thought of as 'chick-flicks'. (Spoiler alert! If you haven't seen these movies yet, this section will reveal aspects of the plot of the movies discussed.)

The basic set-up for these films is the way that the male and female leads conflict but eventually fall in love, and Hollywood has been making these films since the silent days. I shall compare the romantic-comedies of the past with their modern equivalents because most movies *strongly reflect the culture in which they were made* and they are therefore a useful indicator as to the beliefs and values of that culture.

The screwball comedies of the 1930s are the archetype of the 'male versus female rom-com' and it is noticeable how, in those classic old films, that the woman and the man are usually evenly matched. He scores points off her and she scores points off him. Their acerbic banter is very much a two-way street. This is what makes them such fun and it means that it is easy for an audience of both sexes to enjoy them.

But these days romantic-comedies have changed a lot. Contemporary society's hostility toward men has generated a very different idea of a rom-com. For example, in "Addicted to Love" (1997) Meg Ryan and Matthew Broderick meet because Ryan's ex-boyfriend 'Anton' has now become the lover of Broderick's ex-girlfriend 'Linda'. Broderick is maintaining a lonely vigil over Anton's apartment because he is still in love with his ex-girlfriend and dreams of winning her back. Ryan turns up and joins him in a shared surveillance of the apartment. In contrast to Broderick, Ryan does not wish to win back her ex-boyfriend, she only wants revenge. She says:

"I don't want him back, I just want him vapourised. Extinguished. When I'm done with him he'll be a twitchy little stain on the floor."

Most of the movie is spent on Ryan taking her revenge upon Anton, assisted by Broderick. They steal all his money, ruin his business, break up his relationship with Linda, cause an outbreak of his chronic skin allergy, and break both of his arms and his ribs. His life is utterly destroyed. *None* of the hostility in the film is directed toward Linda. By the end of the movie Broderick relents and takes sympathy on their victim, whilst Ryan considers herself to have gotten even with her ex-boyfriend. The lovers, Anton and Linda, get back together because, inevitably, Ryan and Broderick have now fallen in love and must come together for the final embrace.

"The War of the Roses" (1989), starring Kathleen Turner and Michael Douglas, is a film in which there is so much hate that, whilst it's about a romance gone sour, I'm not sure whether the movie counts as a romantic-comedy or not. Is there such a thing as an unromance? Throughout the film Douglas and Turner battle against each other but it is noticeable that all of *her* attacks upon *him* are *physical assaults* (she runs him over with a car, she punches him in the face and knocks him down the stairs, etc.) whilst all of *his* attacks upon *her* are attacks against her *possessions* (he cuts the heels off all her shoes, he pisses on the meal she's just cooked, etc). The standard rule that when a woman hits a man, his pain is funny, but it wouldn't be funny if the man hit the woman, is prominent throughout the film, making it an object-lesson in the sexist double-standard about human pain.

Another couple at war are Jennifer Aniston and Vince Vaughn in "The Break Up" (2006), in which each of the lovers attempts to change the behaviour of the other by hurting their feelings, with the competition increasing in severity as the film goes along. (The strap-line for this movie was "pick a side".) The two characters are the conventional caricatures of the superior female and the inferior male. She is presented as a considerate, intelligent, artistic and sensitive person; he is presented as a boorish, immature, sport-obsessed, computer game-obsessed male slob. Leaving aside the question of why such a high-minded and beautiful woman would have fallen in love with so brutish and shallow a man, we might instead ask: where is the *romance* in a rom-com in which gender relations are presented as a conflict between two separate species with nothing in common except, presumably, the satisfaction of their sexual needs?

Where screwball comedies once portrayed sparkling repartee between two people who were attracted to each other despite their adversarial relationship and who expressed that mutual attraction in the form of a reciprocal mocking badinage, "The Break Up" is a portrait of contemporary society's view of male-female domestic partnerships in which two aliens struggle to stay together and ultimately fail to do so.

362

These cruel and slightly depressing movies are not atypical or abnormal in the romantic-comedies of feminist society. On the contrary, they are big box-office examples of Hollywood's current view of the relationship between women and men. It is the 'Men are from Mars, Women are from Venus' *alienation of the sexes*. In the past rom-coms were all about an antagonistic relationship between a woman and a man which ultimately leads to love but the humorous friction of that antagonism was not maliciously hostile in the manner of present day romantic-comedy.

One customary feature of romance has long been the story arc in which a man must earn or win the love of a woman. This goes all the way back to the mediaeval context of the knight who must undergo various trials or ordeals to win the hand of his fair maid. Translated into the context of a modern romantic-comedy, this is now expressed in the way that the male lead (who is humorously inadequate in one way or another) has to suffer a series of amusing humiliations for the audience to laugh at until, by the end of the movie, the female lead has fallen in love with him.

For example, in "Along Came Polly" (2004) Ben Stiller's newly-wed wife commits adultery and dumps him *on the first day of their honeymoon* when she meets an extremely good-looking hunk on the beach. Having established Stiller's character as a risk-averse romantic loser, he then spends the rest of the movie pursuing gorgeously laid-back yet adventurous Jennifer Aniston. During the course of this pursuit he forces himself to eat spicy food which gives him a massive attack of sweating and diarrhoea, he makes a fool of himself dancing at a salsa club, and ends up eating peanuts off the ground (having rubbed them into the dirt) to prove to her that he is capable of taking risks.

Sadly, male humiliation is very much a part of the formula of contemporary romantic-comedy because the woman is almost always the *object of desire* and therefore *the one with all the power*, and the man is in the position of a supplicant, having to bend over backwards to try to get her to like him and fall in love with him. Compare this to a film like "Bringing Up Baby" (1938) in which reckless Katharine Hepburn falls in love with, and pursues, mild-mannered Cary Grant. All manner of misadventures ensue, most of which (but by no means all) happen to Grant. But the tone of his comedic misfortunes is not one of humiliation because *she* is pursuing *him*. Hepburn is not the perfect object of desire in the movie, *Grant* is. But the object of desire *doesn't* have all the power in their relationship because she keeps getting him into embarrassing mishaps. The balance of power in old screwball comedies is much more even-handed than in modern rom-coms.

"When Harry Met Sally" was a huge box-office success. For much of the film everything is fine, they meet, they disagree, they gradually grow closer together. Sally says that heterosexual women and men can be platonic friends. Harry says that sexual desire always messes up female/male friendships. But they become friends without sleeping together. So Sally is right. Then they have sex and it destroys their friendship. So Harry is right. In this story men and women can be platonic friends but sex does mess it up. So they're both right. But now Sally *hates* Harry and so he spends the remainder of the film abjectly humiliating himself in a pathetic attempt to win her back whilst she stands frostily aloof. Ask yourself: why is *he* in the wrong? Is it because he slept with her?

Ironically, the feminist assumption that it is always the man's gendered role to apologise is actually *contrary to what is on the screen* but this seems to have gone unnoticed by film reviewers. The reason the two have sex is that Sally is badly upset that her former lover is getting married. She phones Harry and asks him to come round and comfort her. Being her friend, Harry rushes to her side and provides emotional support. But when he kisses her in a friendly way, she responds by kissing him in a sexual way. Then they have sex. In other words, *she* uses sexual intimacy with him to comfort herself in her distress. The next morning Harry is mortified by what they've done but Sally looks like the cat who got the cream. Yet, although she has used him sexually to make herself feel better, the film tells us that *it is all his fault* and that he must grovel in apology. After all, he's the man, it's his gendered social role to always be in the wrong.

Compare and contrast, as they say. In each of the classic romantic screwball comedies "His Girl Friday", "The Philadelphia Story" and "My Favourite Wife", all released in 1940, Cary Grant plays an ex-husband who spends the film trying to win back his wife after a previous split. But in none of them does he have to pathetically humiliate himself to do it. In fact, in the first two films Grant's ex-husband character tends to be the one with the most self-assurance and personal power. The storylines of these movies could be used in modern cinema (since they all feature broken relationships) but if they were re-made now the characterisations would be very different. They would have to be re-written to reflect society's sneering contempt for men. These days audiences have come to expect the male lead to be shown in a bad light as some childish loser whose life can only be redeemed by his *realising* what a childish loser he is and growing up a bit.

In Nick Hornby's "Fever Pitch" (1997) the male lead is obsessed with Arsenal football club and in Nick Hornby's "High Fidelity" (2000) the male lead is obsessed with music trivia. The female leads in each case are, naturally, proper adults. No doubt Mr Hornby is himself very much a fan of football and music but this has not stopped him from writing several extremely successful novels many of which have been made into major movies. So he surely can't be the complete asshole that he keeps telling us men are. There must be much more to him as a person than just the character he puts on the screen to please a modern audience.

"The African Queen" (1951) has none of today's feminist caricatures. Humphrey Bogart and Katharine Hepburn *both* play people who have a lot of character deficiencies at the beginning of the movie and the point of the film is that as they fall in love they *both* grow into more well-rounded people. To begin with, he is slothful and hedonistic, and she is dictatorial and priggish. Slowly he learns to smarten up and she learns to relax her religious intolerance. The fault is not all on one side. He has some learning to do and so does she. Neither is seen as being always in the right. The film does not take sides. But if they re-made the movie these days, he would start out as the immature child-man and she would endlessly condescend to him until eventually she forces him to grow up, and his maturity would consist in his accepting that her view of everything was the correct one.

The absence of feminist condescension in old movies means that in "His Girl Friday" (1940) Cary Grant understands Rosalind Russell's character so well that he is able to steal her back from her current boyfriend. Can you imagine a modern rom-com where the male lead *understands women?* The only men in modern movies who understand women are the clichéd 'gay friend' and the clichéd treacherous womanizer who is sexually unfaithful and has to be taught a lesson through some condign punishment. It is popularly believed in feminist culture that all women understand men because such shallow and simple-minded creatures are easy to understand but no man ever truly understands a woman because they are so much more emotionally sophisticated and psychologically complex than those crude creatures, men. So there's seldom any sex equality in modern rom-coms.

This is not to deny the presence of sexism in old movies. "That Touch of Mink" (1962), with Cary Grant and Doris Day, is a romantic-comedy that would probably seem freakishly strange to young people in the 21st century. Grant wants to have sex with Day but she wants to marry Grant. So the film is *entirely* about whether Grant can get the virginal Day into bed before their wedding night. The whole film revolves around Doris Day's vagina. Will she, won't she, will she, won't she? When it looks like Day is about to sleep with Grant, she breaks out in a skin rash. After they are married, Grant breaks out in a skin rash. (Apparently, women are allergic to pre-marital sex and men are allergic to marriage.) As I said, *movies reflect the culture in which they were made.* This was true in the past and it is true in the present.

366

Although, not always. There are occasionally some old movies that could have been written by present-day writers in the type of sexism that they display on the screen. In Preston Sturges' "The Lady Eve" (1941) Barbara Stanwyck and her father conspire to cheat rich Henry Fonda out of some of his money. Stanwyck starts the movie by lying to Fonda and manipulating him in order to swindle him. But they fall in love with each other. Then they have a bust-up because he discovers that she is a swindler, so he doesn't believe that she really loves him. Stanwyck swears revenge. She lies to Fonda some more and he is humiliated at a swanky dinner party. Then he apologises to her as they embrace for the happy ending. Wait, just a second. *He* apologises to *her*? What for? *She's* the liar and the confidence trickster. Ah, but *he* is the man, so he's the one who apologises. I can't imagine why someone hasn't done a re-make, it sounds perfect for a modern-day audience.

It's also true that some contemporary romantic-comedies could have been written by someone from a time gone by. What could be more contemporary than "Bridget Jones' Diary" (2001) and yet what actually happens in the film? Renée Zellweger has to choose between those two old stalwart clichés of romantic fiction the rich and handsome but dangerous rogue, played by Hugh Grant, and the reliable and nice but rather boring ordinary chap, played by Colin Firth. Then what happens? They have a fight over her. The white knight and the black knight actually fight each other to win the lady's hand. How antiquated is that? Yet this was a book and movie phenomenon at the beginning of the 21st century.

A crucial film to consider in any comparison of sex equality and sexism in rom-coms past and present is "Adam's Rib" (1949). This is a film which deliberately sets out to present a battle of the sexes, and it could be thought of as a 'feminist' movie made twenty years prior to second wave feminism. In the story a wife shoots (but only wounds) her adulterous husband. The stars of the film, Spencer Tracy and Katharine Hepburn, are a very happily married couple who are both lawyers. Tracy is the attorney who is appointed to prosecute the wife who shot her husband. But Hepburn sees the case as a chance to strike a political blow for women. She is taken on as the defence attorney and argues her case on the basis that there is a sexist double-standard about adultery, implying that if a man had shot his adulterous wife he would receive more lenient treatment from the law than a woman who shoots her adulterous husband, and Hepburn demands that her client be found 'not guilty' as (she apparently assumes) a man would be. Tracy is mainly concerned with an impartial application of the law and views the case as a straightforward act of attempted murder.

Both behave badly at times (notably, Hepburn humiliates Tracy in court with a cheap stunt) but both remain sympathetic characters. However, the battle in court breaks up their formerly happy marriage. Hepburn wins the court case (thereby defeating the man in his 'male' environment) but Tracy exposes Hepburn's hypocrisy when he finds her in a romantic setting with their amorous next door neighbour and he pretends to be about to shoot her (and her reaction is the opposite of what she had said in court). The movie doesn't really side with either party in their dispute since it's concerned to use comedy to explore the issue of (pre-second wave) 'feminism' and what makes the film so interesting is the way that it deals with the issue without a modern bias.

For example, when the amorous neighbour is trying to seduce Hepburn she reproaches him by saying "Now look here Kip, I'm fighting my prejudices but it's clear that you're behaving like a, well I hate to put it this way but, like *a man*" and he replies as if insulted by the word "You watch your language!" In 1949, his *rejection* of the word 'man' was funny, but what would a *male feminist* make of that in 2014? (In chapter 3 I quoted John Stoltenberg who refers to men as "penised people".) Besides, what feminist nowadays would ever admit to having "prejudices" in a culture of female-entitlement where so many women feel *entitled* to despise men?

The film's non-partisan approach would be a tough assignment for any modern writer. At one point Tracy rages "I want a wife, not a competitor!" in a thoroughgoing traditionalist manner, yet the happy ending is contrived when Tracy saves their marriage by pretending to *cry*, using the traditional 'woman's weapon' of tears to manipulate Hepburn into a change of heart. Sex equality is essential for any good rom-com so it's quite revealing that the culture of Spencer Tracy and Katharine Hepburn could make romantic-comedies with a lot more equality than the culture of Jennifer Aniston and Vince Vaughn.

Intriguingly, two modern rom-coms that have a much higher level of sex equality than is usual these days are the Meg Ryan and Tom Hanks vehicles "Sleepless in Seattle" (1993) and "You've got Mail" (1998). What is intriguing is that they both have connections with older movies. The first references "An Affair to Remember" (1957) and the second is a remake of "The Shop Around the Corner" (1940).

Significantly, *neither film presents Hanks as being inadequate.* In the first he is a tender and considerate father. In the second he is a businessman with a sensitively poetic character. He is insulted a lot in the second film but it is clear to the audience that he does not deserve this abuse. When Ryan insults him it tends to make *her* character look bad, rather than his. Tom Hanks, we might remember, is one of the several actors who have been called 'the new Cary Grant'. Hollywood has been looking for another Cary Grant ever since the original retired.

Does the sad degeneration of the rom-com into movies about acrimonious failed relationships tell us anything about equality in gender relations, past and present? One thing is for sure, it's becoming ever more difficult for filmmakers to produce good romantic-comedies because for a romance to work the woman (and the movie) has to be able to display some *respect* for the male character. Otherwise it's just another chick-flick that flatters women by telling them how superior they are, and where's the romance in that?

In a society that systemically *disrespects* men and views domestic relationships in terms of a Mars/Venus alienation of the sexes, romance is an increasingly difficult thing to put on the screen convincingly.

Male Submission

People who are culturally demonized may learn the lesson ('internalize', as the jargon has it) that they are always the ones who are at fault, and they adopt the attitude appropriate to a guilt-object. They learn to apologise. It doesn't matter for what, and it doesn't matter why, since this is simply a cultural norm. It is their gendered social role. It is their place to apologise. It is their station in life.

A mind-set of habitual submission is something which is expressed in a lot of ways, both large and small. It isn't just men's docile acceptance of egregious political insults, such as having a "Minister for Women and Equalities" instead of a Minister for Equality. It isn't just men's passive acquiescence to high-handed economic injustices, such as having women-only shortlists and pro-women affirmative action. It extends deeply into a man's life on a personal level.

Some examples are dramatic, such as the man who does not defend himself when being physically attacked by a domestically violent woman because he has been taught that 'a man should never hit a woman', leaving him defenceless. Some examples are illogical, such as a man subscribing to the belief that society discriminates against women whilst living in a gynocentric culture obsessed with women's well-being. Some examples are tragic, such as the man who deliberately avoids being tactile with other people's children (or even, in extreme cases, with his own children) because he is aware that society's gendered panic over paedophilia means that his actions, unlike those of women, may be misinterpreted. Some examples are a cause of dilemma, such as the man who believes that he must have a personal capacity for violence to put at the service of a woman for her protection, whist feeling guilty about having a capacity for violence because this is seen as a threat to women. Some examples are a 'Catch 22' situation, such as the man who accepts that a woman is entitled to criticize him for failing to display his vulnerability as she would wish, but who also accepts that a woman is entitled to criticize him when he does display his vulnerability in a way

370

which she has not sanctioned (e.g. the 'weakling' who can't stand up for himself, or the 'wimp' who complains about misandry). The reader can add their own examples to the list.

But perhaps the most pervasive and insidious form of habitual male submission is seen in the cultural conformist's meek subservience to the belief that *women are the proper judges of things;* the belief that *woman are always right.* This is a spin-off from the female-entitlement culture that is most familiar to us when feminists are applying it to cases like (a) women employed in formerly 'male' working environments are entitled to 'improve' those environments by making them operate on feminine gendered norms of behaviour; (b) women respondents in feminist research are entitled to be believed whatever they say; (c) women who make an allegation of rape are entitled to be believed and to see the accused man arrested and convicted; etc.

This idea that it is always the *female* perspective that is the *correct* perspective has been repeated so often and has become so normalized that it has generated a more personalized *sense of entitlement* by which some (by no means all, but some) women have become entitlement-junkies. I'm not talking about state benefits and welfare entitlements here, I'm talking about the generalized feminist attitude that women are *entitled* to what they *want* because they want it.

For example, an entitlement-junkie will feel entitled to being emotionally understood by her man, who must constantly be aware of her feelings (regardless of whether she understands him or considers his feelings). At the same time she also feels entitled to complain that men lack women's natural empathy and depth of emotional understanding. So she feels entitled to something from him which, according to her own sexist stereotype of men, he is not equipped to provide. But that doesn't matter because *she's entitled.* An entitlement-junkie will feel entitled to be listened to by her man even if she isn't saying anything that is of interest to him (but not vice versa because, hey, you know how men just talk about stupid sport or boring cars all the time).

371

Actually, we're all entitled to speak as we please in our personal relationships, but no one is entitled *to be listened to.* As Quentin Crisp used to say: "we'd all like to have friends but if it means you've got to listen the price is ridiculous!"

An entitlement-junkie will feel entitled to sex equality whenever it suits her, but still feel entitled to be treated with gentlemanly deference because she is a 'lady'. An entitlement-junkie will feel entitled to criticize her man for the way he dresses, but also feel entitled to condemn men for judging women on their appearance because that is sexism. An entitlement-junkie will feel entitled to decide upon the interior décor of the marital home on the grounds that men have such bad taste, and feel entitled that her man should agree with her about this. And so on *ad infinitum.*

The point of mentioning this is not merely to ridicule entitlement-junkies (although, why shouldn't we?) but to note *the extent to which men submit to this sort of behaviour.* The idea that women are entitled to have things their own way has become so well-established that it seems to be taken for granted that it is the judgement of the woman, in any given situation, which determines what is or is not the truth.

One enlightening example of this male submission to female superiority is manifested in something as humble and humdrum as going to the toilet. It's a useful example because it is so ubiquitous and so personal. I became aware of this many years ago because (if you'll pardon my mentioning it) it is my practice to lower both the seat and the seat cover after using the toilet. Call me weird if you please but it seems to me that the toilet cover is there for a reason, it is to cover the toilet bowl when not in use, and so I use for that purpose. Why wouldn't I? It's designed that way. But this practice is evidently unusual. Whenever I had male and female guests I discovered that the men would leave both the seat and the cover up after using the toilet, whereas the women would leave the seat *down* and the cover *up* after using the toilet. (Neither left it in the condition in which they found it.) The reason was obvious: both sexes left the toilet seat and cover in the position in which they had used the facility and were likely to use it again the next time. In other words, both sexes do exactly the same thing: they leave the seat and cover in whatever position is *most convenient for themselves.*

Again, why not? There is no such thing as a 'correct' position for a toilet seat and cover. You can suit yourselves. If someone were to absolutely insist upon some position being designated as the correct position, then I would maintain that the only position that could reasonably be called correct is to have both the seat and the cover down after use. That's what the cover is there for, right? There is no point in having a toilet bowl cover if it is never used. But let's not be dictatorial about it, let's accept that it is a matter of purely personal preference and agree that there is no 'correct' position for the seat and cover of the domestic toilet.

Why, then, is it the case, all over the country (all over the western world?), that one of the most frequent and scornful reprimands women make to their menfolk is that the wretched man hasn't left the toilet seat in the correct position? Where is the argument to say that *the woman's personal preference* is more than just a personal preference; that it is the objectively correct position?

One lesson to learn from this is how something that people superficially take to be *evidence of gender difference* (i.e. that men are selfish, inconsiderate beasts who don't show a proper respect for women whereas selfless women would never behave so badly) is, in fact, *evidence of how women and men are not different.* They do the same thing for the same reason; they both leave the toilet seat and cover in whatever position is most convenient for themselves.

But another lesson to learn from this is how it is customarily assumed that whenever the sexes are in conflict over some issue, it must be men who are at fault. Men have nothing to apologise for when they leave the toilet seat up, yet for years and years men have been criticized for leaving the seat in the 'wrong' position; that is, contrary to the wishes of the female

373

with whom they live. And this is where the mind-set of male submission becomes apparent. Men commonly accept this criticism *as justified.* They *apologise* for the umpteenth time for being so selfish and so inconsiderate as to leave the toilet seat up, and they promise to do better in future.

This example will be dismissed as unimportant by those who care nothing about men, but I mention it to show how everything, large and small, profound and mundane, trivial and significant, can express the ever-increasing submission of men in a feminist society. Men can't even take a piss without having to apologise for it. And if you still think that this is too trifling a matter to take seriously, then take a look at how a firmly established gender-supremacist habit of mind can move swiftly in the direction of social *enforcement.* In 2010 a home shopping company marketed a toilet *to train men to lower the toilet seat:*

"Our solution – the Lav Nav - a small device which attaches to the toilet lid, lighting up the toilet in the dark and shining green when the seat is down and red if it is left up. The Lav Nav is ideal for fed up women everywhere - not only is it now easier to find the loo in the dark but the red light is a handy reminder to forgetful men that leaving the seat up is just not on." http://www.blog.24studio.co.uk/2010_08_01_archive.html

Notice how engrained and unchallenged is the assumption that *whatever women want* must therefore be the *correct* thing to do and that they are *entitled to expect compliance* from their men. A retail company is even marketing a commercial product on the unassailable assumption of female correctness and male incorrectness. But it doesn't end there. The real indicator of the future comes from the political sphere.

Viggo Hansen, a county counsellor from the Left Party in Sweden, attempted to pass a law that required men to sit down to urinate. http://digitaljournal.com/article/352108 This was presented in terms of hygiene and improved prostate/bladder health. But does anyone really believe that this feminist party is trying to force men to urinate like women because of their concern for

374

men's health? After millennia in which men have pissed standing up, they now have to piss sitting down for the sake of their health? No, it's the usual assumption that the woman's way is the best way and the only proper way. And men will never leave the toilet seat up again.

The degradation of men in the appalling "A Man's Apology" video https://www.youtube.com/watch?v=5SVQrBDcMTw that went viral online is the epitome of the belief that male self-abasement at the feet of women is virtuous. A series of young men appear on screen to say how sorry they are for all the terrible things that men do to women. They go on to praise women so fulsomely that any sane woman would blush at such asinine flattery and balk at such grovelling sycophancy. This video is the essence of male feminism (it also has a Christian undertone). The men on screen present themselves and all other men as being always in the wrong, as inadequate and undeserving, whereas they present women as perfect creatures who deserve infinite love and respect.

The video unconditionally accepts society's female supremacist attitudes and the reduction of men to guilt-objects. These young men have learned the lesson that if they seek the respect and approval of women, then *abject servility* is the persona they must adopt. But is that truly what women want from their men? Has feminism elevated feminine vanity to the level where they expect men to kneel in worship to them? If so, then this would be entirely in keeping with feminism's view of what 'gender equality' means.

Men are the Ideological Niggers of Feminism

For many years the word 'nigger' has been the most taboo word in the English language because it is this word, more than any other, that is evocative of society's shame. It is the word that most stinks of prejudice; that is most associated with the crime of bigotry. It speaks of the wilful denial of a human being's intrinsic value as an individual autonomous person in their own right, in order to socially embed those people in a

375

group-identity which reduces their status to that of a social utility. This word most powerfully expresses the way that a culture can socially engineer a concept of inferiority and impose it arbitrarily upon anyone who falls within that category of person. It is the word that most shockingly reminds us of how the people of one skin colour, or one ethnicity, or one creed, or one sex, can be viewed (and be taught to view themselves) as inherently inferior and deserving of a lower level of respect than the rest of society.

In western countries in the past it was negroes who were socially embedded in this group-identity, which is obviously where the word 'nigger' comes from, but today in the West there is another group-identity that is well on its way to becoming the niggers of a society dominated by the beliefs and values of feminism: men. There are some who would argue that men have already been reduced to the status of society's nigger but I am not arguing this, I am arguing that *ideologically* feminism views men as niggers (i.e. from a feminist perspective, 'nigger' is men's *ideological group-identity*) and that, as a result, men in feminist society are rapidly heading toward having that status.

It's a society's beliefs about a group of people, it's the collective identity those people are given, that determines the level of dignity and respect they receive in that society. It wasn't the *colour of their skin* that turned negroes into 'niggers', it was the *beliefs and values* of a society that saw them and treated them as niggers. White people were held to be intrinsically better than black people in all the ways that mattered. The word 'nigger' was society's verbal expression of the lower level of dignity and respect which it considered 'appropriate' for black people and therefore imposed upon them.

It's the same in feminist society which has established a set of mainstream cultural beliefs and values that treat women as being intrinsically better than men in all the ways that matter. When movies and television shows and media advertising routinely treat men with overt disrespect, it is an expression of those cultural values. When people habitually speak disparagingly of the male sex, and men are expected to put up with this indignity, it is an expression of those cultural values.

As this book has described, the demonisation of men over the last forty years has created a society in which men are systemically disrespected and treated as guilt-objects. Men are the 'oppressors', men are the rapists and domestic abusers, men are the absent fathers or deadbeat dads, men are the paedophiles, men are the aggressive and violent sex, men are the woman-haters, men are the people who need to be 'civilized' by women, men are the domestically incompetent slobs, men are the immature boys who never grow up, men are the emotionally shallow game-players, men are the absurdly posturing macho clowns, men are the selfish and socially irresponsible people, men are the group of people who are always to blame.

To best understand how the ideological beliefs of feminism cast men into a social role which can reasonably be called *the niggers of feminism*, we should make the historical comparison and see what this tells us. Let's compare feminism with white-supremacism in 1930s Alabama.

We'll begin with comparative attitudes about rape, since the theory of 'rape culture' is such a prominent feature of feminism's current political agenda. In 1931, nine black males between 13 and 19 years of age were convicted of the rape of two white women in Scottsboro, Alabama. They are known to history as the 'Scottsboro Boys'. http://www.scottsboro-boys.org/history.html The accused men were innocent but for black men to be accused of rape by white women was enough to get the men found guilty in such a bigoted society. At a subsequent retrial, one of the alleged 'victims' retracted her accusation, admitting that it was false. The men remained incarcerated anyway and it was years before they were finally released. The 'Scottsboro Boys' case is a famous example of injustice committed by a prejudiced legal system and today most feminists would be quick to condemn it for its racism against those falsely accused black men.

But this is the question: if nine young men (of whatever colour) were charged with exactly the same offence today on exactly the same testimony, *wouldn't feminists be just as prejudiced in their rush to a judgment of guilty* as that white Alabama jury in 1931? As we saw in chapter 5, feminism has a presumption of guilt for men accused of rape. Feminism treats all allegations of rape as actually being rapes because it insists that the woman should always be believed. The Alabama racists would have had a presumption of guilt toward the nine accused because they were *black men* and today the sexist feminists would have a presumption of guilt toward the nine accused because they are *men*. But what difference does it make if a person is treated as a nigger because of their sex or because of their skin colour?

Ironically, the generation of hypocrites who created second wave feminism were adoringly admiring of Harper Lee's novel 'To Kill A Mockingbird' where a black man is falsely accused and falsely convicted of raping a white woman. They identified themselves with the liberal attorney for the defence. But if you think about it, you'll see that they identified themselves with the wrong character. Feminism's ideological presumption of guilt for men accused of rape and its belief in a 'rape culture' where men in general are seen as being guilty of 'normalizing' rape (and therefore share in the blame for any rapes which actually occur) is the opposite of the liberal attorney's belief that each individual man should not be condemned for something that he has not done, nor should he be condemned for something that he simply *is*, whether it be black or male. In today's society feminists are actually *the jury* who falsely convict the accused. It's just that they convict him, not for being black, but for being a man. The theory of 'rape culture' convicts all men, and it convicts them without trial.

Feminism's depiction of men as a class of persons who are a constant and imminent sexual threat to women as a class of persons *exactly mirrors* the attitude of a jury of 1930s Alabama racists toward all black men being a sexual threat to all white women. Just as the racists feared the sexuality of black men, bigoted feminists fear the sexuality of men. But feminists lack the self-knowledge to see themselves as they truly are. They don't realise that they are *not* the nice liberal defence lawyer in 'To Kill A Mockingbird', *they* are the bigoted jury. *Men are the niggers of feminism.*

The parallels do not end there. In a white-supremacist culture, wouldn't you expect to find that black people were more likely than white people to be homeless? That, as a percentage of their relative populations, black people were more likely than white people to be sent to prison? That black people would on average die at a younger age than white people? That black people would be less likely than white people to attend university? That black people would be more likely to do the dirtiest and most dangerous jobs?

All of these things are true of men comparative to women in contemporary society. Men are more likely to be homeless, they're more likely to be sent to prison, on average they die younger than women, they are less likely to attend university than women, and they are more likely to do the dirtiest and most dangerous jobs.

The parallels keep on coming. Society has a much greater concern for the safety, well-being, and emotional sensibilities of women (e.g. the speech-codes, the 'acceptable' behavioural norms, and the legal protections brought in to facilitate the feminisation of the workplace) which require men to abide by female gendered norms. This feminist version of chivalry expects men to exhibit a subservient deference to women as the people whose interests *must be prioritised over their own*, just as black people in a white-supremacist culture had to exhibit a subservient deference toward white people whose interests took precedence.

In a white-supremacist culture, if a black man were assaulted by a white man the victim might be reluctant to fight back because he would be aware that the law would be much harsher on a black man who hit a white man than it would be the other way around. This is exactly the position that men are in under feminist oppression. A man who is assaulted by a woman must remember that if he hits her back, it is likely that he will be arrested for assaulting her, even though she started the fight.

Some Men's Rights Activists even argue that the control that women have over men's fertility, deciding whether a man will become a father or not, and using the custody courts to take a father's children away from him without his consent, echoes the slavery of times past when slaves were required to breed by their slaveowners and had their children involuntarily taken away from them. I would not go so far as to argue this, but you can see their point, can't you?

One of the objections that is likely to made against the argument that men are the niggers of feminism is the claim that it is still men who have the greatest economic power because *overall* men as a class of persons earn more money than women as a class of persons. So men on average earn more than women on average. But the assumption behind this objection is so wilfully misleading that we need to expose it's deception in three different ways.

(1) To say that men *on average* earn more money than women *on average* is not the same thing as saying that women and men earn unequal salaries for working the same hours at the same job. The conflation of those two very different things is an example of feminism's total lack of intellectual integrity. [This feminist myth has been proven false innumerable times. Two examples can be found at https://www.youtube.com/watch?v=EwogDPh-Sow and https://www.youtube.com/watch?v=1oqyrflOQFc]

The reality is that men on average earn more because they work at jobs which command higher salaries (e.g. business, science, engineering, and work that is physically uncomfortable or dangerous). These are jobs that woman could do but generally don't want to do. Men on average earn more because they work longer hours, and choose whatever job pays the best rather than jobs that are self-satisfying or personally fulfilling. They tough it out to get the money. Men on average earn more because they don't take career breaks to have children. No one is offering them six months paid paternity leave. There are plenty of reasons why men on average earn more than women (and let's focus on that word 'earn'. If you earn it, then it's not a privilege) but feminism expects everyone to just assume that there is only one conceivable explanation of a disparity in earnings: misogyny.

The assertion that men have more power than women because women on average earn less than men on average ignores *the role of women* in creating an overall disparity in earnings. Is it men's fault if women choose to work in middle-salary jobs like social services and healthcare and education (where they work in hygienic comfortable 'office' environments) rather than getting a higher paid job as a mechanic on an oil rig or an engineer in a power plant? Men can't force women to work in those higher paid jobs, can they? Women currently have the advantage of greater life-choices than men (in alternating between career and the domestic sphere) and one consequence of this is that it affects their capacity to earn money. If women worked full-time for the whole of their career without taking any career breaks to raise their children, whilst *men* took time out to raise their kids and *men* chose part-time employment so that *they* could have more time with their kids, then it would be women's salaries that would be higher overall. Career women who never have babies earn as much, or more than, their male counterparts.

Remember, it is not men who have control over women's fertility, it is *women* who have control over *men's* fertility. In feminist society it's 'a woman's right to choose', not a man's right to choose. If the domestic sphere were, as feminism likes to paint it, a terrible prison in which women are forced to 'shoulder the burden' of child-care, then there wouldn't be so many women choosing to be mothers. The best way to equalise the overall earnings of men and women would be for society to give fathers an *equal entitlement* to the role of primary child-carer; to give *men* equality with *women* in regard of their own children. But would feminism permit this, or would feminism oppose it?

(2) Earning ability in the workplace is not a reliable indicator of personal power. We should remember that it is not who *earns* the money that really matters, it is *who spends the money* and *upon whom the money is spent*. People who work in advertising have long known that successful marketing targets women. Why? Because women spend more money than men. But how can it be that women are earning less but spending more? Simple. It's because women are not only spending their own money, they are spending men's money too.

This applies also to taxation and the distribution of tax revenues. Men earn more money overall, so men pay more tax overall. Yet governments' public spending is directed more toward women than toward men. Women pay less but receive more. (Incidentally, can you imagine what feminists would say if these roles were the other way around? If women paid more tax than men, whilst men received more of the benefits of public spending than women? They'd hit the roof.)

So, if (a) a large percentage of men are contributing their income to a marriage or cohabitation or family, and (b) a certain percentage of men contribute to the financial support of their ex-wives or ex-partners or children, and (c) society favours women in its redistribution of wealth through the taxation system, then nothing can be reliably deduced from the crude statistics for what is earned by men on average and what is earned by women on average.

Perhaps the complaint that men earn more overall than women is not a complaint that *women* should be making, but rather is a complaint that *men* should be making. As a result of their comparative life-choices, men still find themselves in the position of having to earn more than women during the course of their working lives because the women in their lives are taking time off from earning or are working part-time. Consequently, men are making a larger financial contribution to *society as a whole*.

This ought to be balanced out by the fact that women are making a larger contribution to the work of raising children, but this balance is upset by the fact that nowadays many men are denied significant access to their children and have no contact with other people's children. The reward that men receive for their work in terms of *family life* and a *personal investment in society's future* is diminishing. It is diminishing rapidly. Yet, through taxation, men still bear the greater financial burden for society as a whole. Remember, it is not the oppressor class that works for the oppressed class, it is the oppressed class that works for the oppressor class. So which sex is the oppressed?

(3) Even if someone *did* believe that whichever sex earns the most money overall was a reliable indicator of which sex had the greater power, we would have to ask them if they can see past the end of their own nose. How will things be in ten years? In twenty years? Girls are now so advantaged over boys in education, with an increasing female domination of higher education, and an increasing number of unemployable young men, how long will it be before men in feminist society earn less on average than women?

Of course, this triumph of feminism will require that one of two changes take place in society. Either (a) women stop having babies (in which case society has no future) or (b) men be permitted to stay at home with their kids while women go out to earn money so that they can financially support their husbands and families. Were the latter to occur, women would discover that the traditional female gender role is preferable to the traditional male gender role, and feminism would have to rewrite its theories on 'male privilege'. We'd then be told that the gender who stays home and raises the kids is the privileged sex, and how it's unfair that women have to earn the money to support their lazy men.

So the objection that men have more power because they earn more money does not refute my argument that men are the ideological niggers of feminism. I am arguing that *ideologically* feminist women view men as their niggers and that, as a result, men in contemporary society are rapidly heading toward actually having that status. For example, we are all familiar with stories about black entertainers in the 1950s who appeared on stage as the well-paid headliner act at Las Vegas hotels but who were not allowed to rent a room in those hotels and who had to enter the building through the back door. It is easy to imagine a parallel case where a male feminist is appearing as a speaker at a feminist conference who is told that he must enter the building by the back door because the whole auditorium has been declared a women-only 'safe space'. The only disanalogy would be that the male feminist *would not resent this*, he would see it as 'appropriate' that he should not violate a women-only area.

University campuses are a Petri dish for the feminist future and they have long had advocates for all manner of women-only 'safe spaces' on campus, attempting to justify these on the grounds that women can feel uncomfortable in the presence of men and need a place where they can truly relax amongst other women. Would the manager of a Las Vegas hotel in the 1950s have attempted to justify a whites-only policy on the same basis, that his white clientele would feel uncomfortable mixing with black people?

When society's beliefs about people reduce one particular group in the population to the status that is encapsulated by the word 'nigger', then the people within that group have been devalued as human beings. Instead of all persons having their intrinsic value as human beings recognised, this one group are seen purely in terms of their *utility value* to the people who are seen as being properly human. So, in a racist society of the past, black people were valued solely for their ability to perform work for society. Men are now becoming a parallel case.

In the current systemically feminist society, devoted to the well-being of women and their offspring, the existence of the adult male is only seen to have value in relation to how that male offers some benefit to women or children. Can he provide money, can he provide protection, can he ease their way through life? The male bachelor (without children) has *no merit* from a feminist perspective. All he contributes to women and children is the paying of his taxes, so what good is he? He is ideologically depicted solely in terms of an overgrown juvenile surfing porn sites on the internet. His only role in the feminist agenda is to portray the potential rapist contributing to 'rape culture'. Feminist society does not value men for themselves. Men are not seen as being intrinsically valuable as individual human beings. Men's only recognised value under feminism is their use-value, their instrumental value, to women and children.

Notoriously, Hillary Clinton once said:

"Women have always been the primary victims of war. Women lose their husbands, their fathers, their sons in combat. Women often have to flee from the only homes they have ever known. Women are often the refugees from conflict and sometimes, more frequently in today's warfare, victims. Women are often left with the responsibility, alone, of raising the children." http://clinton3.nara.gov/WH/EOP/First_Lady/html/generalspeeches/1998/19981117.html

For a feminist like Clinton, the dead husbands, the dead fathers, the dead sons, are *not* the primary victims of war. Male lives have no *intrinsic value* to a feminist and so when a husband is killed in a war, the primary victim is his wife; when a father is killed, the primary victim is his daughter; when a son is killed, the primary victim is his mother. And if the husbands never get to see their own children grow up because the husbands are dead, the feminist's primary sympathy is for the wife who has raise her child alone, or maybe with a little financial help from her new boyfriend.

In the UK it's no different. The senior politician Harriet Harman (is it some kind of cosmic joke that the leading feminist in parliament has the name Harm Man?), when standing in for Gordon Brown at Prime Minister's Question Time, was asked by John Maples MP: what is the military objective of the war in Afghanistan? http://news.bbc.co.uk/1/hi/uk_politics/8140086.stm

It was the summer of 2009 and by that time 170 British troops had died, 169 of them men, not to mention all the wounds and amputations and so on. Harman had actually begun her replies at that Question Time by listing the names of the seven British men who had been killed in Afghanistan in the previous week, and had expressed her condolences to their families. So what did Harman say as a justification for all this death and injury? She first went through the official government waffle about opposing terrorism but then she went on to say that what *she* thought was important was that the war in Afghanistan had considerably improved the education system for Afghan children. So, by her own account, that was why Harriet Harman thought her government was sending all those British men to their deaths.

But how many *women's* lives do you think she would have sacrificed to help a larger number of Afghan kids go to school? The question would never arise, would it? Harman's view of male deaths has the same *traditionally sexist and feminist* double-standard about the value of human life that is so evident in Clinton's comment. Whilst women's lives have intrinsic value, the only value a man's life can have is the use to which it can be put to benefit women and their children. *Any* women and their children. Even those who live far away in another country.

This idea, that one group of people are intrinsically valuable in themselves but the other group of people only have instrumental value, is an expression of the very essence of what it means to be a 'nigger' in any society. Under racist oppression, especially at its most extreme under slavery, black people were not seen as having intrinsic value as human beings, they only had instrumental value to their owners. They had value as workers, as the producers of wealth for their owners, and as domestic servants. They were valued solely *for the uses to which they could be put.*

The feminist attitude of seeing no value in men except insofar as they might be useful to women and children as producers and providers, functions on the same principle. Men are valued *for what they can do.* Women simply *are* valuable. If a society has this attitude toward Arabs, then Arabs are the niggers in that society. If a society has this attitude toward Jews, then Jews are the niggers in that society. If a society has this attitude toward men, then men are the niggers in that society. Have black men in the West worked so hard to overcome being treated as niggers because they are black, only to find that they are treated as niggers because they are men?

Another prominent example which displays this same attitude of valuing men only insofar as they serve the interests of women can be found in the way that male 'maturity', if it is spoken of at all, is spoken of in terms of a man's willingness to get married and father children.
https://www.youtube.com/watch?v=troj3dlyQ8k

The 'confirmed bachelor' is assumed to be either (a) gay, or (b) so self-absorbed in his own puerile pleasures that he is selfishly unconcerned with the important things in life, namely women and children. For a man to have any hope of being thought 'mature' he must have demonstrated his capacity for 'commitment' by accepting the traditional responsibilities of husbandry and fatherhood, otherwise he'll be labeled a 'permanent adolescent'.

This is why men are constantly criticized for lacking commitment to relationships and marriage, *even though it is women who initiate the majority of divorces*. Logically, we would have to conclude that as women file for divorce more often than men, then if one sex is more lacking in commitment to their relationships than the other sex, it must be women. But, of course, that is *never* said. Instead, it is men who are pressured into marriage by the taunt that they lack commitment. That a single man's life could have intrinsic value whilst pursuing his own interests and concerns is discounted. Instead, the only 'mature' lifestyle is the life in which men are of *some value to others*, to women and children, since men have no value in themselves.

So the traditional misandry of *valuing a man by his capacity to perform work* rears its ugly head in the current attitude of female-entitlement to the domestic sphere, where women's

387

greater entry into paid employment must not rob them of their access to family life with the support of male partners. Women are entitled to everything that men traditionally had, but they are still entitled to everything that women traditionally had, too. And men must help. Feminist society has reconstructed men to stop them from being traditional men, but they still have to 'man-up' and fulfill their traditional role in the family or be condemned for their immaturity.

But what's in it for the men? The relationship-media are continually demanding to know 'where have all the good men gone?' and 'why aren't men marrying anymore?'. The way in which those two questions are treated as equivalent questions is revealing in itself. The 'good' men that women are looking for are synonymous with the *marriageable* men. Men are only 'good' men if they are the sort that women wish to marry; the men who are being of use to the women. Again, what's in it for the men? https://www.youtube.com/watch?v=BoXQf2f2Yxo

Predictably, the sensible male decision of not wishing to get married in a feminist society is usually presented as a problem to be blamed on the men themselves. They are derided as immature 'man-boys'. The blame is not put where it belongs, on the society that created a situation where a man has to accept his own status as a *legally inferior person* if he chooses to live with a woman or father children with her. Gay men may well be safe to enter into civil partnerships but the despised hetero-male would be well-advised to withdraw from signing any legal contracts that are governed by the cultural norms which reduce him to the status of a nigger of feminism.

There is now a political party in the UK called "Justice 4 Men & Boys" http://j4mb.wordpress.com/ If you believed feminists when they told you that feminism was all about sex equality, or if you still believe them when they tell you this lie, then ask yourself why there is now a political party for the defence of men and boys whose name is "Justice". Black people cast off the pejorative term 'nigger' with the civil rights movement of the 1960s. Now that men are the ideological niggers of feminism, will we see a civil rights movement for men?

388

MGTOW: Men Going Their Own Way and Herbivore men

One of the many flagrant hypocrisies of feminist entitlement culture is the way that women have been taught to feel that *they* are entitled to decide what men ought to be and how men ought to live. Feminism has fought long and hard to *deny men* any say whatsoever in how *women* see themselves or what life-choices they make. If a man so much as finds a woman attractive, she'll be said to have suffered the coercive and controlling objectification of the male gaze. If any man were to dare to offer an opinion as to what women ought to be, he would be shot down in flames as the vilest misogynist alive. Yet, at the same time, feminist society is continually telling men what men are not allowed to be and what *women require men to be*. Feminism, as we've seen so many times, is all about benefiting and advantaging women.

In contrast, from a sex-equalitarian perspective, just as women can refuse to permit men to decide what a woman should be, the same goes for men. Men are also *entitled* to choose their own identity as men, and to make their own life-choices as men. Men can and should refuse to allow women to decide what a man ought to be.

However, authoritarian feminism believes itself to be entitled to tell *everyone* what they are and what they ought to be. It does this to both women and men with it's glowingly positive gender-stereotype of the former and its appallingly negative gender-stereotype of the latter. But now that men have been reduced to a cultural joke of male inadequacy and demonized as the universal scapegoats, women in society are deciding that the men they've created simply aren't *worthy* of sublimely wonderful princesses like themselves. Hence the ubiquitous question: 'where have all the good men gone?' https://www.youtube.com/watch?v=kRikFf7rSel What a strange question. We all know from the last half a century of highly vocal feminism that it's an ideology which *does not believe in* good men. It only believes in bad men. It believes in 'toxic masculinity' and 'pathological maleness'.

The real kicker comes in the description of these 'good' men that women say they are looking for. (For example https://www.youtube.com/watch?v=s9-v4yOteTg) It seems that the 'good' men are the romantic and physically attractive men who have a good job that pays well and who know how to be financially supportive as well as how to show a woman a good time in bed and who want to make a lifelong loving commitment to their wife and who yearn to father children and who can deal with life's adversities with mature self-confidence because they are a 'take charge' guy and . . . . hang on a minute, these 'good' men sound remarkably similar to the despised *traditional man*, don't they? They are the old fashioned alpha-male. This is a description of the male success-object desired by women in the dark days of 'patriarchal' oppression, isn't it? The sex-object called 'Daddy'.

That can't be right, can it? This is the same guy that these women and their mothers have spent forty years assiduously destroying. And now it's far too late to resurrect him. How can this 'good' man love women after decades of feminism poisoning gender relations and transforming women into entitlement-junkies? How can this 'good' man risk getting married and fathering children when his wife can legally abduct his children from him at any time? How can young men get well-paid jobs to be financially supportive when they've been through a feminised education system that has cut off their access to those jobs and may well have made them unemployable? The days of the 'good' man have gone.

These days we are told, rather smugly, that *men are obsolete*. So if an entitlement-junkie wants her entitlements provided, she's going to have to provide them for herself. Women *are on their own* now. Women 'can have it all' except that the one thing they can't have any more is the old fashioned alpha-male because he's dead and buried. But, no problem. After all, we've known for decades that a woman needs a man like a fish needs a bicycle.

Yet that doesn't seem to stop the constant chorus of complaint that, far from being 'good' men, single men these days are like permanent teenagers who just want to drink beer, eat pizza, and play video games. Women sneer at them and disparage them as 'man-boys', and take this as evidence that men are indeed the immature creatures that feminism always said they were. Is this supposed to bully the degraded men of feminist society back into being the traditional family men that their grandfathers were? Hasn't feminism devoted itself to bullying men into *not being* the traditional men that their grandfathers were?

Any woman who despises the so-called 'man-boy' should remind herself that these guys are *the product of feminism*. Instead of complaining about it, shouldn't she be proud of her achievement? These are the men *that feminism has created*. If you tell someone every day of his life that he's an idiot, he may well behave like one. Tell someone every day of his life that he's emotionally illiterate and immature, and he may well behave accordingly. Tell someone every day of his life that he's obsolete, irrelevant, inferior, and 'the problem' in society, and he may well decide to *opt out* of a society in which he is considered irrelevant and inferior.
https://www.youtube.com/watch?v=3yzUECFwU3U

The attitude of any feminist woman who complains about the 'man-boy' amounts to this: *first, feminism spends forty years degrading men, then it blames men for having allowed themselves to be degraded.* Naturally, feminism isn't going to blame itself for what it has done. Nothing is ever feminism's fault, just as nothing is ever women's fault. Men are the guilt-objects. Men are always to blame. So now feminist society, with a level of hypocrisy that beggars all description, is trying to *impose the traditional gender stereotype of masculinity* by demanding that men must 'man up' and become what women require them to be: financially solvent high-achievers willing to accept responsibility and shoulder the burdens that men have traditionally shouldered from time immemorial.

And if modern young men don't conform to this required gender role, then these 'man-boys' must be punished with spiteful mockery for failing to live up to the type of 'good' socially

391

responsible men that were played in movies by actors like James Stewart and Henry Fonda.

Incidentally, do you hear any complaints coming from *young men* about the death of marriage? All the people bemoaning the demise of the 'good' family man seem to be women, don't they? There must be some young men who mourn its passing but most appear to be just getting on with their own lives. But this raises a more general question. How are men attempting to deal, politically and personally, with living in a feminist society?

With feminism having embedded itself so deeply in the current establishment elite, political resistance to feminism has so far been limited to relatively small-scale struggles against misandrist oppression from groups like fathers rights organisations and men's rights activists (MRAs). The establishment rides roughshod over this kind of protest and doesn't feel at all threatened by it. For as long as the great majority of men go on working and paying and fulfilling their obligations, those in government will have no fear of men as a political force.

But it would be a very different matter if large numbers of men started to withdraw from a full participation in society by merely living their own lives in their own way as individuals, accepting no responsibilities beyond taking care of themselves. This is what the political establishment really fears, and that's why 'man-boys' are so heavily ridiculed in society. The term is, of course, derived from traditional misandry. In traditional society there were any number of occasions which were said to 'separate the men from the boys' where it was clear that the people males were supposed to emulate were not the 'boys' but the 'real men'. Saying that a male human being is not a proper man until he accepts the traditional male familial responsibilities is as sexist as saying that a female human being is not a proper woman until she gives birth and cares for a child. The feminist mainstream would utterly condemn the sexism of the latter sentiment, but they are themselves guilty of the sexism of the former sentiment.

Yet this cultural trend of the 'man-boy' seems to be a sign of the future. This non-compliance with traditional social expectations is the (perhaps unconscious) beginning of male resistance to a misandrist society. Feminist writers speak of these men derisively for "refusing to grow up, retreating to fratriarchal spaces and man caves".

http://thefeministwire.com/2013/03/taking-the-white-man-boy-seriously/

However, the pompous invention of non-existent words like "fratriarchal" explains nothing and makes no difference to what might actually happen in the future. The 'man-boys' are men who aren't getting married, who aren't fathering children, who aren't taking out mortgages, and who aren't *committing themselves to a lifetime of work to pay for all of these things*. They are men who are not taking on the traditional male responsibilities. They are men who are saying 'fuck it, I'd rather play computer games'.

So, although the decision they have made may be influenced by their lack of opportunities (who can afford a mortgage with house prices as high as they are? where are the 'jobs for life' in this economy?), nonetheless their decision is entirely rational and consistent with living in a feminist society. Who *wants* to take out a mortgage with a wife when marriages seldom last? Who wants to father children when father's rights, insofar as they exist at all, are always trumped by mother's rights? Who wants to take on the traditional male gender role when accepting that role is no longer rewarded with any respect? Maybe the 'man-boys' are smart enough to *just say no*. If you live in a society that you know is going to deny you any respect whatever you do, why should you fear being disrespected for being a 'man-boy'?

In Japan there is a similar cultural trend, the social phenomenon of the 'grass-eaters' or 'herbivore men'. http://en.wikipedia.org/wiki/Herbivore_men The 'herbivore man' has not only rejected the traditional Japanese 'salaryman' role of commitment to hard work and financial success, he has also rejected the 'skirt-chasing' sexual appetite of the traditional red-blooded male. These young Japanese men are reluctant to take the sexual initiative with women. The herbivore man's attitude to women is much like that of a girl's gay male friend who enjoys the company of women but has no sexual interest in them. Even if a 'grass-eater' does find a woman sexually attractive, he may judge that she's not worth the effort of starting a sexual relationship. These ineffectual and docile men ought to be feminism's ideological ideal of anti-macho manhood, with their passive and unthreatening asexuality and the way that they take more interest in their physical appearance than in their career, but Japanese women appear to be less enamoured of emasculated men who have little interest in sex, marriage, or fatherhood.

Nor are the powers-that-be very enthusiastic about the 'herbivore men' because their lack of a work ethic is not good for the Japanese economy and their avoidance of sexual relationships is not good for the Japanese birth rate.
http://www.theguardian.com/world/2009/dec/27/japan-grass-eaters-salaryman-macho

But why should 'herbivore men' care what Japanese women or the Japanese government like or dislike? Why should 'man-boys' care if society disapproves of their hedonistic lifestyle? Let's remember that from a sex-equalitarian perspective men are every bit as entitled to choose their own identity as are women. Those in political power have no right to decide what a man ought to be.

In the West an ever-growing number of men are coming to consciously understand this. They are the MGTOW movement of Men Going Their Own Way. Politically this is a very significant development. *Unlike* the 'man-boy' who is simply a *product* of feminist society, the premeditated decision to go MGTOW is a *purposeful response* to feminist society. It is a self-aware and deliberate life choice.

Drawing upon their own personal experience of what it is to be a man in contemporary society, they have asked themselves some tough questions and given themselves some tough answers. Why would they want to participate in a society that treats everything they do or don't do as being wrong and where their traditional avenues for finding respect and meaning in their lives (career, children, individual achievement) are all closing down? If there are no jobs or no job security, why take on responsibilities that require these things? If they can have sex with women without marrying or co-habiting, then why marry or co-habit? If the cost of sex is having to put up with the indignity of being perpetually condescended to by an entitlement-junkie, then maybe the sex isn't worth the price and it's better to do without. Why bother date women who don't respect you?

Consequently, an increasing number of men are beginning to *exercise their personal autonomy* by deliberately withdrawing from a society that is systemically alienating to them and which treats them as deficient and inferior. They have ceased to cooperate in their own oppression. They understand that they must be non-compliant. They are men going their own way. MGTOW is the first explicit articulation of an emerging male social non-compliance.

Here is one brief description of a MGTOW philosophy:

"M.G.T.O.W – Men Going Their Own Way – is a statement of self-ownership, where the modern man preserves and protects his own sovereignty above all else. It is the manifestation of one word: *"No"*. Ejecting silly preconceptions and cultural definitions of what a "man" is. Looking to no one else for social cues. Refusing to bow, serve and kneel for the opportunity to be treated like a disposable utility. And living according to his own best interests in a world which would rather he didn't."
http://www.mgtow.com/about/

Here is another description (this one is written by a woman):

"Now whether or not women will admit it, the fact is for a lot of women there is no male "way" because men only live by the grace and favour of women. Without that grace and favour men will be made feel the full force of female disapproval, which manifests itself in many ways . . . the point is that women feel they reserve the right to arbitrate and exercise approval of male

actions, male behaviour, and in fact male autonomy. Our modern society is now exclusively orientated towards achieving, obtaining and accommodating this female approval. MGTOW comprehensively rejects and delegitimizes any necessity for female approval or sanction. MGTOW is men thumbing their noses, giving the finger to the notion that men live by the grace and favour of women. It literally pulls the rug out from under the feet of women who, whether consciously or not, have internalised the idea that men are a resource *for* women, that men live and die to *serve* women's needs, wants and whims, that men have no other function but to be at the beck and call of women, but only if and when a woman decides *she* had some need that a man is obliged to answer and/or fill."
http://www.avoiceformen.com/sexual-politics/m-g-t-o-w/mgtow-and-female-disapproval-2/

Now compare this world-view with the traditional world-view. The opening two sentences of Jane Austen's classic novel Pride and Prejudice are:

"It is a truth universally acknowledged, that a single man in possession of a good fortune must be in want of a wife. However little known the feelings or views of such a man may be on his first entering a neighbourhood, this truth is so well fixed in the minds of the surrounding families, that he is considered as the rightful property of some one or other of their daughters."

Of course, Austen is writing humorously but, as with all the best comedy, its humour is based on an observation of the real world. A single man living his own life successfully *without a woman* is not something that society was or is readily prepared to accept. Why isn't he doing his duty by the womenfolk? Surely he *cannot* be a whole person *in his own right*. He "must" be in need of a wife. Society has so many women who must be provided for. Why isn't he providing for one of them? He is considered as the "rightful property" of a woman, whoever she may turn out to be, regardless of his own views in the matter.

The novel was published in 1813. Those opening sentences

tell us something important about traditional society. They may also tell us something important about the society we live in today. (The enormously popular book and film "Bridget Jones's Diary" borrowed much its plot from Pride and Prejudice. The works of authors like Austen are still bestsellers and the costume drama movies made from their books are still highly commercial as "chick-flicks".) The old-fashioned idea of men accepting the responsibility to be protectors and providers for women and their children is still alive and thriving in the present day but it can only persist for as long as men volunteer to serve. And only a fool wants to serve at the feet of a feminist entitlement-junkie. I said earlier that feminism was the death of romance. It may also prove to be the death of the male financial provider.

MGTOWs utterly *reject* the idea that men are incomplete without women and *reject* the notion that if a man isn't providing for a woman, then he's a failed man. On the contrary, the very essence of MGTOW is male individual self-definition. Each man decides for himself what he is or wishes to become (hence, Going Their Own Way) without asking for women's permission and without seeking women's approval of his decisions. Having said that, there is considerable diversity amongst MGTOWs when it comes to interaction with women. Some prefer to have as little as possible, others have very active sex-lives. MGTOW doesn't mean that men can't have relationships with women, it simply means that a man will have decided what kind of relationship is *acceptable* to him and what is *not acceptable*. He will engage with women on his own terms.

He'll know that he has to protect himself emotionally, financially and in every other way, because society will not lift a finger to protect him. He'll be aware that very few women in contemporary society even know how to respect a man, after so many decades of the constant denigration of all things male. So if he wants a relationship in which he is respected, then he'll be aware of how difficult that will be to find. He'll know that marriage will place him in a position of legal disadvantage, that parenthood places mothers in a legally advantaged position over fathers, and he won't want to lay himself open to such exploitation and heartbreak. (After all, if a woman knew that by having children she had to accept that her husband was free to kick her out of her home and steal her children at any time he thought fit, then how many women would be willing to accept motherhood on those terms?)

A MGTOW is a man who is not willing to accept the inferior status allotted to him by society and who recognises that this rules out certain life-choices that *ought* to be available to him but *aren't* as society is presently constituted. He will not settle for anything less than equal respect and equal entitlements. He won't collude in his own exploitation or accept society's demands that he must treat a woman better than she treats him, that he must respect a woman while she fails to respect him, that he must support a woman who does not support him. And if this refusal to cooperate with society's demands means that he must live alone, then so be it. MGTOW *doesn't* mean that he has to live without female contact, but it *does* mean that he insists upon living with self-respect.

Men as a class of persons have no political power in the western world because no politicians ever speak in defence of men or in the interests of men. Governments are gynocentric in their priorities and their policies. It follows that no man who believes himself to have a right to equality should ever vote for any political party that does not recognise and advocate men's rights. In a society that has human rights, women's rights and children's rights, there can be no excuse for not having men's rights. This is why there are growing numbers of Men's Rights Activists (MRAs). If politicians begin to understand that there is a large constituency of male votes available to them if they start advocating *impartial* sex equality, maybe this will wake them up. Nothing else will.

But men should not invest any faith in the politicians who have shamefully neglected men for so long. Men must get up off their knees to stand up and answer back. Sex-equalitarian women, too, should join in the demand that equality is a two-way street. Some are doing so. The best speaker on misandry

398

around at the moment is Karen Straughan, a Canadian who has recorded numerous online video-essays (under the name GirlWritesWhat) all of which are absolutely essential listening for anyone interested in genuine sex equality. A few of the best examples are:

"Those privileged blue bundles of joy."
https://www.youtube.com/watch?v=7sAomeiTOKI

"Systemic gendered violence."
https://www.youtube.com/watch?v=gekyg7yy4Dc

"Me, a feminist? No way."
https://www.youtube.com/watch?v=PqEeCCuFFO8

MRAs, as political activists, are distinct from MGTOWS (who have made a lifestyle choice) but together they make up the modern 'Men's Movement'. In stark contrast to feminism the Men's Movement is not ideological. It is not fighting a gender war, it is simply trying to deal with the *injustices* caused by the feminist concept of 'social justice'. It doesn't seek a return to the past (why would men want to return to the burdens of their grandfathers?), it deals with the problems that men face in the present. In this sense it is a reflection of where society is now.

What is it that the three cultural trends of the 'man-boys', the 'herbivore men', and the politically aware MGTOWs, all have in common that makes them so relevant to the future of feminist society? A position of non-compliance. None of them conform to the masculine social role of taking responsibility for women and children. Although the three trends are all very different from each other, they can all be seen as defensive reactions to feminist oppression. These men have nothing to gain from a society that treats maleness as deficient, problematic, and blameworthy. They have closed a door upon that society, to live their own life as best they can. It's better than the alternative, becoming a male feminist and spending the rest of your life apologising for yourself. The frat-boy may not have much human dignity but the male feminist has far less. The male feminist has to live on his knees, never standing up and never answering back. The male feminist even has to piss sitting down.

The great irony of all this is that years ago some feminists started fantasising about a female future in which women would disassociate themselves from the 'male oppressor', imagining a gender-apartheid where women would live in female collectives and spurn male society. But at the moment it looks as if feminism might produce a quite different form of gender-apartheid, one that results not from a withdrawal of collectivist women from male society but rather a withdrawal of individualist men from feminist society.

The Future

There is a cultural convention in political debate that anyone who dares to criticise the mess we're in should also posit the solution that is going to put everything right. Well, you can forget that. It is childish to insist that there must always be a solution to every problem because you don't feel that you can bear to think about the injustices of the world unless you also receive the comforting embrace of a happy ending. What happens in real life is *whatever comes next*. Society is not static and what is the case now will not be the case in the future. Whatever comes next won't be a 'solution'. What followed traditional society (with all of its innumerable injustices) was feminist/multiculturalist society but that society was not a solution to its predecessor, it simply brought a new set of injustices, and feminism even exaggerated traditional misandry to new heights (or depths) of sexism. Whatever form of society follows feminism/multiculturalism will inevitably bring its own injustices with it.

Reality notwithstanding, every establishment culture in every society always seems to think that it will last forever. The previous one did and the present one does too. The current establishment is fixated on an idea of the utopian future that they wish to see realised and in their arrogance and complacency they don't consider what the future *might actually turn out to be.* Anyone who wants to speculate seriously on possible futures will have to discard the immature utopian practice of *imagining what we would like* the future to be and instead take the grown-up approach of looking at the potential realities. Then each reader can decide for themselves whether they believe that their children and grandchildren are going to inherit a Hollywood happy ending or not. So let's consider two possible futures. There are many alternatives, of course, but let's just draw attention to a couple of possibilities.

(1) For the last several years various economists have been predicting as inevitable an economic crash so enormous that it will collapse the financial and social structures of the western world. (e.g. "The End of Britain" https://www.youtube.com/watch?v=-gQ20NL7oqc and "Overdose: the Next Financial Crisis" https://www.youtube.com/watch?v=4ECi6WJpbzE) The two main triggers of this impending collapse are said to be the American dollar losing its status as the world reserve currency and/or the unprecedented levels of national debt which will cause western countries to be unable to pay the interest on their national debt if interest rates rise above rock bottom, and thereby bankrupt those countries.

If this were to happen, then the financial support structure for feminism would disappear. Paying for female-entitlement is very expensive. Where would feminism be without the state machine at its command? For the last few decades feminism (like multiculturalism) has been paid for by an ever-greater accumulation of national debt to meet the demands of a 'grievance and entitlement' culture, but at some point the unsustainable debt of countries like the UK and the USA must surely cause their economies to crash, and *feminism will crash with them.* Massive austerity cutbacks to the welfare state, the loss of large numbers of white-collar jobs, the failure of the banking system, the bankruptcy of private pension schemes, mass riots of the youth on the streets, and ethnic conflicts between the diverse communities of a multicultural society would smash *the material basis* for feminist society. https://www.youtube.com/watch?v=tvFVSfMBw04

If debt-capitalism collapses in the West, the sudden and extreme impoverishment of the average standard of living would completely re-order society in a struggle for survival as everyone desperately tries to earn enough to feed themselves and their families.

This would not be a 'solution' to feminism, it would be a nightmare, but it would mean the end of feminism's constant demands for ever greater female privilege and it would probably entail a radical restructuring of employment practices. One of the many realities that feminism refuses to face up to is *how dependent it is on capitalism* to provide a surrogate-daddy welfare system and a credit culture. It's not a coincidence that feminism began and thrived in the affluent countries of the world. In the absence of that affluence, all bets are off.

(2) If debt-capitalism in the west somehow manages to continue to limp on, carrying its monumental national debts and scraping together enough credit to keep paying the interest on those debts, then ongoing multiculturalism will steadily re-model the west into something very different from its past. The rise of Islam as a (the) major political influence on future government policies is an obvious example of this sort of possible 'next society'. Will Islam tolerate feminism? Will Muslim men kneel at the feet of the Goddess Feminism as western men have done? Or will Islam chew up feminism, swallow it, and shit feminism out of its arse?

Islam is an ideology every bit as intractable and self-righteous as feminism itself. What is the most probable outcome of a conflict between the absolute certainties of feminist belief and the absolute certainties of Islamic belief? There may be a clue in the high conversion rates of western women to Islam. If feminism persists at all, then it might be as some sort of Islamic-feminism, whatever that may turn out to be.
https://www.youtube.com/watch?v=mbKqqai1V-c

Multiculturalism means that the future is likely to be a struggle between a plurality of competing cultures and this will cause the twin pillars of ideological 'correctness' (feminism and multiculturalism) to conflict. There is no way of knowing in advance how this will play out but my guess is that multiculturalism will prove stronger than feminism. For one thing, it has a much higher birth-rate.

In any case, the blindness of the current establishment to the *actual consequences* of the political policies of the last half-century has left them *wholly unprepared* for whatever comes next. The establishment dreams its fantasies of the golden politically correct utopia they are building but the reality of the future may sweep aside all the naïve beliefs and values of political correctness and replace them with something that is based upon a completely different world view. Is whatever replaces the current establishment culture likely to be well-disposed toward feminism as it is presently practiced?

One speculative future that is extremely *unlikely* to happen is the feminist dream of a society either without men, or in which men have been made largely invisible. For a long time feminists have smugly indulged in the fantasy of a female future where obsolete men have ceased to be a significant presence. This fantasy arises from the position of cloistered comfort and affluent ease that those feminists have enjoyed in their own lives. Feminist academics and spokespersons live in such a bubble of privilege that it doesn't seem to occur to them what would happen to society in the absence of the men they so despise. They don't seem to question *where the electricity comes from* (oil workers, power workers, etc.) or *where the telephones and the Internet come from* (workmen laying cables under the roads) or *how the food gets into the supermarket* (drivers making deliveries in huge trucks) or any of the other necessities of modern life that feminists take absolutely for granted. How many women lay cables, work on oil-rigs, or drive monster trucks? Some, but not many. How many women *want* to?

The kinds of employment that are absolutely essential for the basic functioning of society (what we might call the 'hard-hat' jobs) but which pampered feminists never give any thought to, are still mostly performed by men. In the absence of men the entire cosy, comfortable world of the professional feminist would burst like a soap bubble. But this doesn't worry them. With the traditional snobbery of the middle-class they assume that working-class men will always be around to service their needs. They just fantasize a future in which men perform all these necessary tasks unseen. Out of sight and out of mind. Because, of course, for these stuck-up feminists *that has always been the case in their own lives.*

However, with the rise of MGTOWs who are going their own way because the double-standards of feminist domestic violence laws and feminist child-custody courts make marriage and fatherhood a financially and emotionally crippling experience that rational men would rather avoid, how will this affect industrial relations? If the future of many men is an increasingly individualist lifestyle of non-compliance with the traditional role of male familial responsibility as the breadwinner, then their greater financial independence could influence their actions in the one form of male power which ordinary men have been able to use in their own defence in the past: the *withdrawal of labour.*

Men have a glorious history of taking working-class action against their exploiters by means of industrial non-compliance; the work-to-rule and the strike. Will industrial action be very much easier for men who do not have the traditional masculine responsibilities, and instead only have themselves to consider? What effect might that have upon the performance of the kind of fundamentally necessary work which enables society to function? Society can survive without many of its service industries (so what if there are no coffee shops or sandwich cafés or Taiwanese restaurants) but there are some types of labour that society absolutely must have if it is to avoid power-cuts, food shortages, scarcity of newly constructed buildings, water supply, fuel supply, car and road maintenance, and so on. These forms of labour are the infrastructure of civilized life.

The establishment elites who insult men every day with their feminist gender-stereotypes are themselves extremely dependent upon men to supply them with their comfortable lifestyle. The professional feminists of the ideological ruling class would be helpless without ordinary working men. Just imagine what would happen if, the next time there were severe weather conditions, the male workers in the rescue services *refused to do overtime*. If there were six inches of snow and ice, a blizzard had been blowing for the last three days, but the men in the road clearance crews were *working-to-rule*. What would happen if the next time there is a riot the male police officers refused to work overtime and stayed home? Would the women employed in these jobs 'woman up' and fill the gaps?

Or consider, if men increasingly withdrew from a personal responsibility for the financial provision of families, how would *the state* finance the additional welfare payments? Would the government levy a special 'man-tax' or 'bachelor-tax' to enable the state to pay for it? If so, how will the government justify imposing an additional tax upon single men without also applying that tax to single women? Will single women be prepared to pay more tax to finance other women's children?

On the other hand, how many men would be in a position to pay? In a society where boys are so disadvantaged in education, with the knock-on effects which that has for employment, might men increasingly be the *recipients* of state welfare rather than the providers of it? In a society where the only place some young men can find any respect for themselves as men is within street gangs, what is the future of gender relations in feminist society?

If feminised education continues on its current trajectory the future will see a society where women have the majority of the high-paid high-status jobs and a lot of men will be an underclass of low-paid low-achievers. The young heterosexual women of the 2020s and 2030s will not be able to find life-partners if they are looking for men *of their own income and status* because there won't be enough of them to go round. They'll have to 'settle' for a man of lower status and lower income than themselves. Those young heterosexual women will then face a choice. Either they'll choose to not have children because they will not be able to take time off-work from their high-income jobs without a significant drop in their standard of living (because their male partner won't be earning enough money to support them in the style to which they've become accustomed). Or they'll choose to have children but surrender the role of primary child-carer to their male partner and financially support him (and risk losing their children to him in the event of a divorce and have to pay child custody thereafter). Or they'll choose to accept a significant drop in their living standards in order to have children whilst living on their male partner's lower income.

And if these high-paid high-status women choose the third option, what then? What happens when there aren't enough doctors, lawyers, business managers, chemists, financiers, airline pilots, computer programmers, analytical statisticians, etc., available because too many of the people in those jobs are taking three or four years off work to raise a family? The so-called glass ceiling is often said to result from women in general being more inclined than men to split their life-concerns between career and other things in life, so that they don't commit to the career-before-everything attitude of society's top-level movers and shakers. If this is true, then what happens when not enough women *want* to play this economic role and not enough men are *qualified* to play it?

Any sensible, responsible government would be asking itself these questions. But we cannot expect governments in the western world to do so. We have to remember that, firstly, the establishment elite cannot countenance the thought that feminism might be the cause of any social or economic problems. For decades their view has been that all criticism of feminism is just misogynist backlash because feminism can only do good in the world.

Secondly, we have to realise that the dystopian nightmare that may be only a decade or two away would not look dystopian to a hardcore feminist, of which academia and professional politics has a plentiful supply. Quite the contrary. If these young heterosexual women don't have access to male partners or to male partners of their own income bracket, it might be a problem for *women* but it won't be a problem for *feminism* because women and feminism are two different things. Feminism says that *men* are the problem, so from its ideological perspective if women don't have access to men, then they don't have access to *the problem*. And if they don't have access to the problem, then there is no problem.

An underclass of male inferiors is precisely what feminism considers morally appropriate. Feminism is, let's not forget, a gender-supremacist ideology. Where else would you consign a class of biologically inferior, innately violent, sexually predatory, immature, selfish, uncivilized, Y-chromosome rapists and domestic abusers than in an underclass? If the future were to be a society in which childless women occupied all the positions of power and influence, living apart from men in a system of gender apartheid, where they did not engage in heterosexual sex and associated almost entirely with other women . . . that would be the wonderful utopia that feminists have been dreaming of since the 1970s.

A Final Word

Okay, so maybe you've read this whole book and you're still unconvinced that men have anything to complain about. After all, you've had an entire lifetime of swimming through an ocean of lying hypocritical feminist propaganda. You've been soaked and marinated in feminist sexism. Your brain tissues are imbued with it. It's been the way you've viewed the world since you were an infant child. It's what you've always believed, what your friends have always believed, what the television and magazines and movies are constantly telling you to believe; how can feminism possibly be wrong?!

If feminism were wrong, well then, you'd have to revise your entire picture of the world. You'd have to oppose the dominant ideology of the society in which you live. And who's got the courage to do that? So, you say to yourself, sure, men have their problems but hey, 'cowboy up' dude, it's not like men are oppressed the way that *women* are oppressed. Anyway, we all know that men are the oppressors so, hey, if men think they are oppressed, then they must be oppressing themselves, right? We always knew they were just a bunch of Homer Simpson dickheads.

If it is that difficult for you to feel any empathy with men or sympathy for them, if you are so lacking in the ability to feel any compassion for adult male human beings no matter what injustices they suffer, then let's close this book with an encapsulation of feminist society in an easy-to-digest analogy about someone that just maybe you might be capable of caring about.

Imagine a home in which the parents, an abusive dominant mother and a browbeaten submissive father, have a daughter and a son. Every single day the daughter is told that she is a wonderful person; she is clever and talented and charming and capable and moral and everything that a person ought to be. Her parents have great plans for her and have already set aside the money for her university education. All their hopes and dreams reside in their marvellous fabulous daughter. At the same time, every single day the son is told that he is a fucking idiot; he is clumsy and badly behaved and stupid and ugly and violent and vulgar. His parents are not going to waste any of their love or any of their money of this disgusting troublemaker because they know that he is only going to grow up into a rapist and a wife-beater, if any women ever marries such a loser. The son never receives a pocket money allowance because his sister gets a double share, his as well as hers, and whenever the daughter does anything wrong, the son is always blamed for it.

Would you not feel that the son had something to complain about?

I will leave you with this:

1. Feminists have no understanding of men. They never have had. They don't know how to empathise with men and have always judged men superficially from the outside. To them,

408

men are the 'other'. They don't know what men truly are or what men have been in the past. Feminists don't want to know.

2. People fear what they don't understand and people hate what they fear. The feminist negative gender-stereotype of men is an articulation of feminists' fear of what they don't understand. Feminist theory is an articulation of how they hate what they fear.

3. Feminists pursue power because they want to be stronger than the thing that they fear. They have acquired massive power. But no amount of power is ever enough to quell their fear entirely. They still inhabit their fantasy nightmare of 'rape culture' and woman-as-victim. So they always seek more and more power. For as long as feminists exercise their power against that which they do not understand, that which they fear, that which they hate, then *impartial sex equality* will be impossible to achieve.

4. Reader, you have a choice to make. Everyone in this society has a choice to make between the continuation of political and cultural female privilege under a feminist establishment, or standing up and answering back against feminist oppression; standing up in defence of social justice and equality *for all*. It's not a choice you can avoid because if you refuse to make a choice, then that's effectively a choice for the continuation of the present injustice. So, privilege for women or equality for all? Choose.

Perhaps you think that you can evade the choice by telling yourself that some feminists aren't too bad really. Oh sure, the spit-flecked violent radicals are ultra-sexist nut-jobs but, hey, most of the moderate ones aren't like that. But, even leaving aside the thorny question of what on earth constitutes a 'moderate' feminist, this distinction between moderates and radicals entirely misses the point. All feminists endorse patriarchy theory, so they all refuse to acknowledge the historical fact that traditional sexism was a gender system of both misandry and misogyny that victimised both sexes. Instead they believe that one half of the victims oppressed the other half of the victims; that men oppressed women. Through a feminist lens, female human beings are people but male human beings are nothing but guilt-objects of the despised patriarchy. *A guilt-object can never have equality with a person.*

Feminists make a genuinely impartial sex equality impossible because they cannot recognise misandry for what it is, either in the past or in the present. By endorsing patriarchy theory all feminists are opposed sex equality. Moderate feminists are *moderately* opposed to sex equality. Radical feminists are *radically* opposed to sex equality. But what matters is that *both* are opposed to sex equality. Feminism is intrinsically sexist.

It is not merely the fringe loonies of feminism who are sexist, misandry is inherent to feminism root and branch. That's why it's called feminism and not equalitarianism. Feminists wage a sex-war. It hardly matters if some of them wage it *only moderately*. Feminism advocates female gender-supremacist beliefs and any form of gender-supremacism is the *polar opposite* of sex equality. So, in the end, you *do* have to choose between feminism and sex equality. They are mutually exclusive. Choose.

THE END

Afterword to the 2nd Edition

In returning to this book to make a few updates here and there, I thought it worthwhile to add something to the points made in the preface about feminists refusing to accept criticism and the speculations in the final chapter regarding the future.

I began the original 2014 edition by addressing the typical reflex dismissals that could be expected from any feminist reader. These still hold true, but there is also a deeper impediment that prevents any feminist from appreciating the arguments contained in the book. I think this additional reason has ominous repercussions for the future of society, and so I include it now.

The Renunciation of Truth: Feminist Feelings Over Facts

Society has been so intellectually corrupted by feminism that in feminised society the very idea of objective truth has been undermined, perhaps fatally. In what we might loosely call political 'debate', there are now two quite different attitudes which are incompatible with one another. The first examines evidence and evaluates rational argument to seek the truth. The second addresses feelings and seeks a consensus of opinion in the hope of avoiding emotional distress. (Not everyone's feelings count equally, of course. The feelings of protected groups matter enormously whilst the feelings of the demonised straight white male are excluded from consideration.) The 'feelings and consensus' version of truth is derived from feminism.

Once upon a time the idea of "women's intuition" was treated as a joke because women would claim that they knew something even without any evidence or justificatory argument. They just knew. Nothing needed to be proven, no reasons in support of their knowledge needed to be provided. They just knew. It was "women's intuition".

This treated a woman's feelings as being the factor which determines reality. Instead of an objective reality of facts, there is a woman's emotional perception of the world and events. The feminisation of society brought about by feminism has steadily insisted upon this attitude being regarded as a serious position. A feminist will speak of a "woman's lived experience" and this "experiencing" of the world is treated as negating the world of empirical facts. Objective truth is not recognised, acknowledged or valued, it is invalidated. What *actually happened* in reality is replaced by what a woman *feels* to have happened. Reality has become whatever a woman feels reality to be.

For example, when a woman feels that she has been raped a feminist will take that to be the truth because that is the woman's experience of what has happened. It does not matter if the women actually consented. The fact of her consent is irrelevant to the feminist. If there were documentary video evidence proving that the woman had consented, this evidence would be discounted by the feminist. It is surprisingly easy for her to do so.

Convenient excuses could always be found to dismiss the facts revealed in the video evidence. It could be claimed that the woman was feeling psychologically pressured and so her consent was forced. It could be claimed that the woman lives in a "rape culture" and so her consent was coerced by this cultural pressure. It could be claimed that the woman had drunk two glasses of wine, making her intoxicated, and so she was not in a position to give her consent. It could be claimed that the woman changed her mind later and so her consent, as seen in the video evidence, no longer applied.

Anything might be claimed by the feminist to discount the empirical fact of the woman's consent. Such facts occur only in objective reality, not in the "lived experience". This is why feminists continue to refer to women who have made false rape

Feminism <u>is</u> Sexism

allegations as "survivors" even after their allegations have been proven to be false. She has not survived a rape because no rape actually occurred, but she is still a "survivor" as far as feminists are concerned. All that matters is that the woman feels she has been raped, therefore she has.

In America under Title 9, university panels of feminists sit in judgement on rape allegations. They declare the accused man guilty on no evidence and without a trial. But they do not believe that they've done anything wrong in making this judgement and destroying the young man's life because to the feminists on the panel the facts of the case are immaterial. The only thing that is material to the case is the woman's testimony of how she feels. She feels she has been raped, therefore she has.

This intellectual corruption has societally suicidal effects for the future. For one thing it generates a very different concept of the right to freedom of speech. Whereas this right was traditionally valued as a means to discover and explore the truth in a competition of ideas, such an endeavour has no value in a feminised society. If there is no true reality of facts, then the competition of ideas has nothing to discover. Weighing rational argument and evidence in the balance to justify or refute a belief has become redundant. Beliefs are justified by a woman's feelings. Knowledge consists of an accurate account of a "woman's lived experience".

By not valuing the truth, by not recognising an objective reality of facts, the feminist's concept of freedom of speech is understood in terms of a woman's right to express her feelings *and be believed*. To deny her expression of how she feels, or to deny the veracity of her "lived experience", is to violate her right to determine reality on the basis of her feelings.

This is why feminists view it as "offensive" whenever anyone disagrees with them. Feminism is the formalised account of feminist women's feelings about reality. To disagree with feminism is to declare those women's feelings untrue, instead of treating them as the deciding factor in any argument.

413

Feminists behave as if they have suffered an injury whenever their feelings are not held to be an infallible guide to reality. They act as if they have been insulted whenever mere facts or logic are given epistemic precedence over their feelings.

The negative consequences of this intellectual corruption have spread beyond its feminist birth canal. All of political correctness has been infantilised by it. In feminised society Social Justice Warriors (the worst misnomer in the English language) have no interest in a traditional right to freedom of speech. Their concern is that none of the "protected groups" in society should feel offended by anyone's speech. For them there is no need for a competition of ideas to explore a reality of facts because their ideological mother, feminism, *has told them what to think and they think it*. It is their infallible guide to "correct" belief.

A woman is victimised if she feels victimised, and "people of colour" are oppressed if they feel oppressed. Disabled persons are discriminated against if they feel they have suffered discrimination, and white men are privileged if women or people of colour feel that white males are privileged. Facts are nothing, emotional perception is everything. The feminist epistemology of feelings intellectually corrupts an ever-widening circle of "protected groups".

Now transgender activists feel violated when anyone denies them their "personal pronouns". Their feelings determine whether they are male or female. Their feelings determine whether their gender is cisnormative or non-binary. Their feelings are the sole determining factor of reality. They *are* what they *feel themselves* to be. Biological facts are irrelevant. And they are outraged if anyone is so offensive as to suggest that reality might possibly be otherwise.

This is why there is conflict between second wave feminists like Germaine Greer and the young generation of Social Justice Warriors. https://www.theguardian.com/education/2015/oct/23/petition-urges-cardiff-university-to-cancel-germain-greer-lecture Feminism has spent half a century promoting female supremacist beliefs and the privileging of women in society. This requires a firm belief in binary gender because it is impossible to be a gender supremacist unless you believe in gender. But today's transgender activists insist that gender is 'fluid' and any person can identify with the gender that is contrary to their biological sex, or be neither male nor female because their identity is "non-binary". If so, then how can feminism continue with its political agenda that men are the guilty bad guys and women are the innocent good guys?

Now anyone can choose to be either male or female (or neither) and you can't tell which is which by just looking. A biologically female person identifies as a man and is therefore guilty of all the things that feminism blames on men. A biologically male person identifies as a woman and is therefore innocent of all the crimes of the dreadful patriarchy. Biologically female persons who identify as male would not be entitled to female privileges because they are *not* women. Biologically male persons who identify as female would be entitled to join women-only support groups, and be included on women-only shortlists etc., because they *are* women. Transgender politics conflicts with feminist gender politics.

One issue of this sort which has already arisen concerns public toilets. Whilst the law seems to have little concern over biologically female persons who identify as male being entitled to use men's toilets (because the personal dignity of men is not an issue that this society gives a damn about), predictably they are very wary of the idea that biologically male persons who identify as female are entitled to use women's toilets. Nonetheless, this idea is now part of the discourse. The United States Department of Labour has issued guidance on the issue ["Transgender worker access to bathroom: best practices" https://www.osha.gov/html/a-z-index.html] which holds that:

"a person who identifies as a man should be permitted to use men's restrooms, and a person who identifies as a woman should be permitted to use women's restrooms."
https://www.osha.gov/Publications/OSHA3795.pdf

415

Feminism has brought this upon itself. It is feminism which has propagandised the superiority of feminine emotionality over "masculine" logic. Feminism invented the concept of "emotional intelligence" to legitimize the old idea of "women's intuition" as a source of "knowledge". It is feminism that has pursued it's policies and legislation, not by evidence-based logical argument, but simply by making emotional appeals about their alleged victimhood and special vulnerability. It is feminism that has created the contemporary political climate of the *"argument" from feelings*.

Using passive-aggressive bullying as a political tactic has been extremely successful for feminism but now they are losing control of this tactic. (For example, Muslims can use it by crying "Islamophobia", and Islam is no friend to feminism.) On university campuses we've seen feminised student activists, the thuggish cry-babies who are now called "cry-bullies", turning hostile against the very academics who taught them their identity politics. [For example the notorious incident at Yale University https://www.youtube.com/watch?v=Tsgc0k594Js] This is rather like seeing a flock of sheep turning on their shepherd. It's an odd phenomenon. All they can do is bleat but the collective bleating is so loud that the noise becomes intimidating.

Wounded feelings, offended feelings, indignant feelings, outraged feelings, upset feelings; these are given precedence in contemporary political debate. They matter more than evidence-based logical argument. Emotional rhetoric rules the day. Victimhood, weakness, and self-pity were weaponized by feminists. Now feminists may be devoured by the Frankenstein monster that they have created. Unfortunately, the rest of us may be destroyed along with them.

There is a phrase for this ideologically conformist feminised world. It is called the "post-truth" world. (This is the Oxford Dictionaries word of the year for 2016.) This Orwellian phrase is a measure of how far intellectual enquiry, popular opinion, and political policy have been degraded by feminist society. "Post-truth" is defined as:

"Relating to or denoting circumstances in which objective facts are less influential in shaping public opinion than appeals to emotion and personal belief." [Oxford English Dictionary https://www.oxforddictionaries.com/press/news/2016/11/17/WOTY-16]

"Post-truth politics (also called post-factual politics) is a political culture in which debate is framed largely by appeals to emotion disconnected from the details of policy, and by the repeated assertion of talking points to which factual rebuttals are ignored." [Wikipedia https://en.wikipedia.org/wiki/Post-truth_politics]

The American conservative speaker Ben Shapiro famously said: "Facts don't care about your feelings". It is an admirable slogan and deserves to be written on a million tee-shirts. Sadly, it will be unlikely to sway opinion in a feminised society in which feelings are paramount. The slogan of a feminised society is: *my feelings don't care about your facts.*

So in addition to the feminist reader's typical reflex dismissals, with which I began this book, she now has a type of dismissal that is far more absolute and terminal. The contemporary feminist will dismiss the arguments in this book because she has discarded and abandoned the very concept of truth itself.

417

Other publications by JP Tate

The JP Tate website

http://jptate.jimdo.com

Sex-Objects: a little book of liberation

How often have you heard feminists reproaching men for the sexual objectification of women? Nothing is more commonplace in the politics of gender as practiced over the last fifty years. The phrase 'sexual objectification' is invariably used negatively, in an act of censure to reprimand the perpetrator for a gross offence. In contemporary society it is taken for granted that sexual objectification is immoral and that it is a 'male crime'.

This book offers a radically anti-establishment re-evaluation of the concept of sexual objectification. It argues that far from being sexually aberrant, erotic objectification is an integral part of human sexual desire. Far from being a social harm created by systemic political misogyny, it is a naturally occurring phenomenon which is found in all human sexualities. It is entailed in your own sexuality no matter what your sexuality happens to be. Everybody does it, both women and men. People sexually objectify others, and are sexually objectified by others, in all sorts of different ways. It is simply a part of how we perceive the erotic.

"Sex-Objects: a little book of liberation" pulls no punches in challenging conventional opinion and it offers a guilt-free sexuality to those whose minds are open to being liberated from the prison of feminist political orthodoxy.

The Identity Wars: Utopia is Dystopia (a novel)

Where will you be in the year 2035?

Most novels about a dystopian future have little to do with the real world. They either take place in some post-apocalypse wasteland full of zombies that has no connection with the present day, or they are old-fashioned visions of far-right totalitarianism on the out-of-date 20th century model.

"The Identity Wars" is very different. It is a new type of dystopian novel based upon the actual society that we live in today. It portrays a dystopian future which arises directly out of the politics and policies of contemporary society.

This novel puts together three features of your world. (1) An impending, and much predicted, serious crash of capitalism causing economic collapse. (2) Western societies becoming ever more divided by multiple ethnic cultures. (3) The growing gender segregation of men and women, such as the social phenomenon of Men Going Their Own Way (MGTOW), as a result of the iniquities of feminism.

Given these three features of the world you live in, "The Identity Wars" looks twenty years into the future and asks: what will society become? What will happen to a feminist-multiculturalist society under the impact of a global financial meltdown?

It is also the story of three men on their fortieth birthdays. The grandfather, Alf Eldridge, who was forty in 1975. The father, Michael Eldridge, who was forty in 2005. The son, Kyle Eldridge a.k.a. Ritzy, who is forty in 2035. Each of them is a product of the culture they live in. Each of them lives in a culture entirely different from the other two. Each of them has a wholly different conception of manhood. Across these three generations, from grandfather to grandson, the world changed radically and dramatically. There will be no going back.

This is the news from tomorrow. The future is coming.

The Most Hated Man (a novel)

A series of bloody deaths is causing panic in a city in England. Someone is murdering teenagers among the underclass by disseminating a lethal recreational drug which, with morbid humour, the mainstream media have termed 'snuff'. But is the snuff-killer just some crazy drug dealer who is pushing a deadly narcotic regardless of the consequences or is he killing these young people deliberately for a deeper motivation of his own?

Two police officers, Detective Inspector Bapoto Smith and Detective Sergeant Gloria Kovač, are a part of the task force unit working the case. Lacking any forensic evidence or public support, they must pursue their investigation hindered further by the puerile restraints of the political directives, policies, and procedures that make up modern policing priorities.

At the same time a second murderer, Hereward, is on a deadly mission of his own. He is abducting members of the political and cultural establishment. For fifty years these reactionaries of 'correctness' have adamantly refused to listen to anyone who disagreed with them. Now Hereward is *making* them listen. The corpses of those to whom he speaks are subsequently found dead by dehydration, bruised from the chains which had bound them. Confronted with this terror the ruling elite are frantic.

Two killers, two fatal agendas, two harassed cops, one broken nation. In a society spiralling out of control, the establishment elites of political correctness have been targeted and their time is running out.

These storylines slowly come together in a chilling vision of the social alienation brought about by those who exercise authoritarian power over the ordinary citizen with the strict speech-codes and thought-police taboos of political conformity. Set against a background of economic decline, the rise of Islamic Jihad, and the social engineering imposed by the ideologies of multiculturalism and feminism, "The Most Hated Man" is unlike any other cops-and-killers thriller you have ever read. It is a story for our times.

All God Worshippers Are Mad: a little book of sanity

This little book seeks to demonstrate in a logical common sense manner that the fundamental beliefs held by all monotheists are incomprehensible and lunatic. It attempts to show that god worshippers themselves do not understand the things they claim to believe, and by which they live their lives. Then it goes on to draw attention to why this matters so urgently in our own era, with the global rise of religious fascism.

What is said in this little book will no doubt be found impolite and overly-provocative by those authoritarian people within the politically correct establishment who think that we should live in a permanent state of apology for the crime of having minds of our own. But religions are not above criticism and they have no right to a special privileged status. Religions can and should be challenged like any other political ideologies.

Topics covered:
01. God
02. Prayer
03. Worship
04. God the Infinite
05. Immortality and Heaven
06. Soul / Spirit
07. Salvation
08. Faith
09. Spreading The Word
10. Theocracy
11. Theocracy and Nuclear Armageddon
12. God, Guilty of Genocide
13. Religion and Morality are Mutually Exclusive
14. God worship is Immoral
15. God worship is Obscene
16. Everything is God's Fault
17. If it's in The Book, then it Must be True
18. Claiming Incomprehensible Beliefs
19. Is Islamism the New Fascism?
20. The Moderates

19631124R00236

Printed in Great Britain
by Amazon